**Lawrenceville
Press**

An Introduction to Programming Using Microsoft® Visual Basic®

Versions 5 and 6

Beth Brown
Bruce Presley

**All orders including educational, Canadian, foreign,
FPO, and APO may be placed by contacting:**

Lawrenceville Press, Inc.
P.O. Box 704
Pennington, NJ 08534-0704
(609) 737-1148
(609) 737-8564 fax

This text is available in hardcover and softcover editions.

16 15 14 13 12 11 10 9 8 7 6 5 4

W e have strived to make this the most comprehensive, yet easy to understand Visual Basic text available. Our primary objective in this text is to present material in clear language with easy to follow examples. To meet this objective, we and our reviewers have thoroughly classroom tested the text.

We believe that students should be instructed in what constitutes good programming style so that their applications are easy to understand, modify, and debug. Good programming techniques are presented throughout the text.

As programming teachers, we have reviewed many of the currently available Visual Basic texts and have found them too often lacking in the clarity required to explain difficult concepts. Also, we have discovered that the teacher support material provided with these texts is both limited and inadequate. This text and its comprehensive Teacher's Resource Package are our answer to these problems.

It is our belief that learning to program offers the student an invaluable opportunity to develop problem-solving skills. The process of defining a problem, breaking it down into a series of smaller problems, and finally writing a computer program to solve it is an exercise in learning to think logically. In addition, the student is made aware of the capabilities and limitations of the computer and soon realizes that the programmer—the human element—is more important than the machine.

An Introduction to Programming Using Microsoft Visual Basic is written for a one or two-term course. No previous programming experience is required or assumed. It is the goal of this text to provide students the best possible introduction to programming using Visual Basic, whether they will continue on to more advanced computer science courses or end their computer education with this introductory course.

Topic Organization

Chapter One presents a brief history of computing and introduces the student to computer and programming terminology.

In Chapter Two students are introduced to Windows 98.

Chapter Three introduces Visual Basic and the Visual Basic IDE. From the beginning, the importance of employing good programming style is emphasized.

Chapter Four introduces variables and constants. The Case Study that ends the chapter produces a Calculator application.

The emphasis of Chapter Five is on decision structures. Concepts presented include random numbers, pseudocode, and counters. Students are shown how to make global declarations and understand logic errors. In the Case Study, a Pizza Order application is created.

Chapter Six presents looping structures. Students are also taught the String and Space functions, and how to compare strings. In the Case Study, a Hangman application is created.

User-defined procedures are discussed in Chapter Seven, as well as static variables. A Game of 21 application is created in the Case Study.

Chapter Eight covers mathematical and business functions. Windows application standards, such as focus, access keys, and tab order are also discussed. The Case Study presents a Mortgage Analyzer application.

Variable arrays and dynamic arrays are explained in Chapter Nine. Two dimensional matrices are discussed, as well as control arrays. Lucy's Cuban Cafe application is created in the Case Study.

In Chapter Ten, adding color, graphics, and sound to applications is covered. Applications with simulated animation are created. In the Case Study, a Race Track application is created.

Chapter Eleven explains sequential access files. File systems controls are also discussed. A Display File application is created in the Case Study.

Random access files are discussed in Chapter Twelve. The **Type** statement is also presented for declaring user-defined types. A Theater Box Office application is developed in the Case Study.

Chapter Thirteen introduces sorting and searching. Algorithms for bubble sort, selection sort, insertion sort, and binary search are introduced.

Menus, dialogs, and using multiple forms are presented in Chapter Fourteen. The Case Study for this chapter is a Gift Order Form application.

Chapter Fifteen introduces using Microsoft Office applications including Excel, Word, and Access with Visual Basic applications.

Design and Features

Classroom Tested All of the material in this text has been tested and developed in the authors' classrooms. The text has also been reviewed as it was being written by more than sixty experienced computer educators.

Programming Concepts This text emphasizes learning the fundamental concepts of programming so that this knowledge can be applied to other programming languages.

Problem Solving   From the very beginning, students are taught to solve problems using proper programming techniques.

Programming Style   Throughout the text separate sections are devoted to explaining in detail the concepts of proper programming style so that students will make their applications easy to read, modify, and debug.

Demonstration Applications and Runs   Many demonstration applications are included, complete with sample runs, so that students are shown both proper programming techniques and the output actually produced by their computer.

Format   Each Visual Basic statement is clearly defined, shown in sample code, and then used in an application.

Objectives   An outline of the significant topics that will be covered is presented at the beginning of each chapter.

Reviews   Numerous reviews are presented throughout each chapter which provide immediate reinforcement to newly learned concepts. Solutions to the reviews are given in the Teacher's Resource Package.

Case Studies   Beginning in Chapter Four, most chapters end by stating a problem and then developing the appropriate algorithm. The process of specification, design, coding, and debugging and testing is clearly outlined for producing the problem's solution.

Chapter Summaries   At the end of each chapter is a summary that briefly discusses the concepts covered in the chapter.

Vocabulary Sections   At the end of each chapter is a vocabulary section that defines new terms. A separate section lists Visual Basic operators, controls, keywords, statements, methods, and functions.

Exercises   Each chapter includes a large set of exercises of varying difficulty, making them appropriate for students with a range of abilities. Many of the exercises contain a demonstration run to help make clear what output is expected from the student's application. Exercises based on previous work are marked with a ✿ symbol. Advanced exercises are indicated as such, and require a carefully thought-out algorithm as part of their solution, similar in form to that used in solving the Case Study. Answers to the exercises are included with the Teacher's Resource Package.

Indexes   In addition to a standard index, an index of the applications in the text is also included.

Appendices   An appendix about standard Visual Basic naming conventions and keywords is included, as well as an appendix listing many of the Visual Basic built-in functions.

Teacher's Resource Package

When used with this text, the Lawrenceville Press *Teacher's Resource Package* provides all the additional material required to offer students an excellent introductory Visual Basic programming course. These materials place a strong emphasis on developing the student's problem-solving skills. The Package divides each of the chapters in the text into lessons that contain the following features:

- **Assignments** Suggested reading and problem assignments.

- **Teaching Notes** Helpful information that we and our reviewers have learned from classroom experience.

- **Discussion Topics** Additional material that supplements the text and can be used in leading classroom discussions.

- **Transparency Masters** Diagrams of different topics that can be copied onto film.

- **Quizzes** Each lesson contains a quiz to help reinforce programming concepts.

- **Worksheets** Problems that supplement the exercises in the text by providing additional reinforcement of concepts.

In addition to the material in the lessons, other features are included for each chapter:

- **Tests** A comprehensive test for each chapter as well as a midterm and final examination. Each test consists of multiple choice questions and problems that are solved on the computer by writing or editing a Visual Basic application. A full set of answers and a grading key are also included.

- **Answers** Complete answers for the reviews and exercises presented in the text.

A master CD, included with the Package, contains the following files:

- **Application files** All applications presented in the text, as listed in the Applications Index.

- **Tests** The tests are provided in text files so that they can be edited.

- **Answer files** Answers to the reviews, exercises, worksheets, and tests.

Student diskettes containing many of the example applications and Case Studies can be easily made by following the directions included in the Teacher's Resource Package. Student diskettes are also available for purchase in packs of 10.

As an added feature, the Package is contained in a three-ring binder. This not only enables pages to be removed for duplication, but also allows you to keep your own notes in the Package.

An Introduction to Programming Using Microsoft Visual Basic

Previous editions of our programming texts have established them as leaders in their field, with more than two million students having been introduced to computing using one of our texts. With this new Visual Basic text, we have made significant improvements over our earlier programming texts. These improvements are based on the many comments we received, a survey of instructors who are teaching the text, and our own classroom experience.

An Introduction to Programming Using Microsoft Visual Basic is available in softcover and hardcover editions. As an additional feature the softcover edition has an improved sewn lay-flat binding which keeps the text open at any page and gives the book additional strength. Both editions of the text are available with Microsoft Visual Basic 6.0 Working Model Edition on CD.

As classroom instructors, we know the importance of using a well written and logically organized text. With this edition we believe that we have produced the finest introductory Visual Basic programming text and Teacher's Resource Package available.

Acknowledgments

The authors are especially grateful to the following instructors and their students who classroom tested this text as it was being written. Their comments and suggestions have been invaluable:

Robert Arkiletian, British Columbia
Jill Baker, Texas
Dawn Brown, Maryland
Chris Buffington, Pennsylavania
Betsy Burke, New York
Tom Choate, Maryland
Gerald Chung, Alberta
David Coad, British Columbia
Philip Conant, Maryland
Peter Davies, New Jersey
Fouad Dehlawi, Washington
Wendell Dillard, Arkansas
Derrick Eason, Nova Scotia
Lynn Edwards, Michigan
Gary Farbman, New York
Sharon Flinspach, Iowa
Kyle Gillett, Colorado
Tony Girkman, Pennsylvania
Jim Heintz, Washington
Edwin Hensley,Texas
Bill Hollett, Michigan
Roger Kiel, New Jersey

Barbara Kirch, New Jersey
Deborah Klipp, New Jersey
Kathleen Larson, New York
Myra LeMieux, Florida
Jerome MacDonald, Alberta
Jill May, Indiana
Ray McFall, Pennsylvania
Carol Nordquist, South Carolina
Rayetta Palmer, Colorado
Polly Parker, Ohio
Quirico Perez, Florida
Carol Raap, South Dakota
Lynn Ricker, Virginia
Diana Schoenblum, New Jersey
Allen Scott, Texas
Carol Tenpas, Indiana
Brenda Tucker, Florida
Richard Turbeville, Florida
Joel Wagnor, New Jersey
Donovan Williams, Wisconsin
Loretta Wulff, Pennsylvania
Craig Yuranek, Oregon

We thank Amy Stuhlberg and Janie Schwark of Microsoft Corporation for their help. We also thank Rick May at Courier Book Companies, Inc. who supervised the printing of this text.

The success of this and all of our texts is due to the efforts of Heidi Crane, Vice President of Marketing at Lawrenceville Press. Joseph Dupree runs our customer relations department and handles the many thousands of orders we receive in a friendly and efficient manner. Rich Guarascio and Michael Porter are responsible for the excellent service Lawrenceville Press offers in shipping orders.

We thank Vickie Grassman, a technical writer for Lawrenceville Press, for her significant contribution to this text. Vickie edited the entire text and produced many of the exercises. Her extensive work has helped make the text so comprehensive.

Elaine Malfas, director of computer graphics and technical editor at Lawrenceville Press has edited the entire text and designed its layout, which makes the text so easy to use and comprehend.

A note of appreciation is due our colleague Nanette Hert. She has reviewed much of the material in this text and created many of the exercises.

Finally, we would like to thank our students, for whom and with whom this text was written. Their candid evaluation of each lesson and their refusal to accept anything less than perfect clarity in explanation have been the driving forces behind the creation of *An Introduction to Programming Using Microsoft Visual Basic*.

About the Authors

Beth A. Brown, a graduate in computer science from Florida Atlantic University, is director of development at Lawrenceville Press where she has coauthored many programming and applications texts and their Teacher's Resource Packages. Ms. Brown currently teaches computer programming and computer applications.

Bruce W. Presley, a graduate of Yale University, taught computer science and physics and served as the director of the Karl Corby Computer and Mathematics Center located at the Lawrenceville School in Lawrenceville, New Jersey. Mr. Presley was a member of the founding committee of the Advanced Placement Computer Science examination and served as a consultant to the College Entrance Examination Board. Presently Mr. Presley, author of more than twenty computer textbooks, is president of Lawrenceville Press and teaches computer programming and computer applications.

Table of Contents

Chapter One – The History of Computers

1.1	Mechanical Devices	1–1
1.2	Electro-Mechanical Devices	1–3
1.3	First Generation Computers	1–4
1.4	The Stored Program Computer	1–5
1.5	Second Generation Computers	1–6
1.6	High-Level Programming Languages	1–6
1.7	Third Generation Computers	1–7
1.8	Mainframes	1–7
1.9	Fourth Generation Computers	1–8
1.10	The Personal Computer	1–8
1.11	Memory: ROM and RAM	1–9
1.12	The CPU	1–10
1.13	Number Systems	1–10
1.14	Storing Data in Memory	1–11
1.15	Storage Devices	1–12
1.16	Object-Oriented Programming	1–13
1.17	The Social and Ethical Implications of Computers	1–13
1.18	Protecting Computer Software and Data	1–14
1.19	The Ethical Responsibilities of the Programmer	1–15
1.20	Why learn to program?	1–16
	Chapter Summary	1–16
	Vocabulary	1–18
	Review Questions	1–20

Chapter Two – Introducing Windows 98

2.1	Operating Systems	2–1
2.2	Applications Software	2–1
2.3	Using the Mouse	2–2
2.4	The Windows 98 GUI	2–3

2.5	Using Windows	2–4
2.6	Using Menus	2–5
2.7	Using Dialog Boxes	2–6
2.8	Using the Keyboard	2–7
2.9	Starting an Application and Creating a Document	2–8
2.10	Saving a Document	2–9
2.11	Closing a Document	2–10
2.12	Opening a File	2–10
2.13	Printing a Document	2–11
2.14	Screen Scroll	2–11
2.15	Exiting an Application	2–12
2.16	Using Diskettes	2–13
2.17	Using My Computer	2–14
2.18	Using Windows Explorer	2–17
2.19	File and Folder Management	2–18
2.20	Recovering Deleted Files	2–20
2.21	Using Online Help	2–20
2.22	Finding Files	2–21
	Chapter Summary	2–22
	Vocabulary	2–25
	File Menu Commands	2–27
	Windows 98 Commands	2–27
	Review Questions	2–28

Chapter Three – Introducing Visual Basic

3.1	The Visual Basic Programming Language	3–1
3.2	A Visual Basic Application	3–1
3.3	The Visual Basic IDE	3–2
3.4	Adding Objects to a Form	3–4
3.5	Object Property Values	3–4
3.6	Resizing and Moving an Object	3–6
3.7	Saving a Project	3–6
3.8	Running a Visual Basic Application	3–6
3.9	Objects and their Event Procedures	3–8
3.10	Printing a Project	3–9
3.11	Removing a Project from the IDE	3–10
3.12	Using Assignment to Change Property Values	3–11
3.13	The Form_Load Event Procedure	3–12
3.14	Commenting Code	3–13
3.15	Opening a Project	3–13
3.16	Image Objects	3–14
3.17	Operators and Expressions	3–17
3.18	Creating an Executable File	3–17
3.19	Exiting Visual Basic	3–18
3.20	Visual Basic Programming Guidelines	3–19
	Chapter Summary	3–19
	Vocabulary	3–21
	Visual Basic	3–22
	Exercises	3–23

An Introduction to Programming Using Microsoft Visual Basic

Chapter Four – Variables and Constants

4.1	Using Variables	4–1
4.2	Variable Assignment	4–2
4.3	Using Named Constants	4–4
4.4	Choosing Identifiers	4–5
4.5	Built-In Data Types	4–5
4.6	Variable Declarations	4–6
4.7	Syntax Errors	4–7
4.8	Debugging Techniques–The Immediate Window	4–8
4.9	Obtaining a Value from the User	4–10
4.10	Automatic Type Conversion	4–11
4.11	Special Division Operators	4–13
4.12	Option Buttons	4–14
4.13	Visual Basic Programming Guidelines	4–17
	Case Study	4–18
	Chapter Summary	4–22
	Vocabulary	4–24
	Visual Basic	4–25
	Exercises	4–26

Chapter Five – Controlling Program Flow with Decision Structures

5.1	The If…Then Statement	5–1
5.2	Roundoff Error	5–2
5.3	The If…Then…Else Statement	5–3
5.4	Nested If…Then…Else Statements	5–4
5.5	The If…Then…ElseIf Statement	5–4
5.6	Generating Random Numbers	5–5
5.7	Scope	5–9
5.8	Logical Operators	5–12
5.9	Algorithms	5–13
5.10	Message Boxes	5–14
5.11	Creating a Password Application	5–15
5.12	Using Counters	5–17
5.13	Check Boxes	5–19
5.14	Printing the Form	5–20
5.15	Visual Basic Programming Guidelines	5–22
	Case Study	5–22
	Chapter Summary	5–27
	Vocabulary	5–29
	Visual Basic	5–30
	Exercises	5–31

Chapter Six – Controlling Program Flow with Looping Structures

6.1	The Do…Loop Statement	6–1
6.2	Infinite Loops	6–2
6.3	Input Boxes	6–4
6.4	Using Accumulators	6–5
6.5	String Conversion Functions	6–8
6.6	Manipulating Strings	6–9
6.7	The Len Function	6–10
6.8	The InStr Function	6–11
6.9	The For…Next Statement	6–12
6.10	Generating Strings	6–15
6.11	Character Data Storage	6–16
	ASCII Codes	6–17
6.12	Comparing Strings	6–18
	Case Study	6–20
	Chapter Summary	6–23
	Vocabulary	6–24
	Visual Basic	6–24
	Exercises	6–25

Chapter Seven – Procedures

7.1	Sub Procedures	7–1
7.2	Value Parameters	7–4
7.3	Documenting Procedures	7–6
7.4	Reference Parameters	7–8
7.5	Static Variables	7–11
7.6	Function Procedures	7–13
7.7	Using Object Parameters	7–17
	Case Study	7–18
	Chapter Summary	7–24
	Vocabulary	7–25
	Visual Basic	7–25
	Exercises	7–26

Chapter Eight – Mathematical and Business Functions

8.1	Built-in Mathematical Functions	8–1
8.2	The IsNumeric Function	8–2
8.3	The Round Function	8–2
8.4	Formatting Numeric Output	8–3
8.5	Built-in Business Functions	8–3
8.6	List Boxes	8–6
8.7	Combo Boxes	8–9
8.8	Windows Application Standards	8–12
	Case Study	8–15

8.9	Built-in Trigonometric Functions	8–20
8.10	Inverse Trigonometric Functions	8–23
8.11	Logarithmic and Exponential Functions	8–24
	Chapter Summary	8–25
	Vocabulary	8–27
	Visual Basic	8–27
	Exercises	8–28

Chapter Nine – Arrays

9.1	Variable Arrays	9–1
9.2	Using Arrays	9–2
9.3	Range Errors	9–3
9.4	Array Parameters	9–4
9.5	Arrays with Meaningful Indexes	9–5
9.6	Searching an Array	9–8
9.7	Dynamic Arrays	9–9
9.8	Control Arrays	9–12
9.9	Two-Dimensional Arrays	9–15
	Case Study	9–19
	Chapter Summary	9–23
	Vocabulary	9–25
	Visual Basic	9–25
	Exercises	9–26

Chapter Ten – Graphics, Color, and Sound

10.1	Using Color	10–1
10.2	Adding Lines to an Application	10–2
10.3	Adding Shapes to an Application	10–3
10.4	Picture Boxes	10–5
10.5	Moving Shapes and Picture Boxes	10–6
10.6	Using Graphic Methods	10–8
10.7	Container Properties that Affect Graphics	10–11
10.8	Using a Timer Object	10–13
10.9	Moving Line Objects	10–14
10.10	Animation	10–15
10.11	Adding Sound	10–18
	Case Study	10–20
	Chapter Summary	10–25
	Vocabulary	10–27
	Visual Basic	10–27
	Exercises	10–29

Chapter Eleven – Sequential Access Files

11.1	What is a File?	11–1
11.2	Opening a File	11–1
11.3	Reading Text from a File	11–2
11.4	Closing a File	11–3
11.5	Multiline Text Boxes	11–3
11.6	Writing Text to a File	11–5
11.7	Writing Records	11–8
11.8	Appending Data to a File	11–9
11.9	Reading Records	11–11
11.10	Updating and Deleting Records	11–13
11.11	Deleting and Renaming Files	11–14
11.12	Using the File System Controls	11–17
	Case Study	11–20
	Chapter Summary	11–25
	Vocabulary	11–26
	Visual Basic	11–26
	Exercises	11–27

Chapter Twelve – Random Access Files

12.1	User-Defined Types	12–1
12.2	Using User-Defined Types	12–2
12.3	What is a Random Access File?	12–2
12.4	Opening a Random Access File	12–3
12.5	Determining Record Length	12–3
12.6	Closing a File	12–4
12.7	Writing Records	12–4
12.8	Reading Records	12–7
12.9	Updating and Deleting Records	12–9
	Case Study	12–12
	Chapter Summary	12–18
	Vocabulary	12–19
	Visual Basic	12–19
	Exercises	12–20

Chapter Thirteen – Sorting and Searching

13.1	Bubble Sort	13–1
13.2	Timing Code	13–3
13.3	A More Efficient Bubble Sort	13–3
13.4	Selection Sort	13–4
13.5	Insertion Sort	13–7
13.6	Binary Search	13–9
	Chapter Summary	13–13
	Vocabulary	13–14
	Visual Basic	13–14
	Exercises	13–15

Chapter Fourteen – Menus, Dialogs, and Multiple Forms

14.1	Menus in Windows Applications	14–1
14.2	Adding Menus to a Visual Basic Application	14–2
14.3	Common Dialogs	14–5
14.4	Adding a New Form to a Project	14–9
14.5	Using Multiple Forms	14–11
14.6	Adding a Template Form to a Project	14–14
14.7	Splash Screen	14–16
14.8	Startup	14–16
14.9	Adding an Existing Form to a Project	14–18
	Case Study	14–21
	Chapter Summary	14–28
	Vocabulary	14–30
	Visual Basic	14–30
	Exercises	14–31

Chapter Fifteen – Using Microsoft Office with Visual Basic Applications

15.1	OLE	15–1
15.2	Embedding a New Excel Spreadsheet	15–2
15.3	Embedding an Existing Excel File	15–5
15.4	Linking an Existing Excel File	15–8
15.5	Linking and Embedding Word Documents	15–5
15.6	Databases and the Data Control	15–13
	Chapter Summary	15–16
	Vocabulary	15–17
	Visual Basic	15–17
	Exercises	15–18

Appendix A – Visual Basic Naming Conventions and Keywords

Naming Conventions for Constants and Variables	A–1
Naming Conventions for Objects	A–1
Keywords	A–2

Index

Program Index	I–1
Index	I–2

An Introduction to Programming Using Microsoft Visual Basic

Chapter One
The History of Computers

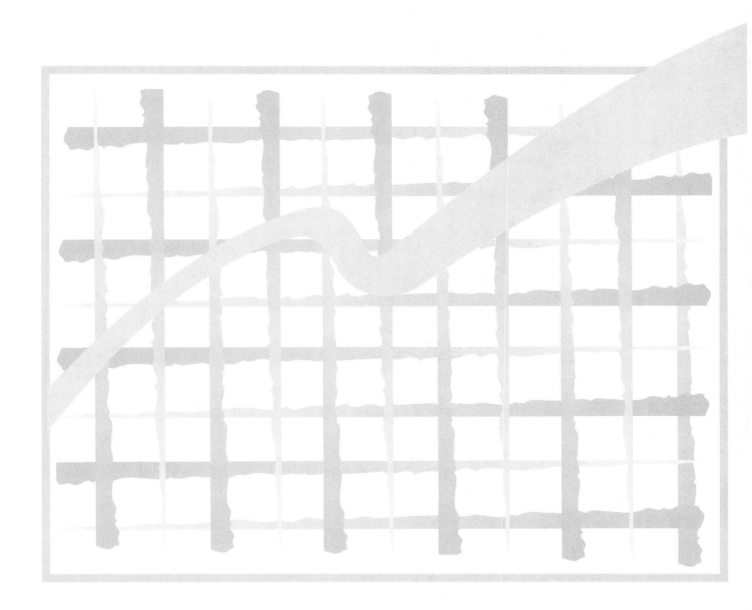

Chapter One Objectives

After completing this chapter you will be able to:

1. Discuss the history of computers.
2. Understand how a microcomputer works.
3. Understand the binary number system.
4. Understand how data is stored in memory.
5. Understand the ethical responsibilities of the programmer.

In this chapter, you will learn about computers, their history, and how they process and store data. Important issues relating to computers and programming are also discussed.

1.1 Mechanical Devices

Pascaline

One of the earliest mechanical devices for calculating was the *Pascaline*, invented by the French philosopher and mathematician Blaise Pascal in 1642. The Pascaline was a complicated set of gears that operated similarly to the way a clock keeps time. It was designed to perform addition only and not multiplication or division. Unfortunately, due to manufacturing problems, Pascal never got the device to work properly.

Blaise Pascal
1623 – 1662

The Pascaline was a mechanical calculating device invented by Blaise Pascal in 1642

Stepped Reckoner

Later in the 17th century Gottfried Wilhelm von Leibniz, a famous mathematician, invented a device that was supposed to be able to add and subtract, as well as multiply, divide, and calculate square roots. His device, the *Stepped Reckoner*, included a cylindrical wheel called the *Leibniz wheel* and a moveable carriage that was used to enter the number of digits in the multiplicand. However, because of mechanically unreliable parts, the device tended to jam and malfunction.

Gottfried Wilhelm
von Leibniz
1646 – 1716

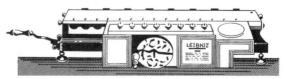

The Stepped Reckoner was another early attempt at creating a mechanical calculating device

Difference Engine

In 1822 Charles Babbage began work on the *Difference Engine*. His hope was that this device would calculate numbers to the 20th place and then print them at 44 digits per minute. The original purpose of this machine was to produce tables of numbers that would be used by ships' navigators. At the time, navigation tables were often highly inaccurate due to calculation errors. In fact, a number of ships were known to have been lost at sea because of these errors. Although never built, the ideas for the Difference Engine lead to the design of Babbage's Analytical Engine.

Analytical Engine

The *Analytical Engine*, designed around 1833, was to perform a variety of calculations by following a set of instructions, or program, stored on punched cards. During processing, the Analytical Engine was to store information in a memory unit that would allow it to make decisions and then carry out instructions based on those decisions. For example, when comparing two numbers it could be programmed to determine which was larger and then follow different sets of instructions. The Analytical Engine was also never built, but its design shown below was to serve as a model for the modern computer.

The History of Punched Cards

In 1810 Joseph Jacquard, a French weaver, used cards with holes punched in them to store weaving instructions for his looms. As the cards passed through the loom in sequence, needles passed through the holes and then picked up threads of the correct color or texture. By rearranging the cards, a weaver could change the pattern being woven without stopping the machine to change threads.

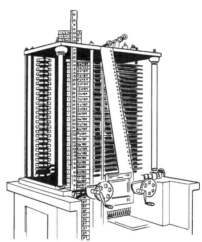

Babbage's Analytical Engine was designed as a calculating machine that used punched cards to store information

Babbage's chief collaborator on the Analytical Engine was Ada Byron, Countess of Lovelace, the daughter of Lord Byron. Interested in mathematics, Lady Byron was a sponsor of the Analytical Engine and one of the first people to realize its power and significance. She also wrote of its achievements in order to gain support for it. Ada Byron is often called the first programmer because she wrote a program based on the design of the Analytical Engine.

Babbage had hoped that the Analytical Engine would be able to think. Ada Byron, however, said that the Engine could never "originate anything," meaning that she did not believe that a machine, no matter how powerful, could think. To this day her statement about computing machines remains true.

Charles Babbage
1792 – 1871

Ada Byron
1815 – 1852

1.2 Electro-Mechanical Devices

Hollerith's tabulating machine

By the end of the 19th century, U.S. Census officials were concerned about the time it took to tabulate the continuously increasing number of Americans. This counting was done every 10 years, as required by the Constitution. However, the Census of 1880 took nine years to compile which made the figures out of date by the time they were published.

In response to a contest sponsored by the U.S. Census Bureau, Herman Hollerith invented a tabulating machine that used electricity rather than mechanical gears. Holes representing information to be tabulated were punched in cards, with the location of each hole representing a specific piece of information (male, female, age, etc.). The cards were then inserted into the machine and metal pins used to open and close electrical circuits. If a circuit was closed, a counter was increased by one.

Herman Hollerith
1860 – 1929

Based on the success of his tabulating machine, Herman Hollerith started the Tabulating Machine Company in 1896. In 1924, the company was taken over by International Business Machines (IBM).

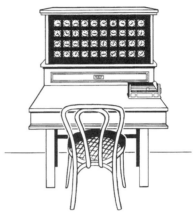

Herman Hollerith's tabulating machine, invented for the Census of 1890, used electricity instead of gears to perform calculations

Hollerith's machine was immensely successful. The general count of the population, then 63 million, took only six weeks to calculate. While the full statistical analysis took seven years, it was still an improvement over the nine years it took to compile the previous census.

Mark I

In 1944, the *Mark I* was completed by a team from International Business Machines (IBM) and Harvard University under the leadership of Howard Aiken. The Mark I used mechanical telephone relay switches to store information and accepted data on punched cards. Because it could not make decisions about the data it processed, the Mark I was not a computer but instead a highly sophisticated calculator. Nevertheless, it was impressive in size, measuring over 51 feet in length and weighing 5 tons. It also had over 750,000 parts, many of them moving mechanical parts which made the Mark I not only huge but unreliable.

Howard Aiken
1900 – 1973

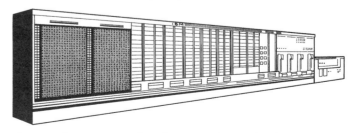

The Mark 1 was 51 feet long and weighed over 5 tons

1.3 First Generation Computers

John Atanasoff
1903 – 1995

Clifford Berry
1918 – 1963

The first electronic computer was built between 1939 and 1942 at Iowa State University by John Atanasoff, a math and physics professor, and Clifford Berry, a graduate student. The *Atanasoff-Berry Computer* (ABC) used the binary number system of 1s and 0s that is still used in computers today. It contained hundreds of vacuum tubes and stored numbers for calculations by electronically burning holes in sheets of paper. The output of calculations was displayed on an odometer type of device.

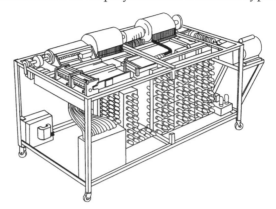

The Atanasoff-Berry Computer used the binary number system used in computers today

The patent application for the ABC was not handled properly, and it was not until almost 50 years later that Atanasoff received full credit for his invention. In 1990, he was awarded the Presidential Medal of Technology for his pioneering work. A working replica of the ABC was unveiled at the Smithsonian in Washington, D.C. on October 9, 1997.

ENIAC

John Mauchly
1907 – 1980

J. Presper Eckert
1919 – 1995

In June 1943, John Mauchly and J. Presper Eckert began work on the *ENIAC* (Electronic Numerical Integration and Calculator). It was originally a secret military project which began during World War II to calculate the trajectory of artillery shells. Built at the University of Pennsylvania, it was not finished until 1946, after the war had ended. But the great effort put into the ENIAC was not wasted. In one of its first demonstrations, ENIAC was given a problem that would have taken a team of mathematicians three days to solve. It solved the problem in twenty seconds.

The ENIAC was originally a secret military project

The ENIAC weighed 30 tons and occupied 1500 square feet, the same area taken up by the average three bedroom house. It contained over 17,000 vacuum tubes, which consumed huge amounts of electricity that produced a tremendous amount of heat requiring special fans to cool the room.

computer

The ABC and the ENIAC are first generation computers because they mark the beginning of the computer era. A *computer* is an electronic machine that accepts data, processes it according to instructions, and provides the results as new data. Most importantly, a computer can make simple decisions and comparisons.

1.4 The Stored Program Computer

The ABC and ENIAC required wire pulling, replugging, and switch flipping to change their instructions. A breakthrough in the architectural design of first generation computers came as a result of separate publications by Alan Turing and John von Neumann, both mathematicians with the idea of the stored program.

In the late 30s and 40s, Alan Turing developed the idea of a "universal machine." He envisioned a computer that could perform many different tasks by simply changing a program rather than by changing electronic components. A *program* is a list of instructions written in a special language that the computer understands.

Alan Turing
1912 – 1954

CPU

In 1945, John von Neumann presented his idea of the stored program concept. The stored program computer would store computer instructions in a *CPU* (central processing unit). The CPU consisted of different elements used to control all the functions of the computer electronically so that it would not be necessary to flip switches or pull wires to change instructions.

EDVAC and EDSAC

Together with Mauchly and Eckert, von Neumann designed and built the *EDVAC* (Electronic Discrete Variable Automatic Computer) and the *EDSAC* (Electronic Delay Storage Automatic Computer). These computers were designed to solve many different problems by simply entering new instructions that were stored on paper tape. The instructions were in *machine language*, which consists of 0s and 1s to represent the status of a switch (0 for off and 1 for on).

machine language

UNIVAC

The third computer to employ the stored program concept was the *UNIVAC* (UNIVersal Automatic Computer) built by Mauchly and Eckert. The first UNIVAC was sold to the U.S. Census Bureau in 1951.

These first generation computers continued to use many vacuum tubes which made them large and expensive. They were so expensive to purchase and run that only the largest corporations and the U.S. government could afford them. Their ability to perform up to 1,000 calculations per second, however, made them popular.

John
von Neumann
1903 – 1957

1.5 Second Generation Computers

transistor

In 1947, William Shockley, John Bardeen, and Walter Brittain of Bell Laboratories invented the *transistor* for which they were awarded the 1956 Nobel Prize in physics. The invention of the transistor made computers smaller and less expensive and increased calculating speeds to up to 10,000 calculations per second.

JohnBardeen, William Shockley, and Walter Brittain

One transistor (on right) replaced many tubes, making computers smaller, less expensive, and more reliable

Model 650

In the early 1960s, IBM introduced the first medium-sized computer named the *Model 650*. It was expensive, but it was much smaller and still capable of handling the flood of paperwork produced by many government agencies and businesses. Such organizations provided a ready market for the 650, making it popular in spite of its cost.

magnetic tape

read, write

Second generation computers also saw a change in the way data was stored. Punched cards were replaced by *magnetic tape* and high speed reel-to-reel tape machines. Using magnetic tape gave computers the ability to *read* (access) and *write* (store) data quickly and reliably.

1.6 High-Level Programming Languages

Second generation computers had more capabilities than first generation computers and were more widely used by business people. This lead to the need for *high-level programming languages* that had English-like instructions and were easier to use than machine language. In 1957, John Backus and a team of researchers completed *FORTRAN* (FORmula TRANslator), a programming language with intuitive commands such as READ and WRITE.

One of the most widely used high-level programming languages has been COBOL, designed by Grace Murray Hopper, a Commodore in the Navy at the time. *COBOL* (COmmon Business Oriented Language) was first developed by the Department of Defense in 1959 to provide a common language for use on all computers. The Department of Defense (DOD) also developed Ada, named after the first programmer, Ada Byron.

Developed in the 1960s by John Kemeny and Thomas Kurtz at Dartmouth University, BASIC was another widely used programming language. *BASIC* (Beginner's All-Purpose Symbolic Instruction Code) has evolved to Visual Basic, which is widely used today for Windows programming.

Grace Murray Hopper
1906 – 1992

While working on the Mark II at Harvard University, Rear Admiral Dr. Grace Murray Hopper found the first computer bug when a moth flew into the circuitry causing an electrical short. While removing the dead moth, she said that the program would be running again after the computer had been "debugged."

An Introduction to Programming Using Microsoft Visual Basic

1.7 Third Generation Computers

integrated circuits

The replacement of transistors by *integrated circuits* (ICs) gave way to the third generation of computers. In 1961, Jack Kilby and Robert Noyce, working independently, developed the IC, sometimes called a *chip*. One IC could replace hundreds of transistors, giving computers tremendous speed to process information at a rate of millions of calculations per second.

ICs are silicon wafers with intricate circuits etched into their surfaces and then coated with a metallic oxide that fills in the etched circuit patterns. This enables the chips to conduct electricity along the many paths of their circuits. The silicon wafers are then housed in special plastic cases that have metal pins coming out of them. The pins allow the chips to be plugged into circuit boards that have wiring printed on them.

A typical chip is about 0.5" wide by 1.5" long

In 1964, the IBM *System 360* was one of the first computers to use integrated circuits and was so popular with businesses that IBM had difficulty keeping up with the demand. Computers had come down in size and price to such a point that smaller organizations such as universities and hospitals could now afford them.

Robert Noyce
1927 – 1990

Noyce developed the integrated circuit while working for Fairchild Semiconductor. In 1968, he left Fairchild to form the company now known as Intel Corporation.

1.8 Mainframes

A *mainframe* is a large computer system that is usually used for multi-user applications. The IBM System 360 was one of the first mainframes available. They are used by large corporations, banks, government agencies, and universities. Mainframes can calculate a large payroll, keep the records for a bank, handle the reservations for an airline, or store student information for a university—tasks that require the storage and processing of huge amounts of information.

Jack S. Kilby
1923 –

Kilby, working for Texas Instruments, developed the first integrated circuit. To demonstrate this new technology, he invented the first electronic hand-held calculator. It was small enough to fit in a coat pocket, but as powerful as the large, desktop models of the time.

Mainframe computers are large and set up in their own rooms

terminals

Most people using mainframes communicate with them using *terminals*. A terminal consists of a keyboard for data input, and a monitor for viewing output. The terminal is connected by wires to the computer, which may be located on a different floor or a building a few blocks away. Some mainframes have hundreds of terminals attached and working at the same time.

1.9 Fourth Generation Computers

microprocessor

Marcian Hoff
1937 –

In 1970, Marcian Hoff, an engineer at Intel Corporation, invented the *microprocessor*, an entire CPU on a single chip. The replacement of several larger components by one microprocessor made possible the fourth generation of computers.

The small microprocessor made it possible to build a computer called a *microcomputer* that fits on a desktop. The first of these was the Altair built in 1975. In 1976, Stephen Wozniak and Steven Jobs designed and built the first Apple computer.

Advances in technology made microcomputers inexpensive and therefore available to many people. Because of these advances almost anyone could own a machine that had more computing power and was faster and more reliable than either the ENIAC or UNIVAC. As a comparison, if the cost of a sports car had dropped as quickly as that of a computer, a new Porsche would now cost about one dollar.

Stephen Wozniak
1950 –

1.10 The Personal Computer

Microcomputers, often called *personal computers* or *PCs*, fit on a desktop. Modern PCs have computing power and storage capacity that rival older mainframes. The computer you will use is a microcomputer:

Steve Jobs
1955 –

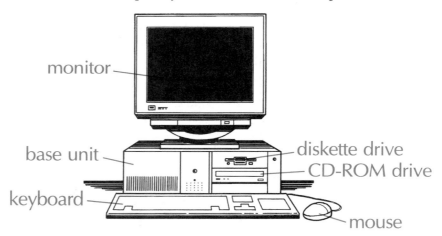

A PC combines a keyboard, monitor, external drives, and a mouse in a desktop-sized package

Microcomputers contain four types of *hardware* components:

1. **Input Devices:** devices from which the computer can accept data. A keyboard, CD-ROM drive, disk drive, and a mouse are all examples of input devices.

2. **Memory:** ICs inside the base unit where data can be stored electronically.

3. **CPU (Central Processing Unit):** an IC inside the base unit that processes data and controls the flow of data between the computer's other units. It is here that the computer makes decisions.

The IBM–PC

In 1981, IBM introduced the IBM–PC. The computer was an instant success because of the availability of spreadsheet, accounting, and word processing software. Sales of the PC skyrocketed even further when Lotus Development Corporation came out with their spreadsheet program 1-2-3, the most successful program in history.

---

4. **Output Devices:** devices that display or store processed data. Monitors and printers are the most common visual output devices. The hard disk, which is inside the base unit, and the diskette and CD-ROM are the most common storage output devices.

The diagram below illustrates the direction that data flows between the separate components of a computer:

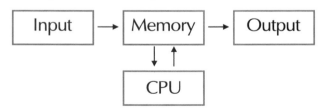

Notice that all information flows through the CPU. Because one of the tasks of the CPU is to control the order in which tasks are completed, it is often referred to as the "brain" of the computer. However, this comparison with the human brain has an important flaw. The CPU only executes tasks according to the instructions it has been given; it cannot think for itself.

software

Microcomputers require software to perform tasks. *Software* is instructions stored as electronic data that tells the computer what to do. *Operating system software* is run automatically when the computer is turned on and enables the user to communicate with the computer by using input devices such as the mouse and keyboard. Additionally, *applications software*, also just called *software*, *application*, or *program*, is written by programmers to perform a specific task.

1.11 Memory: ROM and RAM

Computers have two types of memory contained on chips, *ROM* and *RAM*. Read Only Memory, or ROM, contains the most basic operating instructions for the computer. The data in ROM is a permanent part of the computer and cannot be changed. The instructions in ROM enable the computer to complete simple jobs such as placing a character on the screen or checking the keyboard to see if any keys have been pressed.

Random Access Memory, or RAM, is temporary memory where data and instructions can be stored. Data stored here can be changed or erased. When the computer is first turned on, this part of memory is empty and, when turned off, any data it contains is lost. Because RAM storage is temporary, computers have auxiliary data storage devices. Before turning the computer off, the data in RAM can be saved to a floppy diskette or the hard disk so that it can be used again at a later time.

1.12 The CPU

The CPU (Central Processing Unit) directs the processing of information throughout the computer. It can only follow instructions that it gets from ROM or from a program in RAM.

A CPU chip measures about 2" by 2" and is many times more powerful than the Mark I

Within the CPU is the *ALU* (Arithmetic Logic Unit), which can perform arithmetic and logic operations. The ALU is so fast that the time needed to carry out a single addition is measured in *nanoseconds* (billionths of a second). The ALU can also compare numbers to determine whether a number is greater than, less than, or equal to another number. This ability is the basis of the computer's decision-making power.

1.13 Number Systems

binary

The electrical circuits on an IC have one of two states, off or on. Therefore, the *binary number system* (base 2), which uses only two digits (0 and 1), was adopted for use in computers. To represent numbers and letters, a code was developed with eight binary digits grouped together to represent a single number or letter. Each 0 or 1 in the binary code is called a

bit, byte

bit (BInary digiT) and an 8-bit unit is called a *byte*.

base 10

Our most familiar number system is the decimal, or *base 10*, system. It uses ten digits: 0 through 9. Each place represents a power of ten, with the first place to the left of the decimal point representing 10^0, the next place representing 10^1, the next 10^2, and so on (remember that any number raised to the zero power is 1). In the decimal number 485, the 4 represents 4×10^2, the 8 represents 8×10^1, and the 5 represents 5×10^0. The number 485 represents the sum $4\times100 + 8\times10 + 5\times1$ (400 + 80 + 5) as shown below:

Decimal Number	Base 10 Equivalent
485	$4\times10^2 + 8\times10^1 + 5\times10^0 = 400 + 80 + 5$

base 2

The binary, or *base 2*, system works identically except that each place represents a power of two instead of a power of ten. For example, the binary number 101 represents the sum $1\times2^2 + 0\times2^1 + 1\times2^0$ or 5 in base ten. Some decimal numbers and their binary equivalents are shown below:

Decimal Number	Binary Number	Base 2 Equivalent		
0	0	$= 0\times2^1 + 0\times2^0$	$= 0\times2 + 0\times1$	$= 0 + 0$
1	1	$= 0\times2^1 + 1\times2^0$	$= 0\times2 + 1\times1$	$= 0 + 1$
2	10	$= 1\times2^1 + 0\times2^0$	$= 1\times2 + 0\times1$	$= 2 + 0$
3	11	$= 1\times2^1 + 1\times2^0$	$= 1\times2 + 1\times1$	$= 2 + 1$
4	100	$= 1\times2^2 + 0\times2^1 + 0\times2^0$	$= 1\times4 + 0\times2 + 0\times1$	$= 4 + 0 + 0$

base 16

The hexadecimal system is used to represent groups of four binary digits. The *hexadecimal*, or *base 16*, system is based on 16 digits: 0 through 9, and the letters A through F representing 10 through 15 respectively. Each place represents a power of sixteen. For example, the hexadecimal number 1F represents the sum $1\times16^1 + 15\times16^0$. Some decimal numbers and their hexadecimal equivalents are shown below:

Decimal Number	Binary Number	Hexadecimal Number	Base 16 Equivalent		
0	0000 0000	0	$= 0\times16^0$	$= 0\times1$	$= 0$
10	0000 1010	A	$= 10\times16^0$	$= 10\times1$	$= 10$
15	0000 1111	F	$= 15\times16^0$	$= 15\times1$	$= 15$
20	0001 0100	14	$= 1\times16^1 + 4\times16^0$	$= 1\times16 + 4\times1$	$= 16 + 4$
25	0001 1001	19	$= 1\times16^1 + 9\times16^0$	$= 1\times16 + 9\times1$	$= 16 + 9$
30	0001 1110	1E	$= 1\times16^1 + 14\times16^0$	$= 1\times16 + 14\times1$	$= 16 + 14$

For clarity, a non-base 10 number should have the base subscripted after the number. For example, to show the difference between 100 in base 10 and 100 in base 2 (which represents 4), the base 2 number should be written as 100_2.

ASCII

In order to allow computers to interchange information, the American Standard Code for Information Interchange, or *ASCII*, was developed. In this code, each letter of the alphabet, both uppercase and lowercase, and each symbol, digit, and special control function used by the computer is assigned a number. The ASCII representation of the letters in the name JIM are 74, 73, 77. Both the decimal and binary code representations of those numbers are shown below:

Letter	Decimal	Binary code
J	74	01001010
I	73	01001001
M	77	01001101

ANSI

The ANSI (American National Standards Institute) character set is the first 127 characters of ASCII. The ANSI character set does not vary from computer to computer. The remaining ASCII characters (128 through 256) vary depending on computer.

1.14 Storing Data in Memory

memory size
MB

The size of memory in a computer is measured in bytes. For example, a computer might have 16 MB of RAM. In computers and electronics *MB* stands for *megabytes* where mega represents 2^{20} or 1,048,576 bytes and

GB
K

GB stands for *gigabytes*, which is 2^{30} or 1,073,741,820 bytes. Bytes are sometimes described as *kilobytes*, for example 256K. The *K* comes from the word *kilo* and represents 2^{10} or 1024. Therefore, 64K of memory is really 64×2^{10} which equals 65,536 bytes.

address

Data stored in memory is referred to by an address. An *address* is a unique binary representation of a location in memory. Therefore, data can be stored, accessed, and retrieved from memory by its address. For data to be addressable in memory, it must usually be at least one byte in length. For example, to store JIM in memory each character is stored as binary code in a separate location in memory designated by its address:

	J	I	M
binary code	01001010	01001001	01001101
memory address	01	10	11

Because JIM is a character string, it will probably be stored in adjacent memory addresses.

word   Bits grouped in units of 8 to 64 or more are called *words*. Data stored in a word is also located by an address. The size of a word depends on the computer system.

integers   The binary representation of an integer number is usually stored in two bytes of memory. Because an integer is stored in two bytes, the range

overflow error   of integers that can be stored is –32,768 to 32,767. An *overflow error* occurs when the number of bits that are needed to represent the integer is greater than the size of two bytes.

real numbers   *Real numbers*, also called *floating point numbers*, are numbers that contain decimal points. The binary representation of a real number is usually 4 to 8 bytes of memory. The binary number 111.10 is equivalent to the real decimal number 7.5 and is stored in memory as the binary number 0.11110×2^3. In this form, the bits that represent the *mantissa* (fractional part) are stored in one section of a word and the *exponent*, in this example 3 (11_2), is stored in another section of the word:

The overflow problem discussed for integers can also occur in real numbers if the part of the word storing the exponent is not large enough. A

roundoff error   *roundoff error* occurs when there are not enough bits to hold the mantissa.

1.15 Storage Devices

Most PCs today have three drives: a *diskette drive*, a *CD-ROM drive*, and a *hard disk drive*. The diskette and CD-ROM (compact disc read-only memory) drives are accessible from outside the base unit, and the hard disk is completely contained inside the base unit. All three drives use a different kind of storage media for storing data:

Data can be stored on diskette, CD, or hard disk (internal)

diskette   Sometimes called a floppy disk, *diskettes* are made of a mylar (thin polyester film) disk that is coated with a magnetic material and then loosely

CD   encased in hard plastic. Each diskette has a capacity of 1.44 MB. *CDs* (compact discs) are discs made of mylar with a reflective coating that is sealed in clear, hard plastic. Each CD can store over 650 MB of data, equal

hard disk   to the storage capacity of over 470 diskettes. *Hard disks* are made of an aluminum disk coated with a magnetic material. Unlike diskettes and CDs, hard disks are permanently installed inside the hard disk drive. Each hard drive may have multiple disks inside, and therefore have large storage capacities of 1 GB or more.

An Introduction to Programming Using Microsoft Visual Basic

WORM | Data can be written to and read from diskettes, CDs, and hard disks. However, a PC would need to be equipped with a *WORM* (write once read many) or similar drive to store data on a CD. Therefore, data is usually stored on diskettes or the hard disk drive.

Although not standard with most PCs, there are other storage devices that use media with a much greater capacity than described above. One such drive is a *tape drive*, which stores data on magnetic tape sealed in a cartridge. Each cartridge holds 7 GB or more of data. Another drive is a *removable hard drive* which uses disks constructed like diskettes but larger. Each disk has a capacity of 230 MB or more. Another drive, an Iomega *Zip drive*, is quickly becoming a standard in many PCs. The Zip drive uses disks almost as small as a diskette, but with a 100 MB capacity.

Completely external to the PC is the *hard disk array*. Enormous amounts of data can be made transportable using hard disk arrays. These are towers of several hard drives (not just large diskettes as in the removable hard drives) that combine to equal 72 GB or more. Each hard drive can be removed from the tower and transported to another array tower.

tape drive

removable hard drive

Zip drive

hard disk array

1.16 Object-Oriented Programming

Computers are widely used by virtually every industry. This widespread use is due largely to the development of programs written specifically for a particular need of a business or organization. These programs are called *applications software*, or just *applications*.

With the ever-increasing demand for powerful applications, the need for programmers and programming languages has also increased. Object-oriented programming was developed to more easily create complex applications. An *object* is a collection of data and code that performs a specific task. Object-oriented languages include C++ and Visual Basic.

1.17 The Social and Ethical Implications of Computers

The society in which we live has been so profoundly affected by computers that historians refer to the present time as the *information age*. This is due to the computer's ability to store and manipulate large amounts of information (data). Because of computers, we are evolving out of an industrial and into an information society. Such fundamental societal changes cause disruptions which must be planned for. For this reason it is crucial that we consider both the social and ethical implications of our increasing dependence on computers. By ethical questions we mean asking what are the morally right and wrong ways to use computers.

right to privacy | Probably the most serious problem associated with computers is the possiblility of invading our privacy. Because computers can store vast amounts of data we must decide what information is proper to store, what is improper, and who should have access to the information. Every time you use a credit card, make a phone call, withdraw money, reserve a flight, or register at school a computer records the transaction. These records can be used to learn a great deal about you—where you have been, when you were there, and how much money was spent. Should this information be available to everyone?

The NII

Living in the information age requires access to information stored on computers all over the world. To help make this information available to every school, hospital, business, and library, a U.S. government initiative called the National Information Infrastructure (NII) is working to develop and integrate hardware, software, telecommunications, network standards and much more.

Computers are also used to store information about your credit rating, which determines your ability to borrow money. If you want to buy a car and finance it at a bank, the bank first checks your credit records on a computer to determine if you have a good credit rating. If you purchase the car and then apply for automobile insurance, another computer will check to determine if you have traffic violations. How do you know if the information being used is accurate? To protect both your privacy and the accuracy of data stored about you, a number of laws have been passed.

The **Fair Credit Reporting Act of 1970** deals with data collected for use by credit, insurance, and employment agencies. The act gives individuals the right to see information maintained about them. If a person is denied credit they are allowed to see the files used to make the credit determination. If any of the information is incorrect, the person has the right to have it changed. The act also restricts who may access credit files to only those with a court order or the written permission of the individual whose credit is being checked.

The **Privacy Act of 1974** restricts the way in which personal data can be used by federal agencies. Individuals must be permitted access to information stored about them and may correct any information that is incorrect. Agencies must insure both the security and confidentiality of any sensitive information. Although this law applies only to federal agencies, many states have adopted similar laws.

The **Financial Privacy Act of 1978** requires that a government authority have a subpoena, summons, or search warrant to access an individual's financial records. When such records are released, the financial institution must notify the individual of who has had access to them.

The **Electronic Communications Privacy Act of 1986** (ECPA) makes it a crime to access electronic data without authorization. It also prohibits unauthorized release of such data.

Laws such as these help to insure that the right to privacy is not infringed by the improper use of data stored in computer files. Although implementing privacy laws has proven expensive and difficult, most people would agree that they are needed.

1.18 Protecting Computer Software and Data

Because computer software can be copied electronically, it is easy to duplicate. Such duplication is usually illegal because the company producing the software is not paid for the copy. This has become an increasingly serious problem as the number of illegal software copies distributed through *piracy* has grown. Developing, testing, marketing, and supporting software is an expensive process. If the software developer is then denied rightful compensation, the future development of all software is jeopardized.

piracy

Software companies are increasingly vigilant in detecting and prosecuting those who illegally copy their software. Persons found guilty of using illegally copied software can be fined, and their reputation damaged. Therefore, when using software it is important to use only legally acquired copies, and to not make illegal copies for others.

Another problem that is growing as computer use increases is the willful interference with or destruction of computer data. Because computers can transfer and erase data at high speeds, it makes them especially vulnerable to acts of vandalism. Newspapers have carried numerous reports of computer users gaining access to large computer databases. Sometimes these *crackers* change or erase stored data. These acts are usually illegal and can cause very serious and expensive damage. The Electronic Communications Privacy Act of 1986 specifically makes it a federal offense to access electronic data without authorization.

cracker

One especially harmful act is the planting of a virus into computer software. A *virus* is a series of instructions buried into a program that cause the computer to destroy data when given a certain signal. For example, the instructions to destroy data might check the computer's clock and then destroy data when a certain time is reached. Because the virus is duplicated each time the software is copied, it spreads to other computers, hence the name virus. This practice is illegal and can result in considerable damage. Computer viruses have become so widespread that anti-virus programs have been created to detect and erase viruses before they can damage data.

virus

Contaminated diskettes are one way that viruses are spread from computer to computer

The willful destruction of computer data is no different than any other vandalization of property. Since the damage is done electronically the result is often not as obvious as destroying physical property, but the consequences are much the same. It is estimated that computer crimes cost the nation billions of dollars each year.

1.19 The Ethical Responsibilities of the Programmer

It is extremely difficult, if not impossible, for a computer programmer to guarantee that a program will *always* operate properly. The programs used to control complicated devices contain millions of instructions, and as programs grow longer the likelihood of errors increases. A special cause for concern is the increased use of computers to control potentially dangerous devices such as aircraft, nuclear reactors, or sensitive medical equipment. This places a strong ethical burden on the programmer to insure, as best as he or she can, the reliability of the computer software.

The DOD is supporting research aimed at detecting and correcting programming errors. Because it spends billions of dollars annually developing software, much of it for use in situations which can be life threatening, the DOD is especially interested in having reliable programs.

The Turing Test

In 1950, Alan Turing raised the question "Can machines think?" To answer that question he invented the "Imitation Game." The game involves placing a person and a computer in separate rooms and an interrogator in a third room. Communicating by typed questions and answers, the interrogator questions the human and computer to determine which is the computer. If the interrogator cannot tell the difference between the responses, then the machine has human thought capabilities. Currently, no computer or software program has been shown to be capable of consistently passing the *Turing test*. However, when limited to a specific topic, say sports, several programs have fooled their human interrogators into thinking they were communicating with another human.

As capable as computers have proven to be, we must be cautious when allowing them to replace human beings in areas where judgement is crucial. As intelligent beings, we can often detect that something out of the ordinary has occurred which has not been previously anticipated and then take appropriate actions. Computers will only do what they have been programmed to do, even if it is to perform a dangerous act.

1.20 Why learn to program?

Programming gives a sense of what computers can and cannot do, and is one of the best ways to gain a deep understanding of computer technology. Learning to program leads to a more intuitive feel for why computers and computer programs work the way they do. It also gives an appreciation for the important and difficult task of software creation.

Another benefit of learning to program is the development of problem-solving skills. Problems in real life are often complex, large, and multi-faceted, as are computer programming problems. In learning to program, you will analyze a problem carefully; break it down into small, solvable parts; and put together the solutions to form a complete and correct solution to the problem. This problem-solving ability is what sets apart successful people in all walks of life.

Finally, the most obvious benefit of learning to program is that it is fun. The computer provides an immediate response to your work. When you create a solution to a complex problem, and the solution is embodied in a working program, there is a great feeling of accomplishment.

Chapter Summary

The earliest computing devices were mechanical, requiring gears, wheels and levers, and were often unreliable. The advent of electricity brought about electro-mechanical machines, and later first generation computers that used vacuum tubes and were capable of performing thousands of calculations per minute. The architectural design of computers changed with the idea of a machine that could perform many different tasks by simply changing its program. With the development

transistor of the transistor came second generation computers that were much smaller and faster. Programming languages were developed so programmers could write English-like instructions. Third generation computers

integrated circuit used integrated circuits. Fourth generation computers, the modern microcomputers of today, include an entire CPU on a single chip.

hardware All PCs have several hardware components: (1) input devices (keyboard, mouse, drives) for entering data and commands, (2) memory for storing commands and data, (3) a central processing unit for controlling the operations of the computer, and (4) output devices (monitor, printer, drives) for viewing and storing the processed information. PCs also re-

software quire operating system software and applications software.

RAM Memory is contained on ICs and comes in two forms, RAM, which
ROM can be erased and used over, and ROM, which is permanent. Because the contents of RAM are lost when the computer's power is turned off,

storage devices storage devices such as diskettes, CD-ROMs, and hard disks are used to store data.

CPU
ALU

A CPU directs the processing of information throughout the computer. Within the CPU is the ALU, which is the basis of the computer's decision-making power.

base 2
bit
base 16

Because the electrical circuits of an IC have one of two states, off or on, the binary number system is used to represent the two states: 0 for off and 1 for on. Each 0 or 1 in a binary code is called a bit. In the binary number system, each place represents a power of two. The hexadecimal number system is based on 16 digits: 0 through 9, and the letters A through F. In the hexadecimal number system, each place represents a power of 16.

byte
ASCII

The computer uses binary digits grouped into bytes to express all information. The ASCII code is used to translate numbers, letters, and symbols into a one byte binary code.

memory size
address
word
overflow error

roundoff error

The size of memory is measured in bytes, usually in MB or GB. The location of data stored in memory is referred to by an address. Integers and real numbers are stored in one word in memory. Because the number of bits in a word is limited, an overflow error occurs when the number of bits that represent an integer is greater than the size of the word. A roundoff error occurs when the bits that represent the mantissa of a real number is greater than the section of the word that stores the mantissa.

Applications software are programs developed for a particular need. Object-oriented programming was developed to more easily create complex applications.

Historians refer to the present time as the information age due to the computer's ability to store and manipulate large amounts of data. As the use of computers increases they will profoundly affect society. Therefore, it is important to analyze the social and ethical implications of computers.

right to privacy

A problem created by computers is the potential for invading privacy. Laws have been passed to avoid the misuse of data stored in computers.

piracy

virus

Because computer software is easy to copy, illegal copies are often made. This denies software manufacturers of rightful compensation. Another problem has been the willful destruction of computer files by erasing data or planting virus programs.

As computers are increasingly used to make decisions in situations which can impact human life, it becomes the responsibility of programmers to do their best to insure the reliability of the software they have developed. We must continue to be cautious not to replace human beings with computers in areas where judgement is crucial.

Programming gives a sense of the capabilities of computers and an understanding of computer technology. Learning to program also aids in the development of problem solving skills.

Vocabulary

Address Unique binary representation of the location of data in memory.

ALU (Arithmetic Logic Unit) The part of the CPU that handles arithmetic and logic operations.

Application See Applications software.

Applications software Commercially produced programs written to perform specific tasks.

ASCII (American Standard Code for Information Interchange) The code used for representing characters in the computer.

Base 2 See Binary number system.

Base 10 See Decimal number system.

Base 16 See Hexadecimal number system.

Base unit Unit where the CPU, memory, and internal hard disk drive is housed.

BASIC A high-level computer language developed by John Kemeny and Thomas Kurtz.

Binary number system Number system used by modern computers—uses only digits 0 and 1 (base 2 system).

Bit (BInary digiT) A single 0 or 1 in the binary code.

Byte A group of 8 bits.

CD Disc made of mylar with a reflective coating that is sealed in clear, hard plastic.

CD-ROM drive Drive accessible from outside the base unit. Used to read the data on a CD-ROM.

Chip See Integrated circuit.

Class Contains data and code that define the behavior of an object of its class.

COBOL A high-level language designed by Grace Murray Hopper.

Computer An electronic machine that accepts data, processes it according to instructions, and provides the results as new data.

CPU (Central Processing Unit) The device which electronically controls the functions of the computer.

Cracker A computer user who gains unauthorized access into a computer system.

Data Information either entered into or produced by the computer.

Decimal number system A common number system used by people—uses digits 0 through 9 (base 10 system).

Diskette Sometimes called a floppy disk. Made of mylar coated with a magnetic material and then loosely encased in hard plastic.

Diskette drive Drive accessible from outside the base unit. Used to read and write data to a diskette.

Floating point number See Real number.

FORTRAN A high-level programming language developed by John Backus.

GB (gigabyte) Measurement of computer memory capacity. 1,073,741,820 bytes.

Hardware Physical devices that make up the computer.

Hard disk Made of aluminum coated with a magnetic material. Permanently installed inside the hard disk drive.

Hard disk array A tower of several hard drives where each drive can be removed and transported to another array.

Hard disk drive Drive completely enclosed in the base unit. Used to read and write to disks within the hard drive.

Hexadecimal number system Number system used to group four binary digits—uses digits 0 through 9, and the letters A through F (base 16 system).

High-level programming language A programming language that uses English-like instructions.

Inheritance The ability for a class to also use the properties of another class.

Input Data used by the computer.

Instantiated The creating of an object from a class.

IC (Integrated Circuit) Also called a chip. A silicon wafer with intricate circuits etched into its surface and then coated with a metallic oxide that fills in the etched circuit patterns.

Interpreter A program that executes each line of a program as it is entered.

K (kilobyte) Measurement of computer memory capacity. 1024 bytes.

Keyboard Device resembling a typewriter used to input data into a computer.

Machine language Instructions in binary code (0s and 1s).

Magnetic tape A storage device.

Mainframe Computer system that is usually used for multi-user applications.

Mantissa The fractional part of a number.

MB (megabyte) Measurement of computer memory capacity. 1,048,576 bytes.

Memory Electronic storage used by the computer.

Microcomputer A computer that fits on a desktop and uses a microprocessor.

Microprocessor An entire CPU on a single chip.

Monitor Used to display computer output.

Mouse An input device from which the computer can accept information.

Nanosecond One billionth of a second.

Object A collection of data and code that performs a specific task.

Operating system software Software that allows the user to communicate with the computer.

Output Data produced by a computer program.

Overflow error Occurs when the number of bits that represent an integer is greater that the size of the word in memory.

PC (Personal Computer) A small computer employing a microprocessor.

Piracy The illegal copying of software.

Program Series of instructions written in a special language directing the computer to perform certain tasks.

RAM (Random Access Memory) Memory that the computer can both read and write.

Read Accessing data from a storage medium.

Real number A number that contains a decimal point.

Removable hard drive Drive used to read and write data to a removable disk.

ROM (Read Only Memory) Memory that the computer can only read and not write.

Roundoff error Occurs when there are not enough bits to hold the mantissa of a number.

Software See Applications software.

Tape drive Drive used to read and write the data to a magnetic tape.

Terminal A keyboard and monitor used to communicate with a mainframe.

Transistor An electronic device that replaced the vacuum tube making computers smaller and less expensive and increased calculating speeds.

Virus A series of instructions buried into a program that cause the computer to destroy data when given a certain signal.

Word Bits grouped in units of 8 to 65 bits.

WORM (Write Once Read Many) A device used to store data on a CD.

Write Storing data on a storage medium.

Zip disk A disk, almost as small as a diskette, that stores 100 MB of data. Used in a Zip drive.

Zip drive Drive used to read and write data to a Zip disk.

Review Questions

Sections 1.1 — 1.4

1. Briefly describe the Pascaline and explain what mathematical operations it was designed to perform.

2. a) What mathematical operations was the Stepped Reckoner supposed to perform?
   b) Why was it unreliable?

3. What did Ada Byron mean when she said that the Analytical Engine could never "originate anything"?

4. a) For what purpose did Herman Hollerith invent his tabulating machine?
   b) What were punched cards used for in the tabulating machine?

5. Why wasn't the Mark 1 considered a computer?

6. What number system did the Atanasoff-Berry Computer use?

7. For what purpose was the ENIAC originally designed?

8. What is a computer?

9. In what way did Alan Turning and John von Neumann improve upon the design of the ENIAC?

10. a) What is a program?
    b) What is machine language?
    c) List the first three computers designed to use a stored program.

Sections 1.5 — 1.9

11. Why was the invention of the transistor important to the development of computers?

12. How did the use of magnetic tape improve the performance of computers?

13. a) What is a high-level programming language?
    b) Who designed COBOL?
    c) List three high-level programming languages.

14. Explain what integrated circuits are and why they have been important in the development of computers.

15. a) What is a mainframe?
    b) What is the usual way for a person to communicate with a mainframe?

16. Why was the invention of the microprocessor important to the development of computers?

17. List some of the advantages of a microcomputer compared with the ENIAC or UNIVAC?

Sections 1.10 — 1.16

18. What are input and output devices use for?

19. Describe the flow of data between the components of a computer.

20. In what way was the design of Babbage's Analytical Engine similar to the modern computer?

21. a) What is the difference between ROM and RAM?
    b) How is each affected by turning off the computer?

22. a) Explain what a CPU does.
    b) Why is it called the "brain" of the computer?

23. Why was the binary number system adopted for use in computers?

24. Explain what a bit and a byte are.

25. a) What is decimal equivalent of 111_2?
    b) What is the decimal equivalent of $2C_{16}$?

26. Why was ASCII developed?

27. a) How many bytes of data can 32 MB of RAM store?
    b) How many bytes of data can a 3 GB hard drive store?

28. How is data stored in memory referred to?

29. a) When does an overflow error occur?
    b) When does a roundoff error occur?

30. a) List three storage devices commonly used with a PC.
    b) List three other storage devices used with a PC.

31. What is applications software?

32. Why was object oriented programming developed?

Sections 1.17 — 1.20
33. What is meant by the information age?

34. a) How do you believe society is benefitting from the information age?
    b) What are some of the negative aspects of the information age?

35. How can computers be used to invade your privacy?

36. What can you do if you are turned down for credit at a bank and believe that the data used to deny credit is inaccurate?

37. a) What is necessary for a federal government authority to access an individual's financial records?
    b) What must an authority do after accessing the records?

38. a) What is computer piracy?
    b) What is a computer cracker?
    c) What is a computer virus?

39. a) What ethical responsibilities does a programmer have when writing a program that will impact human lives?
    b) Can the programmer absolutely guarantee that a program will operate properly? Why?

40. List three reasons for learning to progam.

An Introduction to Programming Using Microsoft Visual Basic

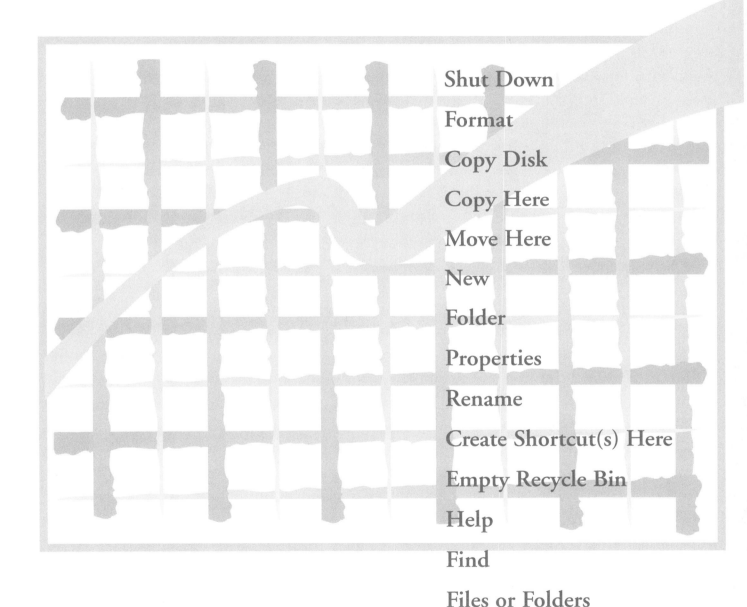

Shut Down

Format

Copy Disk

Copy Here

Move Here

New

Folder

Properties

Rename

Create Shortcut(s) Here

Empty Recycle Bin

Help

Find

Files or Folders

Chapter Two Objectives

After completing this chapter you will be able to:

1. Define what an operating system is.
2. Use the mouse as an input device.
3. Understand the features of the Windows 98 operating system.
4. Identify and describe the features of a window.
5. Manipulate a window.
6. Understand the features of a dialog box.
7. Start and exit an application.
8. Create, save, close, open, and print a document.
9. Scroll a document.
10. Understand how to use and properly handle diskettes.
11. Format, copy, write protect, and backup a diskette.
12. Navigate through the contents of the computer.
13. Copy, move, delete, and rename files and folders.
14. Create shortcuts, read-only files, and folders.
15. Recover deleted files.
16. Use online help and locate files.

This chapter introduces Windows 98. You will use the WordPad application to learn about the common features and commands of most Windows 98 applications. You will also learn how to use the mouse, handle diskettes properly, format a diskette, and make backups of a file.

2.1 Operating Systems

All microcomputers run software that allow the user to communicate with the computer using the keyboard and mouse. This software is called the *disk operating system* (DOS). When the computer is turned on, the operating system software is automatically loaded into the computer's memory from the computer's hard disk in a process called *booting*.

A widely used operating system is Windows 98, which has a *graphical user interface*, or GUI (pronounced "gooey"). A GUI displays pictures called icons on the computer screen. *Icons* are used to perform various tasks.

Through the use of Windows 98, multitasking is possible. *Multitasking* allows for more than one application to run at the same time. For example, with Windows 98 both word processor and spreadsheet applications can run simultaneously.

The Windows 98 GUI also supplies applications and tools that allow you to easily work with the operating system. The Windows 98 GUI is described further in Section 2.4.

2.2 Applications Software

Applications software, also called just software, application, or program, is written by professional programmers to perform a specific application or task. Most applications created for use with Windows 98 have a similar interface. The *interface* of an application is the way it looks on the screen and the way in which a user provides input to the application. For example, two elements of Windows 98 applications are dialog boxes and windows. A *dialog box* allows the user to choose and enter information that is needed to complete an action, and a *window* is the area on the screen that contains an open application or file. A *file* is the material that you create using an application.

William H. Gates III
1955 -

In 1975, while a freshman at Harvard University, Bill Gates and his friend Paul Allen created a Basic language interpreter for the Altair computer. With the success of Basic for the Altair, Gates and Allen founded the Microsoft Corporation in 1977. The huge success of Microsoft began in 1981 when Gates developed MS-DOS (Microsoft Disk Operating System) for the new IBM-PC. Today Microsoft is known for its Windows operating system, Visual Basic programming languge, and many applications software packages.

2.3 Using the Mouse

The computer comes equipped with a special input device called a *mouse,* which is used to perform a variety of tasks. A mouse has two or three buttons and looks similar to:

The mouse

mouse pointer

When the mouse is in use, the *mouse pointer* is displayed on the screen. One common shape of the mouse pointer is an arrow:

The mouse pointer

The mouse pointer may change shape depending on the current operation being performed. For example, an hourglass shape () is displayed when the computer is performing a task and cannot accept additional input at that time.

moving

Sliding the mouse on the top of a desk causes the mouse pointer to move on the screen. Slide the mouse to the left and the mouse pointer moves to the left; slide the mouse to the right and the mouse pointer moves to the right.

pointing

Moving the mouse to place the pointer on an icon or other object is called *pointing.* In this text, when we say to point to an object on the screen, we mean to move the mouse until the mouse pointer is placed on the object.

screen tips

When pointing to an object that performs an action and pausing for a few seconds, a screen tip appears near the pointer. The *screen tip* provides information about the object and often describes what action(s) the object can perform.

selecting

An object on the computer screen can be *selected* by pointing to it and pressing the left mouse button and releasing it quickly. This type of se-

clicking

lection is called *clicking.* When we say to select, or click on, an item, we mean to point to it and then press and release the left mouse button.

right-clicking

Right-clicking is pressing the right button on the mouse and releasing it quickly. Pointing to an object on the screen and then right-clicking displays a list of commands that are related to that object.

double-clicking

A special form of clicking is *double-clicking.* As the name implies, double-clicking means to point to an object and then press the left mouse button twice in rapid succession.

dragging

The last mouse technique is called *dragging.* When we say to drag, we mean to press and hold the left mouse button while moving the mouse. In some cases, an object can be moved by dragging it. When we say to drag an object, we mean to point to it and then hold down the left mouse button while moving the mouse. When the object is in the desired location, release the mouse button. At times, dragging using the *right* mouse button is necessary. The results of dragging with the right mouse button can be very different from dragging with the left mouse button. Unless specified, always use the left mouse button when dragging.

Customizing the Desktop

The Windows 98 Desktop can be customized. Right-clicking on an empty portion of the Desktop and selecting the Properties command from the menu displays a dialog box where you can view and change the Desktop's background, the screen saver, the appearance of windows, and the screen's settings. You can also specify that you have an Active Desktop. An Active Desktop integrates the Web and the Desktop.

You can also modify an object's properties by right-clicking on it and selecting the Properties command.

Moving objects on the Desktop is also possible. The Task bar is usually at the bottom of the screen; however, it can be moved to any corner of the screen by dragging it. The icons can also be dragged to new locations. This allows you to arrange the objects on the Desktop the way you want them to appear.

2.4 The Windows 98 GUI

The *Windows 98 GUI* contains features that allow you to easily use the operating system and applications software. When Windows 98 is running, the computer screen is referred to as the *Desktop*. The Desktop's three most important features are the Start button, Task bar, and icons:

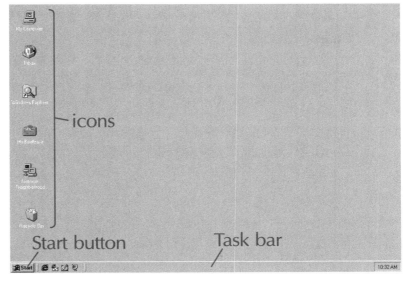

Your Desktop may appear different depending on the properties selected for your computer

Clicking on the Start button displays a list of commands:

Shut Down command

Commands perform specific tasks and actions. Note the Shut Down command. This command should always be selected before you turn off the computer.

The *Task bar* displays the names of every open program. Clicking on a program name on the Task bar displays or minimizes that program's window. The Task bar allows you to easily switch between open programs.

The icons displayed on the Desktop are used to represent files and programs. Icons are double-clicked to perform tasks and run applications.

Review 1

In this review you will view the Windows 98 Desktop, locate the Start button, and view the Start menu.

1) BOOT THE COMPUTER

   a.   Turn on the computer and the monitor. After a few seconds, the computer automatically loads Windows 98.
   b.   After Windows 98 is booted, the Welcome to Windows 98 dialog box may appear. If the dialog box appears, first point to the Close button (☒) in the upper-right corner of the dialog box by moving the mouse until the mouse pointer is on it. Next, click on the Close button by pressing the left mouse button once. The dialog box is removed from the screen.

2) IDENTIFY THE PARTS OF THE DESKTOP

   a.   Identify the icons on the Desktop. How many icons appear on the Desktop?
   b.   Locate the Task bar on the Desktop. Are there any open programs?
   c.   Locate the Start button and point to it. Leave the mouse pointer on the Start button for a few seconds without moving it. What does the screen tip say?

3) VIEW THE START MENU

   a.   Click once on the Start button. Commands are displayed. Note how some of the commands have an arrow (▶).
   b.   Point to Programs. The names of the applications available on your computer are displayed.
   c.   Click once anywhere outside the list to remove the list of commands.

2.5 Using Windows

Applications as well as most documents, are displayed in their own windows. All windows have similar features:

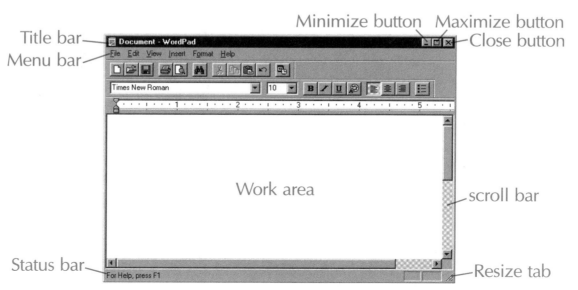

An Introduction to Programming Using Microsoft Visual Basic

- **Title bar** displays the name of the application or document.

- **Menu bar** displays the names of pull-down menus that contain commands.

- **Status bar** displays information about the application or document.

- **Work area** is where information is displayed and entered.

- **Minimize button** (▬) reduces an application's window to its name on the Task bar.

- **Maximize button** (☐) expands the window to fill the screen.

- **Restore button** (▣) is displayed instead of the Maximize button when a window has been maximized. Clicking on this button restores the window to its previous size.

- **Close button** (☒) closes a document window or ends the application and removes the window from the screen.

- **Scroll bar** is used to bring the unseen parts of the Work area into view.

- **Resize tab** is dragged to resize the window. The mouse pointer is displayed as a double-headed arrow (↘) when pointing to the Resize tab. A window can also be resized by pointing to any corner to display a double-headed arrow and then dragging the mouse pointer.

Because numerous windows can be open at the same time, a window may need to be moved. A window can be moved by dragging its Title bar.

File List

Most applications display a list of recently used documents near the bottom of the File menu. Clicking on one of the document names in the list displays that document.

2.6 Using Menus

At the top of an application window is the Menu bar. Each word on the bar is the name of a pull-down menu from which different commands can be selected. Clicking on a menu name displays the commands of that menu. For example, clicking on the word "File" displays the File menu:

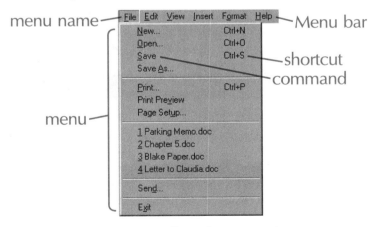

Menus are lists of commands

Pointing to a command on the menu highlights it. Highlighted commands are shown in reversed text (white letters on a dark background). Clicking on the highlighted command selects it. Clicking outside the menu or pressing the Escape key removes the menu from the screen.

Some commands may have an ellipsis (...) following the command name (Open and Save As are examples). This means that a dialog box asking for more information will appear when this command is selected. Dialog boxes are discussed in Section 2.7. When commands are displayed in dim text, they cannot be selected at this time.

Commands and menus may also be selected using the keyboard. Notice that one letter in each of the menu names is underlined. Pressing and holding the Alt key while pressing the underlined letter once displays that menu. For example, holding down the Alt key while pressing the F key displays the File menu. In this text, we denote this sequence of keystrokes as Alt+F.

Each command in a displayed menu also has an underlined letter. Pressing that letter when the menu is displayed selects the command. To execute the Save command from the File menu, first press Alt+F and release the keys, then press the S key. In this text, this sequence is written as Alt+F S.

The Control key (Ctrl) is located at the bottom of the keyboard, near the spacebar and can also be used to select commands without using the mouse. For example, in the File menu the Save command has the shortcut Ctrl+S next to it. This means that holding down the Control key and pressing S once (written in this text as Ctrl+S) selects the Save command.

2.7 Using Dialog Boxes

A dialog box is used to supply the information needed to execute a command. Dialog boxes may have several options:

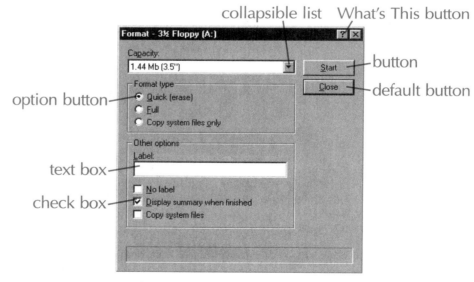

The Format dialog box contains typical dialog box features

- **Button** initiates an action when clicked.

- **Text box** is used to type information that may be needed by a command.

- **Check box** is used to select an option; usually any number of check box options may be selected at the same time.

An Introduction to Programming Using Microsoft Visual Basic

- **Option button**, also called radio button, is used to select an option; usually only one of a set of option buttons may be selected at a time.

- **Collapsible list** displays a list of options to choose from by clicking on the down arrow ( ).

- **Default option** is an entry or option that has already been selected for you. For example, the Close button in the Format dialog box is the default button and has a solid outline. If no other options are selected, the default options are used when the Enter key is pressed.

- **What's This button** ( ) is used to display information about the dialog box options. Clicking on the What's This button displays the ⊗? mouse pointer. Clicking the question mouse pointer on an option in the dialog box displays information about that option.

- **Close button** removes a dialog box without applying any options. A Cancel button is sometimes displayed instead of Close. A dialog box can also be removed by pressing the Escape key.

It is possible to select dialog box options without using the mouse. Each option in a dialog box has an underlined letter. Pressing and holding the Alt key and then pressing the underlined letter selects that option. For example, pressing Alt+S when the Format dialog box is displayed selects the Start button. Pressing the Tab key makes the next option in the dialog box active (ready to receive information).

2.8 Using the Keyboard

The keyboard is used to enter text in the Work area by pressing a letter key. There are also keys on the keyboard that are used to perform a specific action, such as moving the cursor or deleting text:

The keyboard

The *cursor* is a blinking vertical line located in the Work area that indicates where the next character typed will be placed. The cursor can be moved in a document's Work area without erasing or entering text by using the *cursor control keys*. Because these keys are marked with arrows (up, down, left, and right), they are also called *arrow keys*. These keys can only be used to move the cursor where text has already been entered. To move the cursor down one line, press the key marked with a down arrow. To move the cursor up, left, or right, press the key marked with the appropriate arrow. Each of the arrow keys is a *repeat key*, meaning that it will continue moving the cursor as long as it is held down.

To insert new text, the cursor control keys are used to place the cursor where the new text is to appear, and then the new text is typed. Any text following the insertion is moved to the right.

The *Backspace key* (sometimes marked ←) is used to erase the character directly to the left of the cursor. When a character is deleted, any characters to its right are automatically moved over to fill the gap. Do not confuse the Backspace key with the left-arrow key. Both move the cursor to the left, but Backspace erases characters and the left-arrow key does not.

The *Delete key* (sometimes marked Del) is also used to erase a character. Pressing Delete erases the character directly to the right of the cursor. Any characters to the right of the deleted character are automatically moved over to fill the gap made by the deleted character.

The *Escape key* (marked Esc) is used to cancel (escape from) the computer's current operation. The specific effect that pressing the Escape key will have depends on the operation being performed.

The *Enter key* is used to accept a highlighted menu command or selected dialog box options.

Desktop Shortcut

If an icon for an application is displayed on the Desktop, the application can be started by simply double-clicking on the icon.

2.9 Starting an Application and Creating a Document

An application is started by first clicking on the Start button on the Windows 98 Task bar and then pointing to Programs to display a menu of the programs available on your computer. Pointing to a command that has an arrow (▶) displays a group of related items.

The Start button is used to start an application

Clicking on the application in the menu starts the application and displays the application in a window. After an application is running, a document can be created by selecting the New command (Ctrl+N) from the File menu.

All Windows 98 based applications have a File menu with similar commands. The next few sections discuss the commands typically found in the File menu.

2.10 Saving a Document

When a document is *saved*, a copy of what is currently stored in the computer's memory is placed on the computer's internal hard disk or on a diskette. The computer still retains the document in memory so that there are now two copies—one in memory that is displayed on the screen and one saved on disk.

Saving a document is necessary because the computer's memory can only store data while the computer is turned on. When the computer is turned off any data in memory is lost. Once a document has been saved, it can later be loaded into memory for further editing or printing.

Documents saved on disk are called *files* and must be given names to identify them. *Filenames* can be up to 255 characters long and can contain uppercase and lowercase letters, numbers, and spaces. Some special characters such as \, /, :, *, ?, ", <, >, and | are not allowed. Examples of filenames are Cafe Newsletter, CHAPTER 5, and 2nd Memo. It is important to give a file a name that describes what it contains. For example, a file that contains a letter to Suzy Lee is better named Suzy Letter or Letter to Suzy Lee rather than just Letter.

A document can be saved by selecting the Save command (Ctrl+S) from the File menu. The first time a document is saved a dialog box is displayed:

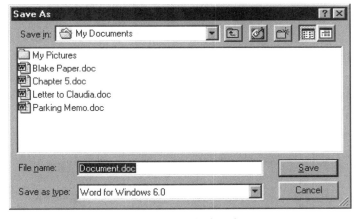

The Save As dialog box

When saving a document using the Save As dialog box, be sure to select the appropriate folder from the Save in collapsible list. Then type a descriptive name in the Field name entry box at the bottom of the dialog box and select the Save button to place a copy of the document to the hard disk using the name you supplied.

It is important to realize that any changes made to a previously saved file are not stored unless the file is saved again. It is also important to realize that saving a changed file replaces or *overwrites* the original copy on disk.

2.11 Closing a Document

Most Windows 98 based applications display documents in their own windows. When you are finished working on a document, it should be saved and then closed. *Closing a document* means that its window is removed from the screen and the document is no longer in the computer's memory. A document can be closed by selecting the Close command (Ctrl+W) from the File menu. If you attempt to close a document that has been edited but not saved, the application warns you before proceeding:

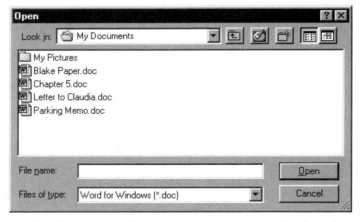

A warning is displayed before closing a modified document

If you want to save the changes before closing, select the Yes button. If you want to close the document without saving the edited version, select the No button. If the Close command was selected by accident, selecting the Cancel button returns the cursor to the Work area.

2.12 Opening a File

A saved file that has been closed must be loaded from disk to the computer's memory before it can be edited. This process is called *opening a file*. A file is opened by selecting the Open command (Ctrl+O) from the File menu to display a dialog box:

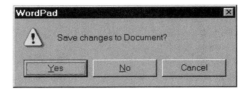

The filenames of saved documents are displayed in the Open dialog box

Selecting the appropriate folder where your document is stored from the Look in collapsible list and then clicking on the desired filename from the list and selecting the Open button transfers a copy of the document to the computer's memory and displays it in a window.

2.13 Printing a Document

A document can be printed by selecting the Print command (Ctrl+P) from the File menu to display a dialog box similar to:

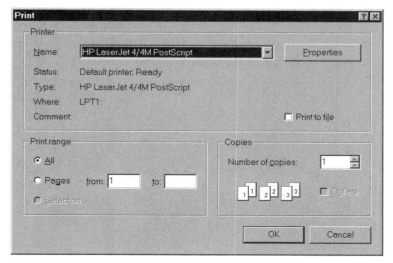

The Print dialog box

Print dialog boxes may appear different depending on the printer you have selected and the application being used. However, most Print dialog boxes contain options for specifying the number of copies to be printed and what pages to print. Because the default options are most commonly used, you will usually just select OK to begin printing. Some Print dialog boxes may contain a Print button instead of OK.

Before printing, a document should be saved because any problems involving the printer could cause the document to be lost.

2.14 Screen Scroll

Most documents are too long to be displayed entirely on the screen. Bringing hidden parts of a document into view is called *screen scroll*. The *scroll bars* on the right side and bottom of the window are used to scroll a document:

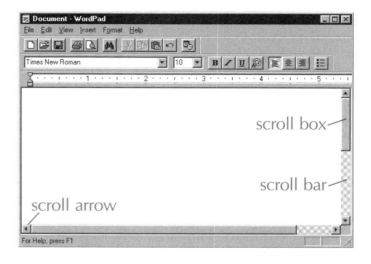

Clicking on the *scroll arrows* in the vertical and horizontal scroll bars will move the document accordingly. Any information scrolled off the screen is not lost, it is just not displayed at that time.

There are several ways to scroll a document:

- Clicking once on the down scroll arrow moves the document up one line, and clicking once on the up scroll arrow moves the document down one line.

- Dragging the *scroll box* moves the document in larger increments. For example, dragging the scroll box to the middle of the scroll bar displays the middle of the document.

- Clicking directly on the scroll bar above or below the scroll box moves the document by one screen towards the top or bottom of the document, respectively.

The cursor does not move when the scroll bars are used. To move the cursor when scrolling, the keyboard must be used. The up-arrow and down-arrow keys move the cursor one line at a time.

2.15 Exiting an Application

When you are finished working with an application, it should be exited properly. This is important because if the application is not exited properly, an open document can be damaged or lost. *Exiting an application* means that its window is removed from the screen and the program is no longer in the computer's memory. An application is exited by selecting the Exit command from the File menu. After selecting the Exit command, a warning is displayed if you have an open document that has not been saved:

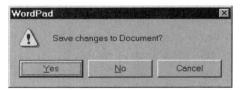

A warning is displayed if you exit without saving a modified document

Selecting the Yes button will save the changes before exiting. Selecting the No button leaves the document unchanged. If the Exit command was selected by accident, selecting the Cancel button returns to the application.

Review 2

In this review you will create, save, and print a document using WordPad. The Windows 98 Desktop should still be displayed from the last review.

1) START WORDPAD

    a. Click on the Start button on the Windows 98 Task bar. A menu is displayed.

    b. Point to Programs. A submenu is displayed.

    c. Point to Accessories and then click on the WordPad command. The WordPad application is started and displayed in a window. A new document is automatically displayed.

An Introduction to Programming Using Microsoft Visual Basic

2) ENTER TEXT USING THE KEYBOARD

Type a paragraph about why you are taking this class and what you hope to learn from the class. Use the Backspace and arrow keys to correct any typing errors that you have made.

3) RESIZE THE WINDOW

a. If the window is maximized, click on the Restore button (▣) to decrease the size of the window, otherwise click on the Maximize button (▣).

b. Click on the minimize button (▣). The window is reduced to the WordPad button on the Task bar.

c. Click on the Document - WordPad button on the Task bar. The window is again displayed.

d. Click on the Restore or Maximize button to return the window to its original size.

4) SAVE THE DOCUMENT

a. On the Menu bar, click on the word File. The File menu is displayed.

b. Point to the Save command in the displayed menu. Save is highlighted.

c. Click on Save to select the Save command. Since this is the first time the document is saved, a dialog box is displayed that prompts you to enter the filename for the document.

d. In the Save in entry box, select the appropriate folder.

e. In the File name entry box, replace the existing text with My Class.

f. Select the Save button.

5) PRINT THE DOCUMENT

a. From the File menu, select the Print command. The Print dialog box is displayed.

b. Select OK to print one copy of the document.

6) EXIT WORDPAD

From the File menu, select the Exit command. The WordPad window is removed from the screen.

2.16 Using Diskettes

Files are often stored on a diskette. Handling diskettes carefully is important because they store documents in a magnetic format that is vulnerable to dirt and heat. Observing the following rules will help to ensure that your diskettes give you trouble-free service:

1. Keep diskettes away from electrical and magnetic devices such as computer monitors, television sets, speakers, and any type of magnet.

2. Do not expose diskettes to either extreme cold or heat.

3. Store diskettes away from dust, dirt, and moisture.

4. Never touch the diskette's magnetic surface, as doing so can damage it and destroy valuable data.

2.17 Using My Computer

My Computer

Double-clicking on the My Computer icon on the Windows 98 Desktop displays a window with icons representing the hardware components of the computer:

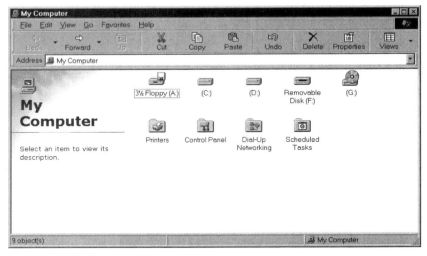

The My Computer window

Double-clicking on one of the disk drives displays the contents of that disk drive in the window. Double-clicking on the Printers icon displays available printers. Double-clicking on one of the available printers while you are printing a document displays a window with the status of your print job.

formatting a diskette

Right-clicking on one of the icons displays a menu of commands. The Format and Copy Disk commands are displayed by right-clicking on the floppy diskette icon (3½ Floppy (A:)).

A new diskette may need to be formatted before it can be used. *Formatting* a diskette prepares it to receive data. The steps for formatting a diskette are:

1. Double-click on the My Computer icon.
2. Place the diskette to be formatted into drive A:
3. Right-click on the 3½ Floppy (A:) icon:

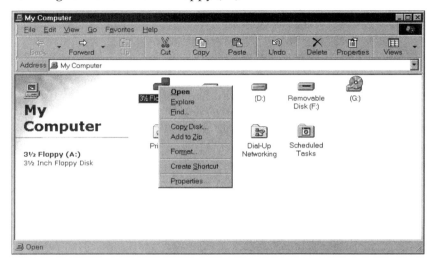

4. Select the Format command. The Format dialog box is displayed:

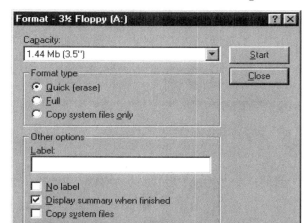

5. Select the Start button.
6. If a dialog box appears saying the diskette cannot be quick for-matted, select the OK button to accept full format. The format-ting process may take a few seconds.
7. Select the Close button to remove the Format Results dialog box and then select Close again to remove the Format dialog box.

copying a diskette   The entire contents of a diskette may be copied to another diskette by using the Copy Disk command. The steps for copying a diskette are:

1. Double-click on the My Computer icon.
2. Right-click on the 3½ Floppy (A:) icon.
3. Select the Copy Disk command. The Copy Disk dialog box is displayed:

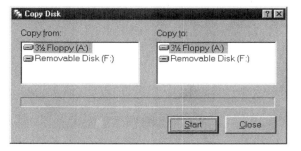

4. Click on the appropriate drive icons in the Copy from and Copy to sections if they are not already selected.
5. Place the diskette to be copied from (source diskette) into the drive and then select the Start button.
6. When prompted, place the diskette that will be copied to (desti-nation diskette) into the drive and then select the OK button.
7. Select the Close button to remove the Copy Disk dialog box when copying is complete.

write protecting a diskette

Because any data on the destination diskette is overwritten when using the Copy Disk command, it is a good idea to *write protect* the source diskette so that it is not accidently used as the destination diskette. To write protect a diskette, turn to the back side of the diskette and slide the write protect tab upward. The write protect tab is located in the upper-left corner on the back of the diskette:

write protect tab —

This diskette is write protected because the write protect tab has been pushed up

making backups

A *backup* is a copy of a file or diskette. Although it is easy to create backups of a file or diskette, many people do not take the time to do so. However, the few minutes it takes to backup a file could save hours if the file is damaged or deleted and must be recreated.

It is important to keep backup diskettes in a different location than the original copies. That way, the chances of both copies being destroyed are low. For example, if you keep your data diskettes in the computer lab, keep the backup copy at home. Businesses often store their backup copies in special fireproof safes, in safe deposit boxes at a bank, or with a company that provides safe "off-site" storage for computer data.

Review 3

In this review you will format a diskette. The following instructions assume that the 3½ floppy diskette drive is the A: drive and that you have a diskette for formatting. Note that any data that is on the diskette will be lost.

1) **OPEN MY COMPUTER**

Double-click on the My Computer icon. The My Computer window is displayed with icons representing the contents of the computer.

2) **FORMAT A DISKETTE**

   a. Place the diskette into drive A:.
   b. Right-click once on the 3½ Floppy (A:) icon.
   c. Select the Format command. The Format dialog box is displayed. Note the different options in the dialog box.
   d. Select the Start button.
   e. If a dialog box appears saying the diskette cannot be quick formatted, select the OK button to accept full format. It may take a few seconds to format the diskette.
   f. Select the Close button to remove the Format Results dialog box and then select the Close button again to remove the Format dialog box.

3) **CLOSE THE MY COMPUTER WINDOW**

Click on the Close button (☒) to remove the My Computer window.

2.18 Using Windows Explorer

Windows Explorer is an application that comes with Windows 98 and is used to view and organize files and folders. Clicking on the Start button, pointing to the Programs command, and then selecting Windows Explorer starts Windows Explorer and displays the Exploring window. The *Exploring window* shows the contents of the computer, including each disk drive and their respective folders, subfolders, and files:

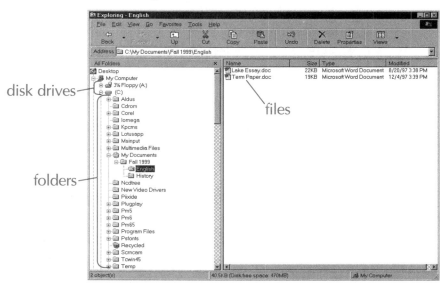

disk drives

files

folders

The Windows 98 Exploring window

A file is simply a collection of data stored on a disk, such as a hard disk or diskette, in a form the computer can read. *Folders* (📁) store and organize related files. Folders can also contain other folders. For example, you could create a folder with the name "Fall 1999" that stores all files related to your classes for the 1999 Fall semester. Additionally, you could have subfolders for each class of that semester stored in the Fall 1999 folder. In the window shown above, History and English are two subfolders in "Fall 1999" that each contain files.

The Exploring window is divided into two sides. The left side displays a list of All Folders stored in the computer and the computer's hardware components, which are represented by icons and their corresponding names. The right side of the Exploring window displays the contents of whichever folder is selected on the left side. The scroll bars can be used to display folders and files that are not currently displayed.

The folders and files displayed in the right side of the window can be displayed in different ways. It is helpful to have information about a file or folder such as the size, type, and the date it was last modified displayed, as in the example above. This can be done by selecting the Details command from the View menu.

Notice how there are plus signs (+) and minus signs (–) to the left of the folder icons in the left side of the Exploring window. If a folder has a plus sign next to it, this indicates subfolders within that folder. Clicking on a plus sign displays these subfolders and changes the plus sign to a minus sign. Clicking on the minus sign will hide the subfolders and change the minus sign back to a plus sign.

Review 4

In this review you will use Windows Explorer to view the files and folders in the computer.

1) OPEN WINDOWS EXPLORER

a. Click the Start button on the Windows 98 Task Bar.
b. Point to Programs and then click on the Windows Explorer command.
c. The Exploring window is displayed. Note the two sides of the window and their contents.

2) VIEW THE FILES AND FOLDERS

a. If not already done, select the My Computer icon on the left side of the Exploring window. Note how all the available hardware are displayed on the right side of the window.
b. On the left side of the Exploring window, click on the C: drive icon. Note how all the contents of that drive are displayed on the right side.
c. Navigate through the contents of the computer by clicking on different folders and subfolders displayed on the left side of the Exploring window.

2.19 File and Folder Management

The Exploring window simplifies the tasks of copying, moving, creating, and deleting files and folders. Files and folders can be copied or moved using a method called *drag and drop*. *Copying* a file leaves the original file in its present location and places an exact copy in a new location. *Moving* a file removes it from its present location and places it in a new location.

copying a file

A file can be copied from one location to another location by using the right mouse button to drag the file's icon to the destination folder. When the mouse button is released a menu is displayed. Clicking on the Copy Here command in the menu copies the file to the new location. This method can be used to copy a file within the same drive or to a different drive.

moving a file

A file can be moved from one location to another location by using the right mouse button to drag a file's icon to the destination folder. When the mouse button is released a menu is displayed. Clicking on the Move Here command in the menu moves the file to the new location. This method can be used to move a file within the same drive or to a different drive.

copying and moving folders

Folders can also be copied and moved using the drag and drop methods described above. When copying or moving folders, all of the subfolders and files are also copied or moved.

creating a folder

A new folder can be created by selecting the existing folder or disk drive that is to contain the new folder and then selecting the Folder command from the New command's submenu in the File menu. A new folder icon is displayed on the right side of the Exploring window. An appropriate name can then be typed to replace the highlighted text "New Folder."

creating read-only files

A file can be made read-only to prevent it from being altered. A *read-only* file cannot have changes made to it. This means that any edits made to the file cannot be retained. A file is made read-only by first right-clicking on the file's name and then selecting the Properties command from the displayed menu. Selecting the Read-only check box in the Properties dialog box and selecting OK makes the file read-only.

deleting a file or folder

A file or folder can be deleted by selecting it and then pressing the Delete key. Windows 98 will then display a warning asking you if you are sure you want to delete the file or folder.

renaming a file or folder   Renaming a file or folder replaces an existing name with a new name. A file or folder can be renamed by first right-clicking on its icon and then selecting the Rename command from the displayed menu. A new name can then be typed and Enter pressed. Files and folders can have names up to 255 characters including spaces. Some special characters such as \, /, :, *, ?, ", <, >, and | are not allowed.

creating a shortcut   A *shortcut* is an icon on the Desktop that when double-clicked will display a file or start a program. A shortcut to a file or application can be created by dragging the icon which represents the desired file or program from the Exploring window to the Desktop using the right mouse button. After releasing the right mouse button, selecting the Create Shortcut(s) Here command from the displayed menu creates the shortcut. When dragging an icon from the Exploring window to the Desktop, part of the Desktop needs to be displayed. Therefore, you may need to resize the Exploring window to display a portion of the Desktop.

Review 5

In this review you will create a folder, copy a file, rename a file, and make the file read-only. The following instructions assume that the 3½ floppy diskette drive is the A: drive and that you have a diskette containing files. The Exploring window should still be displayed from the last review.

1) CREATE A FOLDER

    a. Insert a diskette with files into the A: drive.
    b. Click on the 3½ Floppy (A:) icon in the left side of the window. Any files on the diskette appear on the right side of the window.
    c. From the File menu, select the New command, and from the submenu select the Folder command. A new folder icon with the highlighted name "New Folder" is displayed on the right side of the window.
    d. Type the name Temporary to replace the default name and press Enter. The diskette in the A: drive now contains a folder.

2) COPY A FILE

    a. The files stored on the diskette should still be displayed on the right side of the window. If not, click on the 3½ Floppy (A:) icon.
    b. Using the right mouse button, drag a file's icon to the Temporary folder you created in the step above.
    c. Release the mouse button when the Temporary folder icon is highlighted. From the displayed menu, select on the Copy Here command.
    d. A copy of the file now exists in the Temporary folder on the diskette in the A: drive.

3) RENAME THE COPIED FILE

    a. Click on the plus sign (+) next to the 3½ Floppy (A:) icon on the left side of the window. Any subfolders are displayed.
    b. Click on the Temporary folder icon. The file copied in the last step is displayed in the right side of the window.
    c. Right-click on the file's icon to display a menu.
    d. Select the Rename command from the displayed menu. The name is highlighted and a blinking cursor is displayed.
    e. Enter a new name for the file and then press Enter.

4) CREATE A READ-ONLY FILE

    a. Right-click on the file's icon.
    b. Select the Properties command from the displayed menu.

    c. In the Properties dialog box, click on the General tab and then click on the check box next to the Read-only option and select the OK button.

    d. The file is now read-only and no editing changes may be saved.

5) DELETE A FILE

    a. Click on the 3½ Floppy (A): icon in the left side of the window to display files on the diskette.

    b. Click once on a file's icon to select it.

    c. Press the Delete key. A warning dialog box is displayed.

    d. Select the Yes button. The file is deleted.

6) CLOSE THE EXPLORING WINDOW

2.20 Recovering Deleted Files

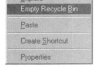

Recycle Bin

When a file is deleted it is not really removed from the hard disk; it is moved to the *Recycle Bin*. Therefore, deleted files can be recovered. A file can be undeleted by double-clicking the Recycle Bin icon on the Desktop to display a list of recently deleted files. Selecting the file to be recovered and then selecting the Recover button undeletes the file. Selecting the Finish button removes the dialog box.

Because deleted files are stored in the Recycle Bin, the deleted files are still taking up space on the computer's hard disk. If you want to permanently delete the files to have more space on the hard disk, right-click on the Recycle Bin icon and then select the Empty Recycle Bin command. Windows 98 will ask if you want to delete the files. Selecting the Yes button will permanently delete the files stored in the Recycle Bin and free up space on the computer's hard disk. It is important to note that Windows 98 automatically empties the Recycle Bin periodically. Therefore, it is not always possible to recover a deleted file.

2.21 Using Online Help

Windows 98 online help

Online help can be used to explore the features in Windows 98. Selecting the Help command after clicking on the Start button displays the Windows Help window:

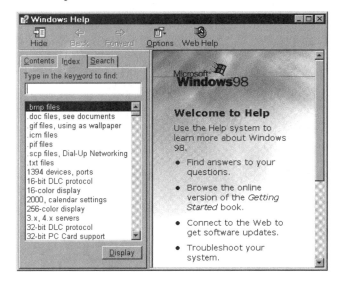

An Introduction to Programming Using Microsoft Visual Basic

Selecting the Index tab allows you to either type a word to search for or select from a list of topics. After entering or selecting the topic you want information on, selecting the Display button will display information pertaining to the selected topic.

Application online help

Online help can also be used to explore the features of an application and help answer questions you might have. Most Windows 98 based applications have a Help menu. Commands from this menu can be used to display information using a dialog box similar to the one shown above for the Windows 98 online help.

2.22 Finding Files

At times you may not know which folder a file is in, or you may only know partial information about a file's name. When this occurs, you can use the Find command to locate files. Clicking on the Start button, pointing to the Find command, and then selecting the Files or Folders command displays the Find window:

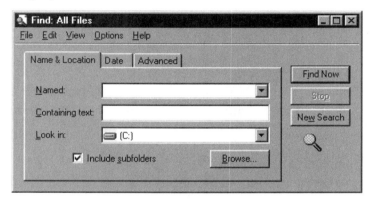

The Find window displays the location of files

If you know the complete name of a file but not the location, type the complete name in the Named entry box, click on the Look in collapsible list and select the appropriate drive, and then select the Find Now button. The contents of the computer is searched and the location of the file is displayed.

If you only know the partial name of a file, you can use the asterisk (*) in place of the unknown characters. For example, suppose you typed a letter to your friend Lisa and included "Lisa" in the name of the file but cannot remember the rest of the file name. Entering *Lisa* in the Named entry box and then selecting the Find Now button will display the location of all the files that contain "Lisa" as part of the file name. The asterisk (*) is used to represent unknown characters.

It is also possible to find a file that you don't know the name of at all, if you know some of the text contained in the file. For example, if you know that the heading "January 7, 1999 Meeting Agenda" is contained in a word processor document but don't know the name of the file enter the text in the Containing text entry box and select the Find Now button. A list of all the files containing the text "January 7, 1999 Meeting Agenda" will be displayed.

Review 6

In this review you will view recently deleted files and use the Windows 98 online help to find information on how to create folders. You will also use the Find command to find a file. The diskette used in the previous review should still be in the A: drive.

1) **OPEN THE RECYCLE BIN**

   Double-click on the Recycle Bin icon on the Windows 98 Desktop. A list of recently deleted files is displayed. The file you deleted in the last review is displayed in the list.

2) **RECOVER A DELETED FILE**

   a. Click once on the name of the file you deleted in the last review.
   b. Select the Recover button. The file has been recovered and is again on the diskette in the A: drive.
   c. Select the Finish button to remove the dialog box.
   d. Use Windows Explorer to verify that the file is on the diskette. Close the Exploring window.

3) **START ONLINE HELP**

   a. Click once on the Start button.
   b. Select the Help command. The Windows Help window is displayed.
   c. Click on the Index tab if it is not already displayed.

4) **VIEW INFORMATION ON FOLDERS**

   a. Type Folders in the entry box. A list of help topics is displayed.
   b. Click on the creating option in the list and then select the Display button. The steps on how to create a new folder is displayed in the window.

5) **CLOSE ONLINE HELP**

   Click on the Close button to remove the window.

6) **FIND A FILE**

   a. Click once on the Start button.
   b. Point to the Find command, and then select the Files or Folders command.
   c. Click on the Name & Location tab if the Named entry box is not already displayed.
   d. Type *.txt in the Named entry box.
   e. Click on the Look in collapsible list down-arrow and select the hard drive if it is not already selected.
   f. Click on the Find Now button. The contents of the hard drive are searched, and the location of any file with the .txt extension is displayed.
   g. Click on the Close button to remove the Find window.

Chapter Summary

This chapter introduced the Windows 98 operating system and some of its applications. The commands and procedures discussed in this chapter can be used in most applications written for use with Windows 98.

 A mouse is an input device used to select an object on the screen by pointing to the object and then pressing the left mouse button once (clicking). Some objects are selected by double-clicking which is pressing the button twice in rapid succession. Dragging is the technique of holding

An Introduction to Programming Using Microsoft Visual Basic

down the mouse button while moving the mouse. In some instances it may be necessary to use the right mouse button instead of the left mouse button, but only when specifically stated to do so.

Once Windows 98 is loaded, the Windows 98 Desktop is displayed. The Start button is used to start an application. The Task bar, at the bottom of the Desktop, displays a button for each open program. This allows you to easily switch between open programs. The icons on the Desktop represent items in the computer.

Applications and documents are usually displayed in their own windows. All windows have similar features such as a Menu bar and the Minimize, Maximize, Restore, and Close buttons.

The Menu bar at the top of an application's window contains the names of pull-down menus. Clicking on a menu name displays a list of commands. In a menu, selecting a command name that is followed by an ellipsis (…) will display a dialog box where information is entered for the command. The Alt and Control keys can be used to select commands without using the mouse.

Dialog boxes are used to supply information needed to execute an action. Common elements found in dialog boxes are buttons, text boxes, check boxes, option buttons, and collapsible lists. A default option is an entry or option that has already been selected. If no other options are selected, the default options are used when the Enter key is pressed. The Alt key can be used to select options and the Tab key can be used to make the next option active.

The keyboard is used to enter text and contains keys used to perform specific actions. The cursor control keys, are used to move the cursor through the document without changing any of the text. The Escape key is used to remove a dialog box or to cancel the current operation. The Backspace and Delete key are used to remove characters. The Enter key is used to accept a highlighted menu command or a dialog box option.

Windows 98 based applications all have a File menu which contains commands to create, save, close, open, and print a document. A new document can be created by selecting the New command. A document can be saved to disk by selecting the Save command. When saved, a document is given a unique name of up to 255 characters which is used to identify it. A document can be printed by selecting the Print command. A document can be removed from the computer's memory by selecting the Close command. Files can be opened by selecting the Open command.

To end an application, the Exit command from the File menu is selected. If an application is not exited properly, an open document can be damaged or lost.

Bringing hidden parts of a document into view is called screen scroll. The scroll bars below and on the right of a window are used to scroll through a document.

My Computer

Diskettes should always be handled carefully to avoid problems. The My Computer icon on the Windows 98 Desktop allows you to format new diskettes and copy the contents of an entire diskette. It is a good idea to write protect your source diskette when using the Copy Disk command. Backing up a file is important because it could save hours of extra work if the file is damaged or deleted and must be recreated. Backup diskettes should always be stored in a different location than the original copies.

file and folder management

Windows Explorer is used to navigate through the files and folders stored in the computer. Folders are used to store and organize related files. The Exploring window displays the contents of a selected disk drive or folder. Files and folders can be copied and moved using a method called drag and drop. Folders are created using the Folder command from the New submenu of the File menu. Read-only files cannot have changes made to them. Files and folders can also be deleted and renamed in the Exploring window. Shortcuts can be created on the Desktop to display a file or start a program.

Recycle Bin

When a file is deleted it is moved to the Recycle Bin. Therefore, deleted files can be recovered from the Recycle Bin. Files are permanently removed from the Recycle Bin using the Empty Recycle Bin command which makes more space available on the hard disk.

Windows 98 online help and the Find command provides information about Windows 98 features, and locates files on the computer, respectively.

Vocabulary

Alt key Used to select a menu, command, or dialog box option.

Applications software Software written by professional programmers to perform a specific task.

Arrow keys See cursor control keys.

Backspace key Erases the character directly to the left of the cursor.

Backup A copy of a file or diskette.

Booting The process by which Windows 98 is loaded into the computer's memory from the hard disk.

Button A dialog box option that initiates an action when clicked.

Check box A dialog box option.

Clicking Placing the mouse pointer on an object and quickly pressing and releasing the left mouse button once.

Close button Square button containing an X in the upper-right corner of a window. Clicking it removes the current window from the screen.

Closing a document The process where a document's window is removed from the screen and the document is no longer in the computer's memory.

Collapsible list A dialog box option that displays a list of choices by clicking on the down-arrow.

Commands Perform specific tasks and actions.

Control key Used to execute a command without using the mouse.

Copying Leaves the original file or folder in its present location and places an exact copy in a new location.

Cursor A blinking vertical line located in the Work area that indicates where the next character typed will be placed.

Cursor control keys Moves the cursor in the Work area without erasing or entering text.

Default A typical entry or option that has already been selected for you.

Delete key Erases the character directly to the right of the cursor.

Dialog box Allows information to be entered that is needed to complete an action.

Disk Operating System Software that allows the user to communicate with the computer using the keyboard and mouse.

Double-clicking Placing the mouse pointer on an object and pressing the left mouse button twice in rapid succession.

Drag and drop A method of copying or moving objects by dragging them to a new location.

Dragging Holding down the left mouse button while moving the mouse.

Enter key Accepts a highlighted menu command or selected dialog box options.

Escape key Cancels the current operation.

Exiting an application The process where the application window is removed from the screen and the program is no longer in the computer's memory.

File A document that is stored on disk.

Filename A unique name for a file stored on disk, up to 255 characters in length. Some special characters such as \, /, :, *, ?, ", <, >, and | are not allowed.

Folder Organizes and stores related files.

Formatting Making a diskette ready to receive data.

GUI (Graphical User Interface) A program that uses icons to communicate with the computer.

Icon A picture on the screen that is used to run programs and perform tasks.

Interface The way an application looks on the screen.

Maximize button Button located in the upper-right corner of a window. Used to expand the window to fill the screen.

Menu bar A horizontal bar located at the top of an application's window that displays the names of pull-down menus.

Minimize button Button located in the upper-right corner of a window. Used to reduce an application's window to its name on the Task bar.

Mouse Input device that is used to move the mouse pointer and perform a variety of tasks.

Mouse pointer A shape displayed on the screen when the mouse is in use.

Moving Removes a file or folder from its present location and places it in a new location.

Multitasking A feature of Windows 98 where more than one application at a time can be running.

My Computer A Windows 98 application used to display the contents of the computer and to format and copy diskettes.

Object Item that appears on the screen. Examples include icons, windows, and dialog boxes.

Opening a file The process where a saved file is transferred from disk to the computer's memory and displayed in a window.

Option button A dialog box option.

Overwrite When a saved file is replaced with an edited version of the file.

Pointing Placing the mouse pointer on an object located on the screen.

Read-only A file that cannot have changes made to it.

Recycle Bin Stores deleted files for a period of time so that they may be recovered.

Renaming Replacing an existing file or folder name with a new name.

Repeat key A key that continues an action as long as it is held down.

Resize tab Located in the lower-right corner of a window and used to change the size of a window.

Restore button Button displayed in the upper-right corner of a window in place of the Maximize button when a window has been maximized. Used to restore a window to its previous size.

Right-clicking Placing the mouse pointer on an object and quickly pressing and releasing the right mouse button once.

Saving a document The process where a copy of a document stored on the computer's memory is placed on the computer's internal hard disk or on a diskette.

Screen scroll Bringing hidden parts of a document into view.

Screen tip Provides information and describes actions that an object can perform.

Scroll arrows Scrolls a document one line at a time.

Scroll bar Brings the unseen parts of the Work area into view.

Scroll box Scrolls a document in large increments.

Selecting The process of clicking on an object on the screen.

Shortcut An icon on the Desktop used to display a file or start a program when double-clicked.

Start button When clicked, displays a list of commands from which applications can be run.

Status bar Located at the bottom of a window and displays information about the program or document.

Tab key Selects the next option in a dialog box.

Task bar Displays a button for each open program.

Text box A dialog box option that accepts typed information.

Title bar Located at the top of a window and displays the name of the application or document.

What's This button Located in the upper-right corner of a dialog box used to display information about a dialog box option.

Window The area of the screen where an open program or document is displayed.

Windows Explorer A Windows 98 applications program used to view and organize files and folders stored in the computer.

Windows 98 An operating system that uses a graphical user interface.

Windows 98 Desktop The computer screen that displays the Start button, icons, and the Task bar.

Work area Where information is displayed or entered in a window.

Write protect Moving the write protect tab on a diskette so it cannot receive data.

An Introduction to Programming Using Microsoft Visual Basic

File Menu Commands

Close command Removes a document from the application's window and the computer's memory.

Exit command Quits an application properly and removes it from the screen.

New command Creates a new document.

Open command Retrieves a previously created file that is stored on disk.

Print command Prints a document.

Save command Transfers a document from the computer's memory to the computer's hard disk or to a diskette.

Windows 98 Commands

Copy Disk command Copies the contents from one diskette to another diskette. Found in the File menu in the My Computer window.

Copy Here command Copies a file or folder from one location to another location. Displayed when dragging a file or folder with the right mouse button.

Create Shortcut(s) Here command Creates a shortcut. Displayed after releasing the right mouse button when dragging a file or folder's icon.

Details command Displays a file or folder's size, type, and the date it was last modified. Found in the View menu in the Exploring window.

Empty Recycle Bin command Removes the contents of the Recycle Bin and frees up hard disk space. Displayed after right-clicking on the Recycle Bin icon on the Desktop.

Find command Locates files in the computer. Displayed after clicking on the Start button on the Task bar.

Folder command Creates a new folder in the currently selected folder or disk drive. Found in the New submenu in the File menu.

Format command Formats a diskette. Found in the File menu in the My Computer window.

Help command Displays information about Windows 98. Displayed after clicking on the Start button on the Task bar.

Move Here command Moves a file or folder to a new location. Displayed when dragging a file or folder with the right mouse button.

Properties command Used to make a file read-only. Displayed by right-clicking on a file name.

Rename command Highlights a file or folder's name so it can be changed. Displayed by right-clicking on a filename.

Shut Down command Should be selected before turning off the computer. Displayed after clicking on the Start button on the Task bar.

Review Questions

Sections 2.1 — 2.8

1. a) What is a disk operating system?
    b) What is a GUI?
    c) What is applications software?

2. a) What is a mouse?
    b) What is pointing?
    c) What is double-clicking?

3. List the steps required to drag an object.

4. a) What is the Windows 98 Desktop?
    b) What does the Task bar allow you to do?
    c) What do icons represent?

5. List the features found in a window and describe them.

6. a) What is a menu and how is one displayed?
    b) List two ways the Save command from the File menu can be executed without using the mouse.

7. a) What is a dialog box?
    b) What are default options?
    c) List four options found in a dialog box and describe them.

8. What are each of the following keys used for?
    a) cursor control keys
    b) Backspace key
    c) Escape key

Sections 2.9 — 2.15

9. a) List the steps required to start an application.
    b) What command is used to create a document?

10. List two reasons why it is important to save a document.

11. a) What is a file?
    b) Why is a file given a name? List five valid filenames.

12. What happens to a document when it is closed?

13. List the steps required to transfer a file from disk into the computer's memory.

14. Why should a document be saved before it is printed?

15. a) What is screen scroll?
    b) Describe two ways to scroll a document.

16. Why is it important to exit an application properly?

Sections 2.16 — 2.22

17. a) Why is it important to take good care of a diskette?
    b) What should be avoided when handling or storing a diskette?

18. List the steps required to format a diskette.

19. a) What command is used to duplicate the entire contents of one diskette to another diskette?
    b) What happens to the original data on a diskette when it is used as a destination diskette?

20. List the steps required to write protect a diskette.

21. a) Why should backups of data be created?
    b) Why is it important to keep backup diskettes in a different location than the originals?

22. a) What is Windows Explorer used for?
    b) Explain what is displayed in the Exploring window.

23. a) What is the difference between copying and moving a file?
    b) What happens to a folder's subfolders and files when it is moved?

24. List the steps required to copy a file.

25. List the steps required to create a subfolder named "Letters" in the My Documents folder.

26. Can changes be made to a read-only file?

27. What is the Recycle Bin used for?

28. a) List the steps required to display information on diskettes in the Windows 98 online help.
    b) What menu in an application can be used to help answer questions you might have?

29. Why would an asterisk (*) be used with the Find command?

An Introduction to Programming Using Microsoft Visual Basic

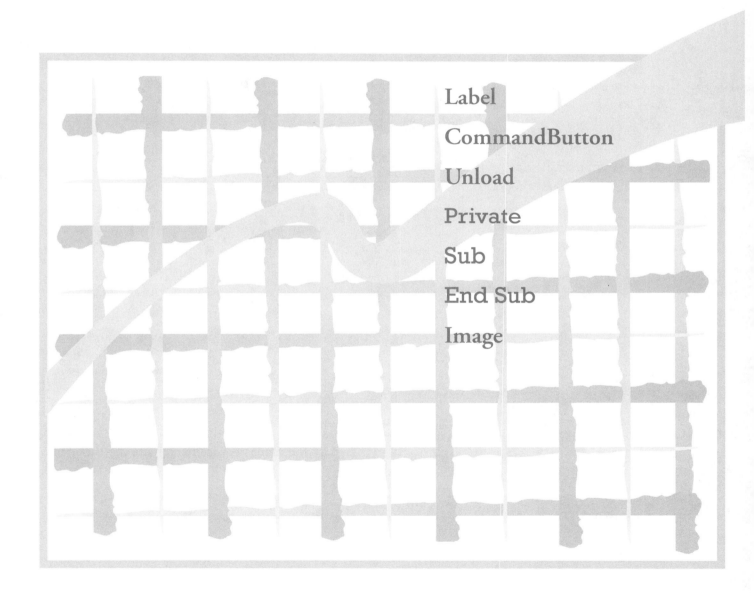

Label

CommandButton

Unload

Private

Sub

End Sub

Image

Chapter Three Objectives

After completing this chapter you will be able to:

1. Understand what an object-oriented language is.
2. Use the Visual Basic IDE.
3. Understand objects and add objects to a form.
4. Create an application.
5. Save, print, and run an application.
6. Understand event procedures.
7. Remove a project from the IDE.
8. Change property values at design time and at run time.
9. Add comments to program code.
10. Open a project.
11. Understand operators and expressions.
12. Create an executable file.
13. Exit Visual Basic.
14. Understand good programming style guidelines.

Visual Basic is used to create applications for Microsoft Windows. It includes tools that allow a programmer to create an application that has features similar to other Windows applications without having to write many lines of code.

3.1 The Visual Basic Programming Language

Visual Basic is based on the BASIC programming language developed in the 1960s by John Kemeny and Thomas Kurtz at Dartmouth University. BASIC stands for Beginner's All-Purpose Symbolic Instruction Code and was used by Kemeny and Kurtz to teach programming to their students.

In 1975, Bill Gates and Paul Allen developed a version of BASIC especially for the Altair personal computer. With the success of this new version of BASIC, Gates and Allen founded the Microsoft Corporation. BASIC then evolved to QuickBasic, a structured language that made programming easier for the rapidly growing number of personal computer users. In 1985, the Windows GUI was introduced. In 1992, Microsoft used QuickBasic and a program called Ruby to develop Visual Basic, an *object-oriented programming (OOP)* environment for creating Windows programs.

Object-Oriented Programming

OOP uses *classes*, which are program code and data, to create objects. In addition to program code, *objects* can have a visual representation such as a dialog box or a button and are used to reduce the complexity of developing graphics-based programs.

event-driven program

Visual Basic programs are event-driven. An *event* is a way in which the user can interact with an object, such as using the mouse to click on a button in a dialog box. An *event-driven program* waits for an event to occur before executing any code, then only code for the current event is executed.

3.2 A Visual Basic Application

Each Visual Basic program, also called an application, consists of an interface and program code. The *interface* is what appears on the screen when the application is running. The *program code* is the instructions that tell an application's objects how to behave.

interface
program code

Ruby

Ruby, originally called Tripod, was developed by Alan Cooper of Coactive Computing Corporation. Tripod was an application that allowed users to create their own computer interface in place of the Windows Desktop. After Cooper demonstrated Tripod to Bill Gates, Microsoft bought the rights to Tripod and renamed it Ruby. Cooper and the team of Mark Merker, Gary Kratkin, Mike Greary, and Frank Raab completed the final Ruby program for Microsoft in 1990.

In this chapter, you will first learn how to create the interface of a Visual Basic application and then how to write the program code that tells the computer what the application should do. Throughout this text, you will learn how to create the application below and many others like it:

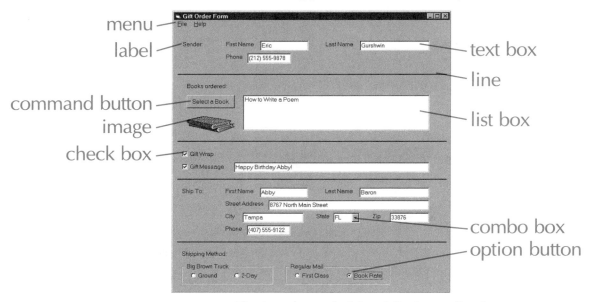

menu
label
command button
image
check box

text box
line
list box

combo box
option button

The interface of a Visual Basic application

3.3 The Visual Basic IDE

creating a new project

The Visual Basic *integrated development environment*, or *IDE*, is used to create a Visual Basic application. A new application is created by first starting the Visual Basic IDE which displays the New Project dialog box:

Starting Visual Basic

Visual Basic can be started by clicking on the Start button on the Task bar, selecting Programs, and then selecting Visual Basic from the submenu. On some computers, selecting Visual Basic displays another submenu where the Visual Basic program can be selected, or there may be an icon on the Desktop that can be double-clicked to start Visual Basic.

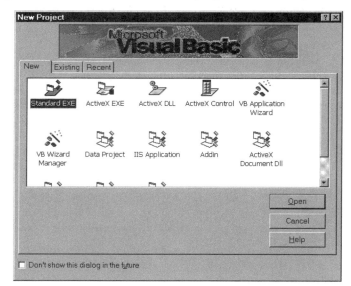

The New Project dialog box

Standard EXE

Selecting the Standard EXE icon and then the Open button in the New Project dialog box displays a project window in the IDE. If Visual Basic is already started, the New Project command (Ctrl+N) from the File menu can be used to create a new project. A *project* contains all the files for the application, including the form and its objects and program code.

The Visual Basic IDE includes all the tools needed to create a Visual Basic application:

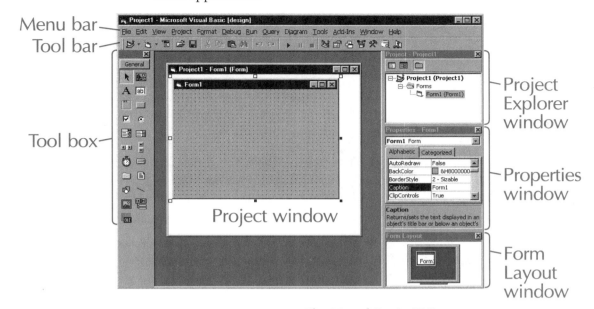

Menu bar—
Tool bar—

Tool box—

Project window

Project Explorer window
Properties window
Form Layout window

The Visual Basic IDE

Screen Tips

Screen tips display the name of a button or control. A screen tip appears near the mouse pointer when pointing (not clicking) to a button or control.

- **Menu bar** contains the names of menus that contain commands.
- **Tool bar** contains buttons that provide shortcuts to commonly performed actions.
- **Tool box** contains controls that are used to create objects.
- **Project window** is where the application interface is created.
- **Project Explorer window** lists the files in the current project.
- **Properties window** lists the properties values of an object.
- **Form Layout window** allows the application's interface to be positioned relative to the computer screen.

Review 1

Follow the instructions below to become familiar with the Visual Basic IDE.

1) **START VISUAL BASIC**

   The New Project dialog box is displayed with the Visual Basic IDE behind it.

2) **CREATE A NEW PROJECT**

   a. In the New Project dialog box, click on the Standard EXE icon if it is not already selected and then select Open. The New Project dialog box is removed and a Project window is displayed.
   b. Note the Tool box, the Project window, and the Project Explorer, Properties, and Form Layout windows.

3.4 Adding Objects to a Form

form   Every Visual Basic application has at least one form. A *form* is a container object for other objects. For example, the Hello World application is a simple Visual Basic application with one form that contains a label and a command button. The Hello World interface appears similar to:

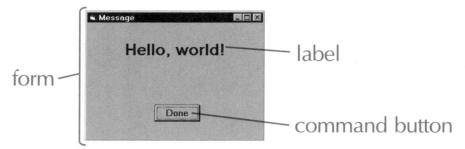

The Hello World application interface

design time   Objects are added to a form at design time. *Design time* refers to the time during which the application interface is being created. An object is added to a form by clicking on the desired control in the Tool box and then drawing the object. For example, the Hello World application has two

label   objects on its form, a label and a command button. A *label* object is used to display information. The label was added to the form by selecting the Label control (A) in the Tool box and then dragging the cross-hairs pointer:

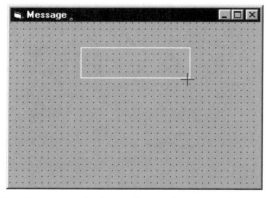

Dragging the cross-hairs pointer displays the size of the object that will appear when the mouse button is released

command button   An object can also be added to the form by double-clicking a control. For example, a command button (the Done button) was added to the Hello World form by double-clicking on the CommandButton control (▣) in the Tool box. A *command button* object is something that the user can click on.

3.5 Object Property Values

An object has *properties* that define its appearance, behavior, position, and other attributes. These properties can be changed in the Properties window by selecting the object's name in the Object collapsible list and then selecting the property in the properties list. Next, a new value is typed or selected for the property. For example, in the Hello World application, the label displays "Hello, world!" because the label object was selected, then Caption was selected, and finally Hello, world! was typed:

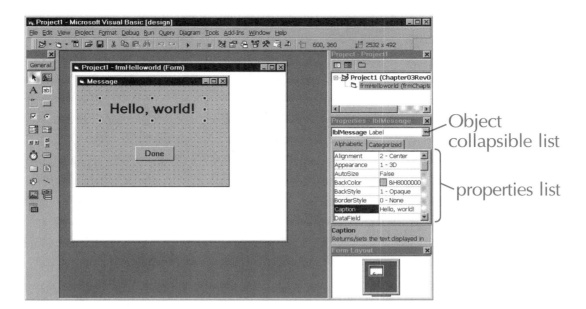

Each type of object has many different properties. Throughout the text, as objects are introduced, their most commonly used properties will also be discussed. So far, the label, command button, and form objects have been introduced. The label object has the properties:

label properties

- **Name** identifies an object and is used by the programmer. It is good programming style to begin label object names with lbl.

- **Caption** changes the text displayed in the label. In the graphic above, the Caption is Hello, world!

- **Font** is used to display a dialog box for changing the font, font style, and size of a label's Caption.

- **Alignment** changes the alignment of text in a label's Caption and can be set to left justify, right justify, or center.

command button properties

The command button object has the properties:

- **Name** identifies an object and is used by the programmer. It is good programming style to begin command button object names with cmd.

- **Caption** changes the text displayed in the command button.

form properties

The form object has the properties:

- **Name** identifies an object and is used by the programmer. It is good programming style to begin form object names with frm.

- **Caption** changes the text displayed in the title bar.

programming style

The Name property is the only property that absolutely should be changed for each object in an application. The Name of an object should begin with the appropriate prefix and then be descriptive of the object's purpose. For example, the form Name for the Hello World application is frmHelloWorld. This name begins with the appropriate prefix (frm) and is descriptive of the form's purpose. Following proper naming conventions is good programming style.

3.6 Resizing and Moving an Object

selecting an object

An object is *selected* by clicking on it to display handles. Once selected, dragging a handle resizes the object. Dragging a corner handle resizes both height and width:

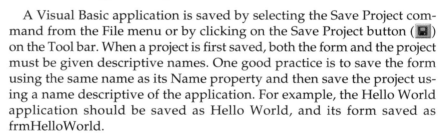

A selected object can be resized by dragging a handle

An object is moved by selecting it and then dragging it (not a handle) to a new location.

Marquee Selection

Multiple objects can be selected using a technique called marquee selection. Selecting the Pointer control and then dragging the mouse pointer on the form creates a dashed-line box called a marquee. Creating this box around several objects and then releasing the mouse button selects all of the objects.

3.7 Saving a Project

A Visual Basic application is saved by selecting the Save Project command from the File menu or by clicking on the Save Project button (▣) on the Tool bar. When a project is first saved, both the form and the project must be given descriptive names. One good practice is to save the form using the same name as its Name property and then save the project using a name descriptive of the application. For example, the Hello World application should be saved as Hello World, and its form saved as frmHelloWorld.

3.8 Running a Visual Basic Application

run time

A Visual Basic application is run by selecting the Start command (F5) from the Run menu or by clicking on the Start button (▶) on the Tool bar. *Run time* refers to the time during which the application is being executed. A Visual Basic application can be run at any time during the development of the program. This allows testing of the application as it is being written. A running application can be terminated by selecting the End command from the Run menu or by clicking on the End button (■) on the Tool bar.

Review 2

Follow the instructions below to create the Hello World application interface described in the previous sections. If not already displayed, start Visual Basic and create a new Standard EXE project.

1) CHANGE THE PROPERTIES OF THE FORM OBJECT

The form object is currently selected because no other objects have been added to the application. The Properties window displays the properties of the selected object, the form.

a. In the Properties window, select the Name property in the properties list if it is not already highlighted. (The Name property is enclosed in parentheses so it is first in the list.)

b. Type frmHelloWorld and then press Enter to replace the current Name Form1. Note the Project window now displays the new name.

    c.   If not already shown, scroll the properties list until the Caption property is displayed and then select Caption.

    d.   Type Message to replace the current Caption and press Enter. Note the Title bar of the form now displays Message.

2) ADD A LABEL OBJECT

    a.   In the Tool box, click on the Label control (A).

    b.   Move the mouse pointer onto the form. Note that the pointer is now a cross-hairs pointer.

    c.   Drag the cross-hairs pointer down and to the right to create a label object.

    d.   Drag the label object (not a handle) so that is centered in the upper third of the form. If necessary, drag a handle to resize the object so that your form looks similar to:

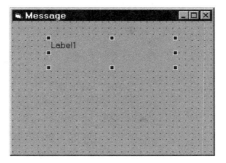

3) CHANGE THE PROPERTIES OF THE LABEL OBJECT

    a.   Click once on the label object to select it, if it is not already selected. Handles are displayed.

    b.   In the Properties window, change the Name property to lblMessage.

    c.   Select the Alignment property. A down arrow is displayed indicating a list of options is available.

    d.   Click on the Alignment down arrow to display a list of options and then select 2 - Center. Note the default text Label1 is now centered in the label object.

    e.   Change the Caption property value to Hello, world!

    f.   Select the Font property. An ellipsis is displayed (…) indicating a dialog box is available.

    g.   Click on the Font ellipsis. The Font dialog box is displayed.

    h.   In the **Font style** list, select Bold.

    i.   In the **Size** list, select 18.

    j.   Select OK. The options are applied to the label. Resize the label, if necessary, so that all the text is displayed.

4) ADD A COMMAND BUTTON OBJECT

    a.   In the Tool box, double-click on the CommandButton control (▢). A command button is placed on the form.

    b.   Drag the command button object (not a handle) so that is centered in the lower third of the form so that your form looks similar to:

5) CHANGE THE PROPERTIES OF THE COMMAND BUTTON OBJECT

a. Click once on the command button object to select it, if it is not already selected. Handles are displayed.
b. In the Properties window, change the Name property to cmdDone.
c. Change the Caption property value to Done.
d. Select the Font property and then click on the ellipsis to display the Font dialog box.
e. In the Size list, select 10 and then select OK.

6) SAVE THE HELLO WORLD PROJECT AND RUN THE APPLICATION

a. From the File menu, select the Save Project command. The Save File As dialog box is displayed.
b. In the Save in entry box, select the appropriate folder.
c. In the File name entry box, type frmHelloWorld if it is not already displayed and then select Save. The Save Project As dialog box is displayed.
d. In the File name entry box, type Hello World and then select Save.
e. On the Tool bar, click on the Start button ( ). The IDE is dimmed and the Hello World application is run.
f. Click on the Done button. Nothing happens because program code has not yet been written to handle this.
g. On the Tool bar, click on the End button ( ). The application is terminated and the IDE is displayed.

3.9 Objects and their Event Procedures

program code
statement

An application, also referred to as a program, contains a set of instructions called *program code* that tells the computer how to perform a specific task. Each line of code is called a *statement*. Programs can contain tens to hundreds, even millions of lines of program code, or statements.

An *event procedure* is a block of code that executes in response to an event. As discussed earlier, an *event* is a way in which the user can interact with an object, such as clicking a button. For example, an application that contains a command button needs to have a click event procedure for that button so that specific actions will be taken when the user clicks on the button.

In a Visual Basic application, each form has a *form module* that is a container for program code. The area displaying the form module is referred to as the Code Editor window. The Code Editor window is viewed by double-clicking on the form or by selecting the Code command from the View menu. The Code Editor window can also be displayed by clicking on the View Code button ( ) in the Project Explorer window. The View Object button ( ) is clicked to view the form.

Event procedures are coded in a form module. For example, the program code for the completed Hello World application appears like:

User Events

A user event is an action performed by the user. For example, a mouse click is a user event. Event procedures can be written for many different user events. For example, a command button click event procedure can be written for each command button.

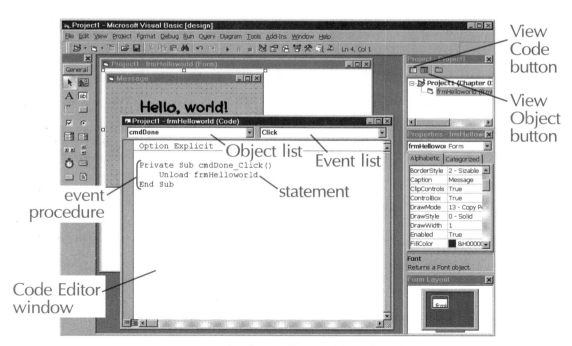

View
Code
button

View
Object
button

The frmHelloWorld Code Editor window

Unload

The cmdDone_Click event procedure is executed when the user clicks on the Done button. This event procedure contains an Unload statement that removes the form from memory and ends the application. The Unload statement requires a form name. If the form to unload is the current form, then Me can be used in place of the form name. For example, the Unload frmHelloWorld statement above could be replaced by Unload Me.

To add an event procedure, the desired object name is selected from the Object list and then a corresponding event is selected from the Event list. When an event procedure is added this way, it contains only two statements and has the form

Private Sub *ObjectName_Event*()

End Sub

where *ObjectName* is the selected object name and *Event* is the selected event name. **Private** indicates that the procedure cannot be accessed outside of the form module. **Sub** declares the procedure and **End Sub** is required to end the **Sub** statement. Between these statements is the *body* of the procedure where statements that tell the application how to respond to the event procedure are added.

Naming Objects

Event procedures require object names as part of the procedure name. For example, cmdDone_Click() is the name of the click event procedure for the **Done** command button. Therefore, objects must be appropriately named before creating any event procedures. Visual Basic will not automatically change an object's name in an event procedure if it is changed on the form after the code is created.

3.10 Printing a Project

The interface and program code of an application are printed by selecting the Print command (Ctrl+P) from the File menu. Selecting Print displays a dialog box similar to:

The Print dialog box

The Print What options in the dialog box are used to print either the form, code, or the form as text. Selecting OK prints the project.

3.11 Removing a Project from the IDE

When finished working with a project, it should be saved and closed. A project is closed by selecting the Remove Project command from the File menu. A dialog box is displayed if the form or project has been modified since it was last saved. Closing a project removes the project window from the IDE.

Review 3

Follow the instructions below to finish the Hello World application. The IDE and frmHelloWorld should still be displayed from the last review.

1) DISPLAY THE CODE EDITOR WINDOW

   a. In the Project Explorer window, click on the View Code button (▣). The frmHelloWorld Code Editor window is displayed.

   b. In the Project Explorer window, click on the View Object button (▦). The form is once again displayed.

   c. In the Project Explorer window, click on the View Code button. The form module is again displayed.

2) ADD THE DONE BUTTON CLICK EVENT PROCEDURE

   a. From the Object list in the Code Editor window (General is currently displayed), select cmdDone. A cmdDone_Click event procedure is added to the program code.

   b. Place the cursor in the blank line below **Private Sub** cmdDone_Click() if it is not already there.

   c. Press the Tab key and then type Unload frmHelloWorld. An Unload statement has been added to the click event procedure. Your procedure should look similar to:

```
Private Sub cmdDone_Click()
    Unload frmHelloWorld
End Sub
```

3) RUN THE APPLICATION

   a. From the File menu, select Save Project or click on the Save Project button (▣) on the Tool bar.

   b. On the Tool bar, click on the Start button (▶). The IDE is dimmed and the Hello World application is run.

   c. Click on the Done button. The application is terminated because the click event procedure contains an **Unload** statement.

   An Introduction to Programming Using Microsoft Visual Basic

4) PRINT THE PROJECT

    a. From the File menu, select the Print command. The Print dialog box is displayed.

    b. Select the Current Module, Form Image, and Code options and then select OK. The application interface and program code are printed.

5) SAVE AND REMOVE THE PROJECT

    a. Save the modified Hello World project.

    b. From the File menu, select the Remove Project command. The project is removed from the IDE.

Review 4

Create a My Name application that displays your name centered, bold, and size 14 and a Done button that terminates the application when clicked. Use the Hello World application as a guide. The application interface should look similar to that shown on the right.

3.12 Using Assignment to Change Property Values

In many applications, it is necessary to change the value of an object's property at run time. For example, the Alignment application below changes the Alignment and Caption properties of the label when the Left, Center, or Right buttons are clicked:

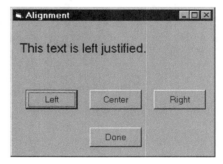

The Alignment application after clicking the Left button

Assignment is used to change the value of an object property at run time. For example, the cmdLeft_Click procedure of the Alignment application contains the following assignment statements:

```
Private Sub cmdLeft_Click()
    lblSample.Caption = "This text is left justified."
    lblSample.Alignment = 0
End Sub
```

An *assignment statement* for changing property values uses the equal sign (=) to give the property on the left of the equal sign the value on the right of the equal sign and has the form:

ObjectName.Property = Value

where *ObjectName* is the object's Name, *Property* is a property name of the object, and *Value* is a valid property setting. *Dot notation* means that a period is used between the *ObjectName* and *Property* to access a property of an object.

Each object property can be assigned only a valid property value. So far, the label, command button, and form objects have been introduced. The valid values of the label object properties are:

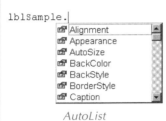
- **Name** cannot be changed at run time through assignment.

- **Caption** can be assigned text enclosed in double quotation marks ("). For example, the statement lblMessage.Caption = "Adios" will change the text of the lblMessage label to "Adios."

- **Font** has several subproperties that are accessed using dot notation and each have their own set of valid property values. **Size** is a numeric value from 0 to 2048. **Bold** and **Italic** are either True or False. **Name** is a valid font name enclosed in double quotation marks. For example:

```
lblMessage.Font.Size = 10
lblMessage.Font.Bold = True
lblMessage.Font.Italic = False
lblMessage.Font.Name = "Arial"
```

- **Alignment** can be assigned 0 (left justify), 1 (right justify), or 2 (center). For example, the statement lblMessage.Alignment = 0 will left justify the text in the lblMessage label.

The valid values of the command button object properties are:

- **Name** cannot be changed at run time through assignment.

- **Caption** can be assigned text enclosed in double quotation marks ("). For example, the statement cmdCancelOrDone.Caption = "Done" will change the Caption of the cmdCancelOrDone button to "Done."

The valid values of the form object properties are:

- **Name** cannot be changed at run time through assignment.

- **Caption** can be assigned text enclosed in double quotation marks. For example, the statement frmUserApp.Caption = "My Application" changes the text in the title bar of the form to "My Application."

3.13 The Form_Load Event Procedure

Event procedures can also be written for form events. The Form_Load event procedure is executed when a form is loaded into memory, such as when an application is started. For example, the following Form_Load procedure changes the Caption and Alignment of a label when the application is started:

```
Private Sub Form_Load()
    lblSample.Caption = "This text is centered."
    lblSample.Alignment = 2
End Sub
```

Changing object property values in the Form_Load event procedure is an alternative to setting property values in the Properties window. Setting object properties through the Form_Load event is referred to as initializing the form. Initializing property values in the Form_Load is a way to document your program. It is easy to look at a printout of the Form_Load procedure to understand what objects are in an application without having to actually start Visual Basic and look at the form, its objects, and the Properties window.

3.14 Commenting Code

programming style

Comments are used to explain and clarify program code for a human reader. They have no effect on the way an application runs. The single quotation mark (') must begin a comment. It is good programming style to include comments wherever code can be ambiguous or misleading. For example, the statement below is easier to interpret with a comment:

```
lblSample.Alignment = 0    'Left justify text in label
```

3.15 Opening a Project

An application is opened for editing by selecting the Open Project command (Ctrl+O) from the File menu or by clicking on the Open Project button ( ) on the Tool bar. After opening a project, it may be necessary to display the form by double-clicking on its name in the Project Explorer window. If folders are displayed in the Project Explorer window, double-clicking on the Forms folder displays the names of the forms in the project.

Review 5

Follow the instructions below to complete the Alignment application described in the previous sections. The Visual Basic IDE should be displayed from the last review.

1) *OPEN THE ALIGNMENT PROJECT*

    a. From the File menu, select the Open Project command. The Open Project dialog box is displayed.

    b. In the Look in entry box, select the appropriate folder.

    c. Click on Alignment and then select Open. The Alignment project is opened.

    d. If the Alignment form is not displayed, use the Project Explorer window to display the form name and then double-click on the name.

2) *ADD THE FORM LOAD EVENT PROCEDURE*

A default message and alignment can be displayed when the application is run by placing code in the Form_Load event procedure.

    a. In the Project Explorer window, click on the View Code button. The Code Editor window is displayed.

    b. From the Object list in the Code Editor window, select Form. A Form_Load event procedure is added to the code.

c. Add the following statements to the Form_Load event procedure:

```
Private Sub Form_Load()
    lblSample.Caption = "This text is centered."
    lblSample.Alignment = 2   'Center text in label (default)
End Sub
```

3) ADD THE LEFT BUTTON CLICK EVENT PROCEDURE

a. From the Object list in the Code Editor window, select cmdLeft. A cmdLeft_Click event procedure is added to the program code.
b. Add the following code so that the event procedure contains:

```
Private Sub cmdLeft_Click()
    lblSample.Caption = "This text is left justified."
    lblSample.Alignment = 0   'Left justify text in label
End Sub
```

4) ADD THE CENTER AND RIGHT BUTTON CLICK EVENT PROCEDURES

Create cmdCenter_Click and cmdRight_Click event procedures that contain the following code:

```
Private Sub cmdCenter_Click()
    lblSample.Caption = "This text is centered."
    lblSample.Alignment = 2   'Center text in label
End Sub
```

```
Private Sub cmdRight_Click()
    lblSample.Caption = "This text is right justified."
    lblSample.Alignment = 1   'Right justify text in label
End Sub
```

5) ADD THE DONE BUTTON CLICK EVENT PROCEDURE

Create a cmdDone_Click event procedure that contains the following code:

```
Private Sub cmdDone_Click()
    Unload Me
End Sub
```

6) SAVE THE PROJECT AND RUN THE APPLICATION

a. Save the modified Alignment project.
b. Run the application. Click on each of the alignment command buttons to test the application.
c. Click on the Done button to end the application.

7) PRINT AND THEN REMOVE THE PROJECT

3.16 Image Objects

An application that includes graphics can be more interesting and easier for a user to interact with. For example, a graphic of a globe could be added to the Hello World application to make it more interesting:

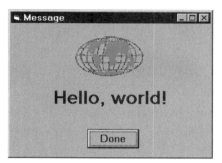

The globe is added with the Image control

 An *image* object is created using the Image control () in the Tool box and has the properties:

- **Name** identifies the object and is used by the programmer. It is good programming style to begin image object names with img.

- **Picture** is used to display a dialog box for selecting the graphic to display in the image area.

- **Stretch** can be either True or False. When Stretch is True, the image is resized if the image box is resized. When Stretch is False, the image remains its original size if the image box is resized. Resizing the image box when stretch is False, crops, or hides, the part of the graphic that no longer fits in the image box.

- **Visible** can be either True or False. Visible is often set at run time to display (Visible = True) or hide (Visible = False) the graphic in the image box.

When an image object is added to a form, it is displayed as a box:

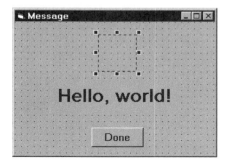

Clicking on the ellipsis in the Picture property from the Properties list displays a dialog box where a graphic can be selected. The image box is then automatically resized to accommodate the selected graphic.

click event A click event procedure is sometimes coded for each image object. The click event is executed when the user clicks on an image. This makes it possible to use image objects as buttons that perform an action when clicked.

File Types

An image control can display graphics in a bitmapped format. Bitmapped graphics are based on a grid, and each graphic is drawn by filling in the squares of the grid. Common bitmapped graphic file extensions are:

BMP   Windows Bitmap
GIF   Graphics Interchange Format
JPEG Joint Photographic Experts Group
WMF   Windows Metafile Format

Review 6

Follow the instructions below to add an image to the Hello World application. The IDE should still be displayed from the last review.

1) OPEN THE HELLO WORLD PROJECT

    a. Open the Hello World project.

    b. In the Project Explorer window, double-click on frmHelloWorld if the Hello World form is not displayed.

2) ADD AN IMAGE OBJECT

Refer to the form below when placing and sizing the form and its objects as instructed in the steps following:

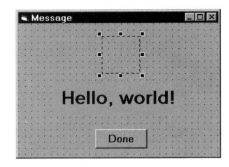

    a. Move the label and command button objects to make room for the image object.

    b. In the Tool box, click on the Image control (▦) and then draw an image box that is approximately 0.5" by 0.5".

3) CHANGE THE PROPERTIES OF THE IMAGE OBJECT

    a. Click once on the image object to select, if it is not already selected. Handles are displayed.

    b. In the Properties window, change the Name property to imgGlobe.

    c. Select the Picture property. An ellipsis is displayed indicating that a dialog box is available.

    d. Click on the Picture ellipsis. The Load Picture dialog box is displayed.

    e. In the Look in collapsible list, select the appropriate folder.

    f. Select Globe in the list of files displayed and then select the Open button. The globe graphic is placed in the image box. The image box was automatically resized to accommodate the globe.

4) CHANGE THE OBJECT SIZE

    a. Drag a corner handle inward to reduce the size of the image. Release the mouse button and note that part of the image is hidden, or cropped, from view.

    b. Drag the corner handle outward until the entire image is again displayed.

    c. In the Properties window, change the Stretch property to True.

    d. Again drag a corner handle inward to reduce the size of the image. The image is resized along with the image box.

    e. Resize the image so that it is approximately 1" wide and 0.5" high and center it above the label.

5) CHANGE THE LABEL PROPERTIES

The label should not display any text when the application is started.

    a. Select the label object.

    b. In the Properties window, select the Caption property if it is not already selected and then delete all of the text in the property. The text displayed in the label object is removed.

6) ADD THE IMAGE CLICK EVENT PROCEDURE

a. Display the Code Editor window.
b. From the Object list in the Code Editor window, select imgGlobe. An imgGlobe_Click event procedure is added to the program code.
c. Add the following statement so that when the user clicks the imgGlobe image the label displays the text "Hello, world!"

```
Private Sub imgGlobe_Click()
    lblMessage.Caption = "Hello, world!"
End Sub
```

7) TEST THE APPLICATION

a. Save the modified Hello World project.
b. Run the application. Click on the globe to display "Hello, world!"
c. Click on the Done button to end the application.

8) PRINT AND REMOVE THE PROJECT

3.17 Operators and Expressions

Visual Basic includes a set of built-in arithmetic operators including exponentiation (^), multiplication (*), division (/), addition (+), and subtraction (–). Arithmetic operators are used to form an *expression*. An expression can be used anywhere a numeric value is allowed. For example, the assignment statement below includes an expression:

```
lblAnswer.Caption = 3.14 * 10^2      'Display area of circle in label
```

An expression is not enclosed in quotation marks because quotation marks indicate text. When the above statement is executed at run time, the Caption for lblAnswer will be changed to 314.

operator precedence

Visual Basic evaluates an arithmetic expression using a specific order of operations, or *operator precedence*. Exponentiation is performed first, multiplication and division next, and then addition and subtraction. Two operators of the same precedence, for example + and –, are evaluated in order from left to right. For example, the expression $5 + 2 * 3 - 1$ evaluates to 10 because multiplication is performed first and then the addition and subtraction.

parentheses

programming style

Operator precedence can be changed by including parentheses in an expression. The operations within parentheses are evaluated first. For example, the result of $(5 + 2) * 3$ is 21 because 5 and 2 were added before multiplication was performed. It is also good programming style to include parentheses when there is any ambiguity or question about the expression so a reader will not have any doubts about what is intended.

3.18 Creating an Executable File

interpreter

Visual Basic uses an *interpreter* that automatically reads each line of program code as it is entered. If a statement has an error, Visual Basic highlights it immediately so that it can be corrected. When a program is run, the interpreter executes the code line-by-line and displays the output in the IDE.

compiler   Visual Basic also includes a *compiler* that translates the program code into a separate executable file. An *executable file* can be run independently of Visual Basic on any computer that uses Windows 95 or later. The Make command from the File menu is used to create an executable file. Note that if you are using the Working Model edition of Visual Basic included on CD with this text, executable files cannot be generated.

3.19 Exiting Visual Basic

When finished working in Visual Basic, it should be exited by selecting the Exit command (Alt+Q) from the File menu. If a project is open and has not been saved since it was last modified, Visual Basic will display a warning dialog box before exiting.

Review 7

For each of the following expressions, indicate the value that will be calculated by Visual Basic. If an expression is not legal, state why.

a) $10 + 3 - 6$ c) $15 / 3 + 2$ e) $15 * (2 + 4)$

b) $15 * 2 + 4$ d) $2^3 + 5 * 4$ f) $"6 + 3 - 2"$

Review 8

The Circle application computes the area of a circle of radius 10. Follow the instructions below to complete the Circle application. Start the Visual Basic IDE if it is not already displayed.

1) OPEN THE CIRCLE PROJECT

a. Open the Circle project.
b. Display the Circle form if it is not already displayed.

2) RUN THE APPLICATION

a. Run the application. Click on the Calculate button. Nothing is displayed because an event procedure has not been written for the Calculate button click event.
b. Click on the Done button. The application is terminated.

3) ADD THE CALCULATE BUTTON CLICK EVENT PROCEDURE

a. Display the frmCircle Code Editor window, if it is not already displayed.
b. From the Object list in the Code Editor window, select cmdCalculate. A cmdCalculate_Click event procedure is added to the program code.
c. The area of a circle is calculated by multiplying π (3.14) and the radius of the circle squared (πr^2). Add the following statement to the cmdCalculate_Click event procedure:

```
Private Sub cmdCalculate_Click()
    lblAnswer.Caption = 3.14 * 10^2      'Display area of circle of radius 10 in label
End Sub
```

4) SAVE THE PROJECT AND RUN THE APPLICATION

a. Save the modified Circle project.
b. Run the application. Click on the Calculate button to test the application. 314 is displayed.
c. Click on the Done button to end the application.

An Introduction to Programming Using Microsoft Visual Basic

5) CREATE AN EXECUTABLE FILE

If you are using the Working Model edition of Visual Basic included on CD with this text, you will not be able to complete this step.

a. From the File menu, select the Make Circle.exe command. The Make Project dialog box is displayed.
b. In the Save in entry box, select the appropriate folder.
c. In the File name entry box, type Circle.exe, if it is not already displayed.
d. Select OK. Visual Basic creates an executable Circle application called Circle. This file may be run from Windows like any other application.

6) SAVE, PRINT, AND THEN REMOVE THE PROJECT

7) EXIT VISUAL BASIC

From the File menu, select the Exit command. The Visual Basic IDE is removed from the screen.

3.20 Visual Basic Programming Guidelines

Visual Basic programs are created using the Visual Basic IDE. Throughout this chapter, several programming style guidelines have been presented. In addition to using these style guidelines, there are a few other guidelines to follow when creating a Visual Basic application:

- Create the application interface first.

- Appropriately name all application objects before writing any code.

- Use the Object list in the Code Editor window to select the object event procedure.

Chapter Summary

object-oriented
event-driven

Visual Basic is an object-oriented programming environment that is used to create event-driven applications for Microsoft Windows. Event-driven programs wait for an event to occur and then respond to it by executing code in an event procedure.

interface
program code

A Visual Basic application consists of an interface and program code. The interface is what appears on the screen when the application is running. The program code is the instructions that tell an application's objects how to behave when the user interacts with them.

The Visual Basic IDE (Integrated Development Environment) includes all the tools needed to create a Visual Basic application. The IDE contains menus with commands for creating, saving, removing, opening, running, ending, and printing a project. The Tool bar has buttons for performing many of these tasks. The IDE also contains windows where the application interface is created, program code is written, and object properties are changed.

creating an object

A form object is used to hold other objects and is automatically added to a project when a project is created. An object is added to the form by clicking on a control in the Tool box and then dragging the cross-hairs pointer on the form or by double-clicking on a control.

A label object is used to display text or the result of an expression and is added to a form with the Label control (). A command button object is an object that can be clicked by the user. It is added to a form with the CommandButton control (). An image object is used to display a graphic and is added to a form with the Image control (). An object can be resized by clicking once on it to select it and then dragging a handle, and moved by selecting it and dragging it.

changing a property value

Properties define the appearance, behavior, position, and other attributes of an object. Every object should have its Name property changed to a descriptive name with the appropriate prefix. Object property values can be changed in the Properties window or through assignment statements that are executed at run time. An assignment statement uses the equal sign to give the property on the left of the equal sign the value on the right of the equal sign.

assignment

event procedures

Event procedures are executed in response to an event and are added to an application's form module in the Code Editor window. An event procedure is created by selecting the object name from the Object list. The Form_Load event procedure is used to execute code when a form is loaded, such as when an application started.

Form_Load

Unload

The Unload statement terminates a program. **Private** indicates that a procedure cannot be accessed outside of the form module. **Sub** indicates the beginning of a procedure, and **End Sub** indicates the end of a procedure.

comments

Comments are used to explain and clarify program code for a human reader. A comment is included in code by preceding text with a single quotation mark ('). It is good programming style to include comments wherever code may be ambiguous or misleading.

Visual Basic includes a set of built-in operators for exponentiation (^), multiplication (*), division (/), addition (+), and subtraction (–). Arithmetic operators are used to form an expression. Expressions are evaluated using a specific operator precedence. Parentheses can be used to change operator precedence.

operator precedence

interpreter
compiler

The Visual Basic IDE includes an interpreter that automatically reads each line of program code as it is entered and highlights errors, and a compiler that translates the program code into a separate executable file.

programming guidelines

When creating a Visual Basic application, the application interface should be created first and the objects appropriately named before writing any code. The object list in the Code Editor window should be used to select the object event procedure.

Vocabulary

Application interface What appears on the screen when a Visual Basic application is running.

Assignment statement Uses the equal sign to give the object property on the left of the equal sign the value on the right of the equal sign.

Body The statements in a procedure.

Class Program code and data to create an object.

Code Editor window The part of the IDE that displays the form module where program code is entered.

Command button An object the user can click.

Comment Information placed in a program to explain and clarify program code for a human reader. Comments are preceded by a single quotation mark.

Compiler A program that translates program code into a separate executable file.

Design time The time during which the application interface is being created.

Dot notation Used in code to access an object property.

Event A way in which the user can interact with an object.

Event-driven program Waits until an event occurs before executing code.

Event procedure Block of code executed in response to an event.

Executable file A file that can be run independently of Visual Basic on any computer that uses Windows 95 or later.

Expression Formed with arithmetic operators.

Form An object used to hold other objects. Each interface has at least one form.

Form Layout window The part of the IDE that allows the application's form position to be selected relative to the computer screen.

Form module A file that contains the program code for a form.

IDE (Integrated Development Environment) Contains all the tools necessary to create a Visual Basic application.

Image An object that displays a graphic.

Interface What appears on the screen when an application is running.

Interpreter A program that automatically reads each line of program code as it is entered.

Label An object used to display information.

Menu bar The part of the IDE that contains the names of menus that contain commands.

Object Has a visual representation and is used to reduce the complexity of graphics-based programs.

OOP (Object-Oriented Programming) Uses classes to create objects and is widely used because it generates reusable, reliable code.

Operator precedence The order in which operators are evaluated in an expression.

Procedure See Event procedure.

Program code Instructions that tell an application's objects how to behave when a user interacts with them.

Project Visual Basic file that maintains all the files associated with an application, including the form and its objects and program code.

Project Explorer window The part of the IDE that lists the files in the current project.

Project window The part of the IDE that contains a form object and is where the interface is created.

Properties window The part of the IDE that lists the properties values of an object.

Property The part of an object that defines its appearance, behavior, position, and other attributes.

Run time The time during which the application is being executed.

Selecting Clicking once on an object to display its handles.

Statement A line of code in a program that tells the computer what to do.

Tool bar The part of the IDE containing buttons that provide shortcuts to commonly performed actions.

Tool box The part of the IDE that contains controls that are used to create objects on a form object.

Visual Basic Object-oriented programming environment used to create Windows applications.

Visual Basic

^ Arithmetic operator used to perform exponentiation.

* Arithmetic operator used to perform multiplication.

/ Arithmetic operator used to perform division.

+ Arithmetic operator used to perform addition.

– Arithmetic operator used to perform subtraction.

() Used to change operator precedence in expressions.

' Precedes a comment.

" Used to enclose text in an assignment statement. Also used to designate a font name in a font name assignment.

= Used in an assignment statement to give the object property on the left of the equal sign the value on the right of the equal sign.

Alignment Object property used to change the alignment of text in a label's Caption. Can be changed at run time.

Bold Font subproperty that can be assigned either True or False. Can be changed at run time.

Caption Object property used to change the text displayed in a Title bar, button, or label. Can be changed at run time.

Code command Displays the form module for a form. Found in the View menu.

CommandButton control Used to create a command button object. Found in the Tool box.

End command Stops the current application. Found in the Run menu. The End button (■) on the Tool bar can be used instead of the command.

End Sub Required to end the Sub Statement.

Exit command Closes the Visual Basic IDE. Found in the File menu.

Font Object property used to display a dialog box for changing the font, font style, and size of an object's caption. Can be changed at run time.

Image control Used to create an image object. Found in the Tool box.

Italic Font subproperty that can be assigned either True or False. Can be changed at run time.

Label control Used to create a label object. Found in the Tool box.

Make command Creates an executable file. Found in the File menu.

Me Used in place of the form name.

Name Object property used to identify the object.

Name Font subproperty that can be assigned a valid font name enclosed in quotation marks. Can be changed at run time.

New Project command Creates a new project. Found in the File menu.

Open Project command Opens an existing project. Found in the File menu. The Open Project button (🖝) on the Tool bar can be used instead of the command.

Picture Object property used to select a graphic.

Print command Prints the interface and program code of an application. Found in the File menu.

Private Indicates the procedure cannot be accessed outside of the form module.

Remove Project command Removes the current project from the IDE. Found in the File menu.

Save Project command Saves the current project. Found in the File menu. The Save Project button (💾) on the Tool bar can be used instead of the command.

Size Font subproperty that can be assigned a numeric value from 0 to 2048. Can be changed at run time.

Start command Runs the current application. Found in the Run menu. The Start button (▶) on the Tool bar can be used instead of the command.

Stretch Object property that can be assigned True or False.

Sub Declares a procedure.

Unload Statement used to terminate a program.

View Code button Clicked to view the form module. Found in the Project Explorer window.

View Object button Clicked to view the form. Found in the Project Explorer window.

Visible Object property that can be assigned True or False. Can be changed at run time.

Exercises

Exercise 1

Create an Address application that displays your name, city, and state in three separate labels. The application interface should look similar to:

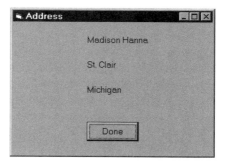

Exercise 2

a) Create a School application that displays your school's name and mascot in two separate labels. The application interface should look similar to:

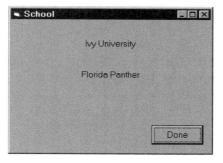

b) Modify the School application to display the Panther graphic and display the text Florida Panther when the image is clicked. The application interface should look similar to the following after clicking on the graphic:

Exercise 3

a) Create an Addition Properties application that displays the associative property of addition, (a+b)+c = a+(b+c), in a label. The application interface should look similar to:

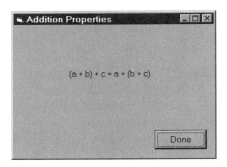

b) Modify the program to display the associative property of addition after clicking on a button and the commutative property, a+b = b+a, when another button is clicked. The application interface should look similar to the following after clicking on the Commutative button:

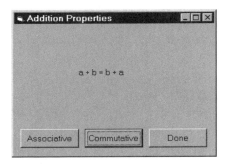

Exercise 4

Create a Size Example application that displays a centered label with Small in size 10, Medium in size 14, or Large in size 18 depending on which button is clicked. The application interface should look similar to the following after clicking on the Medium button:

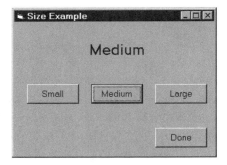

Exercise 5

Create a Style Example application that displays a centered, size 18 Style label that is only bold, only italic, or bold and italic depending on which button is clicked. The application interface should look similar to the following after clicking on the Bold and Italic button:

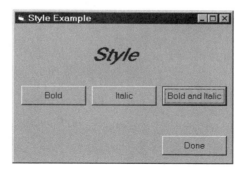

Exercise 6

Create a Font Example application that displays a centered, size 18 Font label that is either in Times New Roman or Arial font depending on which button is clicked. The application interface should look similar to the following after clicking on the Times New Roman button:

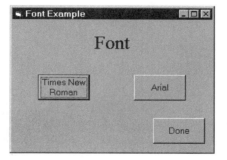

Exercise 7

Create a Hello and Good-bye application that displays Hello! or Good-bye! center aligned, size 18, and bold depending on which button is clicked. Include the Smiley graphic on the interface. The application interface should look similar to the following after clicking on the Hello button:

Exercise 8

Create a Calculations application that displays the result of a calculation after clicking on a button. The application interface should look similar to the following after clicking on the first command button:

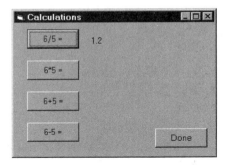

Exercise 9

Create a Circle Circumference application that displays the circumference (2πr) of a circle with radius 10. The application interface should look similar to the following after clicking on the Calculate button:

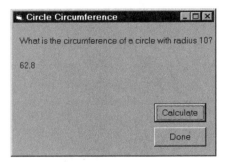

Exercise 10

Create a Rectangle Area and Perimeter application that displays the area (length * width) and perimeter (2l + 2w) of a rectangle of length 5 and width 3. The application interface should look similar to the following after clicking on the Calculate button:

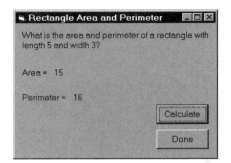

Exercise 11

Create a Car Travel application that calculates and displays the number of kilometers per liter of gasoline a car gets if it travels 700 kilometers on a 70 liter tank of gas. The application should display the Car graphic on the interface when the Calculate button is clicked. The application interface should look similar to the following after clicking on the Calculate button:

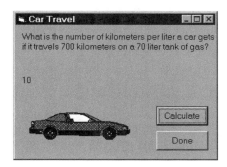

Exercise 12

Create a Long Jump Average application that calculates and displays the average jump length of an athlete whose jumps were 3.3m, 3.5m, 4.0m, and 3.0m. The application interface should look similar to the following after clicking on the Calculate button:

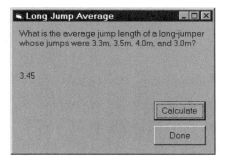

Exercise 13

Create a Guitar Player application that displays the Guitar graphic and the name of your favorite guitar player when the graphic is clicked. The application interface should look similar to the following after clicking on the graphic:

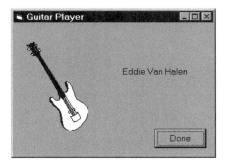

An Introduction to Programming Using Microsoft Visual Basic

Chapter Four
Variables and Constants

Dim

Double

Const

Single

Integer

Long

Currency

String

Boolean

Option Explicit

Debug.Print

TextBox

Mod

OptionButton

Frame

Chapter Four Objectives

After completing this chapter you will be able to:

1. Declare variables in program code.
2. Understand variable assignment statements.
3. Use named constants.
4. Choose legal Visual Basic identifiers that also follow good programming style.
5. Use different data types.
6. Declare multiple variables in program code.
7. Understand and use the **Option Explicit** statement.
8. Understand syntax errors, including run-time errors.
9. Use the **Debug.Print** statement.
10. Use text box objects in applications.
11. Use change event procedures.
12. Understand automatic type conversion.
13. Use special division operators.
14. Use option button objects in frames in applications.
15. Understand good programming style guidelines.

The applications in Chapter Three were limited because they did not allow the user to input data. For example, the Circle application would be more useful if the user could enter the radius of the circle. To get user input, text box and option button objects are used in an application. Variables and constants can be used in program code to represent values.

4.1 Using Variables

programming style

Dim

identifier
data type

A *variable* is a named memory location that stores a value. The use of variables in a program is good programming style because they allow values to be represented by meaningful names that make program code easier to read. Before using a variable it should be declared with a **Dim** statement that includes the identifier and data type. The name of the variable, or *identifier*, is how the value will be referred to within the program. The *data type* of the variable indicates what kind of value it will store. For example, the statement

Dim dblRadius **As Double**

Double

declares a variable dblRadius that stores data of type **Double**. A **Double** is a numeric value that possibly contains a decimal portion. The identifier begins with dbl for good programming style to indicate that the variable stores a **Double**. Other data types are described in Section 4.5.

A variable declaration such as the statement above reserves space in the computer's memory for a value. When a numeric variable is declared in Visual Basic, it is automatically given the value 0:

dblRadius

A variable declaration reserves a space in the computer's memory to hold a value

Dimension

The **Dim** keyword stands for dimension. A declared variable has "dimension" because it has been assigned space in memory.

4.2 Variable Assignment

A variable is given a value through assignment. Variable assignment statements must be written so that the identifier (variable name) is on the left side of the equal sign and the value is on the right. For example, the variable dblRadius is assigned the value 12.3 in the statement:

dblRadius = 12.3

The effect of this assignment statement is that the value 12.3 is stored in the memory location referred to by the name dblRadius:

dblRadius

One common error is to reverse the variable identifier and the value in an assignment statement:

12.3 = dblRadius   'Error!

An expression may also be used on the right side of an assignment statement. For example, in the statement

dblCircleArea = 3.14 * dblRadius ^ 2   'dblCircleArea = 475.05

the expression on the right is evaluated and the result assigned to dblCircleArea. Note that the expression itself includes a variable. A variable can be used wherever a value can be used.

programming style

The program code for the Circle application from Chapter Three can be modified to include variables. Note that as a matter of good programming style, variables are declared at the beginning of the procedure:

```
Project1 - frmCircle (Code)
cmdCalculate                          Click

Private Sub cmdCalculate_Click()
    Dim dblRadius As Double
    Dim dblCircleArea As Double

    dblRadius = 10
    dblCircleArea = 3.14 * dblRadius ^ 2

    lblAnswer.Caption = dblCircleArea
End Sub

Private Sub cmdDone_Click()
    Unload frmCircle
End Sub
```

There are two important ideas to keep in mind when working with variables. First, a variable can store only one value at any given time. For example, after the following statements have executed

Dim dblX **As Double**
dblX = 5.5
dblX = 10

the value stored in dblX is 10 because 10 was the last value assigned to dblX and dblX can hold only one value.

Another important concept is that the expression on the right of an assignment statement is evaluated first and then its value is given to the variable on the left. For example, in the statements

Dim dblSum **As Double**
dblSum = 6
dblSum = dblSum + 3

dblSum is given the value 6 in the first assignment statement. In the second assignment statement, the expression dblSum + 3 is evaluated, which results in 6 + 3 or 9, and then that value assigned to memory location dblSum, overwriting what was previously stored there.

Review 1

What would be the final value of the variable dblResult after execution of the statements below?

a. **Dim** dblNumber **As Double**
   Dim dblResult **As Double**
   dblNumber = 10
   dblNumber = 2*3
   dblResult = dblNumber * 2

b. **Dim** dblNumber **As Double**
   Dim dblResult **As Double**
   dblResult = 5
   dblNumber = 2
   dblResult = dblResult + dblNumber

Review 2

Follow the instructions below to create the Circle Area application that uses variables to compute the area of a circle of radius 6.

1) CREATE A NEW PROJECT

2) ADD OBJECTS TO THE FORM

Refer to the form below when placing and sizing the form and its objects. Use the table below to name and change the properties of the objects.

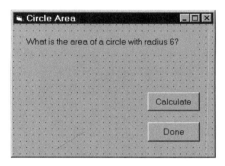

Object	Name	Caption
Form1	frmCircleArea	Circle Area
Label1	lblQuestion	What is the area of a circle with radius 6?
Label2	lblAnswer	*empty*
Command1	cmdCalculate	Calculate
Command2	cmdDone	Done

3) SAVE THE PROJECT

From the File menu, select Save Project. Save the form naming it frmCircleArea. Save the project naming it Circle Area.

4) ADD THE PROGRAM CODE

a. Display the frmCircleArea Code Editor window, if it is not already displayed.
b. The area of a circle is calculated by multiplying π (3.14) and the radius of the circle squared (πr^2). Create a cmdCalculate_Click event procedure that contains the following code:

```
Private Sub cmdCalculate_Click()
    Dim dblRadius As Double
    Dim dblCircleArea As Double

    dblRadius = 6
    dblCircleArea = 3.14 * dblRadius ^ 2

    lblAnswer.Caption = dblCircleArea  'Display area of circle of radius 6 in label
End Sub
```

c. Create a cmdDone_Click event procedure that contains the following code:

```
Private Sub cmdDone_Click()
    Unload Me
End Sub
```

5) RUN THE APPLICATION

a. Save the modified Circle Area project.
b. Run the application. Click on the Calculate button to test the application. 113.04 should be displayed.
c. Click on the Done button to end the application.

6) PRINT AND THEN REMOVE THE PROJECT

4.3 Using Named Constants

A *constant* is a named memory location which stores a value that cannot be changed at run time from its initial assignment. The use of named *programming style* constants is good programming style because they give unchanging values a meaningful name and make program code easier to read. To use a *Const* named constant it must be declared in a **Const** statement that includes an identifier followed by the data type and an assignment. For example, the following statement declares a constant dblPi with a value of 3.14:

```
Const dblPi As Double = 3.14
```

The cmdCalculate_Click procedure in the Circle application can be *programming style* modified to include a named constant. Note that as a matter of good programming style, constants are declared before variable declarations at the beginning of a procedure:

```
Private Sub cmdCalculate_Click()
    Const dblPi As Double = 3.14
    Dim dblRadius As Double
    Dim dblCircleArea As Double

    dblRadius = 10
    dblCircleArea = dblPi * dblRadius ^ 2

    lblAnswer.Caption = dblCircleArea
End Sub
```

By using descriptive variable and constant names, the dblCircleArea assignment statement corresponds to the mathematical formula $A = \pi r^2$.

One common error is to include a program statement that tries to change the value of a constant, as in the following:

```
Const dblPi As Double = 3.14
dblPi = 22/7   'Error
```

4.4 Choosing Identifiers

Case Sensitivity in Indentifiers

Visual Basic does not distinguish case in identifiers. For example, radius and Radius represent the same memory location. However, to avoid confusion for the reader of the program code, Visual Basic maintains identifiers by automatically changing the case of an identifier to match that of the first occurrence.

Legal Visual Basic identifiers:

- must begin with a letter.

- must contain only letters, digits, and the underscore (_) character. Periods, spaces and other special characters are not allowed.

- cannot exceed 255 characters.

There are several identifiers that Visual Basic reserves for use as keywords. A *keyword* has special meaning to the compiler, and therefore cannot be a variable or named constant identifier. For example, **Double** is a keyword. In this text, keywords appear in a different font, just as the word **Double** is formatted. Refer to Appendix A for a list of Visual Basic keywords.

programming style

As a matter of good programming style, variables and constants should be named so that they are quickly and clearly understandable to the reader. This includes using a prefix that describes the type of data the variable or constant will store. For example, dbl should prefix every identifier that represents a **Double** variable. Descriptive identifiers are important for helping you to get your program code working correctly, for later modifying and improving your program code, and for other readers of your program code.

Review 3

Modify the Circle Area application from Review 2 so that a named constant is declared for π and this named constant is used rather than the number 3.14 in the cmdCalculate_Click event procedure.

Review 4

List three legal and three illegal variable identifiers illustrating the rules for identifiers in Visual Basic. Indicate why each illegal name is incorrect.

4.5 Built-In Data Types

Data Type Memory Requirements

Each data type has their own memory requirements for storing values. A Single uses 4 bytes and a Double uses 8. An Integer requires 2 bytes and a Long requires 4. Currency uses 8 bytes and Boolean uses 2. A String requires one byte for each character in the string.

In addition to **Double**, Visual Basic supports several other built-in data types. It is important that a variable or constant be of the appropriate type for the data represented. Visual Basic has several built-in types including:

Type	Used to represent
Single	numbers possibly containing a decimal
Double	numbers possibly containing a decimal
Integer	integers (no decimals)
Long	integers (no decimals)
Currency	numbers representing dollar amounts
String	a set of characters
Boolean	True or False

Single and Double   The **Single** and **Double** types represent positive or negative real numbers. These types are often referred to as *floating point*, meaning that they can represent values with numbers after the decimal point. The difference between the two types is the range of values that can be represented. A **Single** can store values up to $3.4e^{38}$, and a **Double** can store values up to $1.8e^{308}$.

Integer and Long   The **Integer** and **Long** types represent positive or negative integers. The difference between **Integer** and **Long** is the range of values that can be represented. While for many purposes, the **Integer** type is sufficient, it is often necessary to use **Long** for values that may exceed 32,767 (the limit for an **Integer**). If a value with a decimal portion is assigned to an **Integer** or **Long**, the value is rounded. For example, intX = 6.7 gives the value 7 to intX.

While the **Integer** and **Long** types may seem limited, they are the perfect choice for counting or representing whole number quantities. For example, an **Integer** type variable should be used to represent the number of students in a class. Many programs throughout this text use integer variables and constants.

Currency   The **Currency** type represents real numbers that are money values. **Currency** can store values with up to four digits to the right of the decimal place and 15 digits to the left of the decimal place.

String   The **String** type represents a set of characters, also called a *string*. A string can include the letters of the alphabet, digits, and in general any character that can be typed or displayed, such as $, %, and spaces. A **String** assignment requires using double-quotation marks ("):

```
Dim strLastName As String
strLastName = "Grassman"
```

Boolean   The **Boolean** type represents True or False. A **Boolean** variable is useful for representing on/off and yes/no values. For example, blnOpen would be assigned True if open and False if closed.

naming conventions   As discussed in Section 4.4, variable identifiers should be descriptive and begin with an appropriate prefix, as listed below:

Type	Prefix	Type	Prefix
Single	sgl	Currency	cur
Double	dbl	String	str
Integer	int	Boolean	bln
Long	lng		

4.6 Variable Declarations

multiple variables   A single **Dim** statement can be used to declare multiple variables. For example, the following statement declares several variables of different types. Note that commas are used to separate declarations:

```
Dim strName As String, intAge As Integer, dblHeight As Double
```

This style of variable declarations can lead to simpler, easier-to-read code.

variable initialization   Visual Basic initializes variables when they are declared. Variables of numeric types, such as **Double, Single, Integer, Long,** and **Currency**, are initialized to 0. **String** variables are initialized to an empty string (""). **Boolean** variables are initialized to False, which is equivalent to 0.

Visual Basic does not require variables to be declared before they are used. For example, the statements

```
Dim dblRadius As Integer
dblRadis = 10                              'Misspelled variable
dblCircleArea = dblPi * dblRadius ^ 2      'dblCircleArea assigned 0
```

Option Explicit

are legal but do not produce the desired results because dblRadius is never assigned a value and is therefore equal to 0 in the expression. To prevent errors such as this, the **Option Explicit** statement can be added to the General section of the form module. **Option Explicit** displays an error message at run time when a variable is used before it is declared.

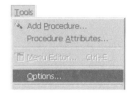

To add the **Option Explicit** statement to existing code, General must be selected from the Object list in the Code Editor window and then the statement typed. To have the **Option Explicit** statement automatically appear in all future form modules, the Options command from the Tools menu is selected and then the Require Variable Declaration option selected from the Editor tab.

Review 5

Write variable declarations to separately represent the first, middle, and last names of a student, the age of a student, and the GPA (Grade Point Average) of a student. Be sure to use good programming style when naming the variables.

4.7 Syntax Errors

A statement that violates the rules of Visual Basic is said to contain a *syntax error*. For example, the statement

```
Dim intX As Integer = 12  'Syntax error!
```

run-time error

is not syntactically correct because assignment is illegal in a variable declaration. Some syntax errors, such as the one above, are immediately detected by Visual Basic which then displays the statement in red in the Code Editor window. Other syntax errors may not be detected until the application is run, at which time a *run-time error* is generated and a dialog box is displayed describing the error:

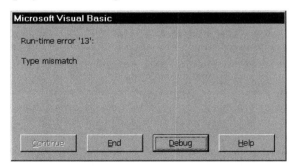

Clicking on the Debug button highlights the statement causing the run-time error:

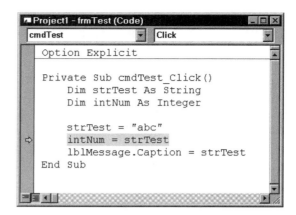

```
Project1 - frmTest (Code)
cmdTest                      Click

Option Explicit

Private Sub cmdTest_Click()
    Dim strTest As String
    Dim intNum As Integer

    strTest = "abc"
    intNum = strTest
    lblMessage.Caption = strTest
End Sub
```

The error can be corrected and then the Run button clicked to continue with program execution.

4.8 Debugging Techniques - The Immediate Window

Debugging is the process of getting an application to work correctly. The Visual Basic IDE has tools that are useful for debugging a program. One tool is the Immediate window, which is displayed by selecting the Immediate Window command (Ctrl+G) from the View window:

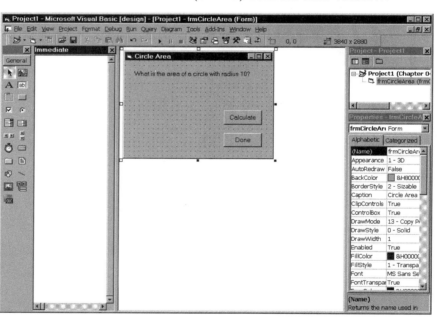

The Immediate window is useful for debugging

The Immediate window displays the output of the **Debug.Print** statement that can be included in program code. The **Debug.Print** statement has the following form:

Debug.Print *item*

item is a variable, a string enclosed in quotation marks, or an expression. Multiple *item*s separated by semicolons (;) can also be included in a **Debug.Print** statement. When a program containing a **Debug.Print** statement is run, the Immediate window displays the output of the statement.

History of Debugging

Grace Murray Hopper was the first person to apply the term "debug" to the computer. In the 1940s, the computer she was using malfunctioned when a moth flew into the circuitry. While removing the dead moth, she said that the program would be running again after the computer had been "debugged." Today the process of removing errors from a program is still called debugging.

For example, **Debug.Print** statements can be added to the Circle Area application to "watch" the value of dblRadius change:

```
Private Sub cmdCalculate_Click()
    Const dblPi As Double = 3.14
    Dim dblRadius As Double
    Dim dblCircleArea As Double

    Debug.Print "dblRadius="; dblRadius
    dblRadius = 10
    Debug.Print "dblRadius="; dblRadius
    dblCircleArea = dblPi * dblRadius ^ 2

    lblAnswer.Caption = dblCircleArea
End Sub
```

Running the Circle Area application and clicking on the Calculate button displays the following:

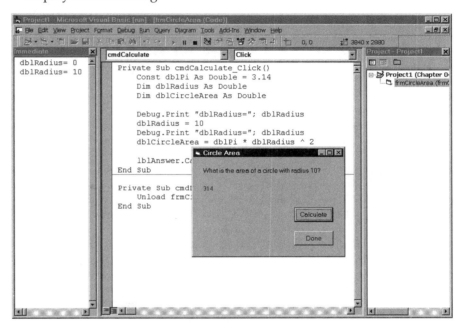

The Immediate window can be removed from the IDE by clicking on its Close button in the upper-right corner.

Review 6

This review uses the Circle Area application created in Review 2 and modified in Review 3. Follow the directions below to add **Debug** statements to the Circle Area application.

1) OPEN THE CIRCLE AREA PROJECT

Display the Circle Area form if it is not already displayed.

2) USE THE IMMEDIATE WINDOW

a. From the View menu, select the Immediate Window command. The Immediate window is displayed.

b. Display the Code Editor window for the Circle Area application.

c. Modify the cmdCalculate_Click procedure to include two Debug statements:

```
Private Sub cmdCalculate_Click()
    Const dblPi As Double = 3.14
    Dim dblRadius As Double
    Dim dblCircleArea As Double

    Debug.Print "dblRadius="; dblRadius        'Debug
    dblRadius = 6
    Debug.Print "dblRadius="; dblRadius        'Debug

    dblCircleArea = dblPi * dblRadius ^ 2

    lblAnswer.Caption = dblCircleArea
End Sub
```

d. Run the Circle Area application and click on the Calculate button. The Immediate window shows the output of the Debug statements. You may need to drag the form to view the output in the Immediate window.

e. Add a third Debug statement to cmdCalculate_Click():

```
...
    dblCircleArea = dblPi * dblRadius ^ 2
    Debug.Print "dblCircleArea="; dblCircleArea        'Debug

    lblAnswer.Caption = dblCircleArea
End Sub
```

f. Run Circle Area and click on the Calculate button. The Immediate window shows the output of the Debug statements.

3) PRINT AND THEN DELETE THE DEBUG STATEMENTS

a. Print the project code.
b. Delete the three Debug statements and then save the modified Circle Area application.

4) REMOVE THE IMMEDIATE WINDOW

In the upper-right corner of the Immediate window, click on the Close button.

4.9 Obtaining a Value from the User

An application can be more useful when the user is able to input values at run time for use in the program code. For example, the Circle Area application would be more useful if the user could enter the radius value for calculating the area of the circle. One way to obtain user input is through a text box:

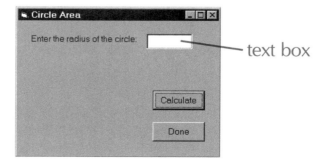

text box

text box A *text box* object is created using the TextBox control () in the Tool box and has the properties:

- **Name** identifies the object and is used by the programmer. It is good programming style to begin text box object names with txt.

- **Text** changes what is displayed in the text box. Text can be changed at run time through assignment. Text is also changed automatically at run time to whatever the user types in the text box.

- **Alignment** sets the alignment of text relative to the text box.

Text box objects do not have a Caption property. Therefore, a label is often placed near the text box to describe its contents or purpose.

change event

A change event procedure is usually coded for each text box. The change event procedure is executed when the user begins to type in a text box. For example, the change event procedure could include code to clear a part of the form by changing the Caption of labels to an empty string (" "). Refer to the txtRadius_Change event procedure below.

At run time, the Text property contains whatever characters the user types into the text box. The value of the Text property (the user's input) can then be used in an assignment statement or an expression, as in the dblRadius assignment statement in the cmdCalculate_Click procedure:

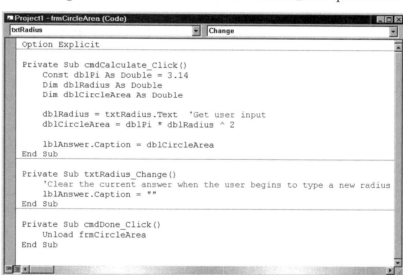

```
Option Explicit

Private Sub cmdCalculate_Click()
    Const dblPi As Double = 3.14
    Dim dblRadius As Double
    Dim dblCircleArea As Double

    dblRadius = txtRadius.Text    'Get user input
    dblCircleArea = dblPi * dblRadius ^ 2

    lblAnswer.Caption = dblCircleArea
End Sub

Private Sub txtRadius_Change()
    'Clear the current answer when the user begins to type a new radius
    lblAnswer.Caption = ""
End Sub

Private Sub cmdDone_Click()
    Unload frmCircleArea
End Sub
```

Rounding

Visual Basic follows certain rules when rounding numbers. A number with a decimal portion greater than .5 is rounded up and a number with the decimal portion less than .5 is rounded down. When the decimal portion equals .5, an odd number is rounded up and an even number is rounded down. The following examples demonstrate this:

```
Dim intX As Integer
intX = 5.5    'intX is assigned 6
intX = 6.5    'intX is assigned 6
```

4.10 Automatic Type Conversion

In an assignment statement, Visual Basic automatically converts data to match the type of the variable it is being assigned to. For example, in the assignment statement below, the value with a decimal portion is automatically rounded to a whole number when assigned to the **Integer** variable:

```
Dim intX As Integer
intX = 6.7        'intX is assigned the value 7
```

Data typed in a text box is a **String** data type. Because Visual Basic automatically converts between data types, the string entered by the user can be assigned to a numeric data type for use in a calculation, as was done in the dblRadius assignment statement in the Circle Area application shown previously (dblRadius = txtRadius.Text).

Visual Basic will try to convert from one data type to another as long as the data is valid for the receiving data type. For example, assigning "123" to an **Integer** variable intX is valid because the characters in the string are also numbers. However, an error will be generated when "abc" is assigned to the **Integer** variable intX.

Review 7

This review uses the Circle Area application created in Review 2 and modified in Review 3 and Review 6. Follow the directions below to modify the Circle Area application to include a text box.

1) OPEN THE CIRCLE AREA PROJECT

Display the Circle Area form if it is not already displayed.

2) MODIFY THE APPLICATION INTERFACE

    a. Change the lblQuestion Caption property to Enter the radius of the circle:

    b. In the Tool box, double-click on the TextBox control (🔤). A text box object is placed on the form.

    c. Resize both the text box and the lblQuestion object and then move the objects so that your form looks similar to:

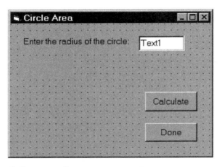

    d. Change the Name property of the text box to txtRadius.

    e. Delete the current text box Text property value so that it is blank.

3) MODIFY THE PROGRAM CODE

    a. Display the Code Editor window.

    b. From the Object list, select General. The cursor is placed in the General section.

    c. Type Option Explicit if it is not already there and then press Enter. Remember that the **Option Explicit** statement will check for undeclared variables at run time.

    d. Modify the cmdCalculate_Click procedure as shown below:

```
Private Sub cmdCalculate_Click()
    Const dblPi As Double = 3.14
    Dim dblRadius As Double
    Dim dblCircleArea As Double

    dblRadius = txtRadius.Text      'Get user input
    dblCircleArea = dblPi * dblRadius ^ 2

    lblAnswer.Caption = dblCircleArea
End Sub
```

    e. From the Object list, select txtRadius. A txtRadius_Change() event procedure is added to the code.

An Introduction to Programming Using Microsoft Visual Basic

f. Add the following statements to the txtRadius_Change() procedure:

```
Private Sub txtRadius_Change()
    'Clear the current answer when the user begins to type a new radius value
    lblAnswer.Caption = ""
End Sub
```

4) **SAVE THE PROJECT AND THEN RUN THE APPLICATION**

a. Save the modified Circle Area project.
b. Run the application.
c. Click in the text box and type 6.
d. Select the Calculate button. The area of the circle is displayed as the Caption of the lblAnswer label.
e. Change the value in the text box and note that the previous circle area is no longer displayed. Select the Calculate button. A new area is calculated and displayed.
f. Select the Done button.

5) **PRINT AND THEN REMOVE THE PROJECT**

Review 8

Create a Rectangle Area application that asks the user for the length and width of a rectangle and then displays the area of the rectangle when the Calculate button is selected. Include a change event procedure that clears the answer label when the user types a new value for the length or width. The application interface should look similar to that shown on the right after entering 5 and 2 and clicking on the Calculate button.

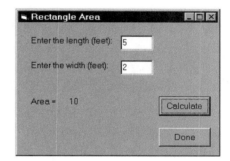

4.11 Special Division Operators

\
Mod

integer division

In addition to the standard built-in operators (^, *, /, +, −), Visual Basic includes two other division operators. The \ operator performs Integer division, and the **Mod** operator performs modulus division.

Integer division truncates the decimal portion of the quotient which results in an integer. For example, in the assignment statement below

Dim intX **As Integer**
intX = 20 \ 7   'intX is assigned 2

the value 2 is assigned to intX because the whole portion of the quotient is 2:

$$
\begin{array}{r}
20 \backslash 7 \\
\textcircled{2}\ r6 \\
7\overline{)20} \\
\underline{14} \\
6
\end{array}
$$

modulus division   *Modulus division* returns the remainder resulting from division. For example, in the assignment statement below

Dim intX **As Integer**
intX = 20 **Mod** 7   'intX is assigned 6

the value 6 is assigned to intX because the remainder of 20 divided by 7 is 6:

$$\begin{array}{r} 2 \;\; \text{(r6)} \leftarrow 20 \text{ Mod } 7 \\ 7\overline{)20} \\ \underline{14} \\ 6 \end{array}$$

Modulus division is often useful in examining the digits of a number, finding the number of minutes left over after hours have been accounted for, and other integer-related tasks.

operator precedence   In arithmetic expressions, integer division is performed after multiplication and division. Modulus division is performed next, and then addition and subtraction. For example, the expression 5 * 2 Mod 3 \ 2 evaluates to 0 because 5 * 2 is performed first, then 3 \ 2, and then 10 Mod 1. Remember that operator precedence can be changed using parentheses.

Review 9

What is assigned to intY when intX is 1998? When intX is 1776? When intX is 38? Explain, in general, the result of this expression:

Dim intX **As Integer**, intY **As Integer**
intY = (intX \ 10) **Mod** 10

Review 10

Skyhook International sells skyhooks in boxes that can hold up to 3 skyhooks. Create a Skyhook International application that allows the user to enter the number of skyhooks ordered, and then after selecting the Compute button displays the number of boxes that will contain three skyhooks and the number of skyhooks left over. Include a change event procedure that clears the interface when the user types a new value for the number of skyhooks ordered. The application interface should look similar to that shown on the right after entering 11 and clicking on the Compute button.

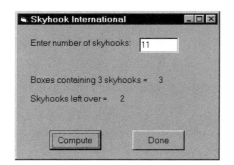

4.12 Option Buttons

radio buttons   Option buttons, sometimes called *radio buttons*, are another way to obtain input from the user. Option buttons are grouped to provide a set of choices and only one option button in a group can be selected at a time. For example, the Hello World International application provides option buttons so that the user can specify the language of the "Hello world!" label:

frame — option button

The Hello World International application after clicking on the Spanish option button

option button

An *option button* object is created using the OptionButton control ( ) in the Tool box and has the properties:

- **Name** identifies the object and is used by the programmer. It is good programming style to begin option button object names with opt.

- **Caption** changes the text displayed as the option button label. Caption can be changed at run time through assignment.

- **Value** can be set to either True or False to display the option button as selected or not selected, respectively. Only one option button can be True at any given time. Therefore, changing the Value of one button to True automatically changes the Values of other buttons to False. Value can be changed at run time through assignment. Value is also changed automatically at run time when the user clicks on an option button.

- **Alignment** moves the option button to either the left or right of its Caption.

click event

A click event procedure is usually coded for each option button. The click event procedure is executed when the user clicks on an option button. For example, the click event procedure could include code to change the Caption of a label when a user clicks on an option button.

frame

A *frame* is a container object to group option buttons relative to a single choice. In the Hello World International application shown above, the option buttons for choosing a language were placed in a frame with the Caption "Select a language." A frame object is created using the Frame control ( ) in the Tool box and must be created before any option buttons are added to the application. A frame has the properties:

- **Name** identifies the object and is used by the programmer. It is good programming style to begin frame object names with fra.

- **Caption** changes the text displayed as the frame label. Caption can be changed at run time through assignment.

option buttons in a frame

When adding option buttons to a frame, they should be drawn in the frame by selecting the OptionButton control and dragging within the frame. When option buttons are drawn in the frame, the frame and option buttons will move together when the frame is dragged.

Review 11

Follow the instructions below to create the Hello World International application.

1) CREATE A NEW PROJECT

2) ADD OBJECTS TO THE FORM

Refer to the form below when placing and sizing the form and its objects. Use the table below to name and change the properties of the objects.

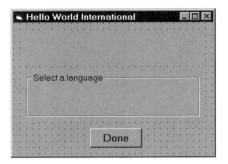

Object	Name	Caption	Font	Alignment
Form1	frmHelloWorldInternational	Hello World International		
Label1	lblMessage	*empty*	Bold 18pt	Center
Frame1	fraLanguage	Select a language		
Command1	cmdDone	Done	10pt	

3) SAVE THE PROJECT

From the File menu, select Save Project. Save the form naming it frmHelloWorldInternational. Save the project naming it Hello World International.

4) ADD OPTION BUTTONS TO THE FORM

Option buttons should be added to a form by drawing them inside a frame. When added this way, a frame and any option buttons inside it function as a group.

a. In the Tool box, click the OptionButton control (⦿) and then drag the cross-hairs pointer in the frame to create an option button.
b. Add two more option buttons inside the frame. Refer to the form below when placing the option buttons. Use the table below to name and change the properties of the objects.

Object	Name	Caption
Option1	optEnglish	English
Option2	optSpanish	Spanish
Option3	optFrench	French

An Introduction to Programming Using Microsoft Visual Basic

5) ADD CLICK EVENT PROCEDURES FOR THE OPTION BUTTONS

a. Display the Code Editor window.

b. From the Object list in the Code Editor window, select optEnglish. An optEnglish_Click event procedure is added to the program code.

c. Add the following statements to the optEnglish_Click procedure:

```
Private Sub optEnglish_Click()
    lblMessage.Caption = "Hello, world!"
End Sub
```

d. Add an optSpanish_Click event procedure with the following statements:

```
Private Sub optSpanish_Click()
    lblMessage.Caption = "Hola mundo!"
End Sub
```

e. Add an optFrench_Click event procedure with the following statements:

```
Private Sub optFrench_Click()
    lblMessage.Caption = "Bonjour le monde!"
End Sub
```

6) ADD A FORM LOAD EVENT PROCEDURE

To make English the default language when the application starts, code must be added to the Form_Load event procedure.

Add a Form_Load event procedure with the following statements:

```
Private Sub Form_Load()
    optEnglish.Value = True          'Select the English option button
    lblMessage.Caption = "Hello, world!"
End Sub
```

7) ADD THE COMMAND BUTTON EVENT PROCEDURE

Add a cmdDone_Click event procedure with the following statements:

```
Private Sub cmdDone_Click()
    Unload Me
End Sub
```

8) RUN THE APPLICATION

Save the modified Hello World International project and then run the application. Select each of the option buttons. Note how the label changes when an option button is selected. End the application.

9) PRINT AND THEN REMOVE THE PROJECT

4.13 Visual Basic Programming Guidelines

programming style   Well-written code is clear and easy to read which makes it easier to debug and modify. Good programming style is essential in creating well-written code. Several programming style guidelines have already been introduced in this and the previous chapter. These guidelines are summarized and expanded in the following list. As you continue through the text, make note of additional programming style guidelines so that you may incorporate them in your code.

A well-written program should include:

- object names that begin with three letters descriptive of the object type.

- comments that explain and clarify code.

- expressions that use parentheses if needed to better understand what is intended.

- variables and constants with meaningful identifiers to represent values. Identifiers should begin with three letters descriptive of the data type.

- an **Option Explicit** statement to insure variables are declared before they are used.

- variables of the appropriate data type.

- variables declared at the beginning of the procedure they are used in.

- constants to represent unchanging values.

- constants declared at the beginning of the procedure they are used in, before any variable declarations.

- statements in a procedure that are indented with a tab so that it is easy to distinguish between procedures.

Case Study

This and all of the subsequent chapters end with a Case Study. *Case Studies* are used to learn problem-solving techniques. Each Case Study illustrates the sequence of steps and thinking that goes into the construction of a substantial application. Learning to program is much more than simply learning a particular language. It is learning how to produce robust, clear, working code. It is learning a *process* for creating an application.

The four steps in creating an application are specification, design, coding, and testing and debugging. In this first Case Study, each of these steps is explained.

specification
The first step in creating an application is clearly defining what the application is to accomplish. This definition is called the *specification*, or *spec*, because it specifies what the application should do. In real-world situations, the specification is developed by talking with the application user and other computer professionals. In this text, the specification will be provided.

The specification for this Case Study is:

A calculator application that allows the user to enter two numbers and then select the operator (^, *, /, \, Mod, +, −) to be used to form an expression with the numbers. Selecting an operator should display the result of the expression. For example, entering 10 and 5, and selecting the + operator displays 15, the result of 10 + 5.

design   The *design* of an application is how the interface will look and how the program code will be written to accomplish the specification. The best way to design the interface is to draw form designs on paper. The code design is a description of each object's event procedures. In this text, each Case Study design will be presented. However, the reviews and exercises will show an application's interface, but will not include code design.

The interface design for this Case Study follows. Note that the label is sketched with dashed lines to indicate that its Caption property will be empty at design time. The label Caption will be changed at run time when an operator has been selected:

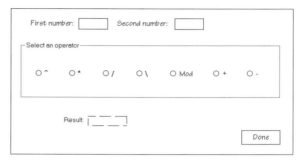

The interface design for the Calculator Case Study

The program code design for this Case Study is:

Each option button click event procedure will be coded to store the text entered in the text boxes in **Double** variables and then display the result of an expression in a label. The text box change event procedures will be coded to clear the option buttons and label. The Done button will be coded to end the program.

coding   *Coding* is creating the interface and writing the program code. In this text, coding will be presented and discussed in the Case Studies but not in the reviews and exercises.

The interface and code for this Case Study are:

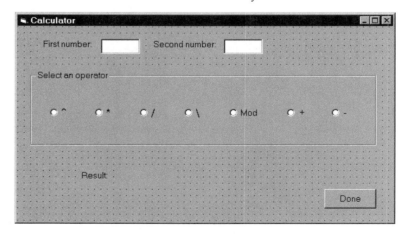

Object	Name	Caption	Text	Font
Form1	frmCalculator	Calculator		
Label1	lblFirstNumber	Enter first number:		
Label2	lblSecondNumber	Enter second number:		
Text1	txtFirstNumber		*empty*	
Text2	txtSecondNumber		*empty*	

Object	Name	Caption	Text	Font
Frame1	fraOperators	Select an operator		
Option1	optExponentiation	^		10pt
Option2	optMultiplication	*		10pt
Option3	optDivision	/		10pt
Option4	optIntegerDivision	\		10pt
Option5	optModulus	Mod		
Option6	optAddition	+		10pt
Option7	optSubtraction	–		10pt
Label3	lblAnswer	*empty*		
Command1	cmdDone	Done		

```vb
Option Explicit

Private Sub txtFirstNumber_Change()
    lblAnswer.Caption = ""          'Clear label

    'Clear option buttons
    optExponentiation.Value = False
    optMultiplication.Value = False
    optDivision.Value = False
    optIntegerDivision.Value = False
    optModulusDivision.Value = False
    optAddition.Value = False
    optSubtraction.Value = False
End Sub

Private Sub txtSecondNumber_Change()
    lblAnswer.Caption = ""          'Clear label

    'Clear option buttons
    optExponentiation.Value = False
    optMultiplication.Value = False
    optDivision.Value = False
    optIntegerDivision.Value = False
    optModulusDivision.Value = False
    optAddition.Value = False
    optSubtraction.Value = False
End Sub

Private Sub optExponentiation_Click()
    Dim dblFirstNumber As Double, dblSecondNumber As Double
    Dim dblAnswer As Double

    dblFirstNumber = txtFirstNumber.Text          'Get first number from user
    dblSecondNumber = txtSecondNumber.Text   'Get second number from user
    dblAnswer = dblFirstNumber ^ dblSecondNumber

    lblAnswer.Caption = dblAnswer
End Sub

Private Sub optMultiplication_Click()
    Dim dblFirstNumber As Double, dblSecondNumber As Double
    Dim dblAnswer As Double

    dblFirstNumber = txtFirstNumber.Text          'Get first number from user
    dblSecondNumber = txtSecondNumber.Text   'Get second number from user
    dblAnswer = dblFirstNumber * dblSecondNumber

    lblAnswer.Caption = dblAnswer
End Sub
```

An Introduction to Programming Using Microsoft Visual Basic

```
Private Sub optDivision_Click()
  Dim dblFirstNumber As Double, dblSecondNumber As Double
  Dim dblAnswer As Double

  dblFirstNumber = txtFirstNumber.Text        'Get first number from user
  dblSecondNumber = txtSecondNumber.Text  'Get second number from user
  dblAnswer = dblFirstNumber / dblSecondNumber

  lblAnswer.Caption = dblAnswer
End Sub

Private Sub optIntegerDivision_Click()
  Dim dblFirstNumber As Double, dblSecondNumber As Double
  Dim dblAnswer As Double

  dblFirstNumber = txtFirstNumber.Text        'Get first number from user
  dblSecondNumber = txtSecondNumber.Text  'Get second number from user
  dblAnswer = dblFirstNumber \ dblSecondNumber

  lblAnswer.Caption = dblAnswer
End Sub

Private Sub optModulusDivision_Click()
  Dim dblFirstNumber As Double, dblSecondNumber As Double
  Dim dblAnswer As Double

  dblFirstNumber = txtFirstNumber.Text        'Get first number from user
  dblSecondNumber = txtSecondNumber.Text  'Get second number from user
  dblAnswer = dblFirstNumber Mod dblSecondNumber

  lblAnswer.Caption = dblAnswer
End Sub

Private Sub optAddition_Click()
  Dim dblFirstNumber As Double, dblSecondNumber As Double
  Dim dblAnswer As Double

  dblFirstNumber = txtFirstNumber.Text        'Get first number from user
  dblSecondNumber = txtSecondNumber.Text  'Get second number from user
  dblAnswer = dblFirstNumber + dblSecondNumber

  lblAnswer.Caption = dblAnswer
End Sub

Private Sub optSubtraction_Click()
  Dim dblFirstNumber As Double, dblSecondNumber As Double
  Dim dblAnswer As Double

  dblFirstNumber = txtFirstNumber.Text        'Get first number from user
  dblSecondNumber = txtSecondNumber.Text  'Get second number from user
  dblAnswer = dblFirstNumber - dblSecondNumber

  lblAnswer.Caption = dblAnswer
End Sub

Private Sub CmdDone_Click()
  Unload Me
End Sub
```

testing and debugging   *Testing* is the process of running the application and entering data to test different possibilities to reveal any bugs. *Debugging* is the process of getting an application to work correctly.

This Case Study should be tested by entering values that are positive, negative, and zero. What will happen when 0 is entered in the second text box? One way to prevent this error is discussed in the next chapter.

Running this Case Study, entering two numbers, and then selecting the * operator displays the following:

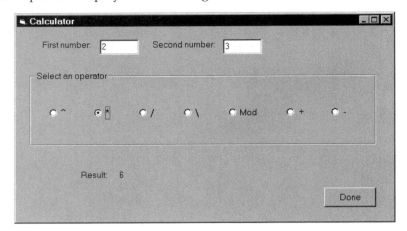

Review 12

Modify the Calculator Case Study to allow the user to enter three numbers.

Chapter Summary

Dim

A variable is a named memory location used to represent a value in a program and is declared in a **Dim** statement that includes the variable identifier and data type. The value of a variable can change throughout program execution. A variable is given a value through assignment.

Const

A constant is used to represent values that cannot be changed at run time from their initial assignment. A **Const** statement is used to declare a constant and includes the constant identifier, data type, and initial assignment.

identifier

keywords

Identifiers in Visual Basic must begin with a letter, must contain only letters, digits, and the underscore character and cannot exceed 255 characters in length. There are several Visual Basic keywords that cannot be used as identifiers. Identifiers should include a prefix that describes the type of data the variable or constant will store and should be clearly and quickly understandable to the reader.

data types

Visual Basic has several built-in data types including **Single, Double, Integer, Long, Currency, String,** and **Boolean.** The appropriate data type should be included in variable or constant declarations. Multiple variables can be declared in a single **Dim** statement by separating each name with a comma. When a numeric variable is declared, Visual Basic automatically initializes it to 0. String variables are automatically initialized to an empty string, and Boolean variables are initialized to False.

Option Explicit

To prevent errors, program code should include the **Option Explicit** statement in the General section of the Code Editor window so that variables are required to be declared before they are used.

An Introduction to Programming Using Microsoft Visual Basic

Immediate window

The Immediate window can be used to debug an application. When a program containing a **Debug.Print** statement is run, the Immediate window displays the output of the statement.

User input can be obtained by including text box and option button objects on a form. A text box object is added to a form with the TextBox control. Option buttons are added to a form with the OptionButton control. Option buttons must be drawn on a frame in order to group the buttons. A frame object is created with the Frame control.

Visual Basic will automatically convert data to match the type of variable it is being assigned to. If data cannot be converted, an error will occur.

\ and Mod

Visual Basic includes an integer division operator (\) that returns the whole portion of the quotient, and a modulus division operator (**Mod**) that returns the remainder of a division operation.

syntax error

A statement that violates the rules of Visual Basic is said to contain a syntax error. Statements with syntax errors are displayed in red in the Code Editor window. Some statements that contain syntax errors will

run-time error

generate a run-time error that halts program execution.

Well-written code is clear and easy to read which makes it easier to debug and modify. Good programming style should be used to create well-written code.

The sequence of steps and thinking that goes into the construction of a substantial application are specification, design, coding, and testing and debugging.

Vocabulary

Coding   Creating an application's interface and writing its program code.

Constant   A named memory location that stores a value that cannot be changed at run time from its initial assignment.

Data type   The kind of value a variable or constant is storing.

Debugging   The process of getting an application to work correctly.

Design   How an application's interface will look and how the program code will be written.

Floating point   A data type that can represent values with numbers after the decimal point.

Frame   A container object used to group option buttons.

Identifier   The name used to represent a variable or constant.

Integer division   Division performed with the \ operator to return only the whole portion of the quotient.

Keyword   Identifier reserved by Visual Basic.

Modulus division   Division performed with the Mod operator to return only the remainder portion of the division operation.

Option button   An object the user can click to provide input.

Radio button   See Option button.

Run-time error   A syntax error that halts a program at run time.

Specification   Definition of what an application should do.

String   A set of characters that can include the letters of the alphabet, digits, symbols, spaces, and any character that can be typed or displayed.

Syntax error   An error caused by a statement that violates the rules of Visual Basic.

Testing   The process of running an application and entering data to test different possibilities to reveal any bugs.

Text box   An object that provides space for the user to enter text.

Variable   A named memory location that stores a value.

Visual Basic

**** Arithmetic operator used to perform integer division.

Boolean A data type used to represent True or False.

Const Statement used to declare a constant.

Currency A data type representing positive or negative numbers that are money values with up to four digits to the right of the decimal place and 15 digits to the left.

Debug.Print Statement used to display output to the Immediate window.

Dim Statement used to declare a variable.

Double A data type representing positive or negative real numbers up to $1.8e^{308}$.

Frame control Used to create a frame object. Found in the Tool box.

Immediate Window command Used to display the Immediate window. Found in the View menu.

Integer A data type representing positive or negative integer numbers up to 32,767.

Long A data type representing positive or negative integer numbers over 32,767.

Mod Arithmetic operator used to perform modulus division.

OptionButton control Used to create an option button object. Found in the Tool box.

Option Explicit Statement used to require a variable declaration before the variable is used.

Options command Used to select the Required Variable Declaration option so that variable declaration is required in a program before a variable can be used. Found in the Tools menu.

Single A data type representing positive or negative real numbers up to $3.4e^{38}$.

String A data type representing a string.

TextBox control Used to create a text box object. Found in the Tool box.

Text Text box object property used to change the value displayed in a text box. Can be changed at run time. Also automatically changed when the user enters a value in a text box.

Value Option button property that can be set to either True or False to display the option button as selected or not selected, respectively. Can be changed at run time. Also automatically changed when the user clicks on an option button.

Exercises

Exercise 1

The height of an object at any given time dropped from a starting height of 100 meters is given by the equation $h=100-4.9*t^2$ where t is the time in seconds. Create an Object Height application that asks the user for a time less than 4.5 seconds and displays the height of the object at that time. The application interface should look similar to:

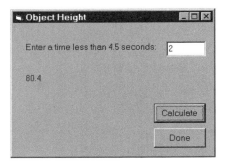

Exercise 2

Create a Temperature Conversion application that asks the user for a temperature in Fahrenheit and displays the temperature in Celsius using the formula $C=\frac{5}{9}(F-32)$. The application interface should display the Thermom graphic on the form. Test the program with values 212, 32, 98.6, and –40. The application interface should look similar to:

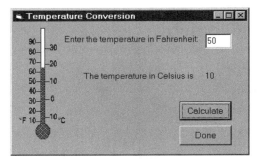

Exercise 3 ☼

Modify the Rectangle Area and Perimeter application created in Chapter Three Exercise 10 to allow the user to enter the length and width of the rectangle. The application interface should look similar to:

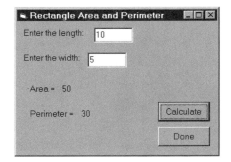

Exercise 4

The cost of making a pizza at Alberto's Pizza Shop is as follows:

- Labor cost is $0.75 per pizza, regardless of size
- Rent cost is $1.00 per pizza, regardless of size
- Materials cost varies by pizza size according to the formula
  $0.05 * diameter * diameter (diameter is measured in inches)

Create a Pizza Cost application that allows the user to enter the size of a pizza and then displays the cost of making the pizza. The application interface should display the Pizza graphic on the form when the Calculate button is clicked. The application interface should look similar to:

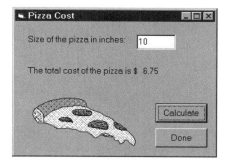

Exercise 5

Einstein's famous formula, $e=mc^2$, gives the amount of energy released by the complete conversion of matter of mass m into energy e. If m represents the mass in kilograms and c represents the speed of light in meters per second (3.0×10^8 m/s), then the result is in the energy units Joules. It takes 360000 Joules to light a 100-watt light bulb for an hour. Create an Energy application that allows the user to enter a mass in kg and displays the energy and the number of light bulbs that could be powered by a given quantity of matter. The application interface should look similar to:

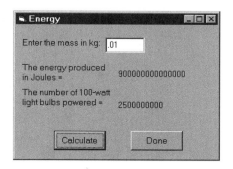

Exercise 6 ☼

Modify the Long Jump Average application created in Chapter Three Exercise 12 to allow the user to enter the values of four long jumps and then display the average jump length. The application interface should look similar to:

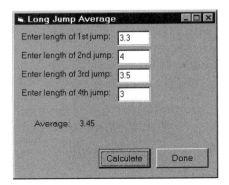

Exercise 7

The Pythagorean Theorem states that $a^2 + b^2 = c^2$ where a and b are the lengths of two sides of a right triangle and c is the length of the side of the triangle opposite the right angle (the hypoteneuse). Create a Pythagorean Theorem application that asks the user for the lengths of sides a and b, and then calculates the length of the hypoteneuse. The application interface should look similar to:

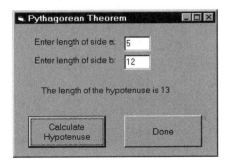

Exercise 8

Create a Change application that displays the minimum number of coins necessary to make the change entered by the user. The change can be made up of quarters, dimes, nickels, and pennies. Assume that the amount of change is less than $1.00. The application interface should display the Coins graphic on the form when the Calculate button is clicked. The application interface should look similar to:

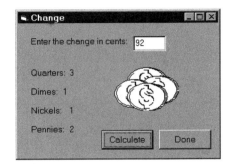

Exercise 9

Create a Digits of a Number application that accepts a two-digit number and displays the digits separately. The application interface should look similar to:

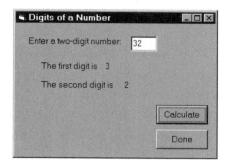

Exercise 10 🔄

Modify the Hello and Good-bye application created in Chapter Three Exercise 7 to display Hello! or Good-bye! depending on which option button is clicked. The application interface should look similar to:

Exercise 11

Create a School Information application that displays the city and state of a school depending on which option button is clicked. Include at least five of your favorite schools. The application interface should look similar to:

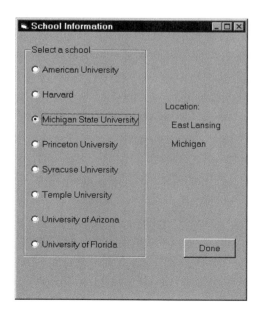

Exercise 12

Create a Band Information application that displays the members of a band depending on which option button is clicked. Include at least three of your favorite bands. The application interface should display the Guitar graphic on the form. The application interface should look similar to the following after clicking on an option button:

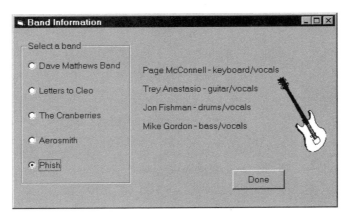

Exercise 13

Create a Time Conversion application that allows the user to enter a time in minutes and then displays the time in seconds or hour:minute format depending on which option button is clicked. Be sure to consider times where the number of minutes left over is less than 10. For example, 184 minutes in hour:minute format is 3:04 (Hint: use the modulus operator). The application interface should look similar to the following after clicking on the Minutes to hour:minute format option button:

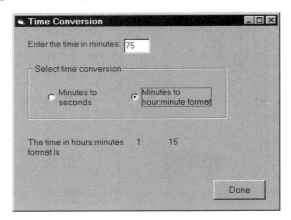

An Introduction to Programming Using Microsoft Visual Basic

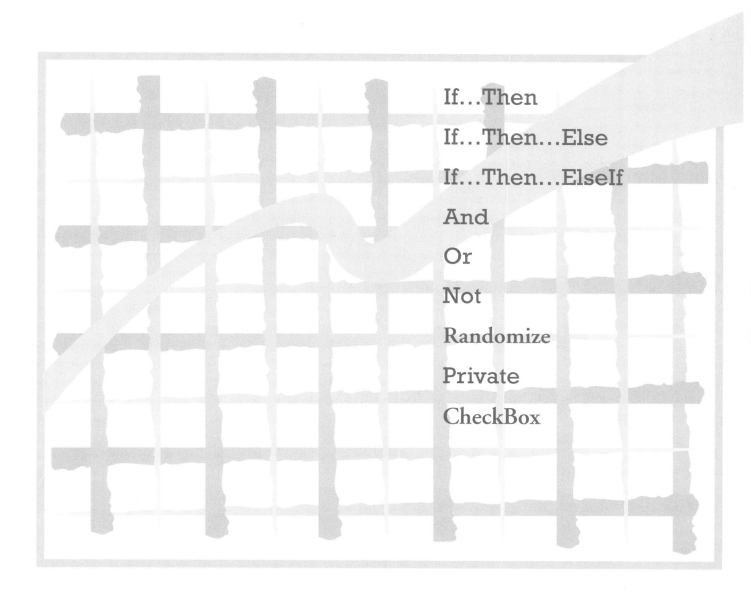

If...Then

If...Then...Else

If...Then...ElseIf

And

Or

Not

Randomize

Private

CheckBox

Chapter Five Objectives

After completing this chapter you will be able to:

1. Use the If…Then, If…Then…Else, and If…Then…ElseIf statements.
2. Understand Nested If…Then…Else statements.
3. Generate random numbers.
4. Return the integer portion of a number without rounding.
5. Understand the scope of a variable or constant.
6. Make global declarations.
7. Use And, Or, and Not in Boolean expressions.
8. Understand algorithms and pseudocode.
9. Understand logic errors.
10. Use message boxes in applications.
11. Use the PasswordChar property of text box objects to create password applications.
12. Use counters in applications.
13. Use check box objects in applications.
14. Use the PrintForm method to print forms.
15. Understand good programming style guidelines.

$\mathbf{I}$n this chapter you will learn about decision structures that control the flow of a program. Decision structures are used to conditionally execute a set of statements. The next chapter introduces looping structures for controlling program flow.

5.1 The If...Then Statement

decision structure

The **If...Then** statement is a *decision structure* that executes code when a condition is true. For example, intGuess = 10 is the condition in the following **If...Then** statement:

```
If intGuess = 10 Then
    lblGuessCheckedMessage.Caption = "You guessed it!"
End If
```

If the value of intGuess is 10, the assignment statement changing the Caption property of the label object is executed. If the value of intGuess is not equal to 10 (i.e. it is greater than or less than 10), then the assignment statement is not executed and program flow continues to the **End If**, which is required to end the **If...Then** statement. Note that the equal sign is used both for comparison and assignment.

The **If...Then** statement takes the form:

```
If condition Then
    statements
End If
```

Boolean expression
relational operators

The *condition* of the **If...Then** statement is a Boolean expression. A *Boolean expression* evaluates to either True or False. *Relational operators* can be used to form Boolean expressions. In the **If...Then** statement above, the equal to relational operator (=) was used. There are five other relational operators in addition to the = operator:

Operator	Meaning
=	equal to
<	less than
<=	less than or equal to
>	greater than
>=	greater than or equal to
<>	not equal to

A Boolean variable may also be used as the *condition* of the **If...Then** statement because its value is either True or False.

The *statements* of an **If...Then** can be a single statement as in the example on the previous page, or multiple statements.

The Guessing Game application below uses an **If...Then** statement:

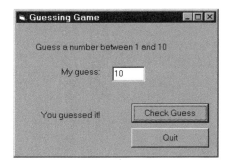

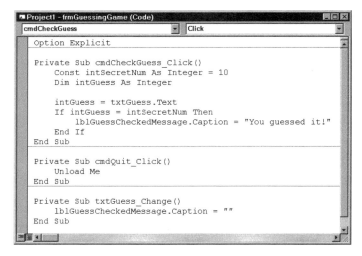

Running the application, typing the number 5, and then clicking on the **Check Guess** button displays no message. Typing the number 10 and clicking on the **Check Guess** button displays the message "You guessed it!"

5.2 Roundoff Error

The condition of an **If...Then** statement should never make an equality comparison between floating point numbers because of the possibility of roundoff error. *Roundoff error* occurs because floating point numbers cannot be exactly represented in binary notation by the computer. For example, the decimal number 0.8 in binary form is a repeating decimal (0.1100110011...). Since there are only a finite number of bits that can be used to represent a number, a repeating decimal must be rounded off, preventing an exact representation.

For example, consider the following statements:

```
If (4.80 * 100 - 480) = 0 Then
    lblComparison.Caption = "Zero"
End If
```

It appears that Zero should be displayed since 4.80 * 100 is 480 and 480 – 480 equals 0. However, the number 4.80 cannot be exactly represented in binary. Therefore, when 4.80 is multiplied by 100 the result is

An Introduction to Programming Using Microsoft Visual Basic

slightly different from 480. This error is called roundoff error. In this case, subtracting 480 from 4.80 * 100 results in a very small number that is not equal to 0 (–1.77635683940025E-14). Refer to Section 1.14 in Chapter One for more on roundof error.

Review 1

Create a Test Grade application that includes a text box for the user to enter a test grade and a **Check Grade** button that when selected displays "Good job!" for a test grade greater than or equal to 70. The application interface should look similar to that shown on the right after entering 88 and clicking on the **Check Grade** button. Be sure to include a change event procedure for the text box.

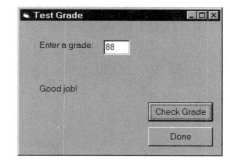

Indenting Code

As program code becomes large and complex, proper indentation of code is necessary for readability. The Tab key is used to indent a line of code. The Indent command from the Edit menu can be used to indent a highlighted block of code. Similarly, the Outdent command from the Edit menu can be used to shift a highlighted block to the left.

5.3 The If...Then...Else Statement

The If...**Then** statement can include an **Else** clause which is executed when the If condition evaluates to False. The If...**Then**...**Else** statement takes the following form:

```
If condition Then
    statements
Else
    statements
End If
```

The *statements* in the **Else** clause can be a single statement or multiple statements.

The cmdCheckGuess procedure of the Guessing Game application could be modified to include an If...**Then**...**Else** statement:

```
Private Sub cmdCheckGuess_Click()
    Const intSecretNum As Integer = 10
    Dim intGuess As Integer

    intGuess = txtGuess.Text
    If intGuess = intSecretNum Then
        lblGuessCheckedMessage.Caption = "You guessed it!"
    Else
        lblGuessCheckedMessage.Caption = "Try again."
    End If
End Sub
```

Running the application, typing a number other than 10, and then clicking on the **Check Guess** button displays the message "Try again." Typing 10 and then clicking on the **Check Guess** button displays the message "You guessed it!"

programming style   The indentation used in the If...**Then**...**Else** statement is good programming style and has no effect on the execution of the statement. When reading the code, the indentation makes it easier to follow the logic of the statement. This is especially important as If...**Then**...**Else** statements become large and complex.

Review 2

Modify the Test Grade application created in Review 1 so that Good job! is displayed for a grade greater than or equal to 70 and Study more. is displayed for a grade less than 70. The application interface should look similar to that shown on the right after entering 65 and clicking on the Check Grade button.

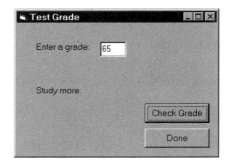

Review 3

Modify the Circle Area application created in the reviews of Chapter Four to display the message Negative radii are illegal. when the radius value entered is negative. If a positive value or zero is entered for the radius, the area of the circle should be displayed. The application interface should look similar to that shown on the right after entering the radius of -5 and clicking on the Calculate button.

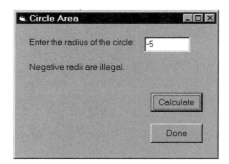

5.4 Nested If...Then...Else Statements

Nested If...Then...Else statements contain another If...Then...Else or If...Then statement. For example, the Guessing Game application could be modified to give the user more of a hint:

```
If intGuess = intSecretNum Then
    lblGuessCheckedMessage.Caption = "You guessed it!"
Else
    If intGuess < intSecretNum Then
        lblGuessCheckedMessage.Caption = "Too low."
    Else
        lblGuessCheckedMessage.Caption = "Too high."
    End If
End If
```

programming style   Nested statements should be indented for good programming style.

5.5 The If...Then...ElseIf Statement

The If...Then...ElseIf statement (note there is no space in ElseIf) is used to decide among three, four, or more actions. For example, there are three possible decisions in the following If...Then...ElseIf:

```
If intGuess = intSecretNum Then
    lblGuessCheckedMessage.Caption = "You guessed it!"
ElseIf intGuess < intSecretNum Then
    lblGuessCheckedMessage.Caption = "Too low."
Else
    lblGuessCheckedMessage.Caption = "Too high."
End If
```

The If...Then...ElseIf statement takes the form:

```
If condition Then
    statements
ElseIf condition Then
    statements
...
Else
    statements
End If
```

The *statements* can be a single statement or multiple statements. There can be multiple **ElseIf** clauses, and the last **Else** clause is optional.

programming style

The logic used in developing an If...Then...ElseIf statement is important. When If conditions are testing a range of numbers, care must be taken to ensure that the conditions are ordered correctly because *statements* are executed only for the first true condition and then program flow continues after the **End If**. When choosing between using nested If...Then...Else statements and a single If...Then...ElseIf statement, the If...Then...ElseIf is easier to read and understand and is considered better programming style.

Review 4

What is the result of the following statements?

```
Dim intScore As Integer
intScore = 25

If intScore >= 100 Then
    lblMessage.Caption = "You won!"
ElseIf intScore < 100 Then
    lblMessage.Caption = "Good try."
ElseIf intScore < 50 Then
    lblMessage.Caption = "Practice more."
End If
```

Does the output reflect what was intended? If not, how should the above statements be rewritten to produce the intended result?

Review 5

Open the Guessing Game project which contains the Guessing Game interface but no program code. Write the Guessing Game code so that 25 is the secret number and an If...Then...ElseIf statement is used to determine the message to display to the user. Base your code and messages on the Guessing Game application discussed in the last four sections. Be sure to include a change event procedure for the text box.

5.6 Generating Random Numbers

Rnd

function

Games, simulators, screen savers, and many other types of applications require random numbers. Visual Basic includes a built-in Rnd function that generates a random number greater than or equal to 0 and less than 1. A *function* is a procedure that performs a task and returns a value. For example, the Random Numbers application generates and displays six random numbers:

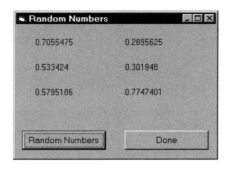

The cmdRandomNumbers_Click procedure uses Rnd to generate each random number:

```
Private Sub cmdRandomNumbers_Click()
    lblRandomNum1.Caption = Rnd
    lblRandomNum2.Caption = Rnd
    lblRandomNum3.Caption = Rnd
    lblRandomNum4.Caption = Rnd
    lblRandomNum5.Caption = Rnd
    lblRandomNum6.Caption = Rnd
End Sub
```

Using Rnd alone generates random numbers greater than or equal to 0 and less than 1. To generate random numbers in a greater range, Rnd is multiplied by the upper limit of the range. For example, to generate random numbers greater than or equal to 0 and less than 10, a statement similar to the following is used:

```
lblRandomNum1.Caption = Rnd * 10
```

Random numbers can also be generated in a range using the following expression:

$$(HighNumber - LowNumber + 1) * Rnd + LowNumber$$

HighNumber represents the maximum value desired and *LowNumber* represents the minimum value. This expression can be used in the cmdRandomNumbers_Click procedure of the Random Numbers application to display six random numbers greater than or equal to 10 and less than 31 ((30 – 10 + 1) * Rnd + 10):

```
Private Sub cmdRandomNumbers_Click()
    lblRandomNum1.Caption = 21 * Rnd + 10
    lblRandomNum2.Caption = 21 * Rnd + 10
    lblRandomNum3.Caption = 21 * Rnd + 10
    lblRandomNum4.Caption = 21 * Rnd + 10
    lblRandomNum5.Caption = 21 * Rnd + 10
    lblRandomNum6.Caption = 21 * Rnd + 10
End Sub
```

When run, the application interface looks similar to:

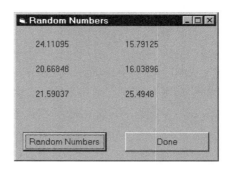

The Int function returns the integer portion of a number without rounding. When used with Rnd, whole random numbers are generated. The Random Numbers application can be modified to display six random integers in the range 10 to 30 inclusive by using the Int function to convert the random numbers to integers in the cmdRandomNumbers_Click procedure:

```
Private Sub cmdRandomNumbers_Click()
    Private Sub cmdRandomNumbers_Click()
    lblRandomNum1.Caption = Int(21 * Rnd + 10)
    lblRandomNum2.Caption = Int(21 * Rnd + 10)
    lblRandomNum3.Caption = Int(21 * Rnd + 10)
    lblRandomNum4.Caption = Int(21 * Rnd + 10)
    lblRandomNum5.Caption = Int(21 * Rnd + 10)
    lblRandomNum6.Caption = Int(21 * Rnd + 10)
End Sub
```

When run, the application interface looks similar to:

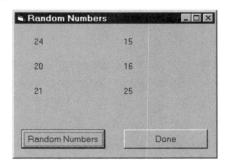

The Fix Function

Fix is a Visual Basic built-in function that is similar to Int. Int and Fix work the same for positive numbers. However, for negative numbers Int returns the first negative integer less than or equal to its argument, while Fix returns the first negative integer that is greater than or equal to its argument. For example, Fix(-5.4) would return –5 and Int(-5.4) would return –6.

How Random Numbers are Generated

The Randomize statement uses the value returned by the computer's clock as a seed. A seed is a value used by the Rnd function to generate a pseudo-random (not truly random) sequence of numbers. Each time Rnd is used, the next number in the sequence is returned.

Randomize

Programs using Rnd should also include a Randomize statement. The Randomize statement initializes the Visual Basic Rnd function so that different random numbers are generated in a program from run to run. The Randomize statement should be executed only once in a program and is therefore best placed in the Form_Load procedure where it is called when the application is started:

```
Private Sub Form_Load()
    Randomize                'Initialize random number generator
End Sub
```

Review 6

Follow the instructions below to create the Random Numbers application.

1) **CREATE A NEW PROJECT**

2) ADD OBJECTS TO THE FORM

Refer to the form below when placing and sizing the form and its objects. Use the table below to name and change the properties of the objects.

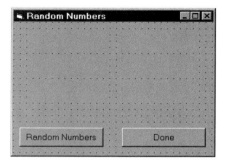

Object	Name	Caption
Form1	frmRandomNumbers	Random Numbers
Label1	lblRandomNum1	*empty*
Label2	lblRandomNum2	*empty*
Label3	lblRandomNum3	*empty*
Label4	lblRandomNum4	*empty*
Label5	lblRandomNum5	*empty*
Label6	lblRandomNum6	*empty*
Command1	cmdRandomNumbers	Random Numbers
Command2	cmdDone	Done

3) SAVE THE PROJECT

From the File menu, select Save Project. Save the form naming it frmRandomNumbers and save the project naming it Random Numbers.

4) DISPLAY THE CODE EDITOR WINDOW

5) ADD THE RANDOM NUMBERS COMMAND BUTTON EVENT PROCEDURE

Add a cmdRandomNumbers_Click event procedure with the following statements:

```
Private Sub cmdRandomNumbers_Click()
    lblRandomNum1.Caption = Rnd
    lblRandomNum2.Caption = Rnd
    lblRandomNum3.Caption = Rnd
    lblRandomNum4.Caption = Rnd
    lblRandomNum5.Caption = Rnd
    lblRandomNum6.Caption = Rnd
End Sub
```

6) ADD THE DONE COMMAND BUTTON EVENT PROCEDURE

Add a cmdDone_Click event procedure with the following statements:

```
Private Sub cmdDone_Click()
    Unload Me
End Sub
```

7) RUN THE APPLICATION

a. Save the modified Random Numbers project and then run the application. Click the Random Numbers button. Write down on a piece of paper the six numbers generated.
b. Select the Done button.

An Introduction to Programming Using Microsoft Visual Basic

c. Run the application again and click the Random Numbers button. Note that the numbers are the same as before.

d. End the application and run it a few more times. Note that the numbers are always the same.

8) ADD THE RANDOMIZE STATEMENT

a. Add a Form_Load event procedure with the following statements:

```
Private Sub Form_Load()
    Randomize
End Sub
```

b. Save the modified Random Numbers project and then run the application a few times. Note that the numbers are always different.

9) GENERATE INTEGERS IN A RANGE

Modify the cmdRandomNumbers_Click event procedure as follows to generate random integers between 10 and 30:

```
Private Sub cmdRandomNumbers_Click()
    lblRandomNum1.Caption = Int(21 * Rnd + 10)
    lblRandomNum2.Caption = Int(21 * Rnd + 10)
    lblRandomNum3.Caption = Int(21 * Rnd + 10)
    lblRandomNum4.Caption = Int(21 * Rnd + 10)
    lblRandomNum5.Caption = Int(21 * Rnd + 10)
    lblRandomNum6.Caption = Int(21 * Rnd + 10)
End Sub
```

10) RUN THE APPLICATION

Save the modified Random Numbers project and then run the application a few times.

11) PRINT AND THEN REMOVE THE PROJECT

5.7 Scope

The *scope* of a variable or constant refers to its accessibility among procedures. For example, the scope of a variable declared in an event procedure is limited to that procedure. No other procedure can refer to that variable or change its value because it is not accessible to any other procedure. Variables and constants declared in a procedure are said to be *local* to that procedure.

local declarations

Variables and constants declared in the General section of a form module are accessible to every procedure in the module. General declarations are said to be *global* to the form module. A global variable declaration should use the keyword **Private** in place of the keyword **Dim**. Global constant declarations should use the keyword **Private** in front of the keyword **Const**.

global declarations
Private

The Local versus Global application code below demonstrates global and local variables:

```
Option Explicit
Private intX As Integer          'Global declaration
Private intY As Integer          'Global declaration

Private Sub Form_Load()
   intX = 30
   intY = 50
End Sub

Private Sub cmdTest1_Click()
   Dim intX As Integer          'Local declaration
   intX = 20

   lblintX.Caption = intX
   lblintY.Caption = intY
End Sub

Private Sub cmdTest2_Click()
   lblintX.Caption = intX
   lblintY.Caption = intY
End Sub
```

Running the Local versus Global application and clicking on the Test 1 button displays the following:

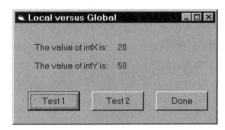

Note that the local declaration of intX in the cmdTest1_Click procedure overrides the global declaration of intX.

Clicking on the Test 2 button displays the following:

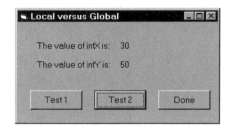

programming style   Local variables should be used whenever possible because their use does not interfere with the operation of other procedures. Even if two procedures declare a variable named strName, the two variables maintain separate values because they were declared locally. Variables declared globally can be changed from within any procedure, making debugging difficult. Use of unnecessary global declarations is poor programming style.

The Guessing Game application can be modified to generate a random number that is assigned to intSecretNum so that the number to guess is different from run to run:

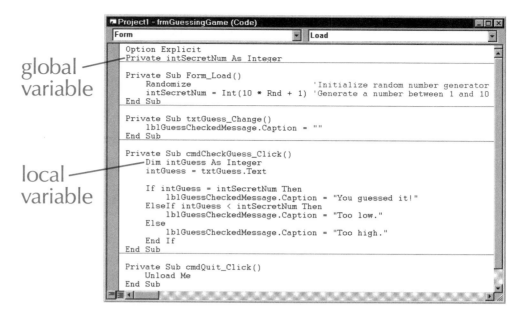

```
Project1 - frmGuessingGame (Code)                                    _ □ ×
Form                              ▼   Load                               ▼
Option Explicit
Private intSecretNum As Integer

Private Sub Form_Load()
    Randomize                        'Initialize random number generator
    intSecretNum = Int(10 * Rnd + 1) 'Generate a number between 1 and 10
End Sub

Private Sub txtGuess_Change()
    lblGuessCheckedMessage.Caption = ""
End Sub

Private Sub cmdCheckGuess_Click()
    Dim intGuess As Integer
    intGuess = txtGuess.Text

    If intGuess = intSecretNum Then
        lblGuessCheckedMessage.Caption = "You guessed it!"
    ElseIf intGuess < intSecretNum Then
        lblGuessCheckedMessage.Caption = "Too low."
    Else
        lblGuessCheckedMessage.Caption = "Too high."
    End If
End Sub

Private Sub cmdQuit_Click()
    Unload Me
End Sub
```

global variable

local variable

intSecretNum is declared as a global variable because both the Form_Load and cmdCheckGuess_Click procedures need access to it. intSecretNum is assigned a random number in Form_Load. If intSecretNum were assigned a random number in the cmdCheckGuess_Click procedure, a new secret number would be generated every time the user clicked on the Check Guess button.

Review 7

Modify the Guessing Game application from Review 5 to use a random number that is greater than or equal to 1 and less than or equal to 50 for intSecretNum. Use global variables only where necessary.

Review 8

Refer to the code below to answer the following questions.

```
Option Explicit
Private Const dblPi As Double = 3.14

Private Sub cmdArea_Click()
    Dim dblRadius As Double
    Dim dblCircleArea As Double

    dblRadius = txtRadius.Text
    dblCircleArea = dblPi * dblRadius ^ 2

    lblAnswer.Caption = dblCircleArea
End Sub

Private Sub cmdCircumference_Click()
    Dim dblRadius As Double
    Dim dblCircleCircumference As Double

    dblRadius = txtRadius.Text
    dblCircleCircumference = 2 * dblPi * dblRadius

    lblAnswer.Caption = dblCircleCircumference
End Sub
```

a. Which variable(s) and constant(s) are global?
b. Which variable(s) and constant(s) are local?

5.8 Logical Operators

A Boolean expression can be formed using the logical operators **And** and **Or**. A *logical operator* joins two expressions to create an expression that evaluates to either True or False. For example, the Guessing Game application could be modified to test for invalid guesses:

```
If intGuess < 1 Or intGuess > 50 Then
    lblCheckedGuessMessage.Caption = "Invalid guess."
ElseIf intGuess = intSecretNum Then
    lblCheckedGuessMessage.Caption = "You guessed it!"
...
```

The condition of the **If...Then...ElseIf** statement above evaluates the first expression, intGuess < 1, and determines if it is True or False. The second expression, intGuess > 50, is then evaluated. If *either* expression is true when the logical operator **Or** is used, then the entire expression is true and "Invalid guess" is displayed.

When the logical operator **And** is used, an expression evaluates to True only when both expressions are True. The table below shows the rules applied when using the logical operators **And** and **Or**:

And				**Or**		
Expression1	*Expression2*	*Result*		*Expression1*	*Expression2*	*Result*
True	True	True		True	True	True
True	False	False		True	False	True
False	True	False		False	True	True
False	False	False		False	False	False

As another example, consider an application that computes a discount depending on the quantity and type of purchase:

```
If strItem = "Pencil" And intQuantity > 50 Then
    curDiscount = 1    '$1.00 discount
End If
```

This **If...Then** statement executes the curDiscount = 1 statement if *both* the strItem is Pencil *and* the intQuantity is greater than 50.

A third logical operator is **Not**. An expression including **Not** is evaluated according to the following rules:

Not	
Expression	*Result*
True	False
False	True

For example, the following statements change the label caption because strItem is not Pencil:

```
Dim strItem As String
strItem = "Pen"

If Not strItem = "Pencil" Then
    lblMessage.Caption = "No discount given."
End If
```

In logical expressions, **Not** is evaluated before **And**. **Or** is evaluated last. For example, the expression **Not** 5 < 6 **Or** 2 > 4 **And** 3 < 6 evaluates to False because **Not** 5 > 6 is performed first, then 2 > 4 **And** 3 < 6, and then False **Or** False. Remember that operator precedence can be changed using parentheses.

Review 9

Given the statements

```
Dim intQuantity As Integer
Dim curPrice As Currency

intQuantity = 20
curPrice = 5
```

determine the value, True or False, for each of the following expressions:

    intQuantity > 10 **And** curPrice > 5

    intQuantity = 15 **Or** curPrice = 5

    intQuantity >= 20 **And** curPrice >=2 **And** intQuantity * curPrice >= 40

    Not curPrice = 5

Review 10 ☼

Modify the Calculator application from Review 12 in Chapter Four so that the event procedures involving division (optDivision_Click, optIntegerDivision_Click, and optModulusDivision_Click) contain **If…Then…Else** statements that display an appropriate message when a divisor (intSecondNumber or intThirdNumber) entered by the user is 0 and displays the result of the expression otherwise.

5.9 Algorithms

Applications with complex specifications require a method of design called an algorithm. An *algorithm* is a series of steps that tell how to solve a problem. An algorithm created using both English and program code *pseudocode* is called *pseudocode*. Often, pseudocode is developed for only the more complex portions of a program. For example, in the Guessing Game application the pseudocode for the Check Guess button click event might be:

```
Private Sub cmdCheckGuess_Click()
   Get guess from a text box
   If guess = secret number Then
      Display equal to message on form
   ElseIf guess < secret number Then
      Display less than message on form
   Else
      Display greater than message on form
   End If
End Sub
```

Creating an algorithm forces a programmer to think through a program before actually coding it. This is helpful in two ways. First, an algorithm is done without a computer, which usually helps a programmer focus on the overall structure of a program. Second, errors in logic are usually reduced.

logic error

A *logic error* is caused by statements that are syntactically correct but produce undesired or unexpected results. Unlike syntax errors, logic errors must be found by the programmer rather than by Visual Basic. These errors can be found only by thorough testing of the application, and by careful reading of the program code. Good programming style that in-

programming style

cludes careful documentation and indentation and descriptive identifiers can be helpful when looking for logic errors.

Review 11

Assuming the comment is correct, determine the logic error in the following statement:

```
If intGrade > 90 Then
    lblGrade.Caption = "You have an A"     'Displays an A for scores greater than or equal to 90
End If
```

5.10 Message Boxes

A *message box* is a Visual Basic predefined dialog box that is used to provide information to the user, such as when invalid data has been entered or when options required for an application to continue have not been selected. For example, the Guessing Game application could be modified to display a message box if the user's guess is out of range:

MsgBox

The MsgBox statement displays a Visual Basic predefined dialog box with a message and an OK button, and has the form:

MsgBox *message*

message is a **String** variable or constant or a string enclosed in quotation marks. The **If...Then...ElseIf** statement in the Guessing Game code modified to display a message box is:

```
If intGuess < 1 Or intGuess > 10 Then
    MsgBox "Guess out of range"
ElseIf intGuess = intSecretNum Then
    lblGuessCheckedMessage.Caption = "You guessed it!"
ElseIf intGuess < intSecretNum Then
    lblGuessCheckedMessage.Caption = "Too low."
Else
    lblGuessCheckedMessage.Caption = "Too high."
End If
```

Review 12 🔄

Modify the Guessing Game application from Review 7 to display a message box if the user's guess is less than 1 or greater than 50. The application interface should look similar to that shown in Section 5.10.

Review 13 🔄

Modify the Test Grade application from Review 2 so that "Invalid test grade" is displayed in a message box if the grade entered is less than 0 or greater than 100. The application interface should look similar to that shown on the right after entering 105 (an invalid test grade) and clicking on the Check Grade button.

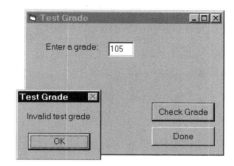

5.11 Creating a Password Application

Many programs are password protected and require the user to enter the correct password to get access to the application. A password dialog box usually looks similar to:

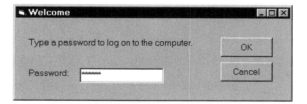

PasswordChar property

The password is kept secret by showing a special character, often an asterisk (*), in place of each letter typed in the text box. This is done at design time by typing * in the PasswordChar property of the text box object. Review 14 develops a Password application that is similar to those used in applications that are password protected.

Review 14

Follow the instructions below to create the Welcome application.

1) **CREATE A NEW PROJECT**

2) **ADD OBJECTS TO THE FORM**

Refer to the form below when placing and sizing the form and its objects as instructed in the steps following:

a. Add two labels, one text box and two command buttons to the form and set their properties:

Object	Name	Caption	Text
Form1	frmWelcome	Welcome	
Label1	lblMessage	Type a password to log on to the computer	
Label2	lblPassword	Password:	
Text1	txtPassword		*empty*
Command1	cmdOK	OK	
Command2	cmdCancel	Cancel	

b. Select the txtPassword object.
c. Change the PasswordChar property to *.

3) SAVE THE PROJECT

From the File menu, select Save Project. Save the form naming it frmWelcome and save the projectnaming it Welcome.

4) WRITE THE PROGRAM CODE

The pseudocode for the OK button click event is:

```
Private Sub cmdOK_Click()
    Get text from text box
    If text = password Then
        Display message in message box
        End program
    Else
        Display message in message box
        Clear previous password
    End If
End Sub
```

Display the Code Editor window and add the following event procedures:

```
Private Sub cmdOK_Click()
    Dim strPassword As String
    strPassword = txtPassword.Text

    If strPassword = "secret" Then
        MsgBox "Password accepted."
        Unload Me
    Else
        MsgBox "The password you entered is incorrect."
        txtPassword.Text = ""
    End If
End Sub

Private Sub cmdCancel_Click()
    Unload Me
End Sub
```

5) RUN THE APPLICATION

Save the modified Welcome project and then run the application. Test the application by entering incorrect passwords and the correct password. Note that the correct password, secret, must be entered as all lowercase.

6) PRINT AND THEN REMOVE THE PROJECT

An Introduction to Programming Using Microsoft Visual Basic

5.12 Using Counters

update

A *counter* is a numeric variable used to store a value that is incremented during run time. The statement for incrementing a counter, often called *updating* a counter, takes the form:

identifier = *identifier* + *constant*

identifier is the numeric variable that is updated. *constant* is the number that is added to the current value of *identifier*. A counter should be initialized and is usually updated by an unchanging amount. For example, the following statement updates a counter by 1:

intNumTries = intNumTries + 1

In the statement above, intNumTries is the name of the counter variable. Each time the statement is executed, 1 is added to the current value of intNumTries and then this new value is assigned to intNumTries.

A counter could be used in the Guessing Game application to keep track of the number of guesses the user has made. To do this, a counter variable needs to be incremented each time the user clicks on the Check Guess button:

```
Option Explicit
Private intSecretNum As Integer
Private intNumGuesses As Integer

Private Sub Form_Load()
    Randomize                           'Initialize random number generator
    intSecretNum = Int(10 * Rnd + 1)    'Generate a number between 1 and 10
    intNumGuesses = 0                   'Initialize intNumGuesses
End Sub

Private Sub txtGuess_Change()
    lblGuessCheckedMessage.Caption = ""
End Sub

Private Sub cmdCheckGuess_Click()
    Dim intGuess As Integer
    intGuess = txtGuess.Text

    intNumGuesses = intNumGuesses + 1   'Increment intNumGuesses

    If intGuess < 1 Or intGuess > 10 Then
        MsgBox "Guess out of range"
    ElseIf intGuess = intSecretNum Then
        lblGuessCheckedMessage.Caption = "You guessed it!"
        lblNumGuessesMessage.Caption = "Number of guesses ="
        lblNumGuesses.Caption = intNumGuesses
    ElseIf intGuess < intSecretNum Then
        lblGuessCheckedMessage.Caption = "Too low."
    Else
        lblGuessCheckedMessage.Caption = "Too high."
    End If
End Sub
```

In the Guessing Game code, intNumGuesses is a counter variable. Visual Basic automatically initializes a numeric variable to 0 when declared. If intNumGuesses were declared in the cmdCheckGuess_Click procedure, it would be initialized to 0 each time the user clicked the Check Guess button. Therefore, by making the scope of intNumGuesses global, it can be incremented in the cmdCheckGuess_Click procedure. Note that

programming style

intNumGuesses is assigned 0 in the Form_Load procedure. It is good programming style to make program code clearer and easier to understand by including a statement to explicitly initialize a counter variable.

Review 15 ⚙ ———————————————————————

Follow the directions below to modify the Welcome application from Review 14 to count the number of times the user incorrectly enters a password.

1) OPEN THE WELCOME PROJECT

2) MODIFY THE PROGRAM CODE

    a. Display the Code Editor window.

    b. Add the following statement to the General section:

```
Private intNumTries As Integer
```

    c. Add a Form_Load event procedure with the following statements:

```
Private Sub Form_Load()
    intNumTries = 0
End Sub
```

    d. Modify the cmdOK_Click procedure as shown below:

```
Private Sub cmdOK_Click()
    Dim strPassword As String
    strPassword = txtPassword.Text

    intNumTries = intNumTries + 1

    If strPassword = "secret" Then
        MsgBox "Password accepted."
        MsgBox intNumTries - 1          'Display number of incorrect tries
        Unload Me
    Else
        MsgBox "The password you entered is incorrect."
        txtPassword.Text = ""
    End If
End Sub
```

3) SAVE THE MODIFIED PROJECT

4) RUN THE APPLICATION

    Run the Welcome application and test it by entering three incorrect passwords and then the correct password. Notice the message box displays the number of incorrect password entries.

5) PRINT AND THEN REMOVE THE PROJECT

Review 16 ⚙ ———————————————————————

Modify the Guessing Game application from Review 12 to include a counter that keeps track of the number of guesses entered by the user. The total number of guesses should be displayed when the user correctly guesses the secret number. Refer to the Guessing Game application code shown in Section 5.11. The application interface should look similar to that shown on the right after entering several numbers and clicking on the Check Guess button.

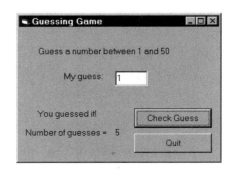

Review 17

Create a Click Counter application that counts the number of times the user has clicked on each of three command buttons. The application interface should look similar to that shown on the right after clicking on each button several times.

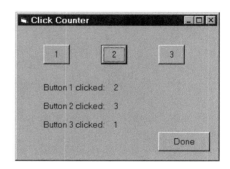

5.13 Check Boxes

Check boxes are used to obtain input from the user. Unlike option buttons, more than one check box can be selected at a time. For example, in the Font Style application, check boxes are used to select style options:

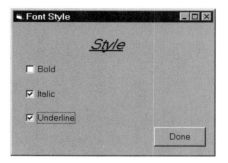

Check boxes are one way to get user input

check box

A *check box* object is created using the CheckBox control ([✓]) in the Tool box and has the properties:

- **Name** identifies the object and is used by the programmer. It is good programming style to begin check box object names with chk.

- **Caption** changes the text displayed as the check box label. Caption can be changed at run time through assignment.

- **Value** can be set to unchecked, checked, or grayed. Value can be changed at run time through assignment using the Visual Basic constants vbUnchecked, vbChecked, and vbGrayed. Value is also changed automatically at run time when the user clicks on a check box.

- **Alignment** moves the check box to either the left or right of the Caption.

click event

A click event procedure is usually coded for each check box. The click event procedure is executed when the user clicks on a check box and should include an If...**Then** statement so that one action is taken if the check box has been selected and another action is taken if the check box has been deselected. For example, the click event procedure could include code to change the Caption of a label when a check box is selected.

5.14 Printing the Form

method
PrintForm

In addition to predefined properties, objects have predefined methods. A *method* is used to perform an action. Form objects have a method called PrintForm that is used to print a form at run time. The PrintForm method is used in a statement that takes the form:

FormName.PrintForm

FormName is the name of the form to print or the keyword Me. Dot notation is used to access a method of an object, just as object properties are accessed.

The Font Style application could be modified to allow the user to print the form:

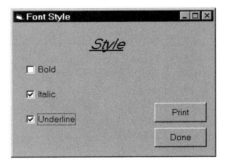

Clicking on the Print button prints the form

The cmdPrint_Click event procedure is:

```
Private Sub cmdPrint_Click()
    Me.PrintForm
End Sub
```

Review 18

Follow the instructions below to create the Font Style application.

1) CREATE A NEW PROJECT

2) ADD OBJECTS TO THE FORM

Refer to the form below when placing and sizing the form and its objects. Use the table on the next page to name and change the properties of the objects.

An Introduction to Programming Using Microsoft Visual Basic

Object	Name	Caption	Font
Form1	frmFontStyle	Font Style	
Label1	lblStyleExample	Style	14 pt
Check1	chkBold	Bold	
Check2	chkItalic	Italic	
Check3	chkUnderline	Underline	
Command1	cmdPrint	Print	
Command2	cmdDone	Done	

3) SAVE THE PROJECT

From the File menu, select Save Project. Save the form naming it frmFontStyle and save the project naming it Font Style.

4) WRITE THE PROGRAM CODE

Display the Code Editor window and add the following event procedures:

```
Private Sub chkBold_Click()
    If chkBold.Value = vbChecked Then
        lblStyleExample.Font.Bold = True
    Else
        lblStyleExample.Font.Bold = False
    End If
End Sub

Private Sub chkItalic_Click()
    If chkItalic.Value = vbChecked Then
        lblStyleExample.Font.Italic = True
    Else
        lblStyleExample.Font.Italic = False
    End If
End Sub

Private Sub chkUnderline_Click()
    If chkUnderline.Value = vbChecked Then
        lblStyleExample.Font.Underline = True
    Else
        lblStyleExample.Font.Underline = False
    End If
End Sub

Private Sub cmdPrint_Click()
    Me.PrintForm
End Sub

Private Sub cmdDone_Click()
    Unload Me
End Sub
```

5) RUN THE APPLICATION

Save the modified Font Style project and then run the application. Test each of the check boxes and command buttons.

6) PRINT AND THEN REMOVE THE PROJECT

5.15 Visual Basic Programming Guidelines

A complex application often contains many different objects to perform its tasks. In addition to previously discussed guidelines, the following steps should be used to code an application. These steps are especially important when an application has many objects or a complex specification:

1. Use the program specification or description to design the application interface.
2. Create the application interface and appropriately name all objects before writing any code.
3. Develop an algorithm for objects with complex tasks. Pseudocode may need to be written for several objects.
4. Code at least one kind of event procedure for each object in an application, excluding label and frame objects.

Step 4 is especially important. Every object in an application, except for label and frame objects, should have an event procedure coded for it. Form objects may not need an event procedure (the Form_Load event) in every application. For example, an application that contains a text box, two check boxes, and two command buttons should have five or six event procedures—a change event procedure for the text box, a click event procedure for each check box, a click event procedure for each command button, and possibly a load event procedure for the form.

Case Study

In this Case Study a Pizza Order application will be created.

specification

The specification for this Case Study is:

A Pizza Order application that allows the user to generate an order. The application should allow the user to select the size of the pizza (regular, large) and the toppings for the pizza (pepperoni, mushrooms, onions, hot peppers). The application should display an order number that is automatically incremented after the previous order is printed, calculate the total of the order as the options are being selected or deselected, print the order, and clear the form for a new order after printing. At startup the order form should display a default size of regular and no toppings selected.

design

When designing the form for this Case Study we need to consider how the user should select the size and toppings of the pizza. For each pizza order there can be only one size, but many toppings. Therefore, option buttons should be used to select the size (only one can be selected at a time), and check boxes should be used to select the toppings (more than one can be selected at a time).

The interface design for the Pizza Order Case Study

Note that the order number label is sketched with dashed lines to indicate that its Caption will not appear until run time. The order number will be initialized to 1 in the Form_Load procedure and then incremented each time an order is printed. The price label will also appear at run time.

The program code design for this Case Study is best done by listing the pseudocode for event procedures:

```
Private Sub Form_Load()
    Select Regular option button
    Clear other option button and all check boxes
    Change price label caption to regular pizza price
    Initialize order number to 1 and display in order number label
EndSub

Private Sub cmdPrint_Click()
    Print the form
    Display message box to inform user that order has been
        printed and the form is being cleared for the next order
    Select Regular option button and clear rest of form
    Change price label caption to pizza price
    Increment the order number and change order number label
End Sub

Private Sub cmdDone_Click()
    Unload the form
End Sub
```

The option button and check box click event procedures will update two global variables in order to determine the total price of the pizza at any time. The dblPizzaPrice global variable will be assigned the value of either the price of a regular pizza or the price of a large pizza. The dblToppingsPrice global variable will be used to maintain the toppings price. When a toppings check box is selected or deselected, this variable will be added to or subtracted from. The pseudocode for an option button and check box click event procedure are:

```
Private Sub optLarge_Click()
    PizzaPrice = LargePizzaPrice
    Display PizzaPrice + ToppingsPrice in TotalPrice Caption
End Sub

Private Sub chkMushrooms_Click()
    If chkMushrooms.Value = vbChecked Then
        ToppingsPrice = ToppingsPrice + MushroomPrice
    Else
        ToppingsPrice = ToppingsPrice - MushroomPrice
    End If
    Display PizzaPrice + ToppingsPrice in TotalPrice Caption
End Sub
```

coding   The interface, object list, and code for this Case Study are:

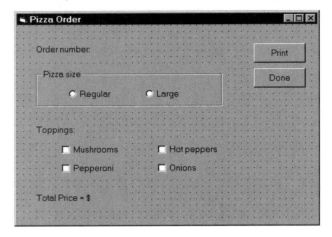

Object	Name	Caption
Form1	frmPizzaOrder	Pizza Order
Label1	lblOrder	Order number:
Label2	lblOrderNumber	*empty*
Frame1	fraPizzaSize	Pizza size
Option1	optRegular	Regular
Option2	optLarge	Large
Label3	lblToppings	Toppings
Check1	chkMushrooms	Mushrooms
Check2	chkHotPeppers	Hot Peppers
Check3	chkPepperoni	Pepperoni
Check4	chkOnions	Onions
Label4	lblTotal	Total Price = $
Label5	lblTotalPrice	*empty*
Command1	cmdPrint	Print
Command2	cmdDone	Done

```
Option Explicit
Private Const curRegularPizzaPrice As Currency = 7
Private Const curLargePizzaPrice As Currency = 10
Private Const curMushroomPrice As Currency = 0.75
Private Const curPepperoniPrice As Currency = 0.75
Private Const curOnionPrice As Currency = 0.75
Private Const curHotPepperPrice As Currency = 0.75

Private intOrderNumber As Integer
Private curToppingsPrice As Currency
Private curPizzaPrice As Currency

Private Sub Form_Load()
  intOrderNumber = 1
  lblOrderNumber.Caption = intOrderNumber

  optLarge.Value = False
  optRegular.Value = True
  curPizzaPrice = curRegularPizzaPrice

  chkPepperoni.Value = vbUnchecked
  chkMushrooms.Value = vbUnchecked
  chkOnions.Value = vbUnchecked
  chkHotPeppers.Value = vbUnchecked
  curToppingsPrice = 0

  lblTotalPrice.Caption = curPizzaPrice + curToppingsPrice
End Sub

Private Sub optRegular_Click()
  curPizzaPrice = curRegularPizzaPrice
  lblTotalPrice.Caption = curPizzaPrice + curToppingsPrice
End Sub

Private Sub optLarge_Click()
  curPizzaPrice = curLargePizzaPrice
  lblTotalPrice.Caption = curPizzaPrice + curToppingsPrice
End Sub

Private Sub chkMushrooms_Click()
  If chkMushrooms.Value = vbChecked Then
    curToppingsPrice = curToppingsPrice + curMushroomPrice
  Else
    curToppingsPrice = curToppingsPrice - curMushroomPrice
  End If
  lblTotalPrice.Caption = curPizzaPrice + curToppingsPrice
End Sub

Private Sub chkHotPeppers_Click()
  If chkHotPeppers.Value = vbChecked Then
    curToppingsPrice = curToppingsPrice + curHotPepperPrice
  Else
    curToppingsPrice = curToppingsPrice - curHotPepperPrice
  End If
  lblTotalPrice.Caption = curPizzaPrice + curToppingsPrice
End Sub

Private Sub chkPepperoni_Click()
  If chkPepperoni.Value = vbChecked Then
    curToppingsPrice = curToppingsPrice + curPepperoniPrice
  Else
    curToppingsPrice = curToppingsPrice - curPepperoniPrice
  End If
  lblTotalPrice.Caption = curPizzaPrice + curToppingsPrice
End Sub
```

```
Private Sub chkOnions_Click()
    If chkOnions.Value = vbChecked Then
        curToppingsPrice = curToppingsPrice + curOnionPrice
    Else
        curToppingsPrice = curToppingsPrice - curOnionPrice
    End If
    lblTotalPrice.Caption = curPizzaPrice + curToppingsPrice
End Sub

Private Sub cmdPrint_Click()
    frmPizzaOrder.PrintForm
    MsgBox "Order printed. Ready for next order."

    intOrderNumber = intOrderNumber + 1
    lblOrderNumber.Caption = intOrderNumber

    optLarge.Value = False
    optRegular.Value = True
    curPizzaPrice = curRegularPizzaPrice

    chkPepperoni.Value = vbUnchecked
    chkMushrooms.Value = vbUnchecked
    chkOnions.Value = vbUnchecked
    chkHotPeppers.Value = vbUnchecked
    curToppingsPrice = 0

    lblTotalPrice.Caption = curPizzaPrice + curToppingsPrice
End Sub

Private Sub cmdDone_Click()
    Unload Me
End Sub
```

testing and debugging   Running Pizza Order displays the following form:

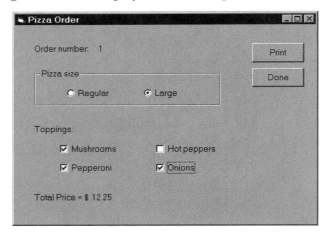

This Case Study should be tested by generating several different pizza orders and checking the price by hand. At least one order should be printed to test the Print button and to test that the order number is properly incremented.

Review 19

Modify the Pizza Order Case Study to include Pickup and Delivery option buttons. If the Delivery option button is selected, $1.50 should be added to the total price of the pizza. The Pickup option button should add $0 to the total price of the pizza and should be the default when the form loads. Hint: A global variable should be used to store the delivery charge.

Chapter Summary

decision structures

Controlling program flow allows the order in which statements are executed to vary. In this chapter the If...**Then**, If...**Then**...**Else**, and If...**Then**...**ElseIf** statements were used to control program flow. These statements are known as decision structures because each evaluates a *condition* to determine program flow. When the *condition* is True, program flow branches to the **Then** portion of the statements. The **Else** portion of the statements are executed when the *condition* is False. The If...**Then**...**ElseIf** statement is used to decide among three, four, or more actions. Indentation used in the If...**Then**...**Else** statement is good programming style and makes it easier to follow the logic of the statement.

Boolean expression

The *condition* of decision structures is a Boolean expression that evaluates to either True or False. A Boolean expression may be a Boolean variable or an expression formed using relational operators ($=$, $<$, $<=$, $>$, $>=$, $<>$). A Boolean expression may also include logical operators (**And**, **Or**, **Not**).

Rnd
function
Int
Randomize

Rnd is a Visual Basic built-in function that generates a random number greater than or equal to 0 and less than 1. A function is a type of procedure that returns a value. The Int built-in function is used to return the integer portion of a number. The Randomize statement is used to initialize the Rnd function so that different random numbers are generated from run to run.

scope
local

global
Private

The scope of a variable or constant refers to its accessibility among procedures. Variables and constants declared in a procedure are local to that procedure because they are not accessible to any other procedures. Variables and constants declared in the General section of the Code Editor window are global to the form module. Global variables and constants should be declared with the keyword **Private** and are accessible to all the procedures in the form module. Global declarations should be used only when absolutely necessary.

algorithm

pseudocode
logic error

An algorithm is a series of steps that tell how to solve a problem. An algorithm created using both English and Visual Basic code is called pseudocode. Creating an algorithm before coding helps reduce logic errors. A logic error is caused by statements that are syntactically correct but produce undesired or unexpected results.

MsgBox

A message box is used to provide information to the user, such as when invalid data has been entered or when options requiring an application to continue have not been selected. The MsgBox statement displays a Visual Basic predefined dialog box using a string as its message.

PasswordChar property

The PasswordChar property of a text box object can be used to display a character in place of each letter typed in the text box. This is often used to create a password application.

counter

A counter is a variable used to store a value that increments, or gets added to at run time. Variables used as counters should be initialized.

check box

Check boxes are used to obtain input from the user. A check box object is created using the CheckBox control in the Tool box. A click event procedure is usually coded for each check box.

PrintForm
method

A form can be printed at run time using the PrintForm method. A method is used by an object to perform an action. Dot notation is used to access a method of an object.

programming guidelines

When coding an application, first use the specification to design the interface and then create the application and appropriately name all the objects, next develop an algorithm for objects and complex tasks. Finally, code at least one event procedure for each object in an application, excluding label and frame objects.

Vocabulary

Algorithm A series of steps that tell how to solve a problem.

Boolean expression An expression that evaluates to either True or False.

Check box An object used to obtain input from the user.

Counter A variable used to store a value that is updated during run time.

Decision structure A statement that executes code depending on a Boolean expression.

Function A type of procedure that returns a value.

Global Variables and constants accessible by every procedure in a form module.

Global declaration Variables and constants declared using the keyword **Private** in the General section of the Code Editor window.

Local Variables and constants accessible by only the procedure in which they are declared.

Local declaration Variables and constants declared in a procedure.

Logic error An error caused by statements that are syntactically correct but produce undesired or unexpected results.

Logical operators Operators (**And, Or,** and **Not**) that may be used to form a Boolean expression.

Method Used by an object to perform an action.

Message box A Visual Basic predefined dialog box that provides information to the user.

Nested statements One or more statements within a statement.

Pseudocode An algorithm created using both English and Visual Basic code.

Relational operators Operators (=, <, <=, >, >=, and <>) that may be used to form a Boolean expression.

Scope The accessibility, or visibility, of variables and constants among procedures.

Update To increment a counter variable.

Visual Basic

= Equal to relational operator used to determine if one value is equal to another.

< Less than relational operator used to determine if one value is less than another.

<= Less than or equal to relational operator used to determine if one value is less than or equal to another.

> Greater than relational operator used to determine if one value is greater than another.

>= Greater than or equal to relational operator used to determine if one value is greater than or equal to another.

<> Not equal to relational operator used to determine if one value is not equal to another.

And Logical operator used to form a Boolean expression. An expression formed using **And** is True only when the expressions it joins are all True.

CheckBox control Used to create a check box object. Found in the Tool box.

If...Then Statement that executes code when a condition is True.

If...Then...Else Statement that executes code in the **Else** clause when a condition is False.

If...Then...ElseIf Statement that is used to decide among three or more actions.

Int Function that returns the integer portion of a number without rounding.

MsgBox Function used to generate a Visual Basic predefined dialog box that displays a message and an OK button.

Not Logical operator used to form a Boolean expression. An expression formed using **Not** is True only when the expression it is used with is False.

Or Logical operator used to form a Boolean expression. An expression formed using **Or** is True when any of the expressions it joins are True.

PasswordChar Text box property used to replace each letter typed in the text box with a special character. The special character is specified at design time.

PrintForm Method used to print a form during run time.

Private Keyword used when declaring a variable or constant global to the form module.

Randomize Statement used to initialize the Visual Basic random number generator.

Rnd Function used to generate a random number greater than or equal to 0 and less than 1.

Value Check box property that can be set to 0, 1, or 2 to display the check box as unchecked, checked, or grayed, respectively. Automatically changed when the user clicks on a check box.

Exercises

Exercise 1

Create a Number of Digits application that allows the user to enter a number less than 100 and then displays a message stating whether the number is a one digit number or a two digit number. The application interface should look similar to:

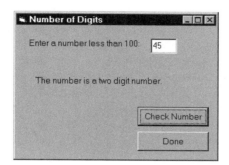

Exercise 2

Express Cafe pays its employees time and a half for every hour worked over 40 hours.

a) Create an Express Cafe Payroll application that calculates gross weekly wages (before taxes) given the hours worked and the hourly rate. The application interface should look similar to:

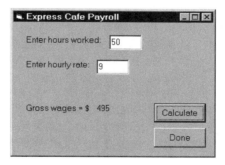

b) Express Cafe employs students who are exempt from taxes and others who are not. Modify the application so that if an employee is not exempt, 18% of the gross wages will be deducted, otherwise NO TAXES DEDUCTED will be displayed in a message box and then the wages displayed:

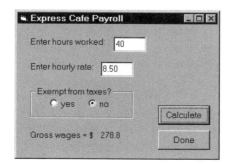

Exercise 3

The Printing Place has different printing prices based on the number of copies to be printed:

0 - 499 copies	$0.30 per copy
500 - 749 copies	$0.28 per copy
750 - 999 copies	$0.27 per copy
1000 copies or more	$0.25 per copy

Create a Printing Prices application that asks the user for the number of copies and then calculates the total price. The application interface should look similar to:

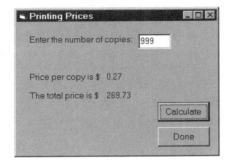

Exercise 4

Speedy Overnight Delivery service does not accept packages heavier than 27 kilograms or larger than 0.1 cubic meters (100,000 cubic centimeters). Create a Package Check application that asks the user to input the weight of a package and its dimensions, and displays an appropriate message if the package does not meet the requirements (e.g., too large, too heavy, or both). The application interface should look similar to:

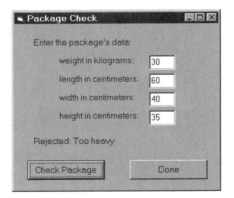

Exercise 5

Create a Computer Troubleshooting application that asks the user if the ailing computer beeps on startup, and if the hard drive spins. If it beeps and the drive spins, have the application display Contact tech support. If it beeps and the drive doesn't spin, have the application display Check drive contacts. If it doesn't beep and the hard drive doesn't spin, have the application display Bring computer to repair center. Finally, if it doesn't beep and the hard drive spins, have the application display Check the speaker connections. The application interface should look similar to:

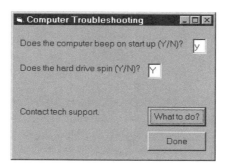

Exercise 6

The Midtown Auto Company produced some models of cars that may be difficult to drive because the car wheels are not exactly round. Cars with model numbers 119, 179, 189 through 195, 221, and 780 have been found to have this defect. Create a Defective Car Models application that allows customers to enter the model number of their car to find out if it is defective. The Carsquare graphic should be displayed when the user enters a defective car model number. If the user enters the model number of a car that is not defective, the application should display Your car is not defective. with no graphic. The application interface should look similar to:

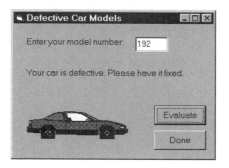

Exercise 7

Create a Grades application that reads in letter grades and continuously displays the number of students who passed (D or better) and the number who failed. The application interface should look similar to the following after entering grades and clicking on the Enter Grade button:

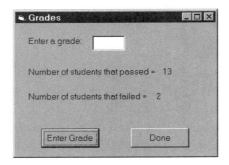

Exercise 8

Create a Slot Machine Game application that acts as a simple slot machine. The user starts with 100 tokens. With each "pull" of the handle, the user loses 1 token and the computer "spins" three wheels, each consisting of the numbers 1, 2, and 3. If all three numbers are 1, the user gets 4 tokens; if all are 2, the user gets 8 tokens; if all are 3, the user gets 12 tokens. The number of tokens that the user has should be displayed on the form and the result of the spin should be displayed in a message box. The application interface should look similar to the following after clicking on the Pull button:

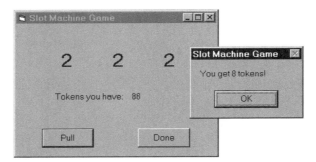

Exercise 9

Create a Game 21 application to simulate a simplified version of the game "21." A deck of cards numbered 1 through 10 is used and any number can be repeated. The computer starts by dealing you (the user) two randomly picked cards, and deals itself three randomly picked cards that are not revealed until the Check Scores button is clicked. You may then draw as many cards as you want, one by one. If both scores are over 21, or if both are equal but under 21, the game is declared a draw. Otherwise, the winner is the one with the highest score less than or equal to 21. If one score is over 21 and the other is 21 or less, the player with 21 or less is declared the winner. The result should be displayed in a message box. The application interface should look similar to the following after cards have been dealt and drawn and the Check Score button clicked:

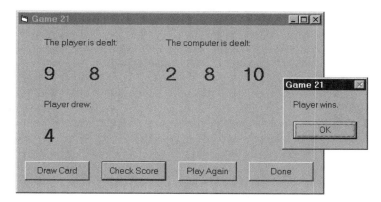

Exercise 10

Create a Math Tutor application that displays math problems by randomly generating two numbers, 1 through 10, and an operator (*, +, -, /), and then allows the user to enter the answer (hint: generate random numbers to represent the operators). The application should be able to check the answer and display a message, display the correct answer, and generate new problems. The Smiley graphic should be displayed when the user enters a correct answer and removed when the user clicks New Problem. The application interface should look similar to the following after entering a correct answer and clicking on the Check Answer button:

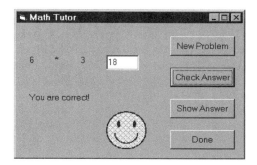

Exercise 11

Create a Sandwich Order application that allows the user to generate a sandwich order that includes the size of the sandwich (small or large) and the fixings for the sandwich (lettuce, tomato, onion, mustard, mayonnaise, cheese). A small sandwich is $2.50 and a large sandwich is $4.00. Mustard and mayonnaise are free, lettuce and onion are $0.10 each, tomato is $0.25, and cheese is $0.50. The defaults should be a small sandwich with no fixings. Remember to update the price appropriately when fixings are deselected or the sandwich size changes. The application should calculate the total price of the order and print the order. The application interface should look similar to:

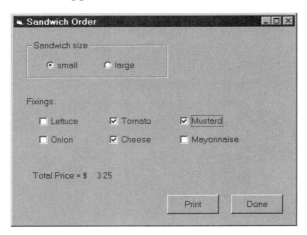

Exercise 12

The Amazing Popcorn company sells gift containers that hold up to six flavors of popcorn. A container costs $15.00. Each regular flavor is $2.00 and each gourmet flavor is $3.00. There is a $4.00 shipping charge if the container holds only regular flavors and a $5.00 shipping charge if the container holds one or more gourmet flavors. Create a Popcorn Order application to process a popcorn order. Remember to update the price appropriately when flavors are deselected or the delivery method changes. The Pick Up option should add $0 to the total price of the order and should be the default when the application is started. The Popcorn graphic should be displayed on the form. The application interface should look similar to the following after selecting popcorn order options:

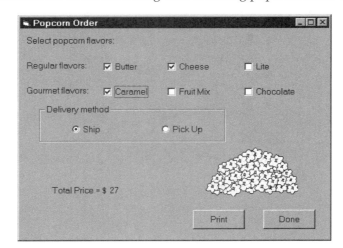

An Introduction to Programming Using Microsoft Visual Basic

Exercise 13

Create a Guess the Blocks application to simulate a modified version of the game Mastermind. In this game, three different colored blocks are lined up and hidden from the player. The player then tries to guess the colors and the correct order of the blocks. There are four colored blocks (red, green, blue, yellow) to choose from. After guessing the color of the three hidden blocks the computer displays how many of the colors are correct and how many of the colors are in the right position. Based on this information the player makes another guess and so on until the player has determined the correct order and color of the hidden blocks. Use R for Red, G for Green, B for Blue, and Y for Yellow. The color of the hidden blocks should be assigned in the form load procedure. The application interface should look similar to the following after making a guess and clicking on the Check Guess button:

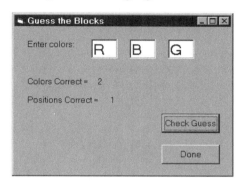

Advanced Exercises

The exercises of this and succeeding chapters will include one or more advanced exercises. These exercises provide the specification; your task is to produce design, coding, debugging, and testing steps just as those used in the Case Study.

Advanced Exercise 14

Create an application that will complete an order for a pet grooming salon. The application should allow the user to generate the price of a pet grooming session based on the services performed on the pet (shampoo, flea dip, trim, and full shave). The application should be able to calculate the total price and print the order.

Advanced Exercise 15

Create an application that will complete an order for a flower arrangement. The application should allow the user to select different types of flowers (roses, carnations, daisies, tulips) and should then calculate the price of the flower arrangement, accept money from the user, display the change, and print the bill.

An Introduction to Programming Using Microsoft Visual Basic

Controlling Program Flow with Looping Structures

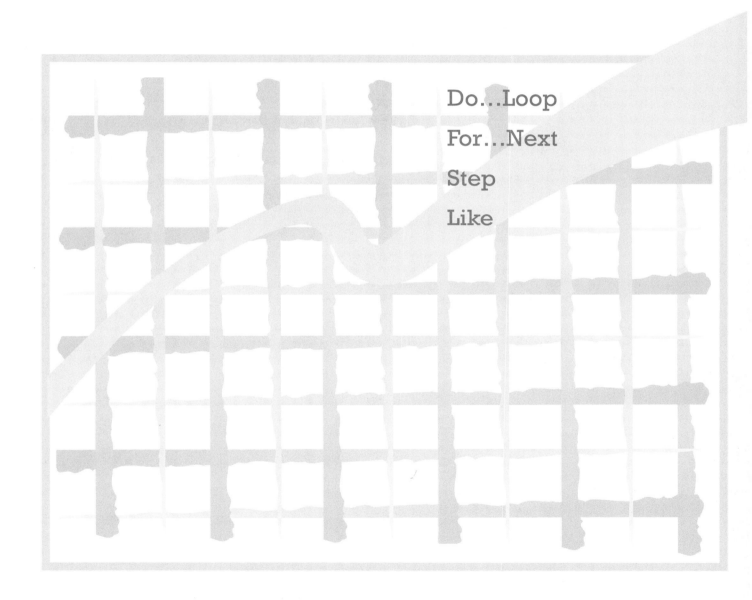

Do...Loop

For...Next

Step

Like

Chapter Six Objectives

After completing this chapter you will be able to:

1. Understand the Do...Loop statement and infinite loops.
2. Use input boxes in applications.
3. Understand accumulators and sentinels.
4. Understand the LCase, UCase, and StrConv functions.
5. Understand the Left, Right, and Mid functions and the Mid statement.
6. Understand the Len and InStr functions.
7. Understand the For...Next statement, and how to use Step.
8. Understand the String and Space functions and the & operator.
9. Understand how characters are stored in memory.
10. Understand the ASCII code and use the Asc and Chr functions in programs.
11. Use textual comparison for comparing strings.
12. Understand pattern matching.

$\mathbf{I}$n this chapter you will learn about looping structures, which control program flow and allow a set of statements to be executed a number of times. String functions will also be discussed.

6.1 The Do...Loop Statement

looping structure

iteration

The Do...Loop statement is a *looping structure* that executes a set of statements as long as a condition is True. Repeating one or more statements is referred to as *looping*, or *iteration*. For example, in the statements

```
Dim intNumber As Integer
intNumber = 0
Do
    intNumber = intNumber + 2        'Increment by 2
Loop While intNumber < 10
```

the body of the Do...Loop executes five times. On the fifth time, intNumber is equal to 10 which makes the loop condition intNumber < 10 False.

The Do...Loop statement takes the form:

```
Do
    statements
Loop While condition
```

statements is the body of the loop and is executed at least once. *condition* is a Boolean expression used to determine if the loop is to be repeated. If *condition* is True, *statements* is executed again and then the *condition* re-evaluated. The loop is repeated until *condition* evaluates to False.

Another form of Do...Loop evaluates the condition before executing the body of the loop and takes the form:

```
Do While condition
    statements
Loop
```

statements is the body of the loop. *condition* is a Boolean expression used to determine if the loop is to be executed or repeated. If *condition* is True, *statements* is executed and then *condition* reevaluated. The loop is repeated until *condition* evaluates to False.

The first form of Do...Loop executes the body of the loop at least once. The second form of Do...Loop may execute zero or more times. This is because, if *condition* is initially False, the body of the loop never executes.

6.2 Infinite Loops

The condition of a loop is used to determine when the loop should stop executing. A Do...Loop continues until its condition is False. What happens, though, if the condition never becomes False? The result is an *infinite loop*—one which continues forever.

A logic error can lead to an infinite loop. For example, the following statements create an infinite loop. Can you see why?

```
Dim intNumber As Integer
intNumber = -1
Do While intNumber < 0
    intNumber = intNumber - 1
Loop
```

Because Number is initially set to –1 and is never changed to a positive number in the body of the loop, the condition of the loop is always True. In Windows 95 and Windows 98, an application that has gone into an infinite loop can usually be interrupted by pressing the key combination Ctrl+Break.

Review 1

Code 1
```
Dim intNumber As Integer
intNumber = 21
Do While intNumber < 21
    intNumber = intNumber + 1
Loop
```

Code 2
```
Dim intNumber As Integer
intNumber = 21
Do
    intNumber = intNumber +1
Loop While intNumber < 25
```

a) How many times is the loop executed in Code 1?
b) What is the value of intNumber after Code 1 has executed?
c) How many times is the loop executed in Code 2?
d) What is the value of intNumber after Code 2 has executed?

Review 2

A prime number is an integer that is evenly divisible by only 1 and itself. For example, 2, 3, and 7 are prime numbers, but 4, 6, and 9 are not. Follow the instructions below to create the Prime Number application.

1) CREATE A NEW PROJECT

2) ADD OBJECTS TO THE FORM

Refer to the form below when placing and sizing the form and its objects. Use the table on the next page to name and change the properties of the objects.

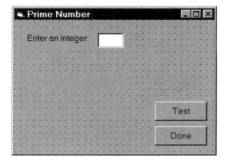

Object	Name	Caption	Text
Form1	frmPrimeNumber	Prime Number	
Label1	lblEnterInteger	Enter an integer:	
Text1	txtInteger		*empty*
Label2	lblPrimeResult	*empty*	
Command1	cmdTest	Test	
Command2	cmdDone	Done	

3) SAVE THE PROJECT

From the File menu, select Save Project. Save the form naming it frmPrimeNumber and save the project naming it Prime Number.

4) WRITE THE PROGRAM CODE

The **Mod** operator can be used to determine if one number evenly divides into another, and a loop can be used to generate divisors between 1 and the number entered. If the only divisor that evenly divides the number entered is the same as the number entered then the user entered a prime number. With this in mind, pseudocode for the Test button click event procedure is:

```
Private Sub cmdTest_Click()
   Get intTestNum from a text box
   intDivisor = 1
   If intTestNum > 1 Then
      Do
         Increment divisor by 1
      Loop While intTestNum is not evenly divisible by intDivisor
   End If
   If intDivisor = intTestNum Then
      Display message that intTestNum is prime
   Else
      Display message that intTestNum is not prime
   End If
End Sub
```

Display the Code Editor window and add the following event procedures:

```
Private Sub txtInteger_Change()
   lblPrimeResult.Caption = ""
End Sub

Private Sub cmdTest_Click()
   Dim intTestNum As Integer
   Dim intDivisor As Integer

   intTestNum = txtInteger.Text
   intDivisor = 1                       'Initialize divisor
   If intTestNum > 1 Then               '1 is a prime number
      Do
         intDivisor = intDivisor + 1    'Increment divisor
      Loop While intTestNum Mod intDivisor <> 0
   End If

   If intDivisor = intTestNum Then
      lblPrimeResult.Caption = "Prime number"
   Else
      lblPrimeResult.Caption = "Not a prime number"
   End If
End Sub
```

```
Private Sub cmdDone_Click()
    Unload Me
End Sub
```

5) RUN THE APPLICATION

Save the modified Prime Number project and then run the application. Test the application using 1, 2, 4, 7, and 9 as entries.

6) PRINT AND THEN REMOVE THE PROJECT

6.3 Input Boxes

An *input box* is a Visual Basic predefined dialog box that has a prompt, a text box, and OK and Cancel buttons. It is used to get information from the user and looks similar to:

input box—

An input box is displayed by using the InputBox function which takes the form:

InputBox(*prompt, title*)

prompt is a **String** variable or a string enclosed in quotation marks. *title* is an optional **String** variable or a string enclosed in quotation marks. When the OK button is selected, the data in the text box is returned by the InputBox function. For example, the following statement displays the input box shown above and then assigns the data typed by the user to the Caption of a label:

lblTextEntered.Caption = InputBox("Enter text", "This is an input box")

When My Text is typed in the input box above and OK selected, the text is displayed in the lblTextEntered label:

If the user selects the Cancel button in an input box, an empty string ("") is returned by the InputBox function. To avoid a run-time error, the text returned by InputBox should be checked before using it:

```
Dim strTextEntered As String

strTextEntered = InputBox("Enter text", "This is an input box")

If strTextEntered = "" Then              'Test string returned
    lblTextEntered.Caption = "Cancel selected."   'Cancel selected
Else
    lblTextEntered.Caption = strTextEntered      'Text entered
End If
```

6.4 Using Accumulators

The Average Score application allows a user to enter as many scores as desired and then displays the average of the scores when the Average button is selected. For example, after entering three scores and clicking on the Average button, the Average Score application looks similar to:

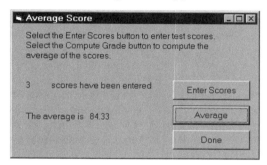

The pseudocode for the Enter Scores button is:

```
Private Sub cmdEnterScores_Click()
    Display input box to receive intScore
    Check if intScore returned by input box is valid score
    Do while intScore <> intSentinel
        Count the score
        Add score to sum of scores
        Display input box to receive intScore
        Check if value returned by input box is valid score
    Loop
End Sub
```

sentinel

A Do...Loop can be used to get multiple values from the user. Note the loop condition compares the entered score to intSentinel. This constant is called a *flag*, or *sentinel*, because its value signifies the end of the loop. When the user enters the sentinel value, the loop no longer executes. This approach provides a clear and easy-to-change method for ending a loop.

The Do...Loop is also used to count and sum the scores as they are entered. A counter in the loop is updated each time the loop iterates. For summing, an accumulator is needed. An *accumulator* is a numeric variable used to store a value that accumulates, or gets added to, during run time. The form for updating an accumulator is:

identifier = identifier + value

identifier is the accumulator that is updated. *value* is the number that is added to the current value of *identifier*. The expression on the right is evaluated first, and then the result stored as the value of the variable on the left. An accumulator should be initialized and is usually updated by a varying amount.

The cmdEnterScores_Click() procedure is:

```
Private Sub cmdEnterScores_Click()
    Const strTitle As String = "Grades"
    Const strPrompt As String = "Enter a test score (-1 to finish):"
    Const intSentinel As Integer = -1          'Loop flag
    Dim intScore As Integer, strTempScore As String

    lblAverageMessage.Caption = ""            'Clear message
    lblAverage.Caption = ""                   'Clear current average
    lblNumberOfScores.Caption = ""            'Clear number of scores
    lblScoresMessage.Caption = ""             'Clear scores message

    intNumberOfScores = 0                     'Initialize global counter
    intTotalPoints = 0                        'Initialize global accumulator

    strTempScore = InputBox(strPrompt, strTitle)       'Get score

    'Determine if Cancel button was selected in input box
    If strTempScore = "" Then                 'Test string returned
        intScore = intSentinel                'Cancel selected
    Else
        intScore = strTempScore               'Score entered
    End If

    Do While intScore <> intSentinel
        intNumberOfScores = intNumberOfScores + 1     'Count score
        intTotalPoints = intTotalPoints + intScore    'Update total

        strTempScore = InputBox(strPrompt, strTitle)       'Get score

        'Determine if Cancel button was selected in input box
        If strTempScore = "" Then             'Test string returned
            intScore = intSentinel            'Cancel selected
        Else
            intScore = strTempScore           'Score entered
        End If
    Loop

    lblNumberOfScores.Caption = intNumberOfScores
    lblScoresMessage.Caption = "scores have been entered"
End Sub
```

Review 3

Part of the Average Score pseudocode was developed in Section 6.4. Follow the instructions below to create the Average Score application.

1) **CREATE A NEW PROJECT**

2) **ADD OBJECTS TO THE FORM**

Refer to the form below when placing and sizing the form and its objects. Use the table on the next page to name and change the properties of the objects.

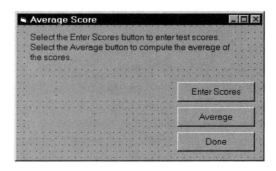

An Introduction to Programming Using Microsoft Visual Basic

Object	Name	Caption
Form1	frmAverageScore	Average Score
Label1	lblHelpMessage	*see text on previous page*
Label2	lblNumberOfScores	*empty*
Label3	lblScoresMessage	*empty*
Label4	lblAverageMessage	*empty*
Label5	lblAverage	*empty*
Command1	cmdEnterScores	Enter Scores
Command2	cmdAverage	Average
Command3	cmdDone	Done

3) SAVE THE PROJECT

From the File menu, select Save Project. Save the form naming it frmAverageScore and save the project naming it Average Score.

4) WRITE THE PROGRAM CODE

Display the Code Editor window and add the following code:

```
Option Explicit
Private intNumberOfScores As Integer, intTotalPoints As Integer

Private Sub cmdEnterScores_Click()
    Const strTitle As String = "Grades"
    Const strPrompt As String = "Enter a test score (-1 to finish):"
    Const intSentinel As Integer = -1              'Loop flag
    Dim intScore As Integer, strTempScore As String

    lblAverageMessage.Caption = ""                 'Clear average message
    lblAverage.Caption = ""                        'Clear current average
    lblNumberOfScores.Caption = ""                 'Clear number of scores
    lblScoresMessage.Caption = ""                  'Clear scores message

    intNumberOfScores = 0                          'Initialize global counter
    intTotalPoints = 0                             'Initialize global accumulator

    strTempScore = InputBox(strPrompt, strTitle)   'Get score

    'Determine if Cancel button was selected in input box
    If strTempScore = "" Then                      'Test string returned
        intScore = intSentinel                     'Cancel selected
    Else
        intScore = strTempScore                    'Score entered
    End If

    Do While intScore <> intSentinel
        intNumberOfScores = intNumberOfScores + 1  'Increment number of scores
        intTotalPoints = intTotalPoints + intScore 'Update total

        strTempScore = InputBox(strPrompt, strTitle)   'Get score

        'Determine if Cancel button was selected in input box
        If strTempScore = "" Then                  'Test string returned
            intScore = intSentinel                 'Cancel selected
        Else
            intScore = strTempScore                'Score entered
        End If
    Loop

    lblNumberOfScores.Caption = intNumberOfScores
    lblScoresMessage.Caption = "scores have been entered"
End Sub
```

```
Private Sub cmdAverage_Click()
    Dim dblAverage As Double
    If intNumberOfScores > 0 Then
        dblAverage = intTotalPoints / intNumberOfScores        'Compute average
        lblAverageMessage.Caption = "The average is"
        lblAverage.Caption = dblAverage                        'Display average
    Else
        lblAverageMessage.Caption = "The average is"
        lblAverage.Caption = 0
    End If
End Sub

Private Sub cmdDone_Click()
    Unload Me
End Sub
```

5) RUN THE APPLICATION

Save the modified Average Score project and then run the application. Test the application.

6) PRINT AND THEN REMOVE THE PROJECT

Review 4

a) Create a Unique Random Numbers application that generates three unique random numbers between 1 and 5. Unique Random Numbers should use a loop that repeatedly generates three random numbers until all three numbers are different. The loop should contain a counter that counts the number of loop iterations required to generate three unique numbers. The application interface should look similar to that shown on the right after clicking on the Generate Numbers button.

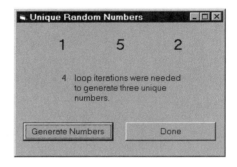

b) Modify the Unique Random Numbers application to allow the user to enter the largest number to generate. Use an input box to get the user's input.

6.5 String Conversion Functions

LCase

Visual Basic includes several built-in functions for converting the case of letters in a strings. These functions include LCase, UCase, and StrConv. The LCase function takes the form:

LCase(*string*)

string is a **String** variable or a string enclosed in quotation marks. LCase returns the string argument as an all lowercase string. The following code demonstrates LCase:

```
Dim strSeason As String
strSeason = "Summer"
lblDisplaySeason.Caption = LCase(strSeason)        'summer
```

UCase The UCase function takes the form:

UCase(*string*)

string is a **String** variable or a string enclosed in quotation marks. UCase returns the string argument as an all uppercase string. The following code demonstrates UCase:

```
Dim strSeason As String
strSeason = "Summer"
lblDisplaySeason.Caption = UCase(strSeason)          'SUMMER
```

StrConv The StrConv function takes the form:

StrConv(*string, conversion*)

string is a **String** variable or a string enclosed in quotation marks. *conversion* is a Visual Basic predefined constant that determines how *string* is to be converted. *conversion* can be vbUpperCase, vbLowerCase, or vbProperCase. StrConv returns the string argument converted according to the constant used. vbUpperCase converts the string to all uppercase, similar to UCase, vbLowerCase converts the string to all lowercase, similar to LCase, and vbProperCase converts the first letter in each word of the string to uppercase. The following code demonstrates StrConv:

```
Dim strTitle As String
strTitle = "summer fun"
lblBook.Caption = StrConv(strTitle, vbProperCase)   'Summer Fun
```

Review 5

Create a Text Case application that displays a word or phrase as all lowercase, all uppercase, or proper case. The Text Case application interface should look similar to that shown on the right after entering to be or not to be and selecting the Proper option button.

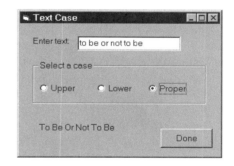

6.6 Manipulating Strings

Visual Basic includes several built-in functions for manipulating strings. These functions include Left, Right, and Mid. Each of these functions re-
Left turns a portion of a string called a *substring*. The Left function takes the form:

Left(*string, length*)

string is a **String** variable or a string enclosed in quotation marks. *length* is the number of characters from the beginning (the left) of the string to return. Left returns *length* number of characters starting from the left of *string*. The following code demonstrates Left:

```
Dim strSeason As String
strSeason = "Summer"
lblDisplaySeason.Caption = Left(strSeason, 3)        'Sum
```

Right

The Right function takes the form:

Right(*string*, *length*)

string is a **String** variable or a string enclosed in quotation marks. *length* is the number of characters starting from the end (the right) of the string to return. Right returns *length* number of characters starting from the right of *string*. The following code demonstrates Right:

```
Dim strSeason As String
strSeason = "Summer"
lblDisplaySeason.Caption = Right(strSeason, 3)          'mer
```

Mid function

The Mid function takes the form:

Mid(*string*, *start*, *length*)

string is a **String** variable or a string enclosed in quotation marks. *start* is the character position to begin taking characters. *length* is the number of characters to return. Mid returns *length* number of characters starting with the *start* character of *string*. The following code demonstrates Mid:

```
Dim strSeason As String
strSeason = "Summer"
lblDisplaySeason.Caption = Mid(strSeason, 2, 4)          'umme
```

Mid statement

Similar to the Mid function is the Mid statement that is used to replace a specified number of characters in a string and takes the form:

Mid(*string1*, *start*, *length*) = *string2*

string1 is a **String** variable or a string enclosed in quotation marks. *start* is the character position to begin replacing characters. *length* is the number of characters to replace. *string2* is a **String** variable or a string enclosed in quotation marks used as the replace characters. The following code demonstrates the Mid statement:

```
Dim strSeason As String
strSeason = "autumn"
Mid(strSeason, 2, 3) = "summer"          'utu is replaced by sum
lblDisplaySeason.Caption = strSeason     'asummn
```

Note that when the Mid statement is used, it appears on the left side of an assignment statement.

6.7 The Len Function

The Len function is a Visual Basic built-in function that returns a count of the number of characters in a string. The Len function takes the form:

Len(*string*)

string is a **String** variable or a string enclosed in quotation marks. Len returns the number of characters in *string*. The following code demonstrates Len:

```
Dim strSeason As String
strSeason = "Summer"
lblDisplayLength.Caption = Len(strSeason)          '6
```

Review 6

Create a String Test application that displays the first letter, last letter, and middle letter of a word or phrase. Use the following algorithm for determining the *position* of the middle character of a string:

```
If Len(strWord) Mod 2 <> 0 Then
   intMiddleCharPos = Len(strWord) \ 2 + 1
Else
   intMiddleCharPos = Len(strWord) \ 2
End If
```

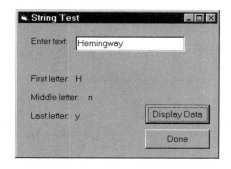

The application interface should look similar to that shown on the right after entering Hemingway and clicking on the Display Data button.

6.8 The InStr Function

The InStr function is a Visual Basic built-in function that returns the starting position of a substring. If the substring is not found, 0 is returned. The InStr function takes the form:

InStr(*start, string1, string2*)

start is the position in *string1* to start searching. If *start* is not included, searching automatically starts at position 1. *string1* is a **String** variable or a string enclosed in quotation marks that will be searched. *string2* is also a **String** variable or a string enclosed in quotation marks that will be searched for. The following code demonstrates InStr. Note that a start position was not indicated so searching started at position 1:

```
Dim strSeason As String, strSubString As String
strSeason = "Summer"
strSubString = "um"
lblDisplayPosition.Caption = InStr(strSeason, strSubString)     '2
```

The following code is another example of InStr. Note that a start position of 3 was indicated so searching started at position 3 (the first letter "m"):

```
Dim strSeason As String, strSubString As String
Dim intStart As Integer
strSeason = "Summer"
strSubString = "um"
intStart = 3

'Displays 0 in a label because the substring is never found
lblDisplayPosition = InStr(intStart, strSeason, strSubString)
```

Review 7

Create a Find String application that displays the first position of a word or phrase in another word or phrase. Use text boxes to allow the user to enter the string to search and the substring to search for. The application interface should look similar to that shown on the right after entering text and search text and clicking on the Find String button.

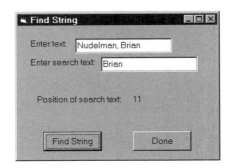

Review 8

Create a Count Letter application that displays the number of times a specific letter occurs in a word or phrase. Use the following algorithm for counting the letter occurrences:

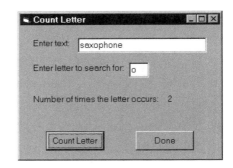

```
intNumOccurences = 0
intSearchPos = 1
Do
    intLetterPos = Position of letter within phrase
    If intLetterPos > 0 Then
        Increment intNumOccurences
        intSearchPos = intLetterPos + 1
    End If
Loop While intSearchPos <= Len(strPhrase) And intLetterPos <> 0
```

The application interface should look similar to that shown on the right after entering saxophone, the letter o, and clicking on the Count Letter button.

6.9 The For...Next Statement

The **For...Next** statement is a looping structure that executes a set of statements a fixed number of times. Unlike **Do...Loop** that executes while a condition is true, **For...Next** executes until a counter reaches an ending value. The **For...Next** statement takes the form:

```
For counter = start To end
    statements
Next counter
```

counter, *start*, and *end* are **Integer** variables, values, or expressions. *counter* is initialized to *start* (*counter* = *start*) only once when the loop first executes, and compared to *end* before each loop iteration. *counter* is automatically incremented by 1 after each iteration of the loop body (*statements*).

With each iteration of the following **For...Next**, a message box is displayed. In this case, 10 message boxes in all will be displayed:

```
Dim intNumber As Integer
For intNumber = 1 To 10
    MsgBox intNumber        'Display message box with intNumber value
Next intNumber
```

programming style   While it is possible to modify the value of the counting variable in the body of a **For…Next** loop or to terminate the loop prematurely, this is generally considered poor programming style.

Step   A **For…Next** statement can include **Step** to change the way the counter is incremented. For example, the following **For…Next** increments the counter by 2 each iteration to sum all the even numbers between 1 and 8:

```
Dim intCount As Integer, intStart As Integer, intEnd As Integer
Dim intStep As Integer
Dim intSum As Integer
intStart = 2
intEnd = 8
intStep = 2
intSum = 0                        'Initialize intSum
For intCount = intStart To intEnd Step intStep
    intSum = intSum + intCount    'Add value of counter to intSum
Next intCount
lblEvenSum.Caption = intSum       '2+4+6+8
```

Step may also be used to decrement a counter. For example, the statements below count down from 10 to 1 with each number being displayed in a message box:

```
Dim intNumber As Integer
For intNumber = 10 To 1 Step -1
    MsgBox intNumber
Next intNumber
```

Review 9

The factorial of a number is the product of all the positive integers from 1 to the number. For example, 3 factorial, written as 3!, is 3 * 2 * 1, or 6. Follow the instructions below to create the Factorial application.

1) CREATE A NEW PROJECT

2) ADD OBJECTS TO THE FORM

Refer to the form below when placing and sizing the form and its objects. Use the table below to name and change the properties of the objects.

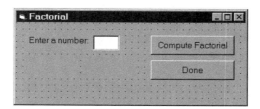

Object	Name	Caption	Text
Form1	frmFactorial	Factorial	
Label1	lblEnterNumber	Enter a number:	
Text1	txtNumber		*empty*
Label2	lblFactorialMessage	*empty*	
Label3	lblFactorial	*empty*	
Command1	cmdComputeFactorial	Compute Factorial	
Command2	cmdDone	Done	

3) SAVE THE PROJECT

From the File menu, select Save Project. Save the form naming it frmFactorial and save the project naming it Factorial.

4) WRITE THE PROGRAM CODE

The pseudocode for the Compute Factorial button click event procedure is:

```
Private Sub cmdComputeFactorial_Click()
   Get intNumber from a text box
   lngFactorial = 1
   For intCounter = 1 To intNumber
      lngFactorial = lngFactorial * intCounter
   Next intCounter
   Display lngFactorial
End Sub
```

Display the Code Editor window and add the following event procedures:

```
Private Sub cmdComputeFactorial_Click()
   Dim intNumber As Integer
   Dim lngFactorial As Long
   Dim intCount As Integer

   intNumber = txtNumber.Text
   lngFactorial = 1

   For intCount = 1 To intNumber
      lngFactorial = lngFactorial * intCount
   Next intCount

   lblFactorialMessage.Caption = "Factorial is:"
   lblFactorial.Caption = lngFactorial
End Sub

Private Sub txtNumber_Change()
   lblFactorialMessage.Caption = ""
   lblFactorial.Caption = ""
End Sub

Private Sub cmdDone_Click()
   Unload Me
End Sub
```

5) RUN THE APPLICATION

Save the modified Factorial project and then run the application. Test the application using 1, 3, 5, and 12 as entries.

6) PRINT AND THEN REMOVE THE PROJECT

Review 10

Create an Odd Numbers Sum application that displays the sum of the odd numbers from 1 to a maximum value entered by the user. The application interface should look similar to that shown on the right after entering 11 and clicking on the Calculate Sum button.

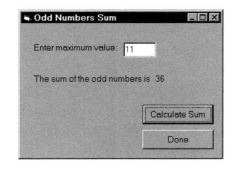

Review 11

Create a Font Size Increment application that displays Size in a label and increases the font size of the label in intervals of 5 starting at size 10 and ending at size 50. A message box should be displayed asking if the user is ready to continue after each font size increase. The application interface should look similar to that on the right after clicking on the Increment Font Size button and selecting OK in the message dialog box a few times.

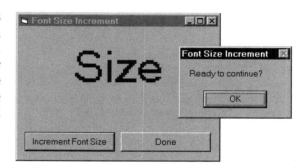

6.10 Generating Strings

String
The String function is a Visual Basic built-in function that returns a string of repeating characters. The String function takes the form:

String(*integer, character*)

integer is an **Integer** variable or value indicating the number of characters in the returned string. *character* is a character enclosed in quotaion marks to be used for the string. The following code demonstrates String:

```
Dim strBar As String
strBar = String(10, "*")
lblDisplayString.Caption = strBar          '**********
```

Space
The Space function is a Visual Basic built-in function that returns a string of spaces. The Space function takes the form:

Space(*integer*)

integer is an **Integer** variable or value indicating the number of spaces in the returned string. The following code demonstrates Space:

```
Dim strBlanks As String
strBlanks = Space(10)
lblDisplayString.Caption  = strBlanks      'Displays        in a label
```

&
The **&** operator is used to concatenate strings. *Concatenation* is the process of joining two or more strings into one string. The & operator is used in an expression similar to the following:

string = string1 & string2

string is a **String** variable that will store the result of the expression. *string1* and *string2* are **String** variables or strings enclosed in quotation marks. The following code demonstrates &:

```
Dim strFirstName As String, strLastName As String
Dim strFullName As String

strFirstName = "Elaine"
strLastName = "Malfas"
strFullName = strFirstName & strLastName
lblShowName.Caption = strFullName          'ElaineMalfas

'Add a space between first and last names
strFullName = strFirstName & Space(1) & strLastName
lblShowName.Caption = strFullName          'Elaine Malfas
```

vbTab
vbCrLf

Visual Basic contains two built-in constants that are useful with strings. The vbTab constant represents the tab character and can be used to place eight spaces in a string. The vbCrLf constant represents a carriage return-linefeed combination and is used to move text to the next line. The following statement displays the message box below:

MsgBox "Hello" & vbTab & "and" & vbCrLf & "Good-bye"

Review 12

Create a Name application that uses two input boxes to get the user's first name and last name and then displays their first and last names in a single label on the form with the same number of underscores as the length of the first and last names with a space. The application interface should look similar to that shown on the right after entering Elaine Malfas.

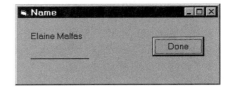

6.11 Character Data Storage

Computers can only store numeric data. As discussed in Chapter One, all data is stored in memory as bytes. Each byte consists of 8 bits, where each bit is either on or off. When a bit is on, it is said to store a 1, when a bit is off, a 0. The 1s and 0s used by a computer represent the binary number system.

When a character, such as a letter of the alphabet, needs to be stored in memory, it is stored as a number. ANSI (American National Standards Institute) developed a code called ASCII (American Standard Code for Information Interchange) for representing characters on a personal computer. The ASCII code uses numbers between 0 and 255 to represent each letter of the alphabet, both uppercase and lowercase, numerals 0 through 9, and many other special characters.

The Asc function is a Visual Basic built-in function that returns the ASCII code corresponding to a character. The Asc function takes the form:

Asc(*string*)

string is a **String** variable or a string enclosed in quotation marks. The value returned by Asc is in the range 0 to 255. The following code demonstrates Asc:

```
Dim strCharacter As String
strCharacter = "A"
lblASCII.Caption = Asc(strCharacter)          '65
```

The Chr function is a Visual Basic built-in function that returns the character corresponding to an ASCII code (decimal number). The Chr function takes the form:

Chr(*integer*)

integer is an **Integer** variable or an integer in the range 0 to 255, inclusive. The following code demonstrates Chr:

```
Dim intASCIICode As Integer
intASCIICode = 65
lblASCII.Caption = Chr(intASCIICode)        'Displays A
```

The table below displays ASCII codes with their character equivalents.

ASCII Codes

bell	7	<	60	Z	90	x	120	¥	165	Ã	195	á	225
tab	9	=	61	[	91	y	121	¦	166	Ä	196	â	226
space	32	>	62	\	92	z	122	§	167	Å	197	ã	227
!	33	?	63	]	93	{	123	¨	168	Æ	198	ä	228
"	34	@	64	^	94	|	124	©	169	Ç	199	å	229
#	35	A	65	_	95	}	125	ª	170	È	200	æ	230
$	36	B	66	`	96	~	126	«	171	É	201	ç	231
%	37	C	67	a	97	ƒ	131	¬	172	Ê	202	è	232
&	38	D	68	b	98	„	132	-	173	Ë	203	é	233
'	39	E	69	c	99	…	133	®	174	Ì	204	ê	234
(	40	F	70	d	100	†	135	–	175	Í	205	ë	235
)	41	G	71	e	101	‰	137	•	176	Î	206	ì	236
*	42	H	72	f	102	‹	139	±	177	Ï	207	í	237
+	43	I	73	g	103	'	145	²	178	Ð	208	î	238
,	44	J	74	h	104	'	146	³	179	Ñ	209	ï	239
-	45	K	75	i	105	"	147	´	180	Ò	210	ð	240
.	46	L	76	j	106	"	148	µ	181	Ó	211	ñ	241
/	47	M	77	k	107	•	149	¶	182	Ô	212	ò	242
0	48	N	78	l	108	–	150	·	183	Õ	213	ó	243
1	49	O	79	m	109	—	151	¸	184	Ö	214	ô	244
2	50	P	80	n	110	~	152	¹	185	×	215	õ	245
3	51	Q	81	o	111	™	153	º	186	Ø	216	ö	246
4	52	R	82	p	112		154	»	187	Ù	217	÷	247
5	53	S	83	q	113	›	155	¼	188	Ú	218	ø	248
6	54	T	84	r	114	œ	156	½	189	Û	219	ù	249
7	55	U	85	s	115		159	¾	190	Ü	220	ú	250
8	56	V	86	t	116	¡	161	¿	191	Ý	221	û	251
9	57	W	87	u	117	¢	162	À	192	Þ	222	ü	252
:	58	X	88	v	118	£	163	Á	193	ß	223	ý	253
;	59	Y	89	w	119	¤	164	Â	194	à	224	þ	254
												ÿ	255

Create a Secret Message Decoder application that decodes a secret message made up of six ASCII codes. After the user enters the ASCII code for each character of the secret message in separate input boxes, the application displays the decoded message on the form. The application interface should look similar to that shown on the right after entering 72, 101, 108, 108, 111, 33 into separate input boxes.

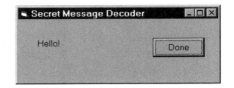

6.12 Comparing Strings

Strings can be compared to determine if one string is the same as another or if one string comes alphabetically before or after another. Chapter Five presented relational operators (=, >, <, >=, <=, <>) for making comparisons. However, relational operators use the internal binary

binary representation representation of characters (ASCII) to determine relationships among strings. For example, the comparison "B" < "a" is unexpectedly True because an uppercase "B" is represented in ASCII by the number 66, which is less than the number 97 used to represent the lowercase "a". As another example, the comparison "Apple" = "apple" is False because uppercase "A" and lowercase "a" are represented by two different ASCII codes.

StrComp
textual comparison The StrComp function is a Visual Basic built-in function that can perform textual comparison on strings. *Textual comparison* is a comparison that does not distinguish between uppercase and lowercase letters. The StrComp function takes the form:

    StrComp(*string1, string2, compare*)

string1 and *string2* are **String** variables or strings enclosed in quotation marks. *compare* is the Visual Basic constant vbTextCompare used to indicate a textual comparison is to be made. StrComp returns 0 if *string1* and *string2* are textually equal. A –1 is returned if *string1* is less than *string2*. When *string1* is greater than *string2*, a 1 is returned. The following code demonstrates StrComp:

```
Dim strFirstWord As String, strSecondWord As String
strFirstWord = "Oranges"
strSecondWord = "apples"

'The following will display: First word comes after second word
If StrComp(strFirstWord, strSecondWord, vbTextCompare) = 0 Then
    lblMessage.Caption = "Both words are the same"
ElseIf StrComp(strFirstWord, strSecondWord, vbTextCompare) = -1 Then
    lblMessage.Caption = "First word comes before second word"
Else
    lblMessage.Caption = "First word comes after second word"
End If

strFirstWord = "Apples"            'Change strFirstWord

'The following will display: Both words are the same
If StrComp(strFirstWord, strSecondWord, vbTextCompare) = 0 Then
    lblMessage.Caption = "Both words are the same"
ElseIf StrComp(strFirstWord, strSecondWord, vbTextCompare) = -1 Then
    lblMessage.Caption = "First word comes before second word"
Else
    lblMessage.Caption = "First word comes after second word"
End If
```

Like   The **Like** operator is also used to perform a textual comparison on strings. However, **Like** can be used to perform pattern matching. *Pattern matching* allows wildcard characters, character lists, and character ranges to match strings. The **Like** operator is used in a statement and takes the form:

result = *string* **Like** *pattern*

result is a Boolean or Integer variable that will store the result of the expression using **Like**. *result* will be True if *string* matches *pattern* and False otherwise. *string* is a **String** variable or a string enclosed in quotation marks. *pattern* can be in many forms, each of which is discussed below:

?   used in place of any single character
*   used in place of many characters
#   used in place of any single number
[] used to enclose a list of characters
–   used to indicate a range of characters in a character list
,   used to separate characters in a character list

The following code demonstrates **Like**:

```
Dim strWord As String, strPattern As String
strWord = "Run"
strPattern = "?un"
lblMessage.Caption = strWord Like strPattern        'Displays True

strWord = "Run"
strPattern = "?um"
lblMessage.Caption = strWord Like strPattern        'Displays False

strWord = "Letter to Suzy"
strPattern = "Letter to *"
lblMessage.Caption = strWord Like strPattern        'Displays True

strWord = "Case 9876"
strPattern = "Case 987#"
lblMessage.Caption = strWord Like strPattern        'Displays True

strWord = "Case 9876"
strPattern = "Case ##6#"
lblMessage.Caption = strWord Like strPattern        'Displays False

strWord = "C"
strPattern = "[A,B,C,D,E,F]"
lblMessage.Caption = strWord Like strPattern        'Displays True

strWord = "B"
strPattern = "[A–F]"
lblMessage.Caption = strWord Like strPattern        'Displays True
```

Review 14

Create a Compare Words application that allows the user to enter two words and then does a textual comparison to determine if the words are equal or if the first word is greater than or less than the second word. The application interface should look similar to that shown on the right after entering miniature and MINIATURE and clicking on the Compare Words button.

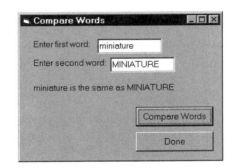

Case Study

In this Case Study a Hangman application will be created.

specification

The specification for this Case Study is:

A Hangman application that allows the user to enter characters and guess a secret word. The application should then display a message if the user guessed the secret word correctly and how many tries it took.

design

The form design for this Case Study is:

The form design for the Hangman Case Study

Note that the label is sketched with a dashed line to indicate that its Caption will not appear until run time. In this case, the label's Caption will display the same number of dashes as characters in the secret word and each time the user guesses a correct letter the corresponding dash is replaced by the correct letter.

The program code design for this Case Study is best done by listing the pseudocode for event procedures:

```
Private Sub cmdDone_Click()
   Unload Form
End Sub

Private cmdPlayGame_Click()
   strSecretWord = "magic"
   strSentinel = "!"
```

Display on form a dash for each character in strSecretWord
intNumberOfGuesses = 0
Get strGuess from an input box
Do While strGuess <> strSentinel
  Increment intNumberOfGuesses
  For intLetterPos = 1 to Len(strSecretWord)
    If strSecretWord letter at intLetterPos = strGuess Then
      Mid(strWordGuessedSoFar, intLetterPos, 1) = strGuess
    End If
  Next intLetterPos
  Display strLettersGuessed on the form
  Get strGuess from an input box
Loop
If strGuess = strSentinel Then
  get strGuess from input box
End If
If strGuess = strSecretWord Then
  Display message
Else
  Display message
End If
Display strSecretWord in label
End Sub

coding   The interface and code for this Case Study are:

Object	Name	Caption
Form1	frmHangman	Hangman
Label1	lblWord	*empty*
Command1	cmdPlayGame	Play Game
Command2	cmdDone	Done

```
Option Explicit

Private Sub cmdPlayGame_Click()
    Const strSentinel As String = "!"

    Dim strSecretWord As String, intSecretWordLength As Integer
    Dim intNumberOfGuesses As Integer
    Dim strGuess As String, strWordGuessedSoFar As String
    Dim intLetterPos As Integer

    strSecretWord = "magic"
    intSecretWordLength = Len(strSecretWord)
```

```
strWordGuessedSoFar = String(intSecretWordLength, "-")
lblWord.Caption = strWordGuessedSoFar

intNumberOfGuesses = 0

strGuess = InputBox("Guess a letter (! to guess word)", "Hangman")
Do While strGuess <> strSentinel
    intNumberOfGuesses = intNumberOfGuesses + 1
    For intLetterPos = 1 To intSecretWordLength
        If StrComp(strGuess, Mid(strSecretWord, intLetterPos, 1), vbTextCompare) = 0 Then
            Mid(strWordGuessedSoFar, intLetterPos, 1) = strGuess
        End If
    Next intLetterPos
    lblWord.Caption = strWordGuessedSoFar
    strGuess = InputBox("Guess a letter (! to guess word)", "Hangman")
Loop

If strGuess = strSentinel Then
    strGuess = InputBox("Guess the word")
End If

If StrComp(strGuess, strSecretWord, vbTextCompare) = 0 Then
    MsgBox "You win! It took you " & intNumberOfGuesses & " guesses."
Else
    MsgBox "You lose. Press OK to display secret word."
End If

lblWord.Caption = strSecretWord
End Sub

Private Sub cmdDone_Click()
    Unload Me
End Sub
```

testing and debugging   This Case Study should be tested by entering correct and incorrect characters and correct and incorrect word guesses.

Running Hangman and guessing two correct letters displays:

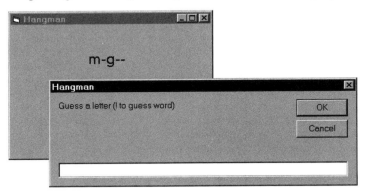

Review 15

Modify the Hangman Case Study to display the number of guesses and the player's score. The number of guesses should be displayed and updated as the game is played. The player should start with a score of 100, and have 10 points taken off for each incorrect guess. The score should be displayed and updated as the game is played.

Chapter Summary

looping structure

Controlling program flow allows for iteration, repeating one or more statements. In this chapter, the Do...Loop statement was used to control program flow. This statement is known as a looping structure because it evaluates a *condition* to determine if the loop is to be repeated. When the *condition* is True, the body *statements* are executed again and then the *condition* reevaluated. The loop is repeated until *condition* is False. Another form of Do...Loop evaluates the *condition* before executing the body of the loop.

infinite loop

Logic errors can result in an infinite loop. An infinite loop is a loop which continues forever. An application that has gone into an infinite loop can usually be interrupted by pressing Ctrl+Break.

InputBox

An input box is used to get information from the user. The InputBox function displays a Visual Basic predefined dialog box with a prompt, title, text box, and OK and Cancel buttons. It returns the text entered by the user or an empty string if the Cancel button is clicked.

accumulator

sentinel

An accumulator is a variable used to store a value that accumulates, or gets added to during run time. A sentinel is a constant that holds a special value to act as a flag signifying the end of a loop. A sentinel provides a clear and easy-to-change method for ending a loop.

LCase, UCase, StrConv

Left, Right, Mid

Len

InStr

Visual Basic includes several built-in functions for converting and manipulating strings. LCase, UCase, and StrConv are used to convert a string argument to all lowercase, uppercase, or proper case respectively. Left, Right, and Mid are used to return a substring of a specified length of the string argument starting from the beginning, end, or a specified starting position, respectively. The Len function returns a count of the number of characters in the string argument. The InStr function returns the position of a substring within a string.

For...Next

Step

The For...Next statement is a looping structure used to execute a set of statements a fixed number of times. This statement executes until *counter* reaches an ending value. The initialization of the loop is performed only once, and *end* is evaluated before each iteration of the loop body. After each iteration of the loop body, *counter* is incremented by 1. Step can be used to increment or decrement *counter* by a set amount.

String

Space

&

The String function is used to generate a string of repeating characters. The Space function generates a string of spaces. Concatenation is the process of joining two or more strings into one string and is performed with the & operator.

ASCII

Asc

Chr

ASCII code uses decimal numbers between 0 and 255 to represent every letter of the alphabet, numbers, and other special characters. The Asc function returns the ASCII code corresponding to a character argument. The Chr function returns the character corresponding to an ASCII code argument.

StrComp

Like

StrComp can be used to textually compare two string arguments. When the two string arguments are equal, 0 is returned. When the first string argument is greater than the second, 1 is returned. When the first string argument is less than the second, –1 is returned. The Like operator can be used to perform pattern matching which allows wildcard characters, character lists, and character ranges to match strings.

Vocabulary

Accumulator A variable used to store a value that accumulates, or gets added to during run time.

ASCII (American Standard Code for Information Interchange) A code that uses decimal numbers between 0 and 255 to represent characters on a personal computer.

Binary comparison Comparing characters by their internal binary representation.

Concatenation The process of joining two or more strings into one string.

Flag See Sentinel.

Infinite loop A loop that continues forever.

Input box A Visual Basic predefined dialog box that is used to get information from the user.

Iteration Repeating one or more statements.

Looping See Iteration.

Looping structure A statement that repeatedly executes code as long as a condition is True.

Pattern matching Allows wildcard characters (?, *, #), character lists, and character ranges ([A–M, Z]) to match strings using the Like operator.

Sentinel A constant that signifies the end of the loop.

Substring A portion of a string.

Textual comparison Comparing characters without distinguishing case.

Visual Basic

& Used to concatenate two or more strings.

Asc Function that returns the ASCII code which corresponds to a character argument.

Chr Function that returns the character corresponding to an ASCII code argument.

Do...Loop Statement that repeatedly executes code as long as a condition is True.

For...Next Statement that executes a loop body a fixed number of times.

InputBox Function used to generate a Visual Basic predefined dialog box that displays a prompt, text box, and OK and Cancel buttons.

InStr Function that returns the position of a substring in a string argument.

LCase Function used to convert a string argument to all lowercase characters.

Left Function that returns a substring of a specified length from the beginning of a string argument.

Len Function that returns a count of the number of characters in a string argument.

Like Operator used to perform textual comparison on strings and pattern matching using characters such as ?, *, #, [].

Mid Function that returns a substring of a specified length from a specified starting point of a string argument. Also, statement that is used to replace a specified number of characters in a string with another set of characters.

Right Function that returns a substring of a specified length from the end of a string argument.

Space Function used to generate a string of spaces.

Step Used in a For...Next statement to increment or decrement the counter by a set amount.

StrComp Function used to textually compare two string arguments.

StrConv Function used to convert a string argument to all uppercase, lowercase, or proper case.

String Function used to generate a string of repeating characters.

UCase Function used to convert a string argument to all uppercase characters.

Exercises

Exercise 1

Create a Password application that uses an input box to accept a password from the user before the interface for the program is displayed. The user can try to enter the correct password five times before a message box is displayed saying the password is not accepted and exits the program. The application should display an input box similar to the following when the program is first run:

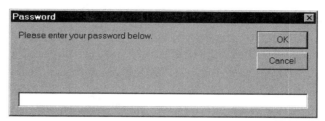

The application should display a message box similar to the following after the user has entered the wrong password five times:

The application interface should look similar to the following after the user has entered the correct password:

Exercise 2

A certificate of deposit (CD) allows you to invest an amount of money at a specified interest rate for a period of time. Create a CD Calculator application that accepts the initial investment amount, the annual interest rate, and the desired ending value in input boxes and then displays the number of years it will take for the CD to be worth the specified ending value when interest is compounded annually. The CD value at the end of each year can be calculated by the formula CD Value = CD Value + (CD Value * Interest Rate). To determine the number of years it will take for the CD to reach the desired ending value, repeatedly execute the formula until the CD Value is equal to or greater than the desired ending value. The application interface should look similar to:

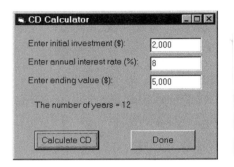

Exercise 3

a) Create a Bowling Scores application that allows the user to enter as many bowling scores as desired and then displays the high score and the low score. The application interface should look similar to the following after selecting the Enter Scores button, entering scores, and then clicking on the Statistics button:

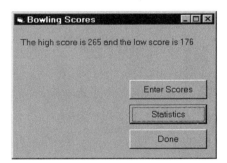

b) Modify the application to also calculate and display the average bowling score.

An Introduction to Programming Using Microsoft Visual Basic

Exercise 4

Create an Initials application that allows the user to enter his or her first and last names and then displays the initials of the name in uppercase. The application interface should look similar to:

Exercise 5

Create a Monogram application that allows the user to enter his or her first, middle, and last names and then displays a monogram with the first and middle initials in lowercase and the last initial in uppercase. The application interface should look similar to:

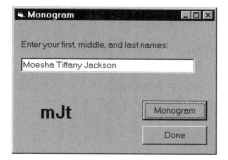

Exercise 6

Create an Average application that calculates the average of a series of numbers from 1 to a number entered by the user. For example, if the user enters 5 then the application would calculate the average of 1, 2, 3, 4, and 5. The application interface should looks similar to:

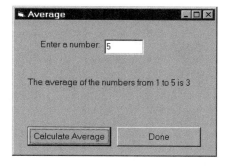

Exercise 7

Create a Sum application that calculates the sum of the numbers between two numbers inclusive entered by the user. For example, if the user enters 10 and 15 then the application would calculate 10+11+12+13+14+15. The application interface should look similar to:

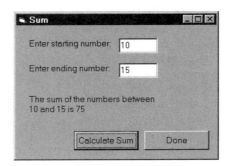

Exercise 8

An acronym is a word formed from the first letters of a few words, such as GUI for graphical user interface. Create an Acronym application that displays an acronym for the words entered by the user. The application should first display an input box asking the user how many words will make up the acronym, then display separate input boxes to get the words, and finally display the acronym in uppercase. The application interface should look similar to the following after clicking on the **Create Acronym** button and entering jelly bean as the words:

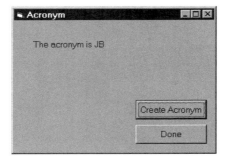

Exercise 9

As a young boy Franklin Roosevelt signed his letters to his mother backwards: Tlevesoor Nilknarf. Create a Name Backwards application that allows the user to enter his or her name and then displays the name backwards in proper case. The application interface should look similar to:

An Introduction to Programming Using Microsoft Visual Basic

Exercise 10

Create a Count Vowels application that counts the number of vowels in a word or phrase. The application interface should look similar to:

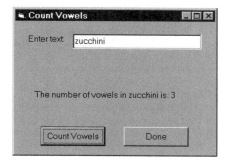

Exercise 11

Create an ASCII application that allows the user to enter a word and then displays the ASCII code for each letter in the word. The application interface should look similar to:

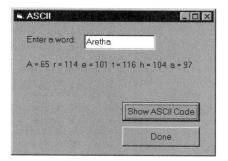

Exercise 12

Create a Spy Helper application to allow the user to encode or decode a message using ASCII codes. The application interface should look similar to the following after selecting the Encode option button and entering Meet me for lunch in the input box:

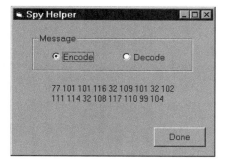

Exercise 13

A palindrome is a word or phrase that is spelled the same backwards and forwards, such as madam or dad. Create a Palindrome application that determines if the word or phrase entered by the user is a palindrome. The application interface should look similar to:

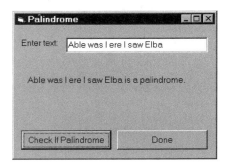

Exercise 14

Create a Student Group application that allows the user to enter a student name and then displays what group the student is in depending on the first letter in the student's last name. Names beginning with A through I are in Group 1, J through S are in Group 2, T through Z are in Group 3. The application interface should look similar to:

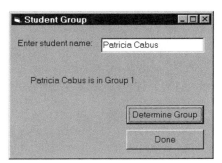

Advanced
Exercise 15

a) You are a spy who must use the computer to produce a secret code. Create an application that allows the user to enter a short message and displays the message in coded form. To produce the coded words, convert each letter in the original message to its corresponding ASCII code number, add 2 to the code number, and then convert back to characters to produce the message. Keep all spaces between the words in their original places and realize that the letters "Y" and "Z" are to be converted to A and B. Note: The user should be able to enter lowercase or uppercase letters and the code should be displayed in all uppercase.

b) Modify the program to decode the message produced in part (a).

An Introduction to Programming Using Microsoft Visual Basic

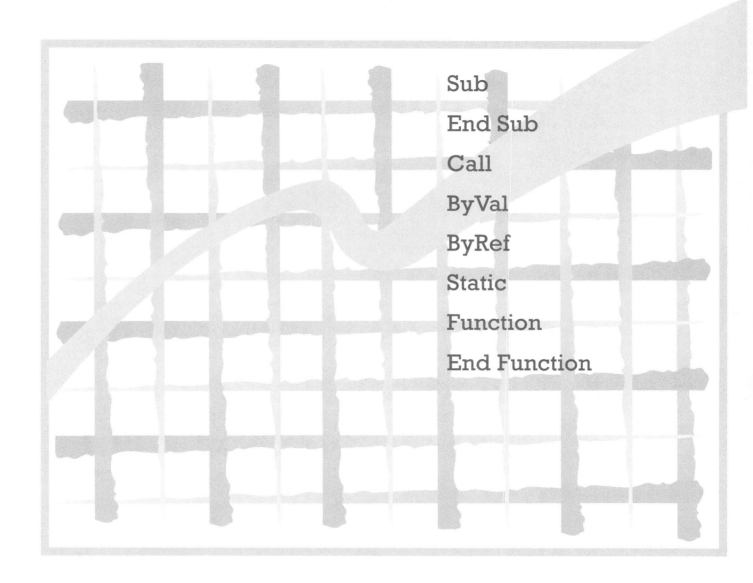

Sub

End Sub

Call

ByVal

ByRef

Static

Function

End Function

Chapter Seven Objectives

After completing this chapter you will be able to:

1. Understand Sub procedures and the **Call** statement.
2. Describe arguments, parameters, and how to pass data to a procedure.
3. Use **ByVal** and **ByRef** for parameters.
4. Document the preconditions and postconditions of a procedure.
5. Understand static variables and how they are initialized.
6. Create function procedures.
7. Use object parameters.

In this chapter you will learn how to write both general and function procedures. You will also use static variables in your programs to maintain a value between procedure calls.

7.1 Sub Procedures

procedure

A *procedure* is a block of code that performs a specific task. For example, the cmdDone_Click event procedure performs the task of ending an application. In Visual Basic, event procedures are referred to as *Sub procedures*.

general procedure

There are two types of Sub procedures, event procedures and general procedures. A general procedure takes the form:

Sub *ProcedureName()*
  statements
End Sub

ProcedureName is a descriptive name of the task performed by the procedure. *statements* is one or more statements that perform the task. **Sub** declares the procedure and **End Sub** is required to end the **Sub** statement.

General procedures are user-defined procedures that simplify a program by dividing it into smaller, more manageable blocks of code. A general procedure reduces redundancy by performing a task that may need to be executed several times throughout the program. For example, the following general procedure can be called whenever the Caption of the label needs to be cleared:

Sub ClearDirections()   'This is a general procedure
  lblDirections.Caption = ""
End Sub

Call

A general procedure must be *called* from another procedure in order to execute. The **Call** statement is used to execute a general procedure, as in the statements below:

Private Sub optBeachDirections_Click()
  Call ClearDirections
  Call ToBeach
End Sub

The event procedure above includes two **Call** statements: one to execute the ClearDirections general procedure, and another to execute the ToBeach general procedure. The event procedure is from the Directions application:

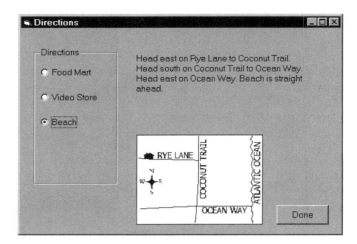

Note that some of the Sub procedures call other Sub procedures. Also note

line continuation

that a line continuation character (_) is used with very long statements:

```
Private Sub Form_Load()
    optFoodMartDirections.Value = False
    optVideoStoreDirections.Value = False
    optBeachDirections.Value = False
End Sub

Private Sub optBeachDirections_Click()
    Call ClearDirections
    Call ToBeach
End Sub

Sub ClearDirections()
    lblDirections.Caption = ""
End Sub

Sub ToBeach()
    Call ToOceanWay
    lblDirections.Caption = lblDirections.Caption & _
        "Head east on Ocean Way. Beach is straight ahead." & vbCrLf
End Sub

Sub ToOceanWay()
    Call ToCoconutTrail
    lblDirections.Caption = lblDirections.Caption & _
        "Head south on Coconut Trail to Ocean Way." & vbCrLf
End Sub

Sub ToCoconutTrail()
    lblDirections.Caption = "Head east on Rye Lane to Coconut Trail." _
        & vbCrLf
End Sub
…
```

When the Beach button is clicked, the optBeachDirections_Click event
procedure is executed. This procedure calls ClearDirections to clear the
lblDirections label. When ClearDirections is finished executing, program
control goes back to optBeachDirections_Click where the next statement
calls the ToBeach procedure. This procedure calls ToOceanWay which
calls ToCoconutTrail. ToCoconutTrail assigns to lblDirections a string of
directions to Coconut Trail and a carriage return-linefeed. ToOceanWay
and ToBeach concatenate additional directions and a carriage return-
linefeed to the lblDirections label. With directions separated into procedures, it is easy to add additional destinations to the application.

An Introduction to Programming Using Microsoft Visual Basic

creating a general procedure

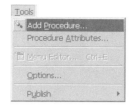

General procedures are added in the Code Editor window by typing Sub followed by the procedure name and then pressing Enter. When this is done, Visual Basic automatically adds an **End Sub** statement and places the cursor in the body of the procedure. A procedure may also be added by selecting the Add Procedure command from the Tools menu. The Add Procedure command displays a dialog box where the procedure name, type, and scope is selected. Selecting OK then places the procedure in alphabetical order in the Code Editor window.

Review 1

The Directions application from Section 7.1 needs to be modified to include directions to a restaurant and a gift shop.

1) OPEN THE DIRECTIONS PROJECT

Display the Directions form if it is not already displayed.

2) MODIFY THE APPLICATION INTERFACE

An option button needs to be added to the form. Refer to the form below when placing the new option button. Be sure to draw the object on the frame so that is it part of the group. Use the table below to name and change the properties of the object.

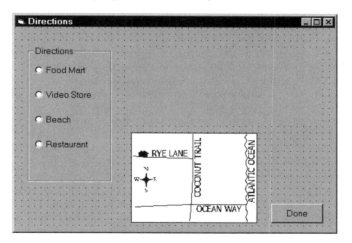

Object	Name	Caption
Option1	optRestaurantDirections	Restaurant

3) MODIFY AND ADD PROGRAM CODE

The restaurant is located on the beach. The Form_Load procedure needs to be modified and the ToRestaurant and optRestaurantDirections_Click procedures need to be added to the program.

a. Display the Code Editor window and add the following statement to the Form_Load event procedure:

```
optRestaurantDirections.Value = False
```

b. Place the cursor after the **End Sub** statement of the ToBeach procedure, press Enter twice, and then add the following procedure:

```
Sub ToRestaurant()
  Call ToBeach
  lblDirections.Caption = lblDirections.Caption & _
    "Smitty's is located at the north end of the beach." & vbCrLf
End Sub
```

c. Add an optRestaurantDirections_Click event procedure with the following statements:

```
Private Sub optRestaurantDirections_Click()
    Call ClearDirections
    Call ToRestaurant
End Sub
```

4) RUN THE APPLICATION

Save the modified Directions project and then run the application. Test the application by selecting each of the option buttons and verifying the corresponding directions are logical.

5) ADD A GIFT SHOP OPTION BUTTON

A popular gift shop is located adjacent to the video store.

a. Modify the Directions application to include a Gift Shop option button that when selected displays the directions to the gift shop.

b. Save the modified Directions project and then run the application. Test the Gift Shop option button by clicking on it.

6) PRINT AND THEN REMOVE THE PROJECT

Review 2

Create an Employee Info application that displays employee information (name, telephone number, birthday) in a single label after entering an employee ID (1, 2, 3, 4, or 5) in a text box and clicking the Display Info button. There should be one general procedure corresponding to each employee ID. The application interface should look similar to that shown on the right after entering 1 and clicking on the Display Info button.

7.2 Value Parameters

passing data

A procedure often needs data in order to complete its task. Data is given, or *passed*, to a procedure by enclosing it in parentheses in the procedure call. For example, the statement below calls the GiveHint procedure and passes two values to it, intSecretNumber and intGuess:

```
Call GiveHint(intSecretNumber, intGuess)
```

argument

A variable or value passed to a procedure is called an *argument*. In the statement above, intSecretNumber and intGuess are the arguments to be used by the procedure.

parameter

A procedure that requires arguments is declared with *parameters* and takes the following form:

```
Sub ProcedureName(ByVal parameter1 As type, ...)
    statements
End Sub
```

ByVal

ProcedureName is the name of the procedure. **ByVal** indicates that the parameter is a value parameter, *parameter1* is the name of the parameter, and *type* is the data type of the parameter. There can be many parameters separated by commas. *statements* is the body of the procedure.

The GiveHint procedure is shown below:

```
Sub GiveHint (ByVal intFirstNum As Integer, ByVal intSecondNum As Integer)
    If intFirstNumber > intSecondNumber Then
        MsgBox "Too low."
    Else
        MsgBox "Too high."
    End If
End Sub
```

When GiveHint is called, the value of the first argument, intSecretNumber, is assigned to the first parameter, intFirstNum, and the value of the second argument to the second parameter. When a procedure is called, the number of arguments must match the number of parameters.

Note how GiveHint is independent of the rest of the program. It does not rely on any other information except what it has been passed, and its parameters were given names meaningful to GiveHint but not necessarily to the calling procedure. Generic procedures such as this one can be easily reused in other programs, making coding more efficient.

The following points are important to keep in mind when working with procedures that have value parameters:

- The order in which arguments are passed is important because the order of the arguments corresponds to the order of the parameters. Therefore, the first argument in the procedure call corresponds to the first parameter, and so on.

- Arguments passed by value can be in the form of constants, variables, values, or expressions. For example, the GiveHint **Call** statement may take any of the following forms:

    ```
    Call GiveHint(intSecretNumber, intGuess)
    Call GiveHint(2*5, 10*2)
    Call GiveHint(10, intGuess)
    Call GiveHint(10, 20)
    ```

- Variable arguments passed by value are not changed by the procedure. For example, consider the following code:

    ```
    Sub Demo ()
        Dim intCounter As Integer
        intCounter = 1
        Call ShowCount(intCounter)
        lblNumber.Caption = intCounter        '1
    End Sub

    Sub ShowCount (ByVal intCounter As Integer)
        intCounter = intCounter + 1
        MsgBox intCounter                     '2
    End Sub
    ```

When the **Call** ShowCount(intCounter) statement executes, a copy of intCounter is passed to the ShowCount procedure. Note that the parameter receiving the value of the argument has the same name, intCounter. ShowCount then increments its local variable intCounter by 1 and then displays 2 in a message box. When ShowCount terminates, the local copy of intCounter is destroyed and program control is sent back to Demo. The lblNumber label is then assigned the value of intCounter, which is still 1 because the value of intCounter is unaffected by the ShowCount procedure.

7.3 Documenting Procedures

Just as comments are used to clarify statements, comments should also be used to describe, or *document*, procedures. Procedure documentation should include a brief description of what the procedure does followed by any preconditions and postconditions. The initial requirements of a procedure are called its *preconditions*. The *postcondition* is a statement of what must be true at the end of the execution of a procedure if the procedure has worked properly. A procedure may not have a precondition, but every procedure must have a postcondition.

precondition
postcondition

Below is the GiveHint procedure with proper documentation. It does not have a precondition. Note that precondition is referred to as pre and postcondition as post:

```
'**********************************************************************
'  Determines if intSecondNum is larger than intFirstNum and then displays an
'  appropriate message
'
'  post: A message is displayed in a message box
'**********************************************************************
Sub GiveHint (ByVal intFirstNum As Integer, ByVal intSecondNum As Integer)
    If intFirstNum > intSecondNum Then
        MsgBox "Too low."
    Else
        MsgBox "Too high."
    End If
End Sub
```

Review 3

Follow the instructions below to modify the Guess Number application.

1) OPEN THE GUESS NUMBER PROJECT

Display the Guess Number form if it is not already displayed.

2) MODIFY THE PROGRAM CODE

Display the Code Editor window and then modify the cmdCheckGuess_Click procedure as shown below and add the GiveHint procedure:

```
Private Sub cmdCheckGuess_Click()
    Dim intUserGuess As Integer

    intUserGuess = txtGuess.Text

    'Add guess to label
    lblNumbersGuessed.Caption = lblNumbersGuessed.Caption & _
        intUserGuess & " "
```

Modify If...Then
```
    If intUserGuess <> intSecretNumber Then
        Call GiveHint(intSecretNumber, intUserGuess)
        txtGuess.Text = ""
    Else
        MsgBox "You guessed it!"
    End If
End Sub
```

```
'*********************************************************************
'   Determines if intSecondNum is larger than intFirstNum and then displays an
'   appropriate message
'
'   post:  A message is displayed in a message box
'*********************************************************************
Sub GiveHint(ByVal intFirstNum As Integer, ByVal intSecondNum As Integer)
    If intFirstNum > intSecondNum Then
        MsgBox "Too low."
    Else
        MsgBox "Too high."
    End If
End Sub
```

3) RUN THE APPLICATION

Save the modified Guess Number project and then run the application. Test the application by entering numbers and clicking on the Check Guess button.

4) PRINT AND THEN REMOVE THE PROJECT

Review 4

The Restaurant Rating application displays an overall rating for a restaurant as a row of stars; 4 stars for excellent, 3 stars for good, 2 stars for fair, and 1 star for poor. The rating is an average of scores. Follow the instructions below to modify the Restaurant Rating application.

1) OPEN THE RESTAURANT RATING PROJECT

Display the Restaurant Rating form if it is not already displayed.

2) MODIFY THE PROGRAM CODE

a. Display the Code Editor window and then add the DisplayRating procedure below the cmdOverallRating_Click procedure:

```
'***************************************************
'   Displays a string of asterisks in a message box
'
'   post: intScore asterisks displayed in a message box
'***************************************************
Sub DisplayRating(ByVal intScore As Integer)
    MsgBox String(intScore, "*")
End Sub
```

b. Add the following Call statement to the cmdOverallRating_Click event procedure:

```
...
    intAvgRating = (intAmbianceRating + intFoodRating + intServiceRating) / 3
    Call DisplayRating(intAvgRating)
End Sub
```

3) RUN THE APPLICATION

Save the modified Restaurant Rating project and then run the application. Test the application by entering different scores for ambiance, food, and service.

4) PRINT AND THEN REMOVE THE PROJECT

7.4 Reference Parameters

A procedure that needs to send values back to the calling procedure should be declared with reference parameters. *Reference parameters* can alter the value of the variable arguments used in the procedure call. A procedure with reference parameters takes the following form:

```
Sub ProcedureName(ByRef parameter1 As type, ...)
    statements
End Sub
```

ByRef

ProcedureName is the name of the procedure. **ByRef** indicates that the parameter is by reference, *parameter1* is the name of the parameter, and *type* is the data type of the parameter. There can be many parameters in a procedure. A procedure can have both reference (**ByRef**) and value (**ByVal**) parameters. *statements* is the body of the procedure.

The TwoDigits procedure returns the first and second digits of a two-digit number in separate variables:

```
'******************************************************************
'  The first digit of intNum is returned as intFirstDigit. The second digit of
'  intNum is returned as intSecondDigit
'
'  pre: intNum is a number less than 100 and greater than -100
'  post: intFirstDigit is a number between 0 and 9 inclusive
'  intSecondDigit is a number between 0 and 9 inclusive
'******************************************************************
Sub TwoDigits (ByVal intNum As Integer, ByRef intFirstDigit As Integer, _
ByRef intSecondDigit As Integer)

    intFirstDigit = intNum \ 10
    intSecondDigit = intNum Mod 10
End Sub
```

The following event below calls TwoDigits:

```
Private Sub DisplayDigits_Click()
    Dim intNum As Integer
    Dim intTensDigit As Integer, intOnesDigit As Integer

    intNum = 27
    Call TwoDigits(intNum, intTensDigit, intOnesDigit)
    lblTensDigit.Caption = intTensDigit        '2
    lblOnesDigit.Caption = intOnesDigit        '7
End Sub
```

address

When TwoDigits is called, a copy of the first argument is assigned to intNum and the addresses of the next two arguments are given to intFirstDigit and intSecondDigit. The *address* of a variable is the location in memory where its value is stored. The **ByRef** parameters refer to argument memory locations:

```
DisplayDigits_Click
    ...
    Call TwoDigits ( 27  intNum,  0  intTensDigit,  0  intOnesDigit)

TwoDigits (  intNum, intFirstDigit, intSecondDigit)
```

The ByVal parameter uses a new memory location to store its corresponding argument's value. The ByRef parameters simply refer to the memory locations of their corresponding arguments.

The LowestToHighest procedure below is another example of a procedure that uses reference parameters:

```
'*************************************************************************
' Determines if intLowest is the lesser of two values and then swaps
' intLowest and intHighest if necessary
'
' post: intLowest is assigned the lesser of the two arguments passed.
' intHighest is assigned the greater of the two arguments passed
'*************************************************************************
Sub LowestToHighest (ByRef intLowest As Integer, ByRef intHighest As Integer)
    Dim intTemp As Integer

    If intLowest > intHighest Then      'swap values
        intTemp = intLowest
        intLowest = intHighest
        intHighest = intTemp
    End If
End Sub
```

When LowestToHighest is called, the values of the passed arguments are switched if the first argument's value is greater than the second. For example, when the following statements are executed

```
intNum1 = 30
intNum2 = 12
Call LowestToHighest(intNum1, intNum2)
lblOrderedNumbers.Caption = intNum1 & " " & intNum2      '12 30
```

LowestToHighest is passed the addresses of intNum1 and intNum2. Since intLowest has a greater value than intHighest, intTemp is assigned 30, then intLowest is assigned 12, and finally intHighest is assigned 30, the value of intTemp. When LowestToHighest has finished executing, the values at the addresses of intNum1 and intNum2 have been swapped, and lblOrderedNumbers displays 12 30.

The following points are important to keep in mind when working with procedures with reference parameters:

- The order of the arguments corresponds to the order of the parameters.

- ByRef parameters accept only variable arguments. For example, a run-time error will be generated when LowestToHighest is called with constants, as in the statement:

  Call LowestToHighest(5, 1)   'Bad Call Statement

- Variable arguments passed by reference may be changed by the procedure.

Parameters

When a variable is passed by value, its value is stored in a new memory location. After the procedure has finished executing, this memory location no longer stores the value. When a variable is passed by reference, the parameter refers to the memory location of the argument passed.

Review 5

Follow the instructions below to modify the Number Breakdown application to display the separate digits of a number up to three digits.

1) OPEN THE NUMBER BREAKDOWN PROJECT

Display the Number Breakdown form if it is not already displayed.

2) MODIFY THE PROGRAM CODE

The ThreeDigits procedure will call TwoDigits to get the first two digits of a number and then use integer division to determine the third digit (the hundreds digit) of the number.

a. Display the Code Editor window and add the ThreeDigits procedure after the TwoDigits procedure:

```
'************************************************************
'  The first digit of intNum is returned as intFirstDigit. The
'  second digit of intNum is returned as intSecondDigit. The third
'  digit of intNum is returned as intThirdDigit.
'
'  pre: intNum is a number less than 1000 and greater than -1000.
'  post: intFirstDigit is a number between 0 and 9 inclusive.
'  intSecondDigit is a number between 0 and 9 inclusive.
'  intThirdDigit is a number between 0 and 9 inclusive.
'************************************************************
Sub ThreeDigits(ByVal intNum As Integer, ByRef intFirstDigit As Integer, _
    ByRef intSecondDigit As Integer, ByRef intThirdDigit As Integer)

    intFirstDigit = intNum \ 100
    intNum = intNum Mod 100
    Call TwoDigits(intNum, intSecondDigit, intThirdDigit)
End Sub
```

b. Modify the cmdBreakDown_Click procedure to break down a three-digit number:

```
        Private Sub cmdBreakDown_Click()
            Dim intNumberEntered As Integer
            Dim intTensDigit As Integer, intOnesDigit As Integer
Add         Dim intHundredsDigit As Integer

            intNumberEntered = txtNumber.Text
            If intNumberEntered < 10 Then
               lblNumberBreakdown.Caption = "The first digit is: " & intNumberEntered
            ElseIf intNumberEntered < 100 Then
               Call TwoDigits(intNumberEntered, intTensDigit, intOnesDigit)
               lblNumberBreakdown.Caption = "The first digit is: " & intTensDigit & _
                  vbCrLf & "The second digit is: " & intOnesDigit
Add ElseIf    ElseIf intNumberEntered < 1000 Then
               Call ThreeDigits(intNumberEntered, intHundredsDigit, intTensDigit, intOnesDigit)
               lblNumberBreakdown.Caption = "The first digit is: " & intHundredsDigit & _
                  vbCrLf & "The second digit is: " & intTensDigit & _
                  vbCrLf & "The third digit is: " & intOnesDigit
            Else
Modify         lblNumberBreakdown.Caption = "Enter a number less than 1,000."
            End If
        End Sub
```

3) RUN THE APPLICATION

Save the modified Number Breakdown project and then run the application. Test the application using single, double, and triple digit numbers.

4) PRINT AND THEN REMOVE THE PROJECT

Review 6

Create a Sort Numbers application that accepts two numbers and then displays them in sorted order when the Sort button is clicked. The program code should use the LowestToHighest procedure discussed in the previous section. The application interface should look similar to that shown on the right after entering 5 and 2 and then clicking on the Sort button.

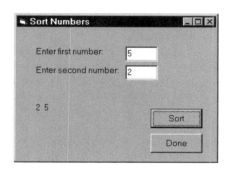

7.5 Static Variables

As discussed in Chapter Five, the scope of a variable is its accessibility among procedures. A local variable is available only to the procedure in which it is declared, while a global variable is available to every procedure in the module. In addition to scope, variables have a *lifetime* in which they exist in memory. The lifetime of a local variable is the duration of the procedure in which it was declared. A global variable's lifetime is the duration of the program.

lifetime

Another way in which a variable may be declared is static. A *static variable's* scope is local to the procedure in which it is declared, but its lifetime is the duration of the program. Static variables are declared using the keyword **Static** instead of **Dim**. Note that as a matter of good programming style static variables are preferred over global variables because their use does not interfere with other procedures.

programming style

The Add Numbers application includes the cmdAdd_Click event procedure which uses a static variable to maintain a running total:

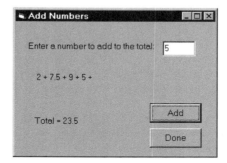

```
Private Sub cmdAdd_Click()
    Dim dblNumberEntered As Double
    Static dblTotal As Double

    dblNumberEntered = txtNewNum.Text
    dblTotal = dblTotal + dblNumberEntered            'running total

    lblNumbersAdded.Caption = lblNumbersAdded & " " _
        & dblNumberEntered & " +"
    lblTotal.Caption = "Total = " & dblTotal
End Sub
```

In the cmdAdd_Click procedure, dblTotal is declared as a static variable. Like all variables, static variables are initialized by Visual Basic when they are declared. Since static variables have a lifetime the duration of the program, their declaration takes place only the first time a procedure is executed. If dblTotal were not a static variable, it would re-declared and re-initialized to 0 each time the user clicked the **Add** button.

initializing a static variable   As discussed in Chapter Four, Visual Basic initializes variables when they are declared. Numeric variables are initialized to 0, **String** variables are initialized to an empty string, and **Boolean** variables are initialized to False. If a static variable needs to be initialized to a value other than that given by Visual Basic, an **If...Then** statement should be used. For example, the following code initializes a static variable to 100:

```
...
Static intX As Integer
If intX = 0 Then          'Initialize to 100
    intX = 100
End If
...
```

Review 7

Follow the directions below to create the Add Numbers application.

1) CREATE A NEW PROJECT

2) ADD OBJECTS TO THE FORM

Refer to the form below when placing and sizing the form and its objects. Use the table below to name and change the properties of the objects.

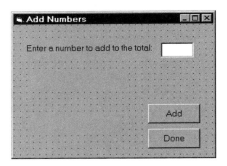

Object	Name	Caption	Text
Form1	frmAddNumbers	Add Numbers	
Label1	lblDirections	*see label text above*	
Text1	txtNewNum		*empty*
Label2	lblNumbersAdded	*empty*	
Label3	lblTotal	*empty*	
Command1	cmdAdd	Add	
Command2	cmdDone	Done	

3) SAVE THE PROJECT

From the File menu, select Save Project. Save the form naming it frmAddNumbers and save the project naming it Add Numbers.

4) ADD THE PROGRAM CODE

Display the Code Editor window and add the following event procedures:

```
Private Sub cmdAdd_Click()
    Dim dblNumberEntered As Double
    Static dblTotal As Double

    dblNumberEntered = txtNewNum.Text
    dblTotal = dblTotal + dblNumberEntered          'running total

    lblNumbersAdded.Caption = lblNumbersAdded & " " _
        & dblNumberEntered & " +"
    lblTotal.Caption = "Total = " & dblTotal
End Sub

Private Sub cmdDone_Click()
    Unload Me
End Sub
```

5) RUN THE APPLICATION

Save the modified Add Numbers project and then run the application. Test the application by entering numbers and clicking on the Add button.

6) PRINT AND THEN REMOVE THE PROJECT

When should a function be used?
A general procedure should be used when a procedure's task includes altering a parameter's value or when a procedure returns more than one value through **ByRef** parameters. Therefore, as a general rule, use a function when a procedure's task should result in a single value.

7.6 Function Procedures

A function procedure, often just called a *function*, performs a specific task and then returns a value. For example, Visual Basic contains several built-in functions including Int, LCase, and Len. A user-defined function takes the following form:

```
Function ProcedureName(ByVal parameter1 As type, ...) As Returntype
    statements
End Function
```

ProcedureName is a descriptive name of the task performed by the function. **ByVal** indicates that the parameter is by value, *parameter1* is the name of the parameter, and *type* is the data type of the parameter. There can be many parameters in a function procedure. *Returntype* indicates the data type of the value returned by the function. *statements* is one or more statements that perform a task. *statements* must include a statement that assigns the return value to *ProcedureName*. **Function** declares the procedure and **End Function** is required to end the **Function** statement.

A function often has at least one parameter for data that is required to perform its task. However, parameters are **ByVal** because a function performs a task and returns a single value. It should not alter the arguments it has been passed.

Functions are called from within a statement that will make use of the return value, as in the assignment statement below:

```
lblStudentGrade.Caption = LetterGrade(dblAverage)
```

The lblStudentGrade label displays the string returned by the LetterGrade function:

```
'**********************************************
'  Returns a letter grade corresponding to dblScore
'
'  post: a letter grade returned
'**********************************************
Function LetterGrade (ByVal dblScore As Double) As String
    If dblScore >= 90 Then
        LetterGrade = "A"
    ElseIf dblScore >= 80 Then
        LetterGrade = "B"
    ElseIf dblScore >= 70 Then
        LetterGrade = "C"
    ElseIf dblScore >= 60 Then
        LetterGrade = "D"
    Else
        LetterGrade = "F"
    End If
End Function
```

Note that in the function above, the letter grade to be returned is assigned to the procedure name.

Functions are useful for validating user input. For example, an application that asks the user to enter a value between 1 and 10 could use the following Boolean function to determine if user input is in the desired range:

```
'*************************************************************
'  Returns True if intUpperLimit < intUserNum < intUpperLimit
'
'  post: True returned if intUpperLimit < intUserNum < intUpperLimit
'        otherwise False returned
'*************************************************************
Function ValidEntry (ByVal intUserNum As Integer, ByVal intUpperLimit As Integer, _
ByVal intLowerLimit As Integer) As Boolean
    If intUserNum > intUpperLimit Or intUserNum < intLowerLimit Then
        ValidEntry = False
    Else
        ValidEntry = True
    End If
End Function
```

The following code uses ValidEntry to check user input:

```
...
intGuess = txtUserGuess.Text
If Not ValidEntry(intGuess, 10, 1) Then
    MsgBox "Invalid Guess. Please try again."
End If
...
```

Note how the Boolean value returned by the function is used as the condition of the If...Then statement.

The following points are important to keep in mind when working with functions:

- The order of the arguments corresponds to the order of the parameters.

- Only **ByVal** parameters should be declared in a function because a function should not alter the arguments it has been passed.

- A function returns a single value and therefore must be used in a statement such as an assignment statement that makes use of the returned value.

Review 8

Follow the directions below to create the Letter Grade application.

1) **CREATE A NEW PROJECT**

2) **ADD OBJECTS TO THE FORM**

Refer to the form below when placing and sizing the form and its objects. Use the table below to name and change the properties of the objects.

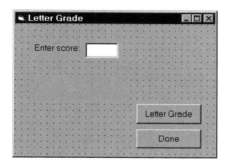

Object	Name	Caption	Text
Form1	frmLetterGrade	Letter Grade	
Label1	lblScore	Enter score:	
Text1	txtScore		*empty*
Label2	lblLetterGrade	*empty*	
Command1	cmdLetterGrade	Letter Grade	
Command2	cmdDone	Done	

3) **SAVE THE PROJECT**

From the File menu, select Save Project. Save the form naming it frmLetterGrade and save the project naming it Letter Grade.

4) **ADD THE PROGRAM CODE**

Display the Code Editor window and add the following code:

```
Private Sub cmdLetterGrade_Click()
    Dim dblScoreEntered As Double

    dblScoreEntered = txtScore.Text
    lblLetterGrade.Caption = "Your grade is " & LetterGrade(dblScoreEntered)
End Sub

Private Sub txtScore_Change()
    lblLetterGrade.Caption = ""
End Sub
```

```
'***********************************************
'  Returns a letter grade corresponding to dblScore
'
'  post: a letter grade returned
'***********************************************
Function LetterGrade (ByVal dblScore As Double) As String
   If dblScore >= 90 Then
      LetterGrade = "A"
   ElseIf dblScore >= 80 Then
      LetterGrade = "B"
   ElseIf dblScore >= 70 Then
      LetterGrade = "C"
   ElseIf dblScore >= 60 Then
      LetterGrade = "D"
   Else
      LetterGrade = "F"
   End If
End Function

Private Sub cmdDone_Click()
   Unload Me
End Sub
```

5) RUN THE APPLICATION

Save the modified Letter Grade project and then run the application. Test the application by entering 90, 75, and 30.

6) MODIFY THE APPLICATION TO CHECK USER INPUT

The Letter Grade application should not accept scores less than 0 or greater than 100. Display the Code Editor window and modify the cmdLetterGrade_Click procedure and add a ValidEntry function, as shown below:

```
          Private Sub cmdLetterGrade_Click()
Add          Const dblLowestScore As Double = 0
Add          Const dblHighestScore As Double = 100
             Dim dblScoreEntered As Double

             dblScoreEntered = txtScore.Text

Add If...Then   If Not ValidEntry(dblScoreEntered, dblHighestScore, dblLowestScore) Then
             MsgBox "Enter a score between " & dblLowestScore & " and " & dblHighestScore
             txtScore.Text = ""
             lblLetterGrade.Caption = ""
          Else
             lblLetterGrade.Caption = "Your grade is " & LetterGrade(dblScoreEntered)
          End If
          End Sub

'*************************************************************
'  Returns True if intLowerLimit < intUserNum < intUpperLimit
'
'  post: True returned if intLowerLimit < intUserNum < intUpperLimit
'  otherwise False returned
'*************************************************************
Function ValidEntry (ByVal intUserNum As Integer, ByVal intUpperLimit As Integer, _
ByVal intLowerLimit As Integer) As Boolean
   If intUserNum > intUpperLimit Or intUserNum < intLowerLimit Then
      ValidEntry = False
   Else
      ValidEntry = True
   End If
End Function
```

An Introduction to Programming Using Microsoft Visual Basic

7) RUN THE APPLICATION

Save the modified Letter Grade project and then run the application. Test the application by entering 101, 80, and -10.

8) PRINT AND THEN REMOVE THE PROJECT

Review 9 ——————————————————————

Using paper and pencil, write a RndInt function that has intLowNum and intHighNum parameters and returns a random integer in the range intLowNum to intHighNum. Properly document the function.

7.7 Using Object Parameters

class

Simple data types include **Integer**, **Double**, and **String**. These data types are used to declare variables and constants. A *class* is a data type used to declare an object. For example, each object in an application interface is of a particular class. An image is an Image class object, a command button is a CommandButton class object, and a label is a Label class object.

Since objects have a data type associated with them, they can be passed as arguments and declared as procedure parameters. For example, the statements below pass a Label object to a procedure that has a Label parameter:

```
...
Call DisplayMessage (lblMessage, "Good job!")
...

'************************************************************
'  Displays a message in a label object
'
'  post: strMessage is assigned to the Caption of lblLabel
'************************************************************
Sub DisplayMessage (ByRef lblLabel As Label, ByVal strMessage As String)
    lblLabel.Caption = strMessage
End Sub
```

When the statements above are executed, the text Good job! is displayed in the Caption of lblMessage. Note that object parameters should be **ByRef**. Objects discussed in this text and their classes are:

Object	Class	Object	Class
Label	Label	Option button	OptionButton
Command button	CommandButton	Frame	Frame
Image	Image	Check box	CheckBox
Text box	TextBox		

Review 10 ☼ ——————————————————————

Follow the instructions below to modify the Guess Number application.

1) OPEN THE GUESS NUMBER PROJECT

Display the Guess Number form if it is not already displayed.

2) MODIFY THE PROGRAM CODE

a. Display the Code Editor window and then add the DisplayMessage procedure below the GiveHint procedure:

```
'***********************************************************
' Displays a message in a label object
'
' post: strMessage is assigned to the Caption of lblLabel
'***********************************************************
Sub DisplayMessage (ByRef lblLabel As Label, ByVal strMessage As String)
    lblLabel.Caption = strMessage
End Sub
```

b. In the cmdCheckGuess_Click event procedure, replace the lblNumbersGuess.Caption assignment with:

```
'Add guess to label
Call DisplayMessage(lblNumbersGuessed, lblNumbersGuessed.Caption & _
intUserGuess & " ")
```

3) RUN THE APPLICATION

Save the modified Guess Number project and then run the application. Test the application by entering different numbers and clicking on the Check Guess button.

4) PRINT AND THEN REMOVE THE PROJECT

Case Study

In this Case Study a Game of 21 application will be created.

specification   The specification for this Case Study is:

The Game of 21 application deals three cards to the user (player) and three cards to the computer. The cards dealt are randomly selected and are in the range 1 to 10, inclusive. The winner is displayed in a message (You won!, Computer won!, or It's a draw!) and a score is updated and displayed (1 point for each win). The user has the option of repeatedly playing the game and the scores are maintained until the user quits the application.

design   The form design for this Case Study is:

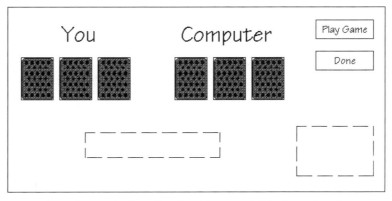

The form design for the Game of 21 Case Study

Note that two labels are sketched with dotted lines to indicate that their Captions will not appear until run time. In this case, one label displays the winner of the hand dealt, and the other label displays the scores. When the application first starts, the backs of the cards are shown. Clicking on Play Game "deals" a hand of cards to both the player and the computer.

The program code design for this Case Study is best done by listing the pseudocode for event procedures:

```
Private Sub Form_Load()
   Randomize
End Sub

Private cmdPlayGame_Click()
   Deal 3 cards to player
   Deal 3 cards to computer

   If Winner = Player Then
      UpdateScore(PlayerScore)
      ShowScore
   ElseIf Winner = Computer Then
      UpdateScore(CompScore)
      ShowScore
   Else
      UpdateScore(DrawScore)
      ShowScore
   End If
End Sub

Private Sub cmdDone_Click()
   Unload Me
End Sub
```

coding   The interface for this Case Study is:

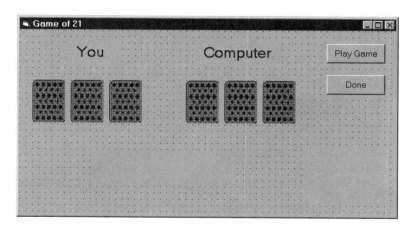

Object	Name	Caption	Picture
Form1	frmGameof21	Game of 21	
Label1	lblYou	You	
Label2	lblComputer	Computer	
Image1	imgPlayerCard1		Cardback.wmf
Image2	imgPlayerCard2		Cardback.wmf

Object	Name	Caption	Picture
Image3	imgPlayerCard3		Cardback.wmf
Image4	imgCompCard1		Cardback.wmf
Image5	imgCompCard2		Cardback.wmf
Image6	imgCompCard3		Cardback.wmf
Label3	lblWinner	*empty*	
Label4	lblScore	*empty*	
Command1	cmdPlayGame	Play Game	
Command2	cmdDone	Done	

The coding for this Case Study will be done in two steps. In the first step, the cmdPlayGame_Click event procedure will be coded. Coding this main procedure will help clarify the coding of the general and function procedures. Global constant declarations, the Form_Load procedure and the cmdPlayGame_Click event procedures are:

```
Option Explicit

Private Const strPlayer As String = "Player"
Private Const strComputer As String = "Computer"
Private Const strDraw As String = "Draw"

Private Sub Form_Load()
  Randomize
End Sub

Private Sub cmdPlayGame_Click()
  Static intPlayerScore As Integer, intCompScore As Integer
  Static intDrawsScore As Integer
  Dim intPlayerTotal As Integer, intCompTotal As Integer

  'Deal 3 cards to Player
  Call DealCard(imgPlayerCard1, intPlayerTotal)
  Call DealCard(imgPlayerCard2, intPlayerTotal)
  Call DealCard(imgPlayerCard3, intPlayerTotal)

  'Deal 3 cards to Computer
  Call DealCard(imgCompCard1, intCompTotal)
  Call DealCard(imgCompCard2, intCompTotal)
  Call DealCard(imgCompCard3, intCompTotal)

  If Winner(intPlayerTotal, intCompTotal) = strPlayer Then
    lblWinner.Caption = "You won!"
    Call UpdateScore(intPlayerScore)
    Call ShowScore(lblScore, intPlayerScore, intCompScore, intDrawsScore)
  ElseIf Winner(intPlayerTotal, intCompTotal) = strComputer Then
    lblWinner.Caption = "Computer won!"
    Call UpdateScore(intCompScore)
    Call ShowScore(lblScore, intPlayerScore, intCompScore, intDrawsScore)
  Else
    lblWinner.Caption = "It's a draw!"
    Call UpdateScore(intDrawsScore)
    Call ShowScore(lblScore, intPlayerScore, intCompScore, intDrawsScore)
  End If
End Sub
```

There are several details to note in the cmdPlayGame procedure above. First, **Static** variables are used for maintaining the number of wins and draws. These variables need to be **Static** so that their values are maintained after the procedure has finished executing. If they were not **Static**, they would be redeclared and reinitialized to 0 by Visual Basic each time the Play Game button is clicked. Second, a DealCard procedure is used to change the card assigned to each image object. Third, a Winner function is used to determine the winner of the hand. Lastly, an UpdateScore procedure and a ShowScore procedure are used to update and display the current score after each hand of cards. The design of the cmdPlayGame_Click procedure can be viewed as:

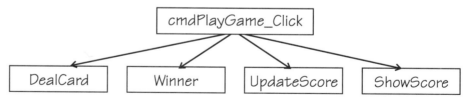

The complete Game of 21 code is shown below:

```
Option Explicit

Private Const strPlayer As String = "Player"
Private Const strComputer As String = "Computer"
Private Const strDraw As String = "Draw"

Private Sub Form_Load()
    Randomize
End Sub

Private Sub cmdPlayGame_Click()
    Static intPlayerScore As Integer, intCompScore As Integer, intDrawsScore As Integer
    Dim intPlayerTotal As Integer, intCompTotal As Integer

    'Deal 3 cards to Player
    Call DealCard(imgPlayerCard1, intPlayerTotal)
    Call DealCard(imgPlayerCard2, intPlayerTotal)
    Call DealCard(imgPlayerCard3, intPlayerTotal)

    'Deal 3 cards to Computer
    Call DealCard(imgCompCard1, intCompTotal)
    Call DealCard(imgCompCard2, intCompTotal)
    Call DealCard(imgCompCard3, intCompTotal)

    If Winner(intPlayerTotal, intCompTotal) = strPlayer Then
        lblWinner.Caption = "You won!"
        Call UpdateScore(intPlayerScore)
        Call ShowScore(lblScore, intPlayerScore, intCompScore, intDrawsScore)
    ElseIf Winner(intPlayerTotal, intCompTotal) = strComputer Then
        lblWinner.Caption = "Computer won!"
        Call UpdateScore(intCompScore)
        Call ShowScore(lblScore, intPlayerScore, intCompScore, intDrawsScore)
    Else
        lblWinner.Caption = "It's a draw!"
        Call UpdateScore(intDrawsScore)
        Call ShowScore(lblScore, intPlayerScore, intCompScore, intDrawsScore)
    End If
End Sub
```

```
'***************************************************************************
'  Displays a card corresponding to a random number in the range 1 to 10
'
'  pre: Randomize called
'  post: imgCard displays a card in the range 1 to 10 and updates intPlayerTotal score
'***************************************************************************
Sub DealCard(ByRef imgCard As Image, ByRef IntPlayerTotal As Integer)
   Dim intCardNum As Integer

   intCardNum = Int(10 * Rnd + 1)
   If intCardNum = 1 Then
      imgCard.Picture = LoadPicture("Card1.wmf")
   ElseIf intCardNum = 2 Then
      imgCard.Picture = LoadPicture("Card2.wmf")
   ElseIf intCardNum = 3 Then
      imgCard.Picture = LoadPicture("Card3.wmf")
   ElseIf intCardNum = 4 Then
      imgCard.Picture = LoadPicture("Card4.wmf")
   ElseIf intCardNum = 5 Then
      imgCard.Picture = LoadPicture("Card5.wmf")
   ElseIf intCardNum = 6 Then
      imgCard.Picture = LoadPicture("Card6.wmf")
   ElseIf intCardNum = 7 Then
      imgCard.Picture = LoadPicture("Card7.wmf")
   ElseIf intCardNum = 8 Then
      imgCard.Picture = LoadPicture("Card8.wmf")
   ElseIf intCardNum = 9 Then
      imgCard.Picture = LoadPicture("Card9.wmf")
   ElseIf intCardNum = 10 Then
      imgCard.Picture = LoadPicture("Card10.wmf")
   End If
   intPlayerTotal = intPlayerTotal + intCardNum
End Sub

'***************************************************************************
'  Returns a string indicating the winner
'
'  post: global constant strPlayer, strComputer, or strDraw returned
'***************************************************************************
Function Winner(ByVal intPlayerTotal As Integer, ByVal intCompTotal As Integer) As String
   Const intLimit As Integer = 21

   If (intPlayerTotal = intCompTotal) Or _
      (intPlayerTotal > intLimit And intCompTotal > intLimit) Then
      Winner = strDraw
   ElseIf (intCompTotal > intLimit) Or _
      (intPlayerTotal > intCompTotal And intPlayerTotal <= intLimit) Then
      Winner = strPlayer
   Else
      Winner = strComputer
   End If
End Function

'***************************************************************************
'  Updates the score of intWinner
'
'  post: intWinner has been increased by intWinPoints
'***************************************************************************
Sub UpdateScore(ByRef intWinner As Integer)
   Const intWinPoints As Integer = 1

   intWinner = intWinner + intWinPoints
End Sub
```

An Introduction to Programming Using Microsoft Visual Basic

```
'*******************************************************************************
'  Displays the current score of Player, Computer, and draws
'
'  post: scores displayed in a label
'*******************************************************************************
Sub ShowScore (ByRef lblLabel As Label, ByVal intPlayerScore As Integer, _
ByVal intCompScore As Integer, ByVal intDrawsScore As Integer)
    lblScore.Caption = "You: " & intPlayerScore & vbCrLf _
        & "Computer: " & intCompScore & vbCrLf _
        & "Draws: " & intDrawsScore
End Sub

Private Sub cmdDone_Click()
    Unload Me
End Sub
```

LoadPicture

The DealCard procedure uses a random number in the range 1 to 10 to determine the card to display in the image box. With this random number, the Visual Basic built-in function LoadPicture is then used to change the image in the image box. The argument passed to LoadPicture is the name of the graphic file in quotation marks. A complete path is also required when the graphic file is not in the home directory. DealCard then returns the value of the card so that this number can be added to the appropriate total.

The Winner function compares the totals of the two hands and returns the winner. The UpdateScore procedure adds 1 to the winner's score, and the ShowScore procedure displays the current scores in a label.

testing and debugging

This Case Study should be tested by verifying by hand that the correct winner of a hand has been selected. The scores should be noted over several hands to be sure they are being updated correctly.

Running Game of 21 and clicking on the Play Game button displays the following:

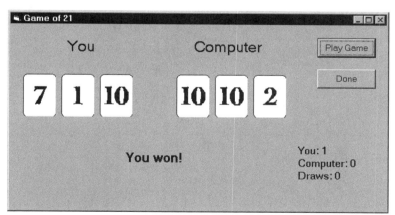

Review 11

The cards dealt in the Game of 21 Case Study application are unrealistic in that it is just as likely to draw a 1 as a 10. A regular deck of cards also has Jacks, Queens, and Kings that all count as ten-point cards. Modify the Game of 21 Case Study application so that cards are drawn from 1 to 13, with cards 1 to 10 counting as their value, and cards 11, 12, and 13 counting as ten points. Use the Jack, Queen, and King.wmf graphics for cards 11, 12, and 13.

Chapter Summary

general procedure

A procedure is a block of code that performs a specific task. Sub procedures include event and general procedures. General procedures are user-defined procedures that simplify a program by dividing it into smaller, more manageable blocks of code. A general procedure reduces redundancy by performing a task that may need to be executed several times throughout the program.

creating a general procedure

Call

General procedures are created by typing them in the Code Editor window or by using the Add Procedure command from the Tools menu. The Call statement is used to execute a general procedure.

argument
parameter

ByVal, ByRef

A procedure can be passed data for use in completing its task. The data passed is called the arguments and a procedure that requires arguments is declared with parameters. ByVal parameters create a local copy of the argument passed and cannot alter the actual value of the variable. ByRef parameters use the actual variable passed and can alter the value of the variable.

documentation

pre, post

Procedures need to be documented using comments. Documentation should include a brief description of what the procedure does followed by any preconditions and postconditions.

Static

lifetime

Static variables are used when a procedure's variables need to maintain their value for the duration of the program. A static variable's scope is local to the procedure in which it is declared, but its lifetime is the duration of the program. The lifetime of a variable is the time in which it exists in memory. Static variables are declared using the keyword Static instead of Dim. If a static variable needs to be initialized to a value other than that given by Visual Basic, an If...Then statement should be used.

function procedure

A function is a procedure that returns a value. Functions often have at least one parameter for data that is required to perform its task. However, parameters are ByVal because a function performs a task and returns a value. It should not alter the arguments it has been passed. Functions are called from within a statement that make use of the return value.

class

A class is a data type used to declare an object. For example, an image is an Image class object and a command button is a CommandButton class object. Since objects have a data type associated with them, they can be passed as arguments and declared as procedure parameters.

Vocabulary

Address A variable's location in memory where its value is stored.

Argument A variable or value passed to a procedure.

Class A data type used to declare an object.

Documentation Comments that describe a procedure and any preconditions or postconditions of the procedure.

Function procedure A procedure that performs a specific task and then returns a value. Also just called a "function."

General procedure A user-defined Sub procedure.

Lifetime The time in which a variable exists in memory.

Parameter A variable declared in a procedure to accept the value or address of an argument.

Pass Giving data to a procedure.

Postcondition A statement of what must be true at the end of the execution of a procedure if the procedure has worked properly. Also just called "post."

Precondition The initial requirements of a procedure. Also just called "pre."

Procedure A block of code that performs a specific task. Procedures simplify a program by dividing it up into smaller, more manageable tasks.

Reference parameter A variable declared in a procedure to accept the address of an argument. Reference parameters can alter the value of the variable arguments used in the procedure call.

Static variable A variable with scope local to the procedure in which it is declared and a lifetime the duration of the program.

Sub procedure A procedure that is an event procedure or a general procedure.

Value parameter A variable declared in a procedure to accept a copy of an argument. Value parameters cannot alter the value of the arguments used in the procedure call.

Visual Basic

Add Procedure command Used to add a procedure to the Code Editor window. Found in the Tools menu.

ByRef Keyword used to declare a reference parameter in a general procedure.

ByVal Keyword used to declare a value parameter in a general or function procedure.

Call Statement used to execute a general procedure.

End Function Statement used to end the Function statement.

End Sub Statement used to end the Sub statement.

Function Statement used to declare a function procedure.

LoadPicture Function that is used to change the image in an image box.

Static Keyword used in place of Dim to declare a static variable.

Sub Statement used to declare a procedure.

Exercises

Exercise 1

Create a Diskette Tips application that displays one of the following messages when the user clicks on the Tip button:

> Keep diskettes away from electrical and magnetic devices.
> Do not expose diskettes to either extreme cold or heat.
> Store diskettes away from dust, dirt, and moisture.
> Never touch the diskette's magnetic surface.

The application interface should look similar to the following after clicking on the Tip button:

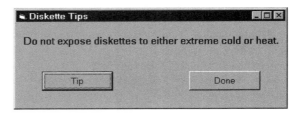

Your program code should use a DisplayTip procedure to randomly assign one of the tips listed above to the label on the form.

Exercise 2

Create an Add Coins application that allows the user to enter numbers of quarters, dimes, nickels, and pennies and then displays the total dollar amount. The application interface should look similar to:

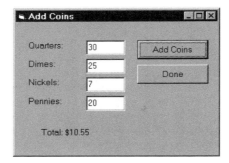

Your program code should use a TotalDollars procedure that has intQuarters, intDimes, intNickels, and intPennies value parameters to assign the result to the label on the form.

Exercise 3

Create a Reduce Fraction application that takes an integer numerator and denominator of a fraction and then displays the fraction reduced or a message stating the fraction cannot be reduced. A fraction may be reduced by finding the largest common factor and dividing both the numerator and denominator by this factor. The application interface should look similar to:

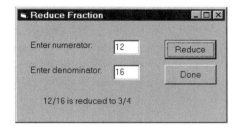

Your program code should use a Reduce procedure that has intNum and intDenom reference parameters and changes the value of these parameters, if necessary, to the reduced values.

Exercise 4

Create a Test Build application that breaks up and then rebuilds numbers 100 through 125 and displays them in a label on the form. The application interface should look similar to the following after clicking on the Break Up and Rebuild button:

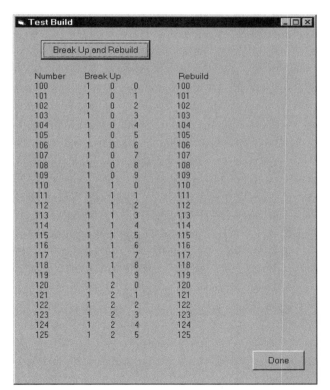

Your program code should use:

- the ThreeDigits procedure from Review 5.
- a Build procedure that has intFirstDigit, intSecondDigit, and intThirdDigit value parameters and returns, in an intBuiltNumber reference parameter, a value that consists of the number represented by the three digits.

Exercise 5

Create an Addition Calculator application that is based on the Add Numbers application presented in Section 7.5. In the Addition Calculator application, the + button should be coded similar to the Add button in the Add Numbers application. The application interface should look similar to the following after clicking on the 1, 2, +, 2, +, 5, +, 3 buttons. Note that 3 has not been added to the sum yet because the + button has not been clicked:

Exercise 6

Your office building uses an alarm system that requires those wishing to gain entry to enter a master code and then press Enter. The master code for your office building is 62498. Create an Alarm System application that displays a message box with an appropriate message if the user clicks on the correct numbers and then clicks on Enter. The application interface should look similar to the following after clicking five number buttons:

Your program code should use a VerifyCode function that has an intCode parameter and returns True if intCode matches the master code and False if intCode does not match the master code.

Exercise 7

The following formulas can be used to convert English units of measurement to metric units:

inches * 2.54 = centimeters
feet * 30 = centimeters
yards * 0.91 = meters
miles * 1.6 = kilometers

Create a Metric Conversion application that allows the user to enter a number and then convert from inches to centimeters, feet to centimeters, yards to meters, and miles to kilometers and vice versa. The application interface should look similar to:

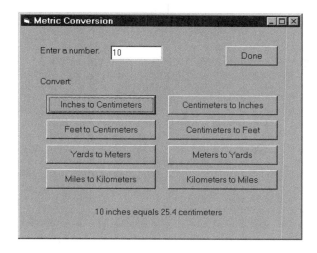

Your program code should also use separate functions to determine the English to metric and metric to English conversion calculations.

Exercise 8

Validating user input is often required in programs. Create a Test Entries application that allows the user to enter an integer, decimal number, and letter and then displays if the values entered by the user are valid. The application interface should look similar to:

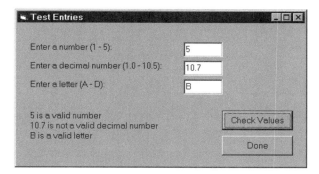

Your program code should use:

- a ValidInt function that has intHighNum, intLowNum, and intNumber parameters and returns True if intNumber is in the range intLowNum to intHighNum, and False otherwise.

- a ValidDouble function that has dblHighNum, dblLowNum, and dblNumber parameters and returns True if dblNumber is in the range dblLowNum to dblHighNum, and False otherwise.
- a ValidChar function that has strHighChar, strLowChar, strCharacter parameters and returns True if strCharacter is in the range strLowChar to strHighChar, and False otherwise.

Exercise 9

The basic unit of lumber measurement is the board foot. One board foot is the cubic content of a piece of wood 12 inches by 12 inches by 1 inch thick. For example, a board that is 1 inch thick by 8 feet long by 12 inches wide is 8 board feet:

$$((1 * (8 * 12) * 12) / (12 * 12 * 1)) = 8$$

Milled wood is cut to standardized sizes called board, lumber, and timber. A board is one-inch thick or less, timber is more than four inches thick, and lumber is anything between one and four inches thick. Create a Lumberyard Helper application allows the user to enter the thickness, length, and width of a piece of wood and then displays the board feet and the name of the wood. The application interface should look similar to:

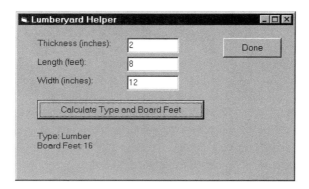

Your program code should use:

- a BoardFeet function that has dblThickness, dblLength, and dblWidth parameters and returns the number of board feet.
- a WoodName function that has a dblThickness parameter and returns the name of the wood.

An Introduction to Programming Using Microsoft Visual Basic

Exercise 10

In the Hi-Lo Game, the player begins with a score of 1000. The player enters the number of points to risk and chooses High or Low. The player's choice of high or low is compared to a random number between 1 and 13, inclusive. If the number is between 1 and 6 inclusive, it is considered "low." If it is between 8 and 13 inclusive, it is considered "high." The number 7 is neither high nor low, and the player loses the points at risk. If the player guesses correctly, he or she receives double the points at risk. If the player guesses incorrectly, he or she loses the points at risk. Create a Hi-Lo Game application that allows the user to enter the number of points to risk and pick either high or low and then displays the result. The application interface should look similar to:

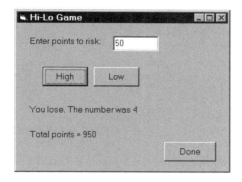

Your program code should use the RndInt function from Review 9 to generate the random number between 1 and 13 inclusive.

Exercise 11

Create a Dice Game application where the player begins with a score of 1000. The player enters the number of points to risk and then clicks on Roll Dice. The points on each die is displayed. If the total is even, the player loses the points at risk. If the total is odd, the player receives double the points at risk. The Dice Game application interface should look similar to:

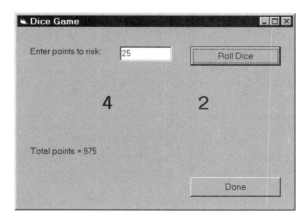

Your program code should use the RndInt function from Review 9 to generate a random number between 1 and 6 inclusive for each die.

Exercise 12

The game of Nim starts with a random number of stones between 15 and 30. Two players alternate turns and on each turn may take either 1, 2, or 3 stones from the pile. The player forced to take the last stone loses. Create a Nim application that allows the user to play against the computer. In this version of the game, the application generates the number of stones to begin with, the number of stones the computer takes, and the user goes first. The application interface should look similar to:

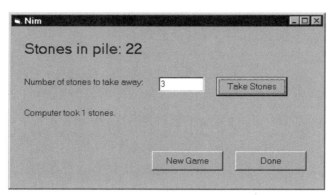

Include code that prevents the user and the computer from taking an illegal number of stones. For example, neither should be allowed to take three stones when there are only 1 or 2 left. Your program code should use:

- the ValidEntry function presented in Section 7.6 to check the number entered by the user.
- the RndInt function from Review 9 to generate a random number from 1 to 3 for the computer's turn to remove stones from the pile.
- separate procedures for the user's turn and the computer's turn.

Exercise 13

The game of Mastermind is played as follows: one player (the codemaker) chooses a secret arrangement of colored pegs and the other player (the codebreaker) tries to guess it. After each guess, the codemaker reports two numbers:

1. The number of pegs that are the correct color in the correct position.
2. The number of pegs that are the correct color regardless of whether they are in the correct position.

Create a Mastermind application where the computer is the codemaker and the player is the codebreaker. For simplicity, do not allow the secret arrangement of colored pegs to have duplicate colors and do not allow the codebreaker to guess duplicate peg colors. The application interface should look similar to:

An Introduction to Programming Using Microsoft Visual Basic

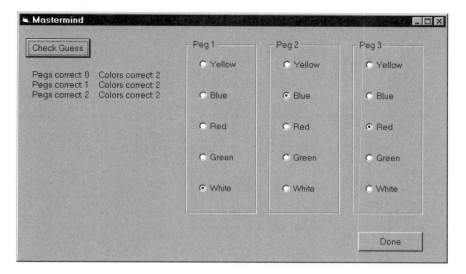

Your program code should:

- use a ChooseColors procedure that has intPeg1Color, intPeg2Color, and intPeg3Color reference parameters to generate unique colors for the secret arrangement of the colored pegs. Use numbers 1 through 5 to represent colors and use the RndInt function from Review 9 to generate a random number.
- generate the secret arrangement of the colored pegs in the cmdCheckGuess_Click procedure. intPeg1Color, intPeg2Color, and intPeg3Color should be static variables that get assigned a number representing a color the first time the player makes a guess. The following pseudocode can be used to assign a color to a peg:

```
If intPeg1Color = 0 Then     'First time variable used
    Call the ChooseColors procedure
End If
```

- use separate functions to determine the number of correct colors and the number of correct pegs each time the player makes a guess.

Exercise 14

Create a Funny Sentences application that allows the user to enter a noun, verb, and adjective and then displays a sentence using these words. The application interface should look similar to:

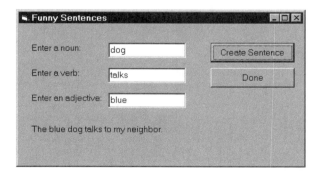

Your program code should use a MakeSentence procedure that has strNoun, strVerb, and strAdjective value parameters and returns, in a lblLabel reference parameter, the sentence displayed in the Caption of the label object. Use numbers 1 through 5 to represent five different sentences of your choosing and use the RndInt function from Review 9 to generate a random number.

Advanced
Exercise 15

Computers are used to test a student's ability to solve arithmetic problems. Create an application that will test a student on addition, subtraction, or multiplication using random integers between 1 and 100. The student begins by choosing the type of problem and is then asked 10 problems with 3 chances to answer each correctly. If after 3 chances the answer is still incorrect, the correct answer is displayed. A score is calculated by awarding 10 points for a correct answer on the first try, 5 points on the second try, 2 points on the third try, and 0 points if all three attempts are wrong. Your program code should contain procedures, functions, and static variables.

Advanced
Exercise 16

A new pet store has opened up in your neighborhood and needs an application to keep track of their inventory. The pet store currently has 15 puppies, 10 kittens, 8 canaries, and 52 fish. Create an application that keeps a running total of how many pets are in stock by subtracting animals that are sold and adding new animal deliveries to the stock.

An Introduction to Programming Using Microsoft Visual Basic

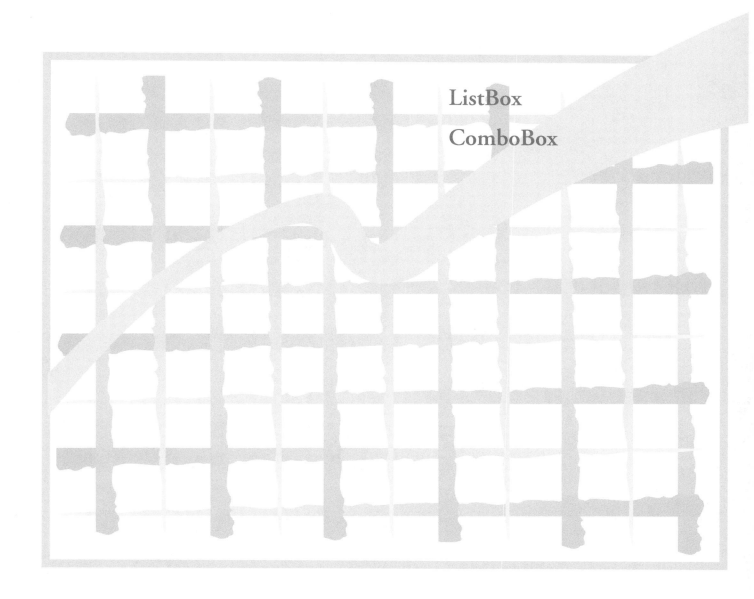

ListBox

ComboBox

Chapter Eight Objectives

After completing this chapter you will be able to:

1. Use the Abs, Sqr, and Sgn mathematical functions.
2. Use the IsNumeric and Round functions.
3. Format numeric output.
4. Use the Pmt, PV, and FV business functions.
5. Use list box objects and combo box objects in applications.
6. Understand Windows application standards, including focus, access keys, tab order, and disabled objects.
7. Use the Sin, Cos, and Tan trigonometric functions.
8. Convert degrees to radians and the reverse.
9. Use the Atn function to determine the arctangent, arcsine, and arccosine of an angle.
10. Use the Log and Exp functions.

Most of the earliest uses for computers were for performing mathematical calculations. One of the very first programming languages was called FORTRAN, which stands for FORmula TRANslator. Another programming language is COBOL (COmmon Business Oriented Language), which was written for creating business applications. Visual Basic has many built-in functions for creating math and business applications.

8.1 Built-in Mathematical Functions

Abs

Visual Basic includes several built-in mathematical functions, such as Abs, Sqr, and Sgn. The Abs function returns the absolute value of a number and takes the form:

Abs(*number*)

number is a numeric variable or value. The following code demonstrates Abs:

```
Dim intNegativeNumber As Integer
intNegativeNumber = -5
lblAnswer.Caption = Abs(intNegativeNumber)        '5
```

Sqr

The Sqr function returns the square root of a number and takes the form:

Sqr(*number*)

number is a positive numeric variable or value. The following code demonstrates Sqr:

```
Dim intNumber As Integer
intNumber = 9
lblAnswer.Caption = Sqr(intNumber)                '3
```

If a negative argument is used in the Sqr function a run time error occurs.

Sgn

The Sgn function returns 1, –1, or 0 when the numeric argument is positive, negative, or 0 respectively. The Sgn function takes the form:

Sgn(*number*)

number is a numeric variable or value. The following code demonstrates Sgn:

```
Dim intNumber As Integer
intNumber = -5
lblAnswer.Caption = "The sign of " & intNumber & _
    " is " & Sgn(intNumber)              'The sign of -5 is -1
intNumber = 3
lblAnswer.Caption = "The sign of " & intNumber & _
    " is " & Sgn(intNumber)              'The sign of 3 is 1
```

8.2 The IsNumeric Function

The IsNumeric function is a Visual Basic built-in function that returns True if its argument can be evaluated as a number and False if it cannot. The IsNumeric function takes the form:

IsNumeric(*argument*)

argument can be a numeric or string expression or variable. The following code demonstrates IsNumeric:

```
Dim strString As String
strString = "123"
lblAnswer.Caption = IsNumeric(strString)    'True

strString = "abc"
lblAnswer.Caption = IsNumeric(strString)    'False

lblAnswer.Caption = IsNumeric("2+4")        'False
lblAnswer.Caption = IsNumeric(2 + 4)        'True
```

Note that "123" evaluates to a number because the string contains only numbers. However, "2+4" is False because the string contains characters other than numbers. In this case, since the + character is not a number, the expression evaluates to a string.

Review 1

Create a Mathematical Functions application that includes a text box for the user to enter a number and command buttons that when clicked display the absolute value, square root, or whether the number is positive, negative, or zero. Use the IsNumeric function to verify user input is numeric. Display an appropriate message if the user enters non-numeric data. The application interface should look similar to that shown on the right after entering 9 and clicking on the **Square Root** button.

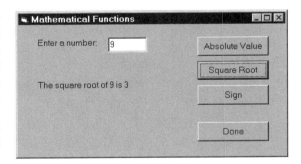

8.3 The Round Function

The Round function can be used to round numeric data to a specified number of decimal places. The Round function takes the form:

Round(*number, decimal places*)

number is a numeric variable or value and *decimal places* is the number of decimal places *number* is rounded to. The following code demonstrates Round:

```
Dim dblNumber As Double
dblNumber = 3.4567
lblAnswer.Caption = Round(dblNumber, 2)     '3.46
```

Review 2

Create a Round the Number application that includes text boxes for the user to enter a number and the number of decimal places to round to and a command button that when clicked displays the rounded number. The application interface should look similar to that shown on the right after entering 23.45788 and 3 and clicking on the Round button.

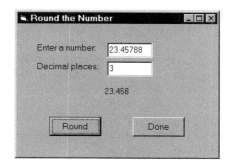

8.4 Formatting Numeric Output

Format

The Format function can be used to format, or change the appearance of, numeric data. The Format function takes the form:

Format(*number*, "*format type*")

number is a numeric variable or value and *format type* is a predefined Visual Basic format. The following code demonstrates Format and the different format types:

```
lblAnswer.Caption = Format(8789, "General Number")   '8789
lblAnswer.Caption = Format(8789, "Currency")         '$8,789.00
lblAnswer.Caption = Format(8789, "Fixed")            '8789.00
lblAnswer.Caption = Format(8789, "Standard")         '8,789.00
lblAnswer.Caption = Format(89, "Percent")            '8900.00%
lblAnswer.Caption = Format(8789, "Scientific")       '8.79E+3
lblAnswer.Caption = Format(1, "Yes/No")              'Yes
lblAnswer.Caption = Format(0, "True/False")          'False
lblAnswer.Caption = Format(1, "On/Off")              'On
```

Formatting a number changes only its appearance in the application, unlike rounding a number, which changes the value stored in memory.

8.5 Built-in Business Functions

Pmt

Visual Basic includes built-in business functions such as Pmt, PV, and FV. Pmt returns the periodic payment for an installment loan. The Pmt function takes the form:

Pmt(*rate*, *term*, *principal*)

rate is the interest rate per period, *term* is the total number of payments to be made, and *principal* is the amount borrowed. For example, the Pmt function would be used to determine the monthly payment on a mortgage loan. The statements below calculate the monthly payments on a 30-year, $100,000 loan with an annual interest rate of 6%:

```
Dim dblPayments As Double
dblPayments = Pmt(0.06 / 12, 360, -100000)          'calculate payment
lblAnswer.Caption = Format(dblPayments, "Currency") '$599.55
```

Since the payments are monthly, the interest rate must also be computed monthly by dividing the annual rate of interest 6% by 12. The number of payments is 360, 30 years * 12 months. The principal is negative because it is the amount borrowed.

PV   PV returns the present value of an investment. The PV function takes the form:

PV(*rate, term, payment*)

rate is the interest rate per period, *term* is the total number of payments to be made, and *payment* is the amount invested per period. For example, the PV function would be used to determine the cost of financing a car. The statements below calculate the cost of financing when $250 per month over a 4-year period is applied to a loan with an interest rate of 8%:

```
Dim dblAmountSpent As Double
Dim dblFinancing As Double
Dim dblPresentValue As Double

dblAmountSpent = 250 * 12 * 4                          '12000
dblPresentValue = PV(0.08 / 12, 48, –250)             '10240.48
dblFinancing = dblAmountSpent – dblPresentValue       '1759.52
lblAnswer.Caption = Format(dblFinancing, "Currency")  '$1,759.52
```

This means that when you apply $250 a month for 4 years to an 8% loan, $1,759.52 is spent on financing, and $10,240.48 is available for purchasing the car. Note that the interest rate and term are expressed as months.

As another example, the following statements determine the amount you can afford to borrow with a 15-year mortgage at 10% when you desire monthly payments of $650:

```
Dim dblBorrowAmount As Double
dblBorrowAmount = PV(0.10 / 12, 180, –650)
lblAnswer.Caption = Format(dblBorrowAmount, "Currency") '$60,487.34
```

FV   FV returns what a series of equal payments invested at a fixed interest rate will be worth after a period of time. The FV function takes the form:

FV(*rate, term, investment*)

rate is the interest rate per period, *term* is the total number of investment payments to be made, and *investment* is the amount invested per period. For example, assume you invest $500 per month in a retirement plan earning 8% interest per year. The statements below determine how much the retirement plan will be worth after 20 years:

```
Dim dblFutureValue As Double
dblFutureValue = FV(0.08 / 12, 240, -500)             'calculate future value
lblAnswer.Caption = Format(dblFutureValue, "Currency") '$294,510.21
```

Note again that the interest rate and term are expressed as months.

Amortization

Amortization is a method for computing equal periodic payments for an installment loan. Car loans and mortgages are often installment loans. Each installment, or payment, is the same and consists of two parts: a portion to pay interest due on the principal for that period and the remainder which goes to reducing the principal. The principal is the amount of money owed which decreases with each payment made.

Data Entry with Business Applications

The IsNumeric function recognizes the $ character and returns True if the characters after the $ are numeric. In addition, values assigned to a **Currency** variable may contain a $ character.

Review 3

Follow the instructions below to create the Installment Loan Payments application.

1) CREATE A NEW PROJECT

2) ADD OBJECTS TO THE FORM

Refer to the form below when placing and sizing the form and its objects. Use the table below to name and change the properties of the objects.

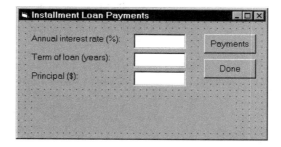

Object	Name	Caption	Text
Form1	frmInstallmentLoanPayments	Installment Loan Payments	
Label1	lblInterestRate	Annual interest rate (%):	
Text1	txtInterestRate		*empty*
Label2	lblTerm	Term of the loan (years):	
Text2	txtTerm		*empty*
Label3	lblPrincipal	Principal:	
Text3	txtPrincipal		*empty*
Label4	lblAnswer	*empty*	
Command1	cmdPayments	Payments	
Command2	cmdDone	Done	

3) SAVE THE PROJECT

From the File menu, select Save Project. Save the form naming it frmInstallmentLoanPayments and save the project naming it Installment Loan Payments.

4) WRITE THE PROGRAM CODE

Display the Code Editor window and add the following event procedures:

```
Private Sub txtInterestRate_Change()
    lblAnswer.Caption = ""
End Sub

Private Sub txtTerm_Change()
    lblAnswer.Caption = ""
End Sub

Private Sub txtPrincipal_Change()
    lblAnswer.Caption = ""
End Sub

Private Sub cmdPayments_Click()
    Dim dblInterestRate As Double, intTerm As Integer, curPrincipal As Currency
    Dim curAnswer As Currency

    dblInterestRate = txtInterestRate.Text / 100
    intTerm = txtTerm.Text
    curPrincipal = txtPrincipal.Text
    curAnswer = Pmt(dblInterestRate / 12, intTerm * 12, -curPrincipal)
    lblAnswer.Caption = "The monthly payments for a loan of " & _
        Format(curPrincipal, "Currency") & " at " & Format(dblInterestRate, "Percent") _
        & " for " & intTerm & " years is " & Format(curAnswer, "Currency")
End Sub

Private Sub cmdDone_Click()
    Unload Me
End Sub
```

5) RUN THE APPLICATION

Save the modified Installment Loan Payments project and then run the application. Test the application by entering 7.5 as the interest rate, 5 as the term, and 20,000 as the principal.

6) PRINT AND THEN REMOVE THE PROJECT

Review 4

Create a How Much Can I Borrow application that includes text boxes for the user to enter the annual interest rate, term, and the payment to be made each month on a loan and a command button that when clicked displays the amount of the loan (present value). The application interface should look similar to that shown on the right after entering the displayed loan information and clicking on the Loan Amount button.

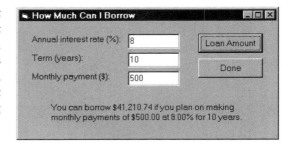

Review 5

Create a Watch Your Money Grow application that includes text boxes for the user to enter the annual interest rate, term, and the amount invested each month and a command button that when clicked displays the value of the investment at the end of the time period. The application interface should look similar to that shown on the right after entering the displayed investment information and clicking on the Future Value button.

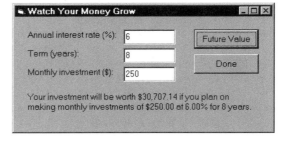

8.6 List Boxes

List boxes allow the user to select a value from a set of values. For example, in the Tuition Calculator application, list boxes are used to select the course level:

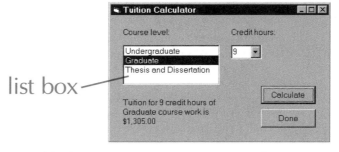

List boxes are one way to get user input

list box   A *list box* object is created using the ListBox control () in the Tool box and has the properties:

• **Name** identifies the object and is used by the programmer. It is good programming style to begin list box object names with lst.

- **List** stores a group of strings that make up the list.

- **Sorted** displays the items in the list in alphabetical order. Sorted is only available at design time.

- **Text** stores the selected list item. Text is only available at run time.

- **ListCount** can be used only at run time to determine the number of items in the list.

click event   A click event is sometimes coded for a list box. The click event procedure is executed when the user clicks on an item in the list box. The value of the item is stored in the text property of the list box object.

A scrollbar automatically appears in the list box if the number of list items exceeds the size of the list box.

AddItem   The AddItem method is used to add an item to the end of the list at run time and takes the form:

lstControl.AddItem *Item*

lstControl is the name of the list box object and *Item* is a **String** variable or a string in quotation marks that is to be added to the list. The AddItem method and the List property are both used to add items to the list. The difference is AddItem is used at run time and List is used at design time. The AddItem method is useful for displaying output in a list box. The following code demonstrates AddItem:

```
Private Sub Form_Load()
    lstCourseLevel.AddItem strUndergrad
    lstCourseLevel.AddItem strGrad
    lstCourseLevel.AddItem strThesis
End Sub
```

Clear   The Clear method is used to delete the contents of the list box at run time and takes the form:

lstControl.Clear

lstControl is the name of the list box object. The following code demonstrates Clear:

```
Private Sub ClearList()
    lstCourseLevel.Clear
End Sub
```

Review 6

Follow the instructions below to create the Tuition Calculator application.

1) CREATE A NEW PROJECT

2) ADD OBJECTS TO THE FORM

Refer to the form on the next page when placing and sizing the form and its objects. Use the table on the next page to name and change the properties of the objects.

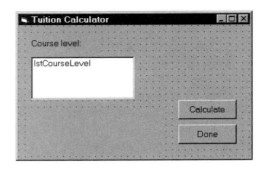

Object	Name	Caption
Form1	frmTuitionCalculator	Tuition Calculator
Label1	lblCourseLevel	Course level:
List1	lstCourseLevel	
Label2	lblAnswer	*empty*
Command1	cmdCalculate	Calculate
Command2	cmdDone	Done

3) **SAVE THE PROJECT**

From the File menu, select Save Project. Save the form naming it frmTuitionCalculator and save the project naming it Tuition Calculator.

4) **WRITE THE PROGRAM CODE**

Display the Code Editor window and add the following code:

```
Option Explicit
Private Const strUndergrad As String = "Undergraduate"
Private Const strGrad As String = "Graduate"
Private Const strThesis As String = "Thesis and Dissertation"

Private Sub Form_Load()
   lstCourseLevel.AddItem strUndergrad
   lstCourseLevel.AddItem strGrad
   lstCourseLevel.AddItem strThesis
End Sub

Private Sub lstCourseLevel_Click()
   lblAnswer.Caption = ""
End Sub

Private Sub cmdCalculate_Click()
   Const curUndergraduatePerHour As Currency = 75
   Const curGraduatePerHour As Currency = 145
   Const curThesisPerHour As Currency = 145
   Dim strCourseLevel As String
   Dim curTuition As Currency

   strCourseLevel = lstCourseLevel.Text

   If strCourseLevel = strUndergrad Then
      curTuition = curUndergraduatePerHour
   ElseIf strCourseLevel = strGrad Then
      curTuition = curGraduatePerHour
   Else
      curTuition = curThesisPerHour
   End If

   lblAnswer.Caption = "Tuition for " & strCourseLevel & " course work is " & _
      Format(curTuition, "Currency") & " per credit hour."
End Sub
```

```
Private Sub cmdDone_Click()
    Unload Me
End Sub
```

5) RUN THE APPLICATION

Save the modified Tuition Calculator project and then run the application. Test the application by clicking on each of the list items and then the Calculate button.

6) PRINT AND THEN REMOVE THE PROJECT

8.7 Combo Boxes

Combo boxes allow the user to select a value from a set of values. However, in a combo box the user has the option of entering a value that is not in the list of values. For example, in the Tuition Calculator application, a combo box is used to enter the number of credit hours:

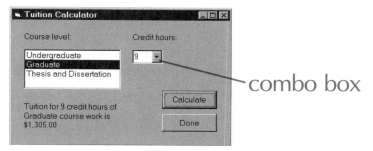

Combo boxes are one way to get user input

combo box   A *combo box* object, sometimes called a *collapsible list*, is created using the ComboBox control () in the Tool box and has the properties:

- **Name** identifies the object and is used by the programmer. It is good programming style to begin combo box object names with cbo.

- **List** stores a group of strings that make up the items in the combo box.

- **Sorted** displays the items in the combo box in alphabetical order. Sorted is only available at design time.

- **Style** can be set to dropdown combo, simple combo, or dropdown list. Dropdown combo has both a drop-down list and a text box that allows the user to enter text. Simple combo has a list that does not drop down and a text box, and drop-down list has only a drop-down list and does not allow the user to type a value. Style can be changed at run time through assignment using the Visual Basic constants vbComboDropDown, vbComboSimple, and vbComboDrop-DownList.

- **Text** stores the selected item in the combo box. Text can also be set at design time to display a default value.

- **ListCount** can be used only at run time to determine the number of items in the list.

click event

change event

Click event and change event procedures can be coded for a combo box. The click event procedure is executed when the user clicks on an item in the list. The selected list item is stored in the Text property. The change event procedure is executed when the user starts to type a value in the combo box.

AddItem

The AddItem method is used to add an item to the end of the combo box list at run time and takes the form:

cboControl.AddItem *Item*

cboControl is the name of the combo box object and *Item* is a **String** variable or a string in quotation marks that is to be added to the list. The AddItem method and the List property are both used to add items to the combo box list, the difference is AddItem is used at run time and List is used at design time.

Clear

The Clear method is used to delete the contents of the combo box and takes the form:

lstControl.Clear

lstControl is the name of the combo box object.

Review 7

Follow the instructions below to modify the Tuition Calculator application to include a combo box.

1) OPEN THE TUITION CALCULATOR PROJECT

Display the Tuition Calculator form if it is not already displayed.

2) ADD A CREDIT HOURS COMBO BOX TO THE APPLICATION

Refer to the form below when placing and sizing the form and its objects as instructed in the steps following:

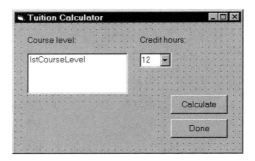

a. Add a label object to the form.
b. In the Tool box, click the ComboBox control (![]) and then drag the cross-hairs pointer in the application after the list box to create a combo box:

c. Use the table below to name and change the properties of the new objects.

Object	Name	Caption	Sorted	Text
Label1	lblCreditHours	Credit hours:		
Combo1	cboCreditHours		True	12

d. Select the combo box if it is not already selected.

e. In the Properties windows, select the List property. Click on the arrow to display a cursor in an empty list.

f. Type 3 and then press Enter.

g. Repeat steps e and f to add 6, 9, 12, and 15 to the list.

3) MODIFY THE PROGRAM CODE

a. Display the Code Editor window and add the following event procedures:

```
Private Sub cboCreditHours_Change()
    lblAnswer.Caption = ""
End Sub

Private Sub cboCreditHours_Click()
    lblAnswer.Caption = ""
End Sub
```

b. Modify the cmdCalculate_Click procedures as shown below:

```
        Private Sub cmdCalculate_Click()
            Const curUndergraduatePerHour As Currency = 75
            Const curGraduatePerHour As Currency = 145
            Const curThesisPerHour As Currency = 145
Add         Dim intCreditHours As Integer
            Dim strCourseLevel As String
            Dim curTuition As Currency

Add         intCreditHours = cboCreditHours.Text
            strCourseLevel = lstCourseLevel.Text

            If strCourseLevel = strUndergrad Then
Modify          curTuition = curUndergraduatePerHour * intCreditHours
            ElseIf strCourseLevel = strGrad Then
Modify          curTuition = curGraduatePerHour * intCreditHours
            Else
Modify          curTuition = curThesisPerHour * intCreditHours
            End If

Modify      lblAnswer.Caption = "Tuition for " & intCreditHours & " credit hours of " & _
                strCourseLevel & " course work is " & Format(curTuition, "Currency")
        End Sub
```

4) RUN THE APPLICATION

Save the modified Tuition Calculator project and then run the application. Test the application by selecting different combinations of course levels and credit hours.

5) PRINT AND THEN REMOVE THE PROJECT

Review 8 ☼ ───────────────────────────

Modify the Installment Loan Payments application created in Review 3 so that it allows the user to enter the interest rate and principal in combo boxes. The application interface should look similar to that shown on the right after entering the loan information and clicking on the Payments button.

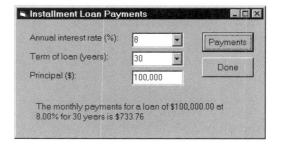

8.8 Windows Application Standards

Applications created for use with Windows 98 have a standard look and feel about them. For example, the application below has several features found in a Windows application:

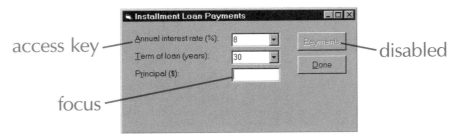

Notice the text box with the cursor in it. This indicates it has the focus. An object with *focus* will receive the user input from the keyboard. The underlined D in the Done button indicates it is an access key. An *access key* is the key pressed while holding down the Alt key to select an object. For example, Alt+D selects the Done button. The *tab order* has been set so that the focus will move from one object to the next in a logical order when the Tab key is pressed. The Payments button is *disabled*, or dimmed, because it is not appropriate to select it at this time since all the loan information has not be entered.

focus
access key

tab order

disabled

Your applications should also adhere to these standards. An application that has features similar to other Windows applications is easier to learn and understand.

A command button object that has the focus appears with a dashed line around it. A text box that has the focus displays a blinking cursor in it and any text typed will be entered in that text box. When a list box or combo box has the focus, the arrow keys can be used to select a list item. Labels cannot receive focus.

creating access keys
&

An ampersand (&) may be used in an object's caption to define an access key. For example, entering &Done in a command button's Caption property displays Done in the command button (Note the underlined D) and allows the user to press Alt+D at run time to select the Done button. When the user presses Alt+D the Done button is said to have the focus.

setting tab order

Tab order allows for easier and faster data entry. For example, when the application above is first started, the interest rate combo box should have the focus and when the Tab key is pressed the focus should move to the term combo box. The tab order is determined by the order in which the objects are created in the application. Obviously, objects are not always created in the desired tab order. The TabIndex property can be used to change the tab order of the objects in the application. Tab index starts at 0.

TabIndex

When using text boxes, list boxes, or combo boxes their associated labels should display an access key so that when the user presses the access key the cursor is displayed in the box. For example, in the application above, pressing Alt+R places the cursor in the principal text box. When setting the tab order for labels and boxes, the label describing the box should have a tab index just previous to the box tab index. This will place the focus in the next object in the tab order because a label cannot receive the focus. For example, in the Installment Loan Payments application the Annual interest rate (%) label has a tab index of 0 and its combo box has a tab index of 1.

disabling an object   There may be times when an object in an application depends on a
Enabled   value used in another object in the application. The Enabled property of an object can be set to False to disable the object which means that the user cannot select it. For example, in the Installment Loan Payments application, the rate, term, and principal needs to be entered before the payments can be calculated. Setting the Enabled property of cmdPayments to False displays the button as gray, and it cannot be selected. Once all the required information is entered, the cmdPayments Enabled property should be set to True.

Visible   The Visible property of an object can be used to hide an object. Setting the Visible property to False does not display the object on the form and True displays the object. This is useful when an object on the form is not relevant to an option selected by the user.

Review 9

Follow the instructions below to modify the Installment Loan Payments application to have access keys and appropriate tab index order.

1) **OPEN THE INSTALLMENT LOAN PAYMENTS PROJECT**

   Display the Installment Loan Payments form if it is not already displayed.

2) **SET COMMAND BUTTON TO DISABLE**

   a. Change the Enable property of the cmdPayments object to False.
   b. Run the application. Note that the Payments button is dimmed and nothing happens when it is clicked.

3) **ADD ACCESS KEYS**

   a. Change the Caption property of lblInterestRate to &Annual interest rate (%):.
   b. Use the table below to change the Caption properties of the objects to include access keys:

Object	Caption
lblTerm	&Term of the loan (years):
lblPrincipal	P&rincipal:
cmdPayments	&Payments
cmdDone	&Done

4) **RUN THE APPLICATION AND TEST THE TAB ORDER AND ACCESS KEYS**

   a. Run the application. Press the Tab key a few times. Notice how the focus from one object to the next is not in a logical order.
   b. Press Alt+A. Note how the interest rate combo box does not receive the focus like it should.

5) **SET TAB INDEX**

   a. Change the TabIndex property of lblInterestRate to 0 if it is not already 0.
   b. Use the table shown on the next page to change the TabIndex properties of the objects as necessary:

Object	TabIndex
cboInterestRate	1
lblTerm	2
cboTerm	3
lblPrincipal	4
txtPrincipal	5
lblAnswer	6
cmdPayments	7
cmdDone	8

6) MODIFY THE PROGRAM CODE

   a. Display the Code Editor window.

   b. Add a CheckValues procedure with the following statements:

```
Sub CheckValues()
    lblAnswer.Caption = ""
    If IsNumeric(cboInterestRate.Text) And IsNumeric(cboTerm.Text) _
        And IsNumeric(txtPrincipal.Text) Then
        cmdPayments.Enabled = True
    Else
        cmdPayments.Enabled = False
    End If
End Sub
```

   c. Add and modify the cboInterestRate_Change, cboInterestRate_Click, cboTerm_Change, cboTerm_Click, and txtPrincipal_Change procedures with the following statements:

```
Private Sub cboInterestRate_Change()
    Call CheckValues
End Sub

Private Sub cboInteretRate_Click()
    Call CheckValues
End Sub

Private Sub cboTerm_Change()
    Call CheckValues
End Sub

Private Sub cboTerm_Click()
    Call CheckValues
End Sub

Private Sub txtPrincipal_Change()
    Call CheckValues
End Sub
```

7) RUN THE APPLICATION

   a. Save the modified Installment Loan Payments project and then run the application. Press the tab key several times. Note how the focus moves in logical order through the objects.

   b. Enter all the necessary loan information. Note how the Payments button is no longer dimmed.

8) PRINT AND THEN REMOVE THE PROJECT

Review 10

Modify the How Much Can I Borrow application created in Review 4 so that the focus is in the first text box when the application is started and the focus moves to the next object in the application in a logical order when the Tab key is pressed. Also set access keys for each text box and both command buttons.

An Introduction to Programming Using Microsoft Visual Basic

Review 11 ⚙

Modify the Tuition Calculator application from Review 7 so that the focus is in the list box when the application is started and the focus moves to the next object in the application in a logical order when the Tab key is pressed. Also set appropriate access keys. The Calculate button should be disabled until all the appropriate information is entered.

Case Study

In this Case Study a Mortgage Analyzer application will be created for the Ivy Real Estate company to help its clients.

specification

The specification for this Case Study is:

A Mortgage Analyzer application that allows the user to enter data to generate the monthly payments of a mortgage or the price of a house the user can afford. The application should allow the user to print the information and clear the form for new input. At startup the order form should display only the available calculations.

design

When designing the form for this Case Study, we need to consider how the user should select what to calculate, how the information should be displayed, and how the user should enter the required information.

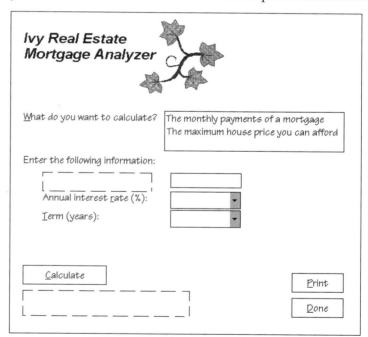

Interface design for the Mortgage Analyzer Case Study

Note that there are two labels sketched with dashed lines to indicate they are not visible at design time. At run time, the first label will display text based on what is selected in the list box and the second label will display the answer when the Calculate button is clicked.

The program code design for this Case Study is best done by listing the pseudocode for event procedures:

```
Private Sub Form_Load()
    Clear form
End sub

Private Sub lstWhatToCalculate_Click()
    Display rate objects with 7 as the default
    Display term objects with 15 as the default
    Display appropriate message in lblPayments depending on
        which item was selected in the list box
    Display payment objects
    Clear answer label
End Sub

Private Sub cboRate_Click()
    Call CheckValues
End Sub

Private Sub cboTerm_Click()
    Call CheckValues
End Sub

Private Sub cmbRate_Change()
    Call CheckValues
End Sub

Private Sub cmbTerm_Change()
    Call CheckValues
End Sub

Private Sub txtPayments_Change()
    Call CheckValues
End Sub

Private Sub CheckValues()
    Display Calculate command button if rate, term, payment
        values are numeric, otherwise hide command button
    Clear answer label
End Sub

Private Sub cmdCalculate_Click()
    Get rate, term, and payment (loan amount) from user
    Convert rate to monthly interest rate
    Convert time in years to term in months
    Calculate answer using Pmt or PV depending on what user
        selected in the list box
    Display answer
End Sub

Private Sub cmdPrint_Click()
    Print the form
    Clear selected item in list box and then clear payments text
        box
    Clear form
End Sub
```

```
Sub ClearForm()
    Set calculation information objects to not visible
    Clear answer label
End Sub

Private Sub cmdDone_Click()
    Unload Me
End Sub
```

coding   The interface and code for this Case Study are:

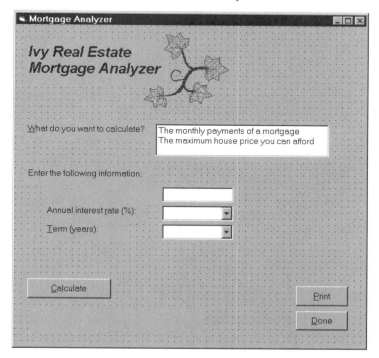

Object	Name	Caption/Text	List	Picture
Form1	frmMortgageAnalyzer	Mortgage Analyzer		
Label1	lblIvyRealestate	*see above (need to format)*		
Image1	imgIvy			Ivy
Label2	lblWhatToCalculate	*see above*		
ListBox1	lstWhatToCalculate		*see above*	
Label3	lblEnterInformation	*see above*		
Label4	lblPayments	*empty*		
Label5	lblRate	Annual interest &rate (%):		
Combo1	cboInterestRate	*empty*	*5.0, 5.5, 6.0...9.0*	
Label6	lblTerm	&Term (years):		
Combo2	cboTerm	*empty*	*5, 10, 15...30*	
Text1	txtPrincipal	*empty*		
Command1	cmdCalculate	&Calculate		
Label7	lblAnswer	*empty*		
Command2	cmdPrint	&Print		
Command3	cmdDone	&Done		

The TabIndex, starting at 0, should be set for each object in the order listed above staring with Label1 and continuing through to Command3. Image1 does not have a TabIndex.

```
Option Explicit

Private Sub Form_Load()
  Call ClearForm
End Sub

Private Sub lstWhatToCalculate_Click()
  lblEnterInformation.Visible = True

  lblRate.Visible = True
  cboInterestRate.Visible = True
  cboInterestRate.Text = 7

  lblTerm.Visible = True
  cboTerm.Visible = True
  cboTerm.Text = 15

  If lstWhatToCalculate.Text = "The monthly payments of a mortgage" Then
    lblPayments.Caption = "&Loan amount ($):"
  Else
    lblPayments.Caption = "&Maximum monthly payments ($):"
  End If

  lblPayments.Visible = True
  txtPrincipal.Visible = True
  lblAnswer.Caption = ""
End Sub

Private Sub cboInterestRate_Click()        'user clicked on new value in the combo box
  Call CheckValues
End Sub

Private Sub cboTerm_Click()                'user clicked on new value in the combo box
  Call CheckValues
End Sub

Private Sub cboInterestRate_Change()       'user typed a value in the combo box
  Call CheckValues
End Sub

Private Sub cboTerm_Change()                'user typed a value in the combo box
  Call CheckValues
End Sub

Private Sub txtPrincipal_Change()          'user types a value in the text box
  Call CheckValues
End Sub

'*********************************************************
' Displays the Calculate command button if combo boxes
' and text boxes contain values greater than 0
'
' post: Calculate command button displayed if rate, term
' and payment values entered by user are greater than 0
'*********************************************************
Sub CheckValues()
  If IsNumeric(cboInterestRate.Text) And IsNumeric(cboTerm.Text) _
    And IsNumeric(txtPrincipal.Text) Then
    cmdCalculate.Visible = True
  Else
    cmdCalculate.Visible = False
  End If
  lblAnswer.Caption = ""
End Sub

Private Sub cmdCalculate_Click()
  Dim dblInterestRate As Double, intTerm As Integer, curPrincipal As Currency
  Dim curAnswer As Currency
```

```
          dblInterestRate = cboInterestRate.Text / 100
          intTerm = cboTerm.Text
          curPrincipal = txtPrincipal.Text

          If lstWhatToCalculate.Text = "The monthly payments of a mortgage" Then
             curAnswer = Pmt(dblInterestRate / 12, intTerm * 12, -curPrincipal)
             lblAnswer.Caption = "The monthly payments would be " _
                & Format(curAnswer, "Currency")
          Else
             curAnswer = PV(dblInterestRate / 12, intTerm * 12, -curPrincipal)
             lblAnswer.Caption = "You can afford a house that is less than " _
                & Format(curAnswer, "Currency")
          End If
          lblAnswer.Visible = True
       End Sub

       Private Sub cmdPrint_Click()
          Me.PrintForm

          lstWhatToCalculate.Text = ""
          txtPrincipal.Text = ""

          Call ClearForm
       End Sub

       Sub ClearForm()
          lblEnterInformation.Visible = False
          lblRate.Visible = False
          cboInterestRate.Visible = False
          lblTerm.Visible = False
          cboTerm.Visible = False
          lblPayments.Visible = False
          txtPrincipal.Visible = False
          cmdCalculate.Visible = False
          lblAnswer.Caption = ""
       End Sub

       Private Sub cmdDone_Click()
          Unload Me
       End Sub
```

Running Mortgage Analyzer displays the following form:

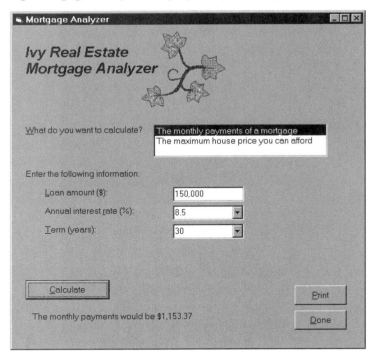

This Case Study should be tested by selecting different items to calculate and different rates, terms, and payments or loan amounts. Entering invalid rates, terms, and loan amounts (text instead of numbers) will test the error handling in the code. At least one calculation should be printed to test the Print button.

8.9 Built-in Trigonometric Functions

Visual Basic includes several built-in trigonometric functions. These functions include Sin, Cos, and Tan. Each of these functions return the *Sin* sine, cosine, and tangent of an angle measured in radians. The Sin function takes the form:

Sin(*number*)

number is a **Double** variable or value, and is in radians. The following code demonstrates Sin:

```
Dim dblRadians As Double
dblRadians = 0.79                    '45 Degrees
lblAnswer.Caption = Sin(dblRadians)  '0.710353
```

Cos The Cos function takes the form:

Cos(*number*)

number is a **Double** variable or value in radians. The following code demonstrates Cos:

```
Dim dblRadians As Double
dblRadians = 0.79                    '45 Degrees
lblAnswer.Caption = Cos(dblRadians)  '0.703845
```

Tan   The Tan function takes the form:

Tan(*number*)

number is a **Double** variable or value in radians. The following code demonstrates Tan:

```
Dim dblRadians As Double
dblRadians = 0.79                       '45 Degrees
lblAnswer.Caption = Tan(dblRadians)     '1.009246
```

converting   The Sin, Cos, and Tan functions require an argument in radians. To
degrees to radians   convert an angle measured in degrees to radians the following formula is used:

```
dblRadians = (dblPi / 180) * dblDegrees     'dblPi = 3.14
```

converting   This formula works because 180 degrees equals π radians. To convert
radians to degrees   from radians to degrees, the following formula is used:

```
dblDegrees = dblRadians * (180 / dblPi)     'dblPi = 3.14
```

Review 12

Using pencil and paper, write a DegreesToRadians function that has a dblDegrees parameter and returns the angle in radians. The function documentation is:

```
'****************************************************************
'  Converts the value dblDegrees in degrees to radians.
'
'  pre: 0 <= dblDegrees <= 360
'  post: The radian equivalent of dblDegrees returned
'****************************************************************
```

Review 13

Using pencil and paper, write a RadiansToDegrees function that has a dblRadians parameter and returns the angle in degrees. The function documentation is:

```
'****************************************************************
'  Converts the value dblRadians in radians to degrees.
'
'  pre: 0 <= dblRadians <= 2pi
'  post: The degree equivalent of dblRadians returned
'****************************************************************
```

Review 14 ⟳

Create a Trigonometric Functions application that includes a text box for the user to enter an angle in degrees and command buttons that when clicked display the sine, cosine, or tangent of the angle rounded to 2 decimal places. Use the DegreesToRadians function from Review 13 in your code. The application interface should look similar to that shown on the right after entering 90 and clicking on the Sine button.

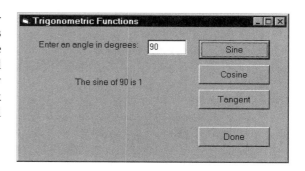

Review 15

Follow the instructions below to create the Sine Cosine Table application.

1) CREATE A NEW PROJECT

2) ADD OBJECTS TO THE FORM

Refer to the form below when placing and sizing the form and its objects. Use the table below to name and change the properties of the objects.

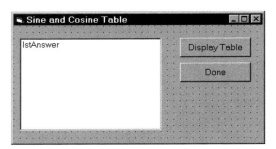

Object	Name	Caption	List
Form1	frmSineCosineTable	Sine and Cosine Table	
List1	lstAnswer		*empty*
Command1	cmdDisplayTable	Display Table	
Command2	cmdDone	Done	

3) SAVE THE PROJECT

From the File menu, select Save Project. Save the form naming it frmSineCosineTable and save the project naming it Sine Cosine Table.

4) WRITE THE PROGRAM CODE

Display the Code Editor window and add event procedures as shown below:

```
Private Sub cmdDisplayTable_Click()
    Dim intAngle As Integer
    Dim dblAngleRadians As Double
    Dim dblSin As Double
    Dim dblCos As Double

    lstAnswer.AddItem "Angle" & vbTab & "Sin" & vbTab & "Cos"

    For intAngle = 0 To 360 Step 15
        dblAngleRadians = DegreesToRadians(intAngle)
        dblSin = Round(Sin(dblAngleRadians), 2)
        dblCos = Round(Cos(dblAngleRadians), 2)
        lstAnswer.AddItem intAngle & vbTab & dblSin & vbTab & dblCos
    Next intAngle
End Sub

'**************************************************************
'   Converts the value dblDegrees in degrees to radians
'
'   pre:  0 <= dblDegrees <= 360
'   post:  The radian equivalent of dblDegrees returned
'**************************************************************
Function DegreesToRadians(ByVal dblDegrees As Double)
    Const dblPi As Double = 3.14
    DegreesToRadians = (dblPi / 180) * dblDegrees
End Function
```

```
Private Sub cmdDone_Click()
    Unload Me
End Sub
```

5) RUN THE APPLICATION

Save the modified Sine Cosine Table project and then run the application. Test it by clicking on the Display Table button.

6) PRINT AND THEN REMOVE THE PROJECT

8.10 Inverse Trigonometric Functions

Atn

Mathematical work often requires finding the angle that corresponds to a trigonometric value. This is called the *inverse* trigonometric function. The inverse of sine is called *arcsine*, the inverse of cosine is called *arccosine*, and the inverse of tangent is called *arctangent*. Visual Basic supplies only one built-in inverse trigonometric function, Atn. Atn returns the arctangent of an angle. The Atn function takes the form:

Atn(*number*)

number is a **Double** variable or value in radians. Atn returns the angle in radians that has tangent *number*. The following code demonstrates Atn:

```
Const dblPi As Double = 3.14
Dim dblTangent As Double
Dim dblAnswerRadians As Double, dblAnswerDegrees As Double
dblTangent = 1.0                                    'radians

'Calculates the angle in radians whose tangent is dblTangent
lblAnswer.Caption = Atn(dblTangent)                '0.785398
```

arcsine

The formula to determine the angle in radians that has sine dblSin is:

dblArcSin = Atn(dblSin / Sqr(-dblSin * dblSin + 1))

arccosine

The formula to determine the angle in radians that has cosine dblCos is:

dblArcCos = Atn(-dblCos / Sqr(-dblCos * dblCos + 1))+ 2 * Atn(1)

Review 16

Using pencil and paper, write an Arcsin function that has a dblSin parameter and returns the arcsine of dblSin in radians. The function documentation is:

```
'**************************************************************
'  Calculates the angle in radians that has sine dblSin.
'
'  pre: -1 <= dblSin <=1
'  post: the arcsine of dblSin returned
'**************************************************************
```

Review 17

Using pencil and paper, write an Arccos function that has a dblCos parameter and returns the arccosine of dblCos in radians. The function documentation is:

```
'****************************************************************
'  Calculates the angle in radians that has cosine dblCos.
'
'  pre: -1 <= dblCos <=1
'  post: the arccosine of dblCos returned
'****************************************************************
```

Review 18

Create an Inverse Trigonometric Functions application that includes a text box for the user to enter a value and command buttons that when clicked display the arcsine, arccosine, or arctangent in degrees rounded to 2 decimal places. Use the functions from Reviews 14, 18, and 19 in your code. The application interface should look similar to that shown on the right after entering 0.5 and clicking on the Arccosine button.

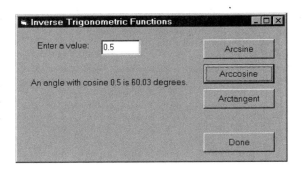

8.11 Logarithmic and Exponential Functions

Log

The Log function (ln) is a Visual Basic built-in function that returns the natural logarithm of a number. The Log function takes the form:

Log(*number*)

number is a **Double** variable or value that is greater than 0. The following code demonstrates Log:

```
Dim dblNumber As Double
dblNumber = 10
lblAnswer.Caption = Log(dblNumber)    '2.3025
```

The natural logarithm of a number is the logarithm base e, where e is 2.718282. The logarithm of *dblNumber* to base *intN* can be calculated using the formula:

Log(*dblNumber*) / Log(*intN*)

Exp

The natural exponential function is the inverse function to the natual logarithm. The Exp function is a Visual Basic built-in function that returns the natural exponential of a value, or e^x. The Exp function takes the form:

Exp(*number*)

number is a numeric variable or value that represents x in e^x. The following code demonstrates Exp:

```
Dim intNumber As Integer
intNumber = 2
lblAnswer.Caption = Exp(intNumber)    '7.389, which is e²
```

Review 19

Create a Logarithmic and Exponential Functions application that includes a text box for the user to enter a number and command buttons that when clicked display the natural logarithm of the number or e raised to that number. The application interface should look similar to that shown on the right after entering 1 and clicking on the Natural Logarithm button.

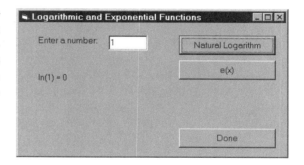

Review 20

Create a Trigonometric Functions List application that includes a text box for the user to enter an angle in degrees and a list box to select a trigonometric function. Use the DegreesToRadians function from Review 13 in your code. The application interface should look similar to that shown on the right after entering 45 and clicking on Tangent in the list box.

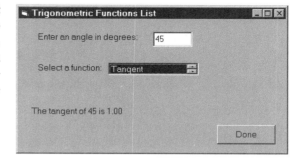

Chapter Summary

This chapter introduced several Visual Basic built-in mathematical and business functions.

Abs
Sqr
Sgn The Abs function returns the absolute value of a number. The Sqr function returns the square root of a number. The Sgn function returns 1, –1, or 0 if a numeric argument is positive, negative, or 0 respectively.

IsNumeric IsNumeric returns True if its argument can be evaluated as a number and False if it cannot.

Round The Round function can be used to round numeric data to a specified number of decimal places.

Format The Format function can be used to format the appearance of numeric data. The different format types are Currency, Fixed, Standard, Percent, Scientific, Yes/No, True/False, and On/Off.

Pmt
PV
FV Visual Basic includes the business functions Pmt, PV, and FV. Pmt returns the periodic payment for an installment loan. PV returns the present value of an investment. FV returns what a series of equal payments invested at a fixed rate of interest will be worth after a period of time.

List boxes and Combo boxes are used to obtain a predefined value from the user. A list box object is created using the ListBox control (▤) in the Tool box, and a combo box object is created using the ComboBox control (▤). List and Combo boxes have List, Sorted, and Text properties. The AddItem method is used to add an item to the list or combo box at run time and the Clear method is used to remove the items.

focus, access key, & An object that has focus receives the user input. An ampersand (&) may be used in an object's caption to define an access key.

tab order In most Windows applications, the Tab key can be used to move through the options in a logical order. The tab order is determined by *TabIndex* the order in which the objects are created in the application. The TabIndex property can be used to change the tab order of objects in an application.

When an option in an application depends on another option being *Enabled* selected, the Enabled property of an object can be set to False so that the user cannot select it, and changed to True when it is appropriate for the *Visible* object to be selected. The Visible property can be used to hide the object.

Sin, Cos, Tan Sin, Cos, and Tan are trigonometric functions that return the sine, *degrees to radians* cosine, and tangent of an angle in radians. A value in degrees is converted to radians using the formula dblRadians = (dblPi /180) * intDegrees. A *radians to degrees* value in radians is converted to degrees using the formula dblDegrees = dblRadians * (180 /dblPi).

Mathematical work often requires finding the inverse trigonometric function, the angle that corresponds to a trigonometric value. Visual Ba- *Atn* sic supplies one built-in inverse trigonometric function, Atn. Atn returns the arctangent of an angle. An angle whose sine is dblSine can be deter- *arcsine* mined with the formula Atn(dblSine / Sqr(−dblSine * dblSine + 1)). An *arcosine* angle whose cosine is dblCosine can be determined with the formula Atn(−dblCosine / Sqr(−dblCosine * dblCosine + 1)) + 2 * Atn(1).

Log Log returns the natural logarithm of a number. Exp returns the value *Exp* of e^x where e = 2.718282.

Vocabulary

Access key The key pressed while holding down the Alt key to select an object.

Arccosine The inverse of cosine.

Arcsine The inverse of sine.

Arctangent The inverse of tangent.

Combo box An object used to obtain a value from a set of values from the user. The user can also enter a value.

Focus Describes an object that will receive the next user input.

List box An object used to obtain a value from a set of values from the user.

Tab order The order in which objects receive the focus when the Tab key is pressed.

Visual Basic

& Used to define an access key.

Abs Function that returns the absolute value of a number.

AddItem Method used to add an item to a list box or combo box.

Atn Function that returns the arctangent of an angle.

Clear Method used to clear the contents of a list box or combo box.

ComboBox control Used to create a combo box object. Found in the Tool box.

Cos Function that returns the cosine of an angle measured in radians.

Enabled Property used to disable an object so that it cannot be selected.

Exp Function that returns the natural exponentials of a value, or e^x.

Format Function used to change the appearance of numeric data.

FV Function that returns the future value of a series of equal payments invested at a fixed rate of interest after a period of time.

IsNumeric Function that returns True if an expression can be a number and False if it is not.

List Property that stores a group of strings that make up the items in a list box or combo box.

ListBox control Used to create a list box object. Found in the Tool box.

Log Function that returns the natural logarithm of a number.

Pmt Function that returns the periodic payment for an installment loan.

PV Function that returns the present value of an investment.

Round Function that returns numeric data rounded to a specified decimal place.

Sgn Function that returns 1, –1, or 0 if a numeric argument is positive, negative, or 0 respectively.

Sin Function that returns the sine of an angle measured in radians.

Sorted Property used to display the items in a list box or combo box in alphabetical order.

Sqr Function that returns the square root of a number.

TabIndex Property used to set the tab index order of a control.

Tan Function that returns the tangent of an angle measured in radians.

Text Property that stores the items selected at run time.

Visible Property used to hide an object.

Exercises

Exercise 1

A perfect square is an integer whose square root is a whole number. For example, 4, 9, and 16 are perfect squares. Create a Perfect Square application that determines if the number entered by the user is a perfect square. Your code should include a PerfectSquare function that has an intNumber parameter and returns True if intNumber is a perfect square and False if it is not (Hint: use the Int function in determining if a square root is a whole number). The application interface should look similar to:

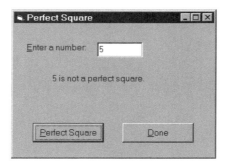

Exercise 2 ♺

Green Lawn Service charges the following prices for irregularly shaped lawns:

lawn cutting	$0.05 per square meter
basic landscaping	$1.00 per square meter
deluxe landscaping	$3.00 per square meter

They charge the following prices for square-shaped lawns:

lawn cutting	$0.025 per square meter
basic landscaping	$0.50 per square meter
deluxe landscaping	$2.00 per square meter

Green Lawn Service assumes that if the total square meters of a lawn has an integer square root, then it is a perfect shaped lawn. Create a Green Lawn Service application that allows the user to enter the lawn size in square meters and select from a list box the type of service, and then displays the total price of the service. Your code should include the PerfectSquare function from Exercise 1. The application should look similar to:

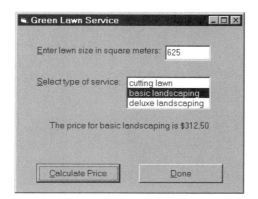

An Introduction to Programming Using Microsoft Visual Basic

Exercise 3

Create a Payment Calculator application the allows the user to enter the loan amount, annual interest rate, length of the loan in years, and how often the payments will be made (daily, monthly, or yearly). How often the payments are made affects the rate and term used in the Pmt function because they have to be in the same units. Assume that there are 30 days in each month and there are 360 days in a year. The application should display the payments, total amount paid over the length of the loan, and the total amount of interest paid. The application interface should look similar to:

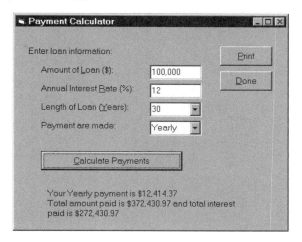

Exercise 4

Create a Loan Calculator application the allows the user to enter the maximum monthly payments, annual interest rate, and length of the loan in years. The application should display the loan amount, total amount paid over the length of the loan, and the total amount of interest paid. The application interface should look similar to:

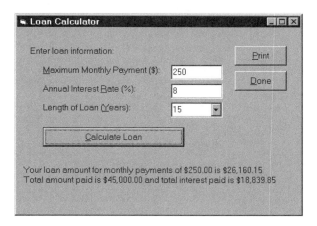

Exercise 5

Create an Investment Calculator application that allows the user to enter the amount invested monthly, annual interest rate, and length of the investment in years. The application should display the value of the investment at 5 year intervals in a list box. The application interface should look similar to:

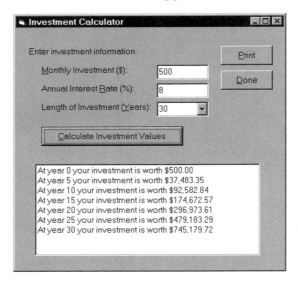

Exercise 6

A Pythagorean triple is a set of three integers that solves the equation $a^2 + b^2 = c^2$. Create a Pythagorean Triples application that displays all Pythagorean triples with values of A and B less than 100. Use the PerfectSquare function from Exercise 1 in your code. The application interface should look similar to the following after clicking on the Compute button:

Exercise 7

Create a Square Root Roundoff Error application that compares the square of the square root of a number with the number itself for all integers from 1 to 100. This difference in values is due to the computer's rounding error. The application interface should look similar to the following after clicking on the Compute button:

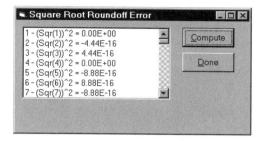

Exercise 8

Create a Bookstore Order Form application the allows the user to select different items and the quantity of the items to purchase and then display the order information in a list box in the Cart graphic. The application interface should look similar to:

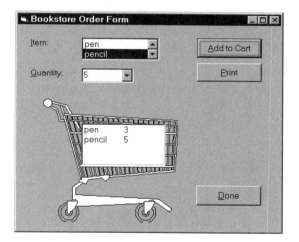

Exercise 9 ✿ *trigonometry required*

Create an Angle Conversion application that converts an angle entered in degrees to radians and vice versa. The application should display 30, 0.52, 45, 0.79, 60, and 1.05 in a combo box. Refer to the functions created in Reviews 2 and 3. The application interface should look similar to the following after selecting an angle and clicking on the degrees to radians option button:

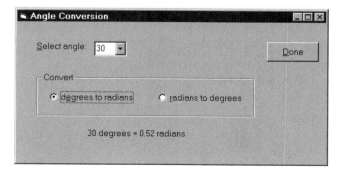

Exercise 10 *trigonometry required*

Create a My Random Number application that produces a sequence of random numbers without using the Rnd function. To do this, let X vary from 1 to 100 in steps of 1. Obtain Sin(X) and multiply this by 1000, which results in the value Y. Then take the absolute value of Y and divide Int(Y) by 16, and let the remainder serve as your random number. The application interface should look similar to the following after clicking on the <u>C</u>alculate Random Numbers button:

Exercise 11 *trigonometry required*

The formula Area = ½ * a * b * sin C is a formula that can be used to find the area of a triangle:

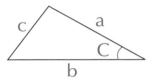

Create a Triangle Area application that allows the user to enter the lengths of sides a and b and the angle of C in degrees, and then displays the area of the triangle using the formula given above. The application interface should look similar to:

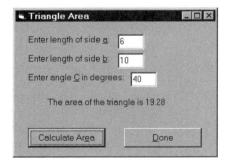

Exercise 12 *trigonometry required* ──────────────────────────

SOH-CAH-TOA is a mnemonic for the trigonometric formulas that can be used to find the sine, cosine, and tangent of an angle in a right triangle:

Sine = Opposite/Hypotenuse   Cosine = Adjacent/Hypotenuse   Tangent = Opposite/Adjacent

For example, the sine of angle A below is calculated by dividing the opposite side (a) by the hypotenuse (c). Likewise, the cosine of angle A is b/c, and the tangent of angle A is a/b:

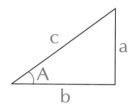

Create a SOH-CAH-TOA application that allows the user to enter the lengths of the three sides of a triangle and uses the formulas given above to calculate the sine, cosine, and tangent of angle A. The application should use the result of that calculation to determine what angle A is in degrees (Hint: use inverse trigonometric functions). Include a CheckSides function that checks the sides entered to see if they are for a right triangle (Hint: refer to Chapter Four, Exercise 7). The function should return True if it is a right triangle and False if not. A message box should be displayed if it is not a right triangle and the text boxes should be cleared. The application interface should look similar to:

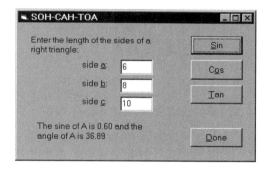

Exercise 13

The formula $y = ne^{kt}$ is a general formula that can be used for estimating growth where:

- y   is the final amount
- n   is the initial amount
- k   is a constant
- t   is the time

For example, this formula could be used for estimating population growth in a region or for estimating cell grown in a lab experiment. Create a Bacteria Growth application that calculates how many bacteria will be present based on this formula. The application interface should look similar to:

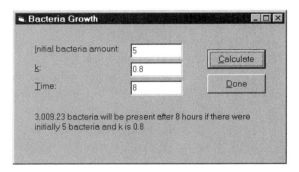

Exercise 14

The formula $V_n = P(1 + r)^n$ is a general formula that can be used to estimate depreciation or appreciation where:

- V_n is the value at the end of n years
- P   is the initial value of the equipment
- r   is the rate of appreciation (positive) or depreciation (negative)
- n   is the time in years

For example, this formula could be used to determine the current value of a mainframe that a company has owned for 10 years. From this formula you can also determine how long it will take a piece of equipment to depreciate to a specific value using the formula: $n = \log(V_n / P) / \log(1 + r)$. Create a Depreciation application that calculates how long it will take a piece of equipment to depreciate using this formula. The application interface should look similar to:

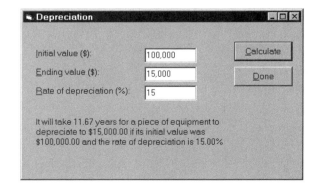

Advanced

Exercise 15 *trigonometry required*

Create an application that will solve a triangle (compute the unknown sides and angles) for the following situations:

- given two sides and the included angle
- given two angles and any side
- given three sides

The application should allow the user to select one of the three choices above, and based on which option is selected allow the user to enter the appropriate known information. Angles should be entered in degrees and displayed in degrees.

Advanced

Exercise 16 *trigonometry required*

The formula used in Exercise 13 for growth problems can also be used in decay problems. In decay problems, k is negative. Create an application that allows the user to select from the following options:

- calculate the final amount: ne^{kt}
- calculate the initial amount: y / e^{-kt}
- calculate the constant (called the half-life): $(\log (y/n)) / (t * \log e)$
  (where $\log e = 0.4343$)

The application should allow the user to select one of the three choices above and then based on which option is selected allow the user to enter the appropriate known information. For example, a radioactive mass of 200 grams will reduce to 100 grams in 10 years. Based on this information, the half-life is calculated to be –0.06931.

An Introduction to Programming Using Microsoft Visual Basic

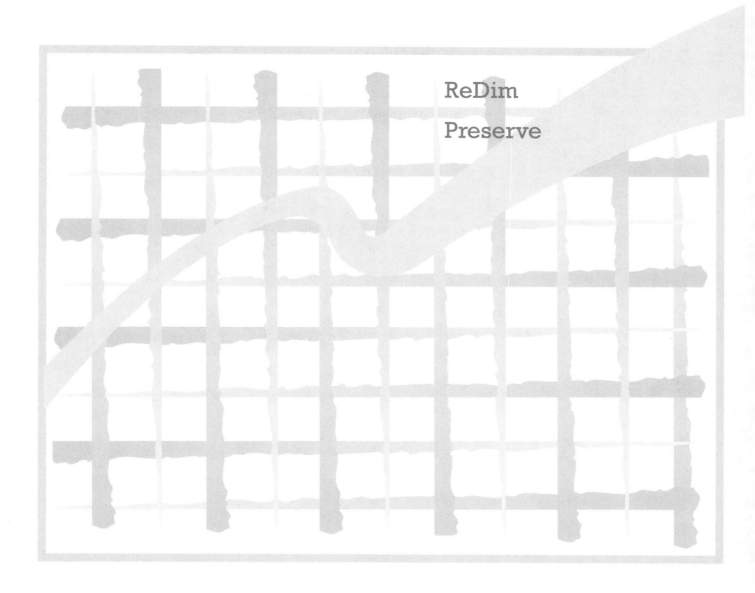

ReDim

Preserve

Chapter Nine Objectives

After completing this chapter you will be able to:

1. Understand variable arrays and the elements of an array.
2. Write variable array declarations and understand how arrays are initialized and their elements accessed.
3. Understand upper bound, lower bound, and the Visual Basic built-in functions LBound and UBound.
4. Use **For…Next** loops with arrays.
5. Understand how to use arrays with meaningful indexes.
6. Search an array using a linear search algorithm.
7. Understand dynamic arrays.
8. Use the **ReDim** and **ReDim Preserve** statements.
9. Understand control arrays.
10. Use the Index property and the Count method.
11. Use control arrays as parameters.
12. Remove an object from a control array.
13. Understand a two-dimensional array.
14. Declare a matrix and understand dynamic matrices.

$\mathbf{I}$n this chapter you will learn about variable arrays and control arrays. The linear search algorithm for searching an array is discussed, as well as using multidimensional arrays.

9.1 Variable Arrays

member, element
index

A *variable array* stores a set of variables that each have the same name and are all of the same type. Each variable of an array is called a *member*, or *element*, and is identified by a number called an *index*. A **String** array with five members could be visualized as:

0	1	2	3	4
Elaine	Vickie	Tristan	Sage	Cory

StrNames

Option Base

The statement **Option Base** 1 is used to change the default starting index of the arrays in a module from 0 to 1. The statement must be placed in the General section.

In Visual Basic, indexing begins with 0 unless specified otherwise. Therefore, in the example above, Sage is the fourth element of the array and has index 3.

array declaration

upper bound

An array is declared with a **Dim**, **Private**, or **Static** statement that includes the identifier followed by the upper bound of the array in parentheses and then the data type. The *upper bound* of an array is the highest index of the array. The data type of the array indicates the type of the elements. For example, the statement

Dim strNames(4) **As String**   '5 elements

declares a strNames array that has five **String** elements with indexes 0, 1, 2, 3, and 4. The starting index of an array can be specified by including a *lower bound* in the array declaration. For example, the statement

lower bound

Dim strNames(1 **To** 5) **As String**

declares a strNames array that has five **String** elements with indexes 1, 2, 3, 4, and 5. The upper bound and lower bound of an array may also be specified using a constant of type **Long**, as in the statements:

Const lngLowerBound **As Long** = 1
Const lngUpperBound **As Long** = 5
Dim strNames(lngLowerBound **To** lngUpperBound) **As String**

array initialization

When an array is declared, its variables are initialized by Visual Basic. Numeric array elements are initialized to 0, **String** array elements to empty strings, and **Boolean** array elements to False values.

9.2 Using Arrays

accessing an element

An element of an array is accessed by including its index in parentheses after the array name. For example, the following statement displays in a label Caption the value of the element with index 4:

```
lblStudentName.Caption = strNames(4)
```

assignment

Assignment to an array element works similarly. For example, the following statement assigns "Tristan" to the element with index 3:

```
strNames(3) = "Tristan"
```

LBound, UBound

The LBound and UBound Visual Basic built-in functions are used to determine the lower bound and upper bound of an array. The LBound and UBound functions take the form:

```
LBound(ArrayName)
UBound(ArrayName)
```

ArrayName is the name of the array. LBound returns the lower bound of *ArrayName*, and UBound returns the upper bound of *ArrayName*.

For...Next

A **For...Next** loop is often used to access the elements of an array because the loop counter can be used as the array index. For example, in the following statements, a **For...Next** loop and an input box are used to assign values to the elements of an array:

```
…
For lngIndex = LBound(strNames) To UBound(strNames)
    strNames(lngIndex) = InputBox("Enter student's first name:", "Students")
Next lngIndex
…
```

In the above statements, an input box is displayed for each loop iteration. The text entered in the input box is then assigned to the element with index lngIndex.

The Display Names application uses input boxes to get five names from the user and then displays the names in a list box:

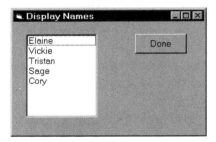

```
Private Sub Form_Load()
    Dim strNames(1 To 5) As String
    Dim lngIndex As Long

    'Load names
    For lngIndex = LBound(strNames) To UBound(strNames)
        strNames(lngIndex) = InputBox("Enter student's first name:", "Students")
    Next lngIndex

    'Display names
    For lngIndex = LBound(strNames) To UBound(strNames)
        lstNames.AddItem strNames(lngIndex)
    Next lngIndex
End Sub
```

```
Private Sub cmdDone_Click()
    Unload Me
End Sub
```

9.3 Range Errors

run-time error

A run-time error occurs if code refers to an index outside the lower bound to upper bound range of an array. For example, the following assignment statement causes a run-time error:

```
Dim strNames(9) As String
strNames(10) = "Constance"
```

The error message produced by the above statements is "Subscript out of range." *Subscript* is another word for index.

subscript

Review 1 ───

Using paper and pencil, write declarations for an array storing 15 test grades (integer values), an array storing 100 prices (currency values), and an array storing 50 true/false test answers (Boolean values).

Review 2 ───

Follow the instructions below to create the Display Names application.

1) CREATE A NEW PROJECT

2) ADD OBJECTS TO THE FORM

Refer to the form below when placing and sizing the form and its objects. Use the table below to name and change the properties of the objects.

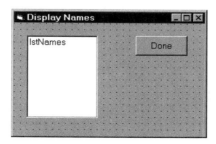

Object	Name	Caption
Form1	frmDisplayNames	Display Names
List1	lstNames	
Command1	cmdDone	Done

3) SAVE THE PROJECT

From the File menu, select Save Project. Save the form naming it frmDisplayNames and save the project naming it Display Names.

4) WRITE THE PROGRAM CODE

Display the Code Editor window and add the following code:

```
Option Explicit

Private Sub Form_Load()
   Dim strNames(1 To 5) As String
   Dim lngIndex As Long

   'Load names
   For lngIndex = LBound(strNames) To UBound(strNames)
      strNames(lngIndex) = InputBox("Enter student's first name:", "Students")
   Next lngIndex

   'Display names
   For lngIndex = LBound(strNames) To UBound(strNames)
      lstNames.AddItem strNames(lngIndex)
   Next lngIndex
End Sub

Private Sub cmdDone_Click()
   Unload Me
End Sub
```

5) RUN THE APPLICATION

Save the modified Display Names project and then run the application. Test the application by entering five names.

6) PRINT AND THEN REMOVE THE PROJECT

9.4 Array Parameters

Arrays can be passed as arguments and declared as procedure parameters by using the array name followed by an empty set of parentheses. However, arrays are required to be passed by reference. For example, the SumOfItems function has an array parameter and returns the sum of the elements in the array. Note that the array parameter is **ByRef**:

```
'**********************************************************
'  Returns the sum of the values in intNumArray
'
'  Pre:   intNumArray contains at least one element
'  Post:  Sum of values in intNumArray returned
'**********************************************************
Function SumOfItems (ByRef intNumArray() As Integer) As Long
   Dim lngIndex As Long
   Dim lngSum As Long

   lngSum = 0     'initialize sum
   For lngIndex = LBound(intNumArray) To UBound(intNumArray)
      lngSum = lngSum + intNumArray(lngIndex)
   Next lngIndex
   SumOfItems = lngSum
End Function
```

The array name followed by an empty set of parentheses is used in a procedure call. For example, the following statement passes intDataArray to the SumOfItems function:

```
lngTotal = SumOfItems(intDataArray())
```

A single element of an array may also be passed as an argument. Single array elements can be passed by value or by reference. For example, the DisplayElement procedure displays intNumber in lblLabel. Single elements may be passed **ByVal** or **ByRef**:

```
'*************************************************************
'   Assigns intNumber to the Caption of lblLabel
'
'   Post:  intNumber displayed in lblLabel
'*************************************************************
Sub DisplayElement (ByVal intNumber As Integer, ByRef lblLabel As Label)
    lblLabel.Caption = intNumber
End Sub
```

Only the array element is included in a procedure call. For example, the following statement passes the intDataArray element with index 3 to the DisplayElement procedure:

```
Call DisplayElement(intDataArray(3))
```

9.5 Arrays with Meaningful Indexes

An index value can indicate the data stored by its element. For example, an intTestScores array with 100 elements indexed from 1 to 100 could store a count of all the scores of 90 in the element with index 90, the scores of 82 in element 82, etc. Many algorithms make use of this aspect of an array's structure to simplify storage. The Dice Rolls and Letter Occurrences applications described in this section implement such algorithms.

The Dice Rolls application counts the frequency of dice roll outcomes. Each roll of the dice is simulated by generating a random number from 1 to 6 for each of two dice. The outcome of each roll is used to update the intCounts array, which stores counters. For example, if 3 is rolled, then element 3 of the intCounts array is updated. The Dice Rolls interface and code are shown below:

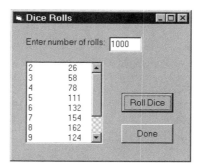

The Dice Rolls application after entering 1000 and clicking on the Roll Dice button

```
Private Sub Form_Load()
    Randomize
End Sub

Private Sub cmdRollDice_Click()
    Dim intNumRolls As Integer
    Dim intCounts(2 To 12) As Integer        'lowest roll is 2, highest is 12

    intNumRolls = txtNumRolls.Text
    Call CountTrials(intNumRolls, intCounts())
    Call DisplayCounts(intCounts(), lstOutcome)
End Sub
```

```
Private Sub txtNumRolls_Change()
   lstOutcome.Clear
End Sub

'****************************************************************
'  Simulates intNumRolls rolls of two dice and stores the
'  counts of each outcome in intCounts()
'
'  pre: intCount() lower bound is 2, upper bound is 12
'  post: intNumRolls dice rolls simulated. Counts of
'  intNumRolls simulated dice rolls stored in intCounts()
'****************************************************************
Sub CountTrials(ByVal intNumRolls As Integer, ByRef intCounts() As Integer)
   Dim intRoll As Integer, intRollOutcome As Integer

   For intRoll = 1 To intNumRolls
      intRollOutcome = Int(6 * Rnd + 1) + Int(6 * Rnd + 1)
      intCounts(intRollOutcome) = intCounts(intRollOutcome) + 1
   Next intRoll
End Sub

'****************************************************************
'  Displays the contents of intCounts() in a list box
'
'  post: Elements of intCounts() displayed in a list box
'****************************************************************
Sub DisplayCounts(ByRef intCounts() As Integer, ByRef lstList As ListBox)
   Dim intRollOutcome As Integer

   For intRollOutcome = LBound(intCounts) To UBound(intCounts)
      lstList.AddItem intRollOutcome & vbTab & intCounts(intRollOutcome)
   Next intRollOutcome
End Sub

Private Sub cmdDone_Click()
   Unload Me
End Sub
```

The Letter Occurrences application counts the frequency of characters in a string. To simplify the storage of the letter counts, an intLetterCounts array will be used. To further simply storage, the intLetterCounts array will have indexes that correspond to the ASCII codes representing the uppercase letters "A" (ASCII 65) through "Z" (ASCII 90). The Letter Occurrences interface and code follow:

The Letter Occurrences application after entering a phrase (a quote by John Kieran) and clicking on the Count Letters button

An Introduction to Programming Using Microsoft Visual Basic

```
Private Sub Form_Load()
  Randomize
End Sub

Private Sub cmdCountLetters_Click()
  Dim strPhrase As String
  '65 is ASCII code for A, 90 is ASCII code for Z
  Dim intLetterCounts(65 To 90) As Integer

  strPhrase = txtString.Text
  Call CountLetters(strPhrase, intLetterCounts())
  Call DisplayCounts(intLetterCounts(), lstOutcome)
End Sub

Private Sub txtString_Change()
  lstOutcome.Clear
End Sub

'**************************************************************************
'  Counts the occurrences of letters a through z, regardless of case, in strPhrase
'
'  pre: intLetterCounts() has 26 elements with 65 lower bound and 90 upper bound
'  post: intLetterCounts() contains the counts of the
'  occurrences of letters a through z and A through Z in strPhrase
'**************************************************************************
Sub CountLetters(ByVal strPhrase As String, ByRef intLetterCounts() As Integer)
  Dim intCharacter As Integer
  Dim strUppercaseLetter As String

  For intCharacter = 1 To Len(strPhrase)
    strUppercaseLetter = UCase(Mid(strPhrase, intCharacter, 1))
    If strUppercaseLetter >= "A" And strUppercaseLetter <= "Z" Then
      intLetterCounts(Asc(strUppercaseLetter)) = _
        intLetterCounts(Asc(strUppercaseLetter)) + 1
    End If
  Next intCharacter
End Sub

'**********************************************************************
'  Displays the contents of intLetterCounts() in a list box
'
'  post: Elements of intLetterCounts() displayed in a list box
'**********************************************************************
Sub DisplayCounts(ByRef intLetterCounts() As Integer, ByRef lstList As ListBox)
  Dim intLetterCount As Integer

  For intLetterCount = LBound(intLetterCounts) To UBound(intLetterCounts)
    lstList.AddItem Chr(intLetterCount) & vbTab & intLetterCounts(intLetterCount)
  Next intLetterCount
End Sub

Private Sub cmdDone_Click()
  Unload Me
End Sub
```

Note that the CountLetters procedure converts each letter of strPhrase to uppercase and then determines if the character is a letter from A to Z. In DisplayCounts, the loop control variable, intLetterCount, is converted to a character to act as a label in the list.

Review 3

The Dice Rolls application discussed in Section 9.5 is coded for rolling two dice. Open the Dice Rolls application and modify it to count and display the rolls of three dice. The application interface should look similar to that shown on the right after entering 1000 for the number of rolls and clicking on the Roll Dice button.

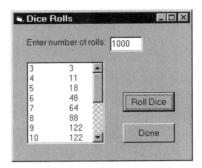

Review 4

Create a Number Occurrences application that displays the counts of the occurrences of each digit in a number entered by the user (Hint: treat the number entered as a string). The application interface should look similar to that shown on the right after entering the number 12664590 and clicking on the Count Numerals button.

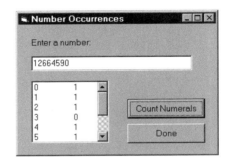

9.6 Searching an Array

linear search

There are many ways to search an array for a specific value. The simplest searching algorithm is called *linear search* and works by proceeding from one element to the next through the array until the desired value is found or until the entire array has been searched. The function FindItemIndex below uses the linear search algorithm:

```
'*************************************************************
'  Returns the index of the first occurrence of intSearchItem in
'  intDataArray() or -1 if intSearchItem not found
'
'  pre: intDataArray upper bound >= 0
'  post: Index of the first occurrence of intSearchItem returned, or
'  -1 returned if intSearchItem not found.
'*************************************************************
Function FindItemIndex(ByRef intDataArray() As Integer, _
ByVal intSearchItem As Integer) As Integer
   Dim intIndex As Integer

   intIndex = LBound(intDataArray)
   Do While (intDataArray(intIndex) <> intSearchItem) _
      And (intIndex < UBound(intDataArray))
      intIndex = intIndex + 1
   Loop
   If intDataArray(intIndex) = intSearchItem Then
      FindItemIndex = intIndex      'Item found
   Else
      FindItemIndex = -1            'Item not found
   End If
End Function
```

An Introduction to Programming Using Microsoft Visual Basic

The loop used in FindItemIndex does not explicitly check the last item in intDataArray. However, if intSearchItem has not yet been found the If...Then compares it to the last array item.

9.7 Dynamic Arrays

A *dynamic array* can vary in size during run time and is used in situations where the size of an array is unknown at the start of a program or when it would be more efficient to vary the size of an array throughout program execution. A dynamic array is declared in a statement similar to the following:

Dim intDataArray() **As Integer**

Note that the array name is followed by an empty set of parentheses, indicating the size is unknown.

ReDim

A ReDim statement allocates space for the elements of a dynamic array. The upper bound for the array must be included. A lower bound may also be included. For example, the following statement allocates space for five elements with indexes 1 through 5:

ReDim intDataArray(1 **To** 5)

ReDim can be executed again and again to resize an array throughout program execution. However, each time a ReDim statement is executed, all the values in the array are lost. To keep the existing values in an array when resizing it, the **ReDim Preserve** statement must be used. The

Preserve

Preserve keyword is legal only when changing the upper bound of an array. A run-time error occurs when the lower bound is changed in a ReDim Preserve statement. For example, the following statements demonstrate **Preserve**:

```
Dim intDataArray() As Integer
Dim intX As Integer, intY As Integer

intX = 1
intY = 2
ReDim intDataArray(intX To intY)
intDataArray(1) = 200
intDataArray(2) = 250
ReDim Preserve intDataArray(intX To intY+1)    'Add an element
lblLabel.Caption = intDataArray(2)             '250
ReDim intDataArray(intX To intY)               'Remove element 3
lblLabel.Caption = intDataArray(2)             '0
```

Note that in the statements above, the value at index 2 remains after the **ReDim Preserve** statement. In the second **ReDim** statement, the value of the array is initialized to 0.

It is important to realize that a **ReDim Preserve** statement is illegal before a dynamic array has been dimensioned because there are no values to preserve. Also, a run-time error will occur when LBound or UBound are used with a dynamic array that has not been dimensioned.

The application shown on the next page demonstrates dynamic arrays. It includes the AddItem and RemoveItem general procedures for adding and removing elements to the array:

Dimension

The **Dim** keyword stands for dimension. A declared variable has "dimension" because it has been assigned space in memory.

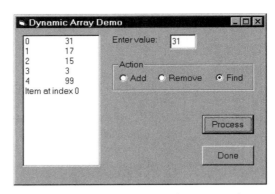

The Dynamic Array Demo application after adding several values, entering a number, selecting Find, and clicking Process

```
Private Sub Form_Load()
   Randomize
   optAdd.Value = True
   optRemove.Value = False
   optFind.Value = False
End Sub

Private Sub cmdProcess_Click()
   Static intDataArray() As Integer        'Declare dynamic array
   Static intNumDataItems As Integer       'Number of items in intDataArray
   Dim intNumEntered As Integer
   Dim intIndex As Integer

   intNumEntered = txtNumEntered.Text
   If optAdd.Value Then
      Call AddItem(intDataArray(), intNumDataItems, intNumEntered)
      Call DisplayData(intDataArray(), intNumDataItems, lstArrayElements)
   ElseIf optRemove.Value And intNumDataItems > 0 Then
      Call RemoveItem(intDataArray(), intNumDataItems, intNumEntered)
      Call DisplayData(intDataArray(), intNumDataItems, lstArrayElements)
   ElseIf optFind.Value And intNumDataItems > 0 Then
      intIndex = FindItemIndex(intDataArray(), intNumEntered)
      lstArrayElements.AddItem "Item at index " & intIndex
   End If
End Sub
'*****************************************************************
'  Increases size of intDataArray() by 1, increments intNumDataItems
'  by 1, and adds intNumToAdd as the last element of the array
'
'  pre: intDataArray() lower bound is 0 if intDataArray() has one or
'  more elements
'  post: intDataArray() increased by 1, intNumDataItems incremented
'  by 1, and intNumToAdd last element of array
'*****************************************************************
Sub AddItem(ByRef intDataArray() As Integer, _
ByRef intNumDataItems As Integer, ByVal intNumToAdd As Integer)
   If intNumDataItems = 0 Then
      ReDim intDataArray(intNumDataItems)     'One element with Index 0
   Else
      ReDim Preserve intDataArray(intNumDataItems)
   End If
   intDataArray(intNumDataItems) = intNumToAdd
   intNumDataItems = intNumDataItems + 1
End Sub
```

An Introduction to Programming Using Microsoft Visual Basic

```
'*******************************************************************
' Decreases size of intDataArray() by 1, decrement intNumDataItems by 1,
' removes first occurence of intNumToRemove from intDataArray() if found
'
' pre: intNumDataItems > 0
' post: intDataArray() decreased by 1, intNumDataItems decremented by 1,
' intNumToRemove deleted from array, if found
'*******************************************************************
Sub RemoveItem(ByRef intDataArray() As Integer, _
ByRef intNumDataItems As Integer, ByVal intNumToRemove As Integer)
   Dim intItemIndex As Integer, intIndex As Integer

   intItemIndex = FindItemIndex(intDataArray(), intNumToRemove)
   If intItemIndex > -1 Then                    'fill spot of removed item
      For intIndex = intItemIndex To (UBound(intDataArray) - 1)
         intDataArray(intIndex) = intDataArray(intIndex + 1)
      Next intIndex
      intNumDataItems = intNumDataItems - 1 'decrement intNumDataItems
      If intNumDataItems > 0 Then             'resize array
         ReDim Preserve intDataArray(intNumDataItems - 1)
      End If
   End If
End Sub

'*************************************************************
' Returns the index of the first occurrence of intSearchItem in
' intDataArray() or -1 if intSearchItem not found
'
' pre: intDataArray() has at least one element
' post: Index of the first occurrence of intSearchItem returned, or
' -1 returned if intSearchItem not found
'*************************************************************
Function FindItemIndex(ByRef intDataArray() As Integer, _
ByVal intSearchItem As Integer) As Integer
   Dim intIndex As Integer

   intIndex = LBound(intDataArray)
   Do While (intDataArray(intIndex) <> intSearchItem) _
      And (intIndex < UBound(intDataArray))
      intIndex = intIndex + 1
   Loop
   If intDataArray(intIndex) = intSearchItem Then
      FindItemIndex = intIndex     'Item found
   Else
      FindItemIndex = -1           'Item not found
   End If
End Function

'*******************************************************************
' Clears list box and then displays the contents of intDataArray() in a list box
'
' post: list box cleared of any previous items. intDataArray() elements
' displayed in a list box
'*******************************************************************
Sub DisplayData(ByRef intDataArray() As Integer, _
ByVal intNumDataItems As Integer, ByRef lstList As ListBox)
   Dim intIndex As Integer

   lstList.Clear
   If intNumDataItems > 0 Then
      For intIndex = LBound(intDataArray) To UBound(intDataArray)
         lstList.AddItem intIndex & vbTab & intDataArray(intIndex)
      Next intIndex
   End If
End Sub
```

There are several things to note about the Dynamic Array Demo application. In the cmdProcess_Click event procedure, intDataArray is declared as a dynamic static array. If it were not a static variable, intDataArray would be reinitialized each time the Process button is clicked. Also in this procedure, a static counter intNumDataItems is declared to keep track of the number of data items stored in the array. This variable is required so that the dynamic array is resized correctly.

The AddItem procedure first appropriately resizes intDataArray. If there are 0 data items, then the **Preserve** keyword is not needed. Note that the array is resized to the number of data items because indexing starts at 0. After the array is resized, the new item is added as the last element and then intNumDataItems is incremented.

The RemoveItem procedure finds the first location of the item to be removed and then moves each following element up one spot to fill the space. intNumDataItems is decremented and then the array resized. Note that the array is made smaller only when there are more than 0 elements in the array because an array cannot be redimensioned to an empty array.

Review 5

Create a Find Name application that allows the user to add, delete, and find names. The application interface should look similar to that shown on the right after adding several names, entering Sage, selecting the Find option button, and then clicking on the Process button.

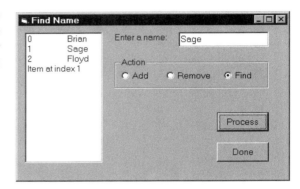

9.8 Control Arrays

A *control array* is a set of objects that each have the same name and are all of the same type. Each object of a control array is identified by the object's *Index property* Index property value, which is set at design time. For example, the Control Array Demo application contains a control array of command buttons:

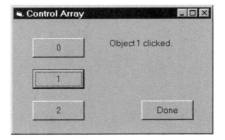

creating a control array   The simplest way to create a control array is to create the first object of the array and change its name as desired. Next, copy and then paste the first object to create the next object in the array. When the second object of the array is pasted, Visual Basic displays a dialog box asking if you want to create a control array:

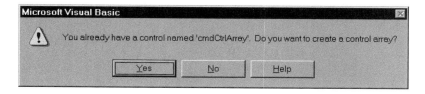

Copying and Pasting

An object is copied by selecting it, which displays handles, and then selecting the Copy command (Ctrl+C) from the Edit menu. Next, the Paste command (Ctrl+V), also from the Edit menu, is selected to place a copy of the object on the form.

Selecting Yes in the above dialog box places the object copy on the form, giving it the same name as the first and changing its Index value to 1. At this time, Visual Basic also changes the Index of the original object to 0. Finally, repeatedly pasting places additional copies of the object on the form, with each having the same name and incrementing Index values.

The advantage of using a control array is that the objects in the array share event procedures. For example, an array of command buttons has only one click event and therefore only one click event procedure is coded. This click event procedure is automatically passed the Index value of the command button clicked. The code for the Control Array Demo application is shown below:

```
Private Sub Form_Load()
    cmdCtrlArray(0).Caption = "0"
    cmdCtrlArray(1).Caption = "1"
    cmdCtrlArray(2).Caption = "2"
End Sub

Private Sub cmdCtrlArray_Click(Index As Integer)
    lblOutput.Caption = "Object " & Index & " clicked."
End Sub

Private Sub cmdDone_Click()
    Unload Me
End Sub
```

The objects of a control array are accessed at run time by using the object name followed by the Index value in parentheses, as in the Form_Load procedure. Note the Index parameter in the cmdCtrlArray_Click event procedure. Visual Basic automatically adds the proper parameter to a control array event procedure when the Object List in the Code Editor window is used to add the event procedure.

LBound, UBound

The LBound and UBound properties may be used with a control array to determine the lowest and highest Index property values of the array objects. LBound and UBound are used in a statement similar to:

```
For Index = cmdCtrlArray.LBound To cmdCtrlArray.UBound
    ...
```

Count

The Count method returns the number of objects in a control array and takes the form:

```
intNumObjects = cmdCtrlArray.Count
```

using control arrays as parameters

A control array can be passed as an argument by using the control array name. When declared as a procedure parameter, a control array must be **ByRef** and is of type **Object**. The Tic-Tac-Toe application in the next section uses a control array parameter.

removing an object from a control array

An object is removed from a control array by changing its name and deleting its Index property value.

Review 6

Follow the instructions below to create the Shell Game application.

1) CREATE A NEW PROJECT

2) ADD OBJECTS TO THE FORM

Refer to the form below when placing and sizing the form and its objects. Use the table below to name and change the properties of the objects.

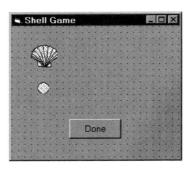

Object	Name	Caption	Picture
Form1	frmShellGame	Shell Game	
Image1	imgShells		Shell
Image2	imgPearls		Pearl
Command1	cmdDone	Done	

3) CREATE TWO CONTROL ARRAYS

Be sure that the two image objects added to the form have been named and the appropriate graphic has been selected using the Picture property.

a. Click on the shell image to select it. Handles are displayed.
b. From the Edit menu, select the Copy command. A copy of the shell image object is placed on the Clipboard.
c. From the Edit menu, select the Paste command. A dialog box is displayed.
d. Select Yes in the dialog box to create a control array. A copy of the shell image is placed on the form.
e. In the Properties window, note that the Index of the new image object is 1.
f. Move the new image object to the center of the form, beside the first image object.
g. Execute the Paste command to paste another image object on the form. Move this image object to the right of the second.
h. Create a control array of pearl image objects. Refer to the interface below for placement:

4) SAVE THE PROJECT

From the File menu, select the Save Project command. Save the form naming it frmShellGame and save the project naming it Shell Game.

5) WRITE THE PROGRAM CODE

a. Display the Code Editor window and add the Form_Load procedure:

```
Private Sub Form_Load()
    Dim intIndex As Integer

    Randomize

    'Hide pearls at start of program
    For intIndex = imgPearls.LBound To imgPearls.UBound
        imgPearls(intIndex).Visible = False
    Next intIndex
End Sub
```

b. From the Object list, select imgShells. A click event procedure containing an **Integer** parameter is added to the module. Complete the imgShells_Click event procedure:

```
Private Sub imgShells_Click(Index As Integer)
    Dim intShellWithPearl As Integer

    'Pick the shell that hides the pearl
    intShellWithPearl = Int((imgPearls.UBound - imgPearls.LBound + 1) * Rnd _
        + imgPearls.LBound)
    imgPearls(intShellWithPearl).Visible = True      'Show the pearl
    If intShellWithPearl = Index Then
        MsgBox "You win!"
    Else
        MsgBox "Sorry, you lose."
    End If
    imgPearls(intShellWithPearl).Visible = False      'Hide the pearl
End Sub
```

Note how control arrays have simplified the above code. With the shell images in a control array, there is only one event procedure, not three. No matter which shell the user clicks, this event procedure is executed. Placing the pearl images in a control array simplifies displaying the "hidden" pearl because only the pearl image with Index value intShellWithPearl is displayed. When the user selects OK in the message box, the pearl is again "hidden."

c. Code the Done command button:

```
Private Sub cmdDone_Click()
    Unload Me
End Sub
```

6) RUN THE APPLICATION

a. Save the modified Shell Game project and then run the application. Try to guess which shell is "hiding" the pearl and then click on that shell. The pearl and a message box is displayed.
b. Select OK in the message box and then play again.

7) PRINT AND THEN REMOVE THE PROJECT

9.9 Two-Dimensional Arrays

matrix A *matrix* is a multidimensional variable array that is used to store related information. Just as one-dimensional arrays can have meaningful indexes for representing data, a two-dimensional array can be used to represent data that relates to a grid. For example, a checkerboard, a tic-tac-toe board, the streets in a city, and seats in a theater can all be represented by a grid. A two-dimensional matrix representing a tic-tac-toe board can be visualized as shown below:

	0	1	2
0	X	O	X
1	X	X	O
2	O	O	O

strTTTBoard

declaring a matrix

A matrix is declared with a **Dim**, **Private**, or **Static** statement that includes the identifier followed by the upper bound of the first dimension (the rows) and the upper bound of the second dimension (the columns) separated by a comma in parentheses and then the data type. For example, the statement

```
Dim strTTTBoard(2, 2) As String      '9 elements
```

declares a 3 x 3 strTTTBoard matrix that has nine **String** elements with rows indexed 0 to 2 and columns indexed 0 to 2. Each element is accessed by including the appropriate row and column indexes in parentheses after the matrix name. For example, the following statement assigns the Caption of cmdBoard to the element in the first row (0) and the second column (1):

```
strTTTBoard(0, 1) = cmdBoard.Caption
```

The lower bound of each dimension of a matrix can be specified in the matrix declaration. For example, the following statement declares a strTTTBoard matrix that has nine **String** elements with rows indexed 1 to 3 and columns indexed 1 to 3:

```
Dim strTTTBoard(1 To 3, 1 To 3) As String
```

LBound, UBound

The LBound and UBound Visual Basic built-in functions may also be used with matrices to determine lower and upper bounds of dimensions. When used with a matrix, the LBound and UBound functions take the form:

```
LBound(MatrixName, Dimension)
UBound(MatrixName, Dimension)
```

MatrixName is the name of the matrix. *Dimension* is 1 for the row dimension and 2 for the column dimension.

nested For…Next

Nested **For…Next** loops are often used to access the elements of a matrix because one loop counter indicates the row of the matrix and the other counter indicates the column. For example, in the following statements, nested **For…Next** loops are used to display the contents of a matrix in a list box:

```
...
Dim strTTTBoard(2, 2) As String
For lngRow = LBound(strTTTBoard, 1) To UBound(strTTTBoard, 1)
    For lngCol = LBound(strTTTBoard, 2) To UBound(strTTTBoard, 2)
        lstMove.AddItem strTTTBoard(lngRow, lngCol)
    Next lngCol
Next lngRow
...
```

An Introduction to Programming Using Microsoft Visual Basic

dynamic matrix

A matrix may also be dynamic. As with a one-dimensional dynamic array, a dynamic matrix is declared in a **Dim** statement with an empty set of parentheses and then a **ReDim** statement is later used to change the dimensions.

The Tic-Tac-Toe application uses a control array to represent the board and a matrix to keep track of player moves. The Tic-Tac-Toe interface and code follow:

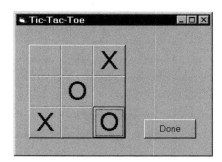

Tic-Tac-Toe after four moves

```
'**********************************************************
' Two players play a game of Tic-Tac-Toe
'
' pre: Board is made of a command button control array with
' empty Captions and Indexes in the following order:
'       0  1  2
'       3  4  5
'       6  7  8
' post: Tic-Tac-Toe has been played until a winner or a
' draw is declared or the Done button clicked.
'**********************************************************
Private Sub cmdTTTSquares_Click(Index As Integer)
    Static strTTT(2, 2) As String    'Store players moves
    Static strPlayer As String       'O or X

    'Initialize strPlayer
    If strPlayer = "" Then
        strPlayer = "X"              'X goes first
    End If

    'Check for existing X or O
    If cmdTTTSquares(Index).Caption <> "" Then
        MsgBox "Invalid move."
    Else
        'Show move
        cmdTTTSquares(Index).Caption = strPlayer

        'Store move in strTTT()
        Call MakeMove(Index, strPlayer, strTTT())

        'Check for winner
        If IsWinner(strTTT()) Then
            MsgBox "Game over!"
            Call NewGame(strPlayer, strTTT(), cmdTTTSquares)
        Else                         'Next player's turn
            If strPlayer = "X" Then
                strPlayer = "O"
            Else
                strPlayer = "X"
            End If
        End If
    End If
End Sub
```

```
'**************************************************************
' Store Tic-Tac-Toe move in strTTT() matrix
'
' pre: 0 <= intIndex <= 8, strTTT() is 3 x 3 matrix with
' indexing starting at 0
' post: Tic-Tac-Toe move stored in strTTT() matrix
'**************************************************************
Sub MakeMove(ByVal intIndex As Integer, ByVal strPlayer As String, _
ByRef strTTT() As String)
    If intIndex <= 2 Then          'Move made in first row
        strTTT(0, intIndex) = strPlayer
    ElseIf intIndex <= 5 Then 'Move made in second row
        strTTT(1, intIndex - 3) = strPlayer
    Else                           'Move made in third row
        strTTT(2, intIndex - 6) = strPlayer
    End If
End Sub

'**************************************************************
' Determines if there is a winner
'
' pre: strTTT() is 3 x 3 matrix with indexing starting at 0
' post: True returned if a winner is found or if all the
' TTTSquares are filled
'**************************************************************
Function IsWinner(ByRef strTTT() As String) As Boolean
    Dim intRow As Integer, intCol As Integer
    Dim blnMovesLeft As Boolean

    IsWinner = False

    'Check all rows
    For intRow = 0 To 2
        If strTTT(intRow, 0) = strTTT(intRow, 1) And _
            strTTT(intRow, 1) = strTTT(intRow, 2) And _
            strTTT(intRow, 0) <> "" Then
            IsWinner = True
        End If
    Next intRow
    'Check all columns
    For intCol = 0 To 2
        If strTTT(0, intCol) = strTTT(1, intCol) And _
            strTTT(1, intCol) = strTTT(2, intCol) And _
            strTTT(0, intCol) <> "" Then
            IsWinner = True
        End If
    Next intCol

    'Check one diagonal
    If strTTT(0, 0) = strTTT(1, 1) And strTTT(1, 1) = strTTT(2, 2) And _
        strTTT(0, 0) <> "" Then
        IsWinner = True
    End If

    'Check other diagonal
    If strTTT(0, 2) = strTTT(1, 1) And strTTT(1, 1) = strTTT(2, 0) And _
        strTTT(0, 2) <> "" Then
        IsWinner = True
    End If
```

An Introduction to Programming Using Microsoft Visual Basic

```
'Check for empty squares
blnMovesLeft = False
For intRow = 0 To 2
  For intCol = 0 To 2
    If strTTT(intRow, intCol) = "" Then
      blnMovesLeft = True
    End If
  Next intCol
Next intRow
If Not blnMovesLeft Then
  IsWinner = True
End If
End Function

'**************************************************************
' Changes player to X, reinitializes strTTT(), and
' Clears cmdTTTSquares
'
' pre: strTTT() is 3 x 3 matrix with indexing starting at 0 and
' cmdSquares is a command button control array of 9 buttons with
' indexing starting at 0
' post: strTTT() matrix initialized and control array captions cleared
'**************************************************************
Sub NewGame(ByRef strPlayer As String, ByRef strTTT() As String, _
ByRef cmdTTTSquares As Object)
  Dim intIndex As Integer, intRow As Integer, intCol As Integer

  'Player X starts
  strPlayer = "X"

  'clear player moves
  For intRow = 0 To 2
    For intCol = 0 To 2
      strTTT(intRow, intCol) = ""
    Next intCol
  Next intRow

  'Clear board
  For intIndex = 0 To 8
    cmdTTTSquares(intIndex).Caption = ""
  Next intIndex
End Sub

Private Sub cmdDone_Click()
  Unload Me
End Sub
```

Case Study

In this Case Study a restaurant order application for Lucy's Cuban Cafe will be created.

specification   The specification for this Case Study is:

> The Lucy's Cuban Cafe application allows the user to click on a menu item to select it. The selected item is then added to the total order and the amount due for the order is updated and displayed.

design   The form design for this Case Study is:

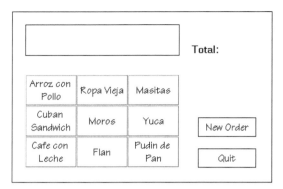

The menu item command buttons are a control array

Lucy's Cuban Cafe

Lucy serves only authentic Cuban food at her restaurant. The menu names are in Spanish and translate to English as Arroz con Pollo (Chicken and yellow rice), Ropa Vieja (shredded beef), Masitas (pork served with plantains), Cuban Sandwich (Cuban bread with meat and cheese), Moros (black beans and rice), Yuca (cassava), Cafe con Leche (coffee with milk), Flan (baked custard), and Pudin de Pan (bread pudding).

There are several things to note about this interface design. The menu items are a control array because each menu item should perform the same task (add it to the list and update the total amount due) when selected, regardless of the menu item. The items ordered will be added to a list box so that many items can easily be accommodated. A New Order button is added so that many orders can be processed while the application is running.

The program code design for this Case Study includes using arrays to hold item names and prices. The array indexes for each item should correspond to the appropriate command button. The pseudocode for the complex event procedures is:

```
Private Sub Form_Load()
    Create an array of item names
    Assign items names to control array
    Create an array of item prices
End Sub

Private cmdFood_Click(Index As Integer)
    Add selected food item to list
    Update total amount due
    Show total
End Sub

Private cmdNewOrder_Click()
    Change total to 0
    Show total
    Clear list box
End Sub
```

Adding the selected food item to the list box is best done in a separate general procedure. Both the cmdFood_Click and cmdNewOrder_Click event procedures update the total displayed. Therefore, a general procedure called ShowTotal should be coded.

An Introduction to Programming Using Microsoft Visual Basic

coding   The interface and code for this Case Study is:

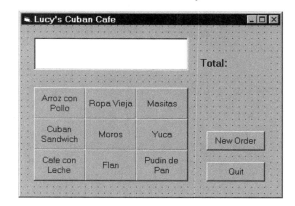

Object	Name	Caption	Index
Form1	frmLucysCubanCafe	Lucy's Cuban Cafe	
List1	lstItemsOrdered		
Label1	lblTotal	*empty*	
Command1	cmdFood		0
	cmdFood		1
	cmdFood		2
	cmdFood		3
	cmdFood		4
	cmdFood		5
	cmdFood		6
	cmdFood		7
	cmdFood		8
Command2	cmdNewOrder	New Order	
Command3	cmdQuit	Quit	

```
Option Explicit
Dim curPriceList() As Currency
Dim strItemList() As String
Dim curTotal As Currency          'Order total

Private Sub Form_Load()
   Const intNumItems As Integer = 9   'number of menu items
   Dim intIndex As Integer

   ReDim strItemList(intNumItems)
   'Load item names
   strItemList(0) = "Arroz con Pollo"
   strItemList(1) = "Ropa Vieja"
   strItemList(2) = "Masitas"
   strItemList(3) = "Cuban Sandwich"
   strItemList(4) = "Moros"
   strItemList(5) = "Yuca"
   strItemList(6) = "Cafe con Leche"
   strItemList(7) = "Flan"
   strItemList(8) = "Pudin de Pan"


   'Assign Captions to cmdFood command buttons
   For intIndex = 0 To intNumItems - 1
      cmdFood(intIndex).Caption = strItemList(intIndex)
   Next intIndex
```

```
        ReDim curPriceList(intNumItems)
        'Load items prices
        curPriceList(0) = 9.95    'Arroz con Pollo
        curPriceList(1) = 9.95    'Ropa Vieja
        curPriceList(2) = 8.95    'Masitas
        curPriceList(3) = 6.95    'Cuban Sandwich
        curPriceList(4) = 2.75    'Moros
        curPriceList(5) = 2.75    'Yuca
        curPriceList(6) = 1.75    'Cafe con Leche
        curPriceList(7) = 2.5     'Flan
        curPriceList(8) = 2.95    'Pudin de Pan
    End Sub

    Private Sub cmdFood_Click(Index As Integer)
        Call AddToList(Index)
        curTotal = curTotal + curPriceList(Index)
        Call ShowTotal(curTotal, lblTotal)
    End Sub

    Private Sub cmdNewOrder_Click()
        curTotal = 0              'reinitialize order total
        Call ShowTotal(curTotal, lblTotal)
        lstItemsOrdered.Clear    'clear items ordered
    End Sub

    Sub AddToList(ByRef intIndex As Integer)
        lstItemsOrdered.AddItem strItemList(intIndex) & vbTab & _
            Format(curPriceList(intIndex), "Currency")
    End Sub

    Sub ShowTotal(ByVal curTotal As Currency, ByRef lblLabel As Label)
        lblLabel.Caption = "Total: " & Format(curTotal, "Currency")
    End Sub

    Private Sub cmdQuit_Click()
        Unload Me
    End Sub
```

testing and debugging   Running Lucy's Cuban Cafe and clicking on several menu items
displays the following:

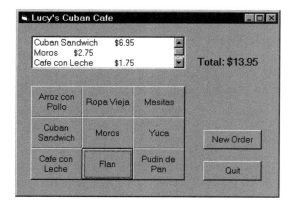

This Case Study should be tested by selecting each of the menu items at
least once and verifying that the items appear correctly in the list and
that the total is updated correctly. The New Order button should also be
clicked to verify that it performs as expected.

An Introduction to Programming Using Microsoft Visual Basic

Review 7

Modify the Lucy's Cuban Cafe Case Study application to include an English command button that when clicked displays the English names of the menu items on the buttons. The English button should become dimmed once it is clicked.

Chapter Summary

member, element
A variable array stores a set of variables that each have the same name and are all of the same type. Each variable of an array is called a member, or element, of the array. An array can be one-dimensional or multidimensional. A multidimensional array is called a matrix.

array declaration
upper bound

lower bound
A variable array is declared using a Dim, Private, or Static statement that includes the identifier followed by the upper bound of the array in parentheses. Multidimensional array declarations must include the upper bound for each dimension. By default, arrays have a lower bound of 0. A different lower bound may be specified in the array declaration. The lower bound and upper bound of an array may be declared using constants of type Long.

array initialization
When an array is declared, its elements are initialized by Visual Basic. Numeric array elements are initialized to 0, String array elements to empty strings, and Boolean array elements to False values.

accessing an element

For...Next
An element of an array is accessed by including the desired index number in parentheses after the variable name. To access an element of a multidimensional array, both the row and column indexes must be used. A For...Next loop is used to access the elements of an array. Nested For...Next loops are used to access the elements of a multidimensional array. A run-time error occurs if code refers to an index outside the lower bound to upper bound range of an array.

LBound, UBound
The LBound and UBound Visual Basic built-in functions are used to determine the lower bound(s) and upper bound(s) of a variable array.

Variable arrays can be passed as arguments and declared as procedure parameters by using the array name followed by an empty set of parentheses. However, arrays are required to be passed by reference. A single array element may be passed by value or by reference by including the array name followed by the desired index(es) in parentheses.

An array's structure can be thought of as a set of storage boxes where the name of each box (the index) indicates the data stored in that box. Many algorithms make use of this aspect of an array's structure to simplify storage.

linear search
A simple algorithm for searching an array is called linear search, which proceeds from one element to the next through the array until the desired value is found or until the array has been searched.

dynamic array

Preserve
ReDim
A dynamic array can vary in size during run time and is used in situations where the size of an array is unknown at the start of a program or when it would be more efficient to vary the size of an array throughout program execution. A ReDim statement allocates space for the elements of a dynamic array and erases existing elements. The keyword Preserve in a ReDim statement leaves existing values in the array.

Index property

A control array is a set of objects that each have the same name and are all of the same type. Each object of a control array is identified by the object's Index property value, which is set at design time. The simplest way to create a control array is to copy and paste an object.

LBound
UBound
Count
Object

The objects of a control array are accessed at run time by using the object name followed by the Index value in parentheses. The LBound and UBound properties are used to determine the lowest and highest Index property values in the array. The Count method returns the number of objects in a control array. A control array is of type **Object** and can be passed as an argument or declared as a procedure parameter. An object is removed from a control array by changing its name and deleting its Index value.

Vocabulary

Control array A set of objects that each have the same name and are of the same type.

Dynamic array An array that can vary in size during run time.

Element A variable of an array.

Index The number used to identify an element of a variable or control array.

Linear search A simple algorithm for searching an array for a specific element.

Lower bound The lowest index of an array.

Matrix A multidimensional array that is used to store related information.

Member A variable of an array.

Subscript Another word for index.

Upper bound The highest index of an array.

Variable array A set of variables that each have the same name and are all of the same type.

Visual Basic

() Parentheses are used with an identifier to indicate an array.

Count Method that returns the number of objects in a control array.

LBound Function that returns the lower bound of an array. Also a control array property that returns the lowest Index value of the objects in the control array.

Preserve Keyword used in a **ReDim** statement to keep the existing values of an array when it is resized.

ReDim Statement used to allocate space for the elements of a dynamic array.

UBound Function that returns the upper bound of an array. Also a control array property that returns the highest Index value of the objects in the control array.

Exercises

Exercise 1

Modify the Display Names application from Review 2 so that the names are displayed in the list box in the reverse order in which they were entered.

Exercise 2

Create a Max and Min Numbers application that generates an array of 10 random numbers between 1 and 99 and then displays the array elements in a list box. The application should display the highest number in the array when the Max button is clicked and the lowest number in the array when the Min button is clicked. The application interface should look similar to:

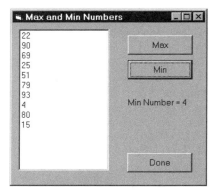

Exercise 3

Create a Generated Numbers application that stores in an array with indexes 1 through 100 numbers generated by the index values. Generate the number to be stored at each index by summing the index and its individual digits. For example, 25 should be stored at index 17 because 17 + 1 + 7 = 25 and 4 should be stored at index 2 because 2 + 0 + 2. The application interface should look similar to:

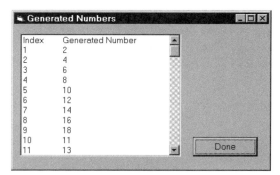

Your program code should use a FillArray procedure to generate the numbers and a DisplayArray procedure that displays each index and its element in the list box.

An Introduction to Programming Using Microsoft Visual Basic

Exercise 4

Modify the Hangman Case Study from Chapter Six to keep track of the letters guessed in an array with meaningful indexes. A message box should be displayed if the user enters the same guess twice.

Exercise 5

a) Create a Generate Numbers application that allows the user to enter the size of the array and then loads the array with random numbers between 1 and 99 and then displays the array index and its element in a list box. The application interface should look similar to:

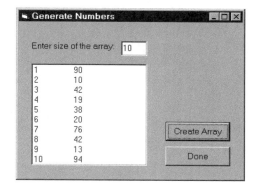

b) *Advanced.* An array is said to be sorted if it's elements are in either increasing or decreasing order. The selection sort algorithm works by repeatedly taking the lowest item from an array and adding it to a new array, so that all the elements in the new array are sorted from low to high. Modify the Generate Numbers application so that it also displays the array sorted from low to high in the list box. Your program code should use:

- FindLowest function that returns the index of the lowest value in the array.
- Sort procedure that repeatedly finds the lowest value in an Array A, removes it, and adds it to an array T. When all the values of A have been moved, the elements of T are copied to A with an assignment statement and a loop. Use the FindLowest function and refer to the AddItem and RemoveItem procedures from the text.

Exercise 6

Create a Matching Index and Element application that allows the user to enter the size of an array in an input box and then randomly fills each element of the array with a number that is in the range of 1 to the size of the array, and then displays the array elements in a list box. Have the application count the indexes of the array that match its corresponding element value. For example, if the random number generated is 2 and stored in index 2, then count it. The application interface should look similar to:

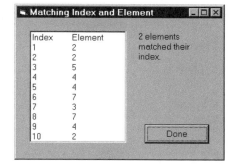

Exercise 7

Create an Even and Odd Numbers application that generates an array of 10 random numbers between 1 and 99, and displays in a list box the entire array, the even numbers, and the odd numbers. The application interface should look similar to:

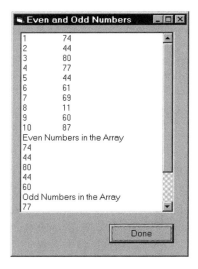

Your program code should use:

- FillArray procedure to generate and store the random numbers in the array
- DisplayArray procedure that displays the index and its element in the list box
- EvenNumbers procedure that adds the even numbers to the list box
- OddNumbers procedure that adds the odd numbers to the list box

Exercise 8

Create a Duplicate Values application that allows the user to enter numbers between 1 and 99 in an input box until a duplicate value is entered. When a duplicate value is entered, the numbers entered before the duplicate value are displayed in a list box and a message is displayed of how many numbers where entered. The application interface should look similar to the following after entering 67, 87, 90, and 67, in input boxes:

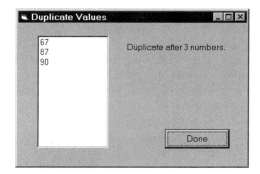

Exercise 9

Modify the Mastermind application from Chapter Seven Exercise 13 to use arrays with the following features:

- Permit the number of pegs (from 1 to 10) to be specified at the start of the application.
- Permit the number of colors (from 1 to 9) to be specified at the start of the program.
- Permit both the guess and the secret code to contain duplicates. This will require extra care when counting the number of pegs of the correct color. For example, if the secret code is 1, 2, 3, 4, 5 and the guess is 2, 1, 1, 2, 2 then the program should only report two correct colors (a single 1 and a single 2).

Exercise 10

Create a Lockers application that simulates a progressive cycle of closing and opening every n^{th} locker in a hall of 100 lockers, with n starting at the 2nd locker and continuing through to the 100th locker. The application should represent the locker status (open or close) as a boolean array with True representing open. When the application first starts, all of the lockers should be open and their status displayed in a list box. When the user clicks the Simulate button, the status of every 2nd locker should be switched (if it is open then close it and if it is closed open it). Then, the status of every 3rd locker should be switched. Continue this process for every 4th through the 100th locker. Display the concluding locker statuses in a list box. The application interface should look similar to that shown on the next page after clicking on the Simulate button:

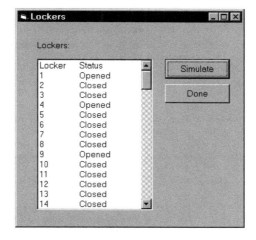

Can you identify what pattern the open lockers represent in the concluding array?

Exercise 11 ⚙ ──────────────────────────────

The Shell Game application from Review 6 gives the user just one chance at choosing the shell with the pearl. Using the following guidelines, modify the Shell Game application to give the user a better chance of finding the pearl:

- After the user selects a shell but before the hidden pearl is displayed, remove (hide) one of the other two shells that does not contain the pearl.
- Use an input box to ask the user if he or she wants to keep the original guess or choose the remaining shell as the new guess.
- Display the result in a message box.

The application interface should look similar to the following after playing one game:

Exercise 12 ──────────────────────────────────

a) Create a Game Board application that represents a game board with 16 spots. Use a control array of command buttons to represent the 16 spots. The application should simulate 100 dice rolls when the user clicks the **100 Dice Rolls** button and store in an array with meaningful indexes the total number of times each spot was landed on based on the dice roll (moving around the board clockwise). The total count should be displayed on each command button. The application interface should look similar to the following after clicking on the **100 Dice Rolls** button:

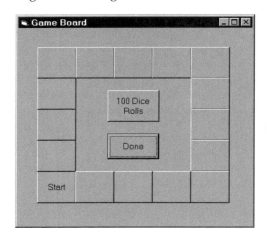 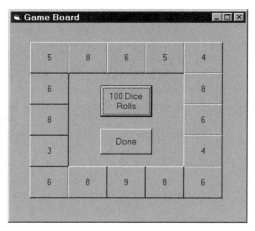

b) *Advanced.* Modify the application so that spot 13 is a "Go Back" location. If spot 13 is landed on, count it as being landed on but go back to spot 5, count it as being landed on and continue from spot 5. Also, if doubles are rolled consecutively then go back to spot 5.

Exercise 13

a) Create a Golf Game application that uses a two-dimensional array representing 4 golfers playing 9 holes of golf (4 x 9 matrix) to store 36 randomly generated golf scores (integer values 1 through 9), and displays the contents of the matrix in a list box. The golfer with the lowest number of strokes on a hole wins that hole. Display how many holes each player won overall. The application interface should look similar to:

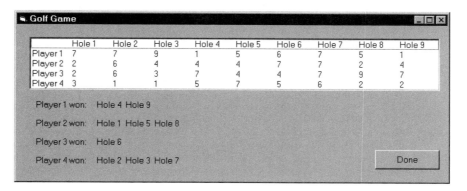

b) *Advanced*. Modify the application to include an option that allows the user to manually enter the golf scores into the array.

Exercise 14

Create a Hidden Prizes application that contains a control array of command buttons to represent a 5 x 5 board. The user is allowed five guesses to find the two randomly selected command buttons that contain the text Comp and uter. If the user finds both of the hidden words, he or she wins. The application interface should look similar to:

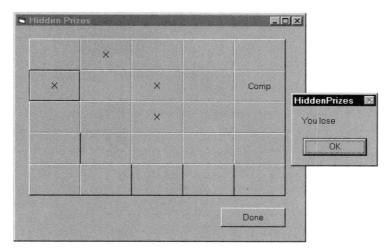

Advanced
Exercise 15

The game of Life was devised by a mathematician as a model of a very simple world. The Life world is a two-dimensional plane of cells. Each cell may be empty or contain a single creature. Each day, creatures are born or die in each cell according to the number of neighboring creatures on the previous day. A neighbor is a cell that adjoins the cell either horizontally, vertically, or diagonally. The rules in pseudocode style are:

- If the cell is alive on the previous day
     Then if the number of neighbors was 2 or 3
          the cell remains alive
          otherwise the cell dies (of either loneliness or overcrowding)
- If the cell is not alive on the previous day
     Then if the number of neighbors was exactly 3
          the cell becomes alive
          otherwise it remains dead.

For example, the world displayed as:

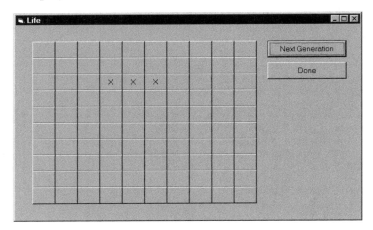

where X's indicate live cells, becomes

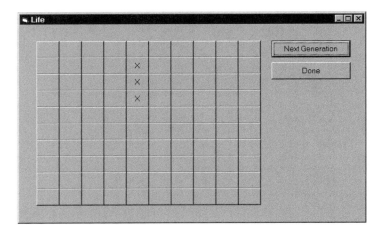

Create an application that uses a 10 x 10 grid. To initialize the grid, have the application randomly generate the coordinates for 20 cells. Show a new generation each time the user clicks on the Next Generation button, or until there are no more live cells.

The Penny Pitch game is popular in amusement parks. Pennies are tossed onto a board that has certain areas marked with different prizes. For example:

PUZZLE		POSTER		DOLL
	POSTER		DOLL	BALL
	PUZZLE	GAME		
PUZZLE	BALL		POSTER	GAME
DOLL	GAME			BALL

The prizes available on this board are puzzle, game, ball, poster, and doll. At the end of the game, if all of the squares that say BALL in them are covered by a penny, the player gets a ball. This is also true for the other prizes. The board is made up of 25 squares (5 x 5). Each prize appears on 3 randomly chosen squares so that 15 squares contain prizes.

Create an application that simulates ten pennies being randomly pitched onto the board. At the end of the game display a list of the prizes won or NONE.

An Introduction to Programming Using Microsoft Visual Basic

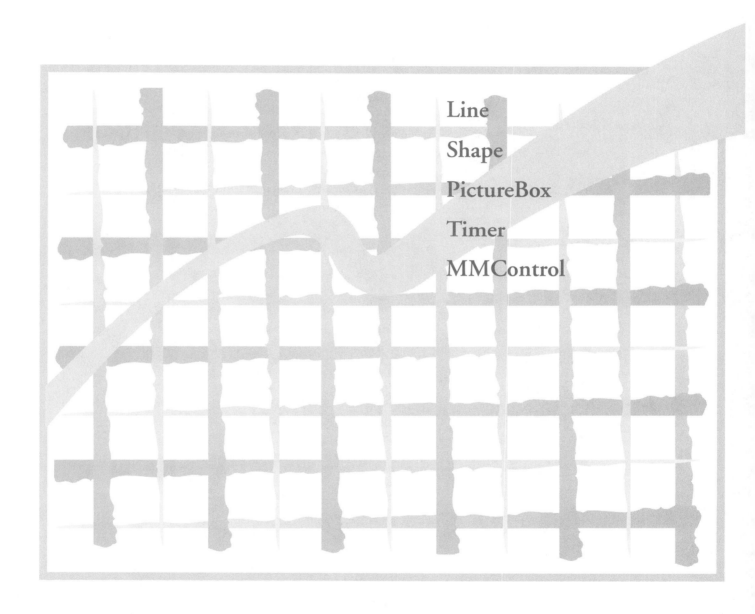

Line

Shape

PictureBox

Timer

MMControl

Chapter Ten Objectives

After completing this chapter you will be able to:

1. Change the color of text, a form, and its objects.
2. Add lines and shapes to an application.
3. Use picture box objects.
4. Move shapes and pictures boxes in a container.
5. Understand twips.
6. Understand graphic methods such as Line, Circle, and PSet.
7. Use container properties that affect graphics, such as AutoRedraw and DrawStyle.
8. Use timer objects and timer event procedures.
9. Move line objects using the x and y coordinate properties X1, Y1, X2, Y2.
10. Add animation to an application using graphics and timer objects.
11. Add sound to an application.

$\mathbf{C}$olors and graphics are used to make applications easier to understand and more interesting. An image can be complex, like those introduced in Chapter Three, or a simple graphic such as a solid circle or square. In this chapter, you will use a picture box object to place images and draw graphics on a form. You will learn to draw graphics on a form at design time and run time using the line and shape objects and the Line and Circle methods. The timer object will be used to include simple animation in an application. Sound will be added to an application using the multimedia object.

10.1 Using Color

Color can be used to enhance an application's interface. For example, a command button can be red and a form can be white. Other objects that have color properties are text boxes, labels, option buttons, check boxes, list boxes, combo boxes, and frames. Object color is changed at design time using the properties:

- **BackColor** changes the background color of an object. Clicking on the BackColor down arrow in the properties list and then clicking the Palette tab displays colors that can be selected. The Style property of a command button must be set to Graphical at design time for the BackColor to be displayed.

- **ForeColor** changes the color of the text displayed on an object. Clicking on the ForeColor down arrow in the properties list and then clicking the Palette tab displays colors that can be selected. There is no ForeColor property for command buttons. The ForeColor property for a form will be discussed later in the chapter.

BackColor and ForeColor can be changed at run time through assignment using the following Visual Basic color constants:

vbBlack	vbMagenta
vbBlue	vbRed
vbCyan	vbWhite
vbGreen	vbYellow

RGB Function

RGB (Red, Green, and Blue) is used to define colors on a computer monitor. Each tiny dot on the monitor is actually composed of three smaller dots, one each of red, green, and blue. To display a color, the computer varies the brightness of the three dots. For example, purple is displayed by having the red and blue dots shine brightly and the green dot dimmed. White is displayed by having the three dots fully on, and black by having them off.

The RGB function can be used at run time in an assignment statement to change a color property and takes the form:

RGB (*red, green, blue*)

where *red, green, blue* are integer variables, values, or expressions between 0 and 255 that represent the brightness of red, green, and blue that make up the color. RGB can be used instead of a Visual Basic color constant, which allows a larger choice of colors to be used. For example

Me.BackColor = RGB (255, 0, 0)

changes the background color of a form to red.

For example, the following assignment statement changes the background color of a form to blue when it is loaded:

Private Sub Form_Load()
 Me.BackColor = vbBlue
End Sub

Image objects do not have color properties.

Review 1

Create a Change Background Color application that changes the background color of the form to the appropriate color when one of the color buttons is clicked. The form and command buttons should initially be white. The application interface should look similar to that shown on the right after clicking on the Yellow button.

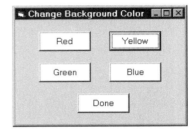

10.2 Adding Lines to an Application

A line is a simple graphic that can be incorporated into an application interface. For example, lines are used on a form to separate information. The Line Examples application displays different line styles:

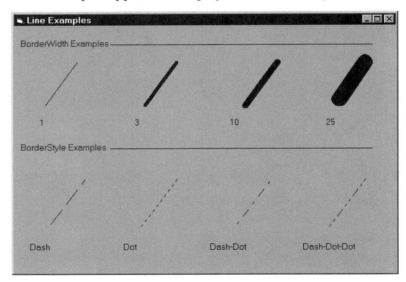

Lines of different BorderStyles and BorderWidths

line   A *line* object is created using the Line control () in the Tool box and has the properties:

- **Name** identifies the object and is used by the programmer. It is good programming style to begin line object names with lin.

- **BorderColor** changes the color of a line. BorderColor can be changed at run time through assignment using the Visual Basic color constants.

- **BorderStyle** can be set to transparent, solid, dash, dot, dash-dot, dash-dot-dot, or inside-solid. BorderStyle can be changed at run time through assignment using the following Visual Basic constants:

vbTransparent	vbBSDashDot
vbBSSolid	vbBSDashDotDot
vbBSDash	vbBSInsideSolid
vbBSDot	

- **BorderWidth** changes the thickness of a line. BorderWidth can be changed at run time through assignment using a numeric variable, value, or expression that evaluates to 1 to 8,192. BorderWidth must be set to 1 for BorderStyles to take effect, except for the solid and inside-solid BorderStyles.

When creating lines, the BackColor of the form should be set first because changing the BackColor of the form erases any graphics drawn on the form.

10.3 Adding Shapes to an Application

Simple graphics can be incorporated in an application interface by adding shapes including circles, squares, and ovals. The Simple Graphic Examples application below displays possible shapes that can be added to an application:

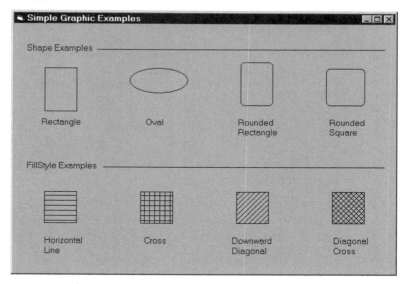

Simple graphics with different Shapes and FillStyles

shape   A *shape* object is created using the Shape control ( ) in the Tool box and has the properties:

- **Name** identifies the object and is used by the programmer. It is good programming style to begin shape object names with shp.

- **BackColor** changes the background color of a shape. When FillStyle is set to solid the BackColor is ignored. BackColor can be changed at run time through assignment using the Visual Basic color constants.

- **BackStyle** can be set to transparent or opaque. When BackStyle is set to transparent, BackColor is ignored. BackStyle can be changed at run time through assignment using 0 for transparent and 1 for opaque.

- **BorderColor** changes the color of the outline of a shape. BorderColor can be changed at run time through assignment using the Visual Basic color constants.

- **BorderStyle** can be set to transparent, solid, dash, dot, dash-dot, dash-dot-dot, or inside-solid. BorderStyle can be changed at run time through assignment using the following Visual Basic constants:

vbTransparent	vbBSDashDot
vbBSSolid	vbBSDashDotDot
vbBSDash	vbBSInsideSolid
vbBSDot	

- **BorderWidth** changes the thickness of the outline of a shape. BorderWidth can be changed at run time through assignment using a numeric variable, value, or expression that evaluates to 1 to 8,192. BorderWidth must be set to 1 for BorderStyles to take effect, except for the solid and inside-solid BorderStyles.

- **FillColor** changes the inside color of a shape. FillColor can be changed at run time through assignment using the Visual Basic color constants.

- **FillStyle** can be set to solid, transparent, horizontal line, vertical line, upward diagonal, downward diagonal, cross, or diagonal cross. When FillStyle is set to transparent the FillColor is ignored. FillStyle can be changed at run time through assignment using the following Visual Basic constants:

vbFSSolid	vbFSTransparent
vbHorizontalLine	vbVerticalLine
vbUpwardDiagonal	vbDownwardDiagonal
vbCross	vbDiagonalCross

- **Shape** can be set to rectangle, square, oval, circle, rounded rectangle, or rounded square. Shape can be changed at run time through assignment using the following Visual Basic constants:

vbShapeRectangle	vbShapeSquare
vbShapeOval	vbShapeCircle
vbShapeRoundedRectangle	vbShapeRoundedSquare

When drawing shapes, the BackColor of the form should be set first because changing the BackColor of the form erases any graphics drawn on the form.

Review 2

Create a Shapes application that displays a variety of different shapes with different color and style properties. Your application should have a minimum of three different shapes, three different colors, three different styles, and a line object. The application interface should look similar to that shown on the right.

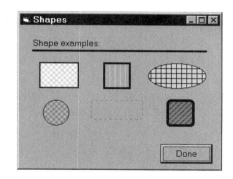

10.4 Picture Boxes

Picture boxes allow the user to place images and graphics on a form. The difference between an image object and a picture box is that an image object uses less system resources because it can only contain an image and has only a few of the properties, events, and methods that the picture box object has. A *picture box* object is created using the PictureBox control () in the Tool box and has the properties:

 picture box

- **Name** identifies the object and is used by the programmer. It is good programming style to begin picture box object names with pic.

LoadPicture

- **Picture** is used to display a dialog box for selecting the image to display in the picture area. Picture can be changed at run time through assignment using the LoadPicture function. The LoadPicture function takes the form:

  picObject.Picture = LoadPicture (*filepath*)

  picObject is the name of the picture object and *filepath* is a **String** variable or a string enclosed in quotation marks that specifies the location of the graphic file on disk. If *filepath* is not included, the picture box object is cleared.

- **BorderStyle** can be set to none or fixed single. BorderStyle can be changed at run time through assignment using 0 for none and 1 for fixed single. When BorderStyle is set to None there is no border around the graphic.

- **AutoSize** can be either True or False. When AutoSize is True, the picture box is resized to the same size as the graphic. When AutoSize is False, the graphic is resized to the same size as the picture box. If the picture box is resized, the graphic is also resized.

- **Visible** can be either True or False. Visible is often set at run time to display (Visible = True) or hide (Visible = False) the graphic in the picture box.

In addition to using a picture box to place an image from a file, the Shape control can be used to create a simple graphic on the picture box. In this case, the picture box is the container for the graphic.

File Types

A picture box can display images that are in the following formats:

BMP	Windows Bitmap
GIF	Graphics Interchange Format
JPG	Joint Photographic Experts Group
WMF	Windows Metafile Format
ICO	Icon

10.5 Moving Shapes and Picture Boxes

A shape or graphic can be moved within its container, which is either a form or a picture box. Note that a picture box can be both an object within a form container and a container of other objects. Shapes and picture box objects have properties that are used to position them in their container:

- **Left** changes the distance between the left edge of the object and the left edge of the form.

- **Top** changes the distance between the top edge of the object and the top edge of the form.

- **Width** changes the width of the object. A form object also has a Width property.

- **Height** changes the height of the object. A form object also has a Height property.

twips   The distance an object moves is expressed in units called *twips*, where 1,440 twips equal 1 inch (567 twips equal 1 cm). For example, the picture box shown below is 600 twips from the left and 800 twips from the top of the form container:

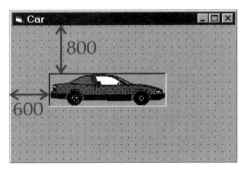

Move method   The Move method is used at run time to move a picture box or shape object to a new location. The Move method is used in a statement that takes the form

    object.Move *left, top, width, height*

where *object* is the name of the picture box or shape object to move and *left* is a required numeric value that specifies the twips between the left edge of *object* and the left edge of the container. *top, width,* and *height* are optional numeric arguments that specify the twips from the top of the container to the top of *object*, the width of *object*, and the height of *object*, respectively. For example, the following statement

    picSmiley.Move picSmiley.Left - 20

moves the picture box named picSmiley 20 twips to the left of its current position. If the picture box is currently 100 twips from the left edge of its container than the expression picSmiley.Left - 20 results in the picSmiley being moved to 80 twips from the left edge of its container.

Review 3

Follow the instructions below to create the Move Graphic application.

1) **CREATE A NEW PROJECT**

2) **ADD OBJECTS TO THE FORM**

Refer to the form below when placing and sizing the form and its objects. Use the table below to name and change the properties of the objects.

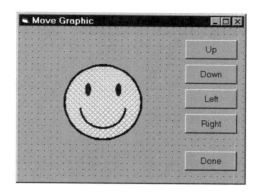

Object	Name	Caption	Picture	BorderStyle	AutoSize
Form1	frmMoveGraphic	Move Graphic			
Command1	cmdUp	Up			
Command2	cmdDown	Down			
Command3	cmdLeft	Left			
Command4	cmdRight	Right			
Command5	cmdDone	Done			
Picture1	picSmiley		Smiley	None	True

3) **SAVE THE PROJECT**

From the File menu, select Save Project. Save the form naming it frmMoveGraphic and save the project naming it Move Graphic.

4) **WRITE THE PROGRAM CODE**

Display the Code Editor window and add the following event procedures:

```
Private Sub cmdUp_Click()     'moves object 40 twips up from its current position
    picSmiley.Move picSmiley.Left, picSmiley.Top - 40
End Sub

Private Sub cmdDown_Click() 'moves object 40 twips down from its current position
    picSmiley.Move picSmiley.Left, picSmiley.Top + 40
End Sub

Private Sub cmdLeft_Click()     'moves object 40 twips to the left of its current position
    picSmiley.Move picSmiley.Left - 40
End Sub

Private Sub cmdRight_Click()  'moves object 40 twips to the right of its current position
    picSmiley.Move picSmiley.Left + 40
End Sub

Private Sub cmdDone_Click()
    Unload Me
End Sub
```

5) RUN THE APPLICATION

Save the modified Move Graphic project and run the application. Test the application by clicking on each command button.

6) PRINT AND THEN REMOVE THE PROJECT

Review 4 ——————————————————————————

Create a Move Graphics application that moves three images and a solid square graphic in a clockwise or counter clockwise motion. Use the Move method in your program code. The application interface should look similar to that shown on the right after clicking on the Clockwise button.

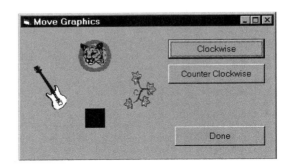

10.6 Using Graphic Methods

Form and picture box container objects have methods that can be used to create and manipulate graphics at run time:

- Line draws a line or rectangle
- Circle draws a circle, ellipse, or arc.
- PSet sets the color of an individual point.
- PaintPicture paints a graphic at a specified location.
- Cls clears all graphics.

coordinate system

These methods use the x and y coordinates of the container object. The coordinate system of a container can be thought of as a two-dimensional grid with the upper-left corner of the container as position 0,0. The x-coordinate is the position in twips from the left of the container and the y-position is the position in twips from the top of the container.

Line method

The Line method is used in a statement that takes the form

object.**Line** (*x1, y1*)-(*x2, y2*), *color*, **BF**

where *object* is the container, *x1* and *y1* indicate the starting point of the line, *x2* and *y2* indicate the ending point, *color* is a Visual Basic color constant that indicates the color of the line(s), B indicates a box should be formed from the points, and F indicates to fill the box with *color*. The x and y coordinates are **Single** variables, values, or expressions. The *color*, B, and F arguments are optional. The following event procedures create a line and a rectangle:

```
Private Sub cmdDrawLine_Click()
    Me.Line (100, 100)-(500, 500), vbBlue
End Sub
```

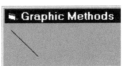

Line drawn using the Line method

Omitted Arguments

The graphic methods discussed in this section have many arguments, some arguments are required and others are optional. When optional arguments are omitted and arguments that come after it are still needed, commas are used as placeholders. For example, to draw a box without specifying any color the statement would be:

Me.**Line** (50, 50)–(200, 200), , **B**

```
Private Sub cmdDrawBox_Click()
    Me.Line (200, 200)-(600, 650), vbRed, B
End Sub
```

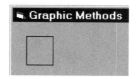

Rectangle drawn using the Line method

Circle method

The Circle method is used in a statement that takes the form

*object.***Circle** *(x, y), radius, color, start, end, aspect ratio*

where *object* is the container, *x* and *y* is the center point of the circle, *radius* is the size of the radius, *color* is a Visual Basic color constant that indicates the color of the circle outline, *start* and *end* are the beginning and ending points of an arc (refer to the side bar on Arcs for more information), and *aspect ratio* specifies a circle or ellipse.

The arguments *x*, *y*, *radius*, *start*, *end*, and *aspect ratio* are **Single** variables, values, or expressions. *start* and *end* are values between -2π and 2π radians and *aspect ratio* is 1 for a circle, less than 1 for a wide ellipse, and greater than 1 for a tall ellipse. The arguments after *radius* are optional. The following event procedures create a circle, arc, and ellipse:

```
Private Sub cmdDrawCircle_Click()
    Me.Circle (500, 300), 200
End Sub
```

Circle drawn using the Circle method

```
Private Sub cmdDrawArc_Click()
    Me.Circle (500, 300), 200, , 3.14, 0
End Sub
```

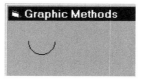

Arc drawn using the Circle method

```
Private Sub cmdDrawEllipse_Click()
    Me.Circle (500, 300), 200, , , , 1.5
End Sub
```

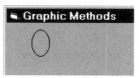

Ellipse drawn using the Circle method

Arcs

An arc is a portion of a circle. The following diagram shows points on a circle measured in radians (2π radians = 360°):

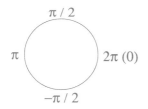

For example, an arc representing a quarter circle could begin at 0 and end at $\pi/2$. When calculating the starting and ending point, keep in mind that the radians are measured counterclockwise.

PSet method

The PSet method is used in a statement that takes the form

object.**PSet** (*x, y*), *color*

where *object* is the container, *x* and *y* are **Single** variables, values, or expressions that specify the position of the dot, and *color* is a Visual Basic color constant that indicates the color of the dot. *color* is optional. The following event procedure creates a dot:

```
Private Sub cmdDrawDot_Click()
    PSet (1000, 500), vbBlue
End Sub
```

— dot

Dot drawn using the PSet method

PaintPicture method

The PaintPicture method is used in a statement that takes the form

object.PaintPicture *object2*.Picture, *x, y*

where *object* is the container, *object2* is the name of an object that has a Picture property, and *x, y* are **Single** variables, values, or expressions that specify the upper-left position of picture. The following event procedure places the image in the imgSmiley object into the picNewLocation picture box:

```
Private Sub cmdPaintPicture_Click()
    picNewLocation.PaintPicture imgSmiley.Picture, 100, 100
End Sub
```

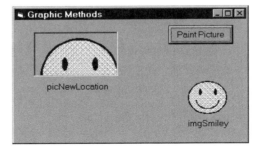

The graphic in the image box was "painted"
into the picture box

Cls method

The Cls method is used in a statement that takes the form

object.Cls

where *object* is the container that is to be cleared of all graphics drawn on it using the graphics methods. The following code demonstrates Cls:

```
Private Sub cmdEraseGraphics_Click()
    Me.Cls 'Erases graphics drawn on the form using graphic methods
End Sub
```

An Introduction to Programming Using Microsoft Visual Basic

b. Change the following properties of the form:

DrawWidth	FillColor	FillStyle	ForeColor
3	a color of your choosing	Solid	a different color than the FillColor

7) RUN THE APPLICATION

Save the modified Draw Shapes project and run the application. Test the application by clicking on each button. Note how the properties set for the container object (the form) affect the appearance of the shapes drawn with the graphics methods.

8) PRINT AND THEN REMOVE THE PROJECT

Review 6

Create a Face application that displays a happy face inside a picture box when the Happy button is clicked and a sad face when the Sad button is clicked. When the application first starts a face with a straight horizontal line for the mouth should be displayed. The eyes should have a black outline and a green inside. The nose should be solid black and the mouth should be a red line with a width of 2. The smile and frown should be an arc. The application interface should look similar to that shown on the right after clicking on the Happy button.

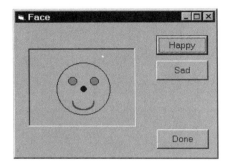

10.8 Using a Timer Object

timer Applications often require code to be executed at regular intervals. For example, some word processors automatically save a document every 10 minutes. A timer object is used to execute code at specified intervals and can also be used to simulate animation. A *timer* object is created using the Timer control ( ) in the Tool box and has the properties:

- **Name** identifies the object and is used by the programmer. It is good programming style to begin timer object names with tmr.

- **Interval** is the amount of time that passes before the Timer event procedure is executed. Interval is specified in milliseconds between 0 and 64,767 where 1,000 milliseconds equals 1 second. Interval can be changed at run time through assignment.

- **Enabled** can be set to either True or False. When Enabled is True, the Timer event will be called. When Enabled is False, the Timer event will not be called.

Although the timer object is displayed on the form at design time, when the application is running it is hidden from the user.

timer event A timer event occurs automatically after the amount of time specified in the Interval property has passed. For example, if Interval is 1000, then a timer event occurs every 1000 milliseconds (every second). A timer event procedure is coded for each timer object on the form, and is automatically called by the application when a timer event occurs. After the code in the timer event procedure has been executed the timer object starts counting down again.

The following timer event procedure changes the BackColor of the form when a timer event occurs:

```
Private Sub tmrBlinkColor_Timer()
    If Me.BackColor = vbBlue Then
        Me.BackColor = vbRed
    Else
        Me.BackColor = vbBlue
    End If
End Sub
```

If the tmrBlinkColor Interval property is set to 1000, then the form changes color every second. In this case it goes from red to blue and then back again.

10.9 Moving Line Objects

Line objects created using the Line control can be moved at run time using the properties:

- **X1** changes the x coordinate of the starting point of the line. X1 can be changed at run time through assignment.

- **Y1** changes the y coordinate of the starting point of the line. Y1 can be changed at run time through assignment.

- **X2** changes the x coordinate of the ending point of the line. X2 can be changed at run time through assignment.

- **Y2** changes the y coordinate of the ending point of the line. Y1 can be changed at run time through assignment.

Changing a line object's X1, X2, Y1, and Y2 properties moves the line to the new coordinates on its container.

Review 7

Follow the instructions below to create the Move Line application.

1) **CREATE A NEW PROJECT**

2) **ADD OBJECTS TO THE FORM**

Refer to the form below when placing and sizing the form and its objects. Use the table on the next page to name and change the properties of the objects.

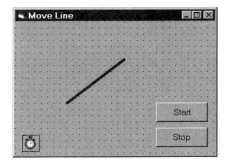

Object	Name	Caption	BorderColor	BorderWidth	Enabled	Interval
Form1	frmMoveLine	Move Line				
Line1	linMoveLine		blue	3		
Command1	cmdStart	Start				
Command2	cmdStop	Stop				
Timer1	tmrMoveLine				False	500

3) SAVE THE PROJECT

From the File menu, select Save Project. Save the form naming it frmMoveLine and save the project naming it Move Line.

4) WRITE THE PROGRAM CODE

Display the Code Editor window and add the following event procedures:

```
Private Sub Form_Load()
    Randomize
End Sub

Private Sub cmdStart_Click()
    tmrMoveLine.Enabled = True
End Sub

Private Sub cmdStop_Click()
    Unload Me
End Sub

Private Sub tmrMoveLine_Timer()
    linMoveLine.X1 = Int(Me.Width * Rnd + 1)  'high number is width of form
    linMoveLine.Y1 = Int(Me.Height * Rnd + 1) 'high number is height of form
    linMoveLine.X2 = Int(Me.Width * Rnd + 1)
    linMoveLine.Y2 = Int(Me.Height * Rnd + 1)
End Sub
```

5) RUN THE APPLICATION

Save the modified Move Line project and run the application. Test the application by clicking on the Start button.

6) PRINT AND THEN REMOVE THE PROJECT

Review 8

Create a Color Dots application that randomly puts a red, blue, or green colored dot on a black form every second. Resize the form using its Width and Height property so that it is a perfect square and then use the value in the Width property as the high number value in calculating random numbers for the x and y coordinates of the dots. The DrawWidth of the dot should be set to 5.

10.10 Animation

Animation can be simulated by having several images on a form and then activating one image at a time. For example, to animate a dolphin jumping, the first image on the following page would be displayed, then the second, and then the third:

Animation can be simulated by using several images

A timer object is used to control the speed of the animation and the three graphics are placed in a picture box control array. A control array is used to easily specify the graphic to be displayed. The following Timer event procedure demonstrates animation:

```
Private Sub tmrDolphinJump_Timer()
    picDolphin(intIncrement).Visible = False
    If intIncrement = 2 Then
        intIncrement = 0
    Else
        intIncrement = intIncrement + 1
    End If
    picDolphin(intIncrement).Visible = True
End Sub
```

The Interval property of tmrDolphinJump is set to 125. This means that every 125 milliseconds the Timer event procedure is called.

Animation can also be created by moving an object. For example, the Move method of a picture box can be used to move an image across the form. The Case Study at the end of this chapter demonstrates this.

Review 9

Follow the instructions below to create the Dolphin application.

1) **CREATE A NEW PROJECT**

2) **ADD OBJECTS TO THE FORM**

Refer to the form below when placing and sizing the form and its objects as instructed in the steps following.

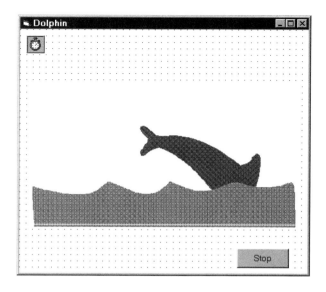

a. Use the table below to name and change the properties of the objects:

Object	Name	Caption	BackColor	Height	Width	Interval
Form1	frmDolphin	Dolphin	white	5000	5500	
Timer1	tmrDolphinJump					175
Command1	cmdStop	Stop				

b. Create a control array of three picture boxes named picDolphin. Use the table below to set the properties for all three picture box objects:

Object	AutoSize	BackColor	BorderStyle	Picture
picDolphin(0)	True	white	None	Dolphin1
picDolphin(1)	True	white	None	Dolphin2
picDolphin(2)	True	white	None	Dolphin3

c. Stack all three picture boxes on top of each other in the center of the form.

3) SAVE THE PROJECT

From the File menu, select Save Project. Save the form naming it frmDolphin and save the project naming it Dolphin.

4) WRITE THE PROGRAM CODE

Display the Code Editor window and add the following event procedures:

```
Option Explicit
Private intIncrement As Integer

Private Sub Form_Load()
    picDolphin(0).Visible = True        'displays first picture box
    picDolphin(1).Visible = False       'hides second picture box
    picDolphin(2).Visible = False       'hides third picture box
    intIncrement = 0
End Sub

Private Sub tmrDolphinJump_Timer()
    picDolphin(intIncrement).Visible = False    'hides currently displayed picture box
    If intIncrement = 2 Then                     'determines next picture box to display
      intIncrement = 0
    Else
      intIncrement = intIncrement + 1
    End If
    picDolphin(intIncrement).Visible = True      'displays next picture box in sequence
End Sub

Private Sub cmdStop_Click()
    Unload Me
End Sub
```

5) RUN THE APPLICATION

Save the modified Dolphin project and run the application.

6) PRINT AND THEN REMOVE THE PROJECT

10.11 Adding Sound

multimedia

adding controls to the Tool box

A multimedia object can be used to add sound to an application. A *multimedia* object is created using the MMControl control ( ). This control is added to the Tool box by first selecting the Components command (Ctrl+T) from the Project menu, which displays the Components dialog box:

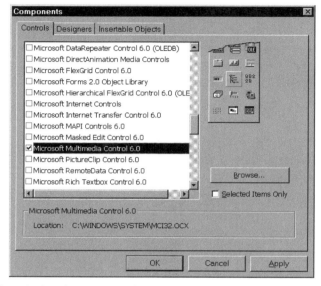

This dialog box is used to add controls to the Tool box

Selecting the Microsoft Multimedia Control check box and then clicking OK adds the MMControl control to the Tool box. A multimedia object has the properties:

- **Name** identifies the object and is used by the programmer. It is good programming style to begin multimedia object names with mmc.

- **DeviceType** changes the type of device that is playing the sound. In this text we will use .wav files so the DeviceType is WaveAudio. To play a music CD in the CD-ROM drive, DeviceType is CDAudio.

- **Enabled** can be set to either True or False. When Enabled is False the multimedia object cannot play sound. When Enable is True the multimedia object can play sound.

- **FileName** is used to display a dialog box for selecting the .wav file to be played. FileName can be changed at run time through assignment. FileName is omitted if the DeviceType is CDAudio.

- **Visible** can be set to either True or False to display (Visible = True) or hide (Visible = False) the multimedia object.

The multimedia object appears as a bar of buttons similar to those used on a CD player:

The multimedia object

Clicking on the Play button at run time plays the sound file specified in the FileName property.

Wave Sound

Sound can be recorded in many different formats. Waveform sound is a popular method for storing sound in a digitized format. The standard Windows file format for audio data has a .wav extension. The .wav file format was developed jointly by Microsoft and IBM.

Command

As an alternative to requiring the user to click on the buttons on the multimedia object, the Command property can be used. The Command property takes the form:

*mmcObject.*Command = *command*

mmcObject is the name of the multimedia object and *command* can be one of the following commands that correspond to the buttons in the multimedia object:

- **Open** opens *mmcObject*

- **Close** closes *mmcObject*. A multimedia object should be closed before ending the application and must be closed before changing the FileName property.

- **Play** plays the sound track specified in the FileName property.

- **Stop** stops playing the current sound track that is running.

- **Prev** sets the sound track back to the beginning.

> ### Multimedia Object Button Properties
>
> Each button on the multimedia object has an Enabled and Visible property associated with it. For example, there are PlayEnabled and PlayVisible properties that are associated with the Play button.

Unload

The following code demonstrates a multimedia object. Note the Form_Unload procedure which is executed when a program is ended. In this case, clicking on the Done command button unloads the form which executes the Form_Unload procedure:

```
Private Sub Form_Load()
    mmcSound.DeviceType = "WaveAudio"
    mmcSound.FileName = "Laser.wav"
    'Opens the mmcSound WaveAudio device
    mmcSound.Command = "Open"
End Sub

Private Sub cmdPlaySound_Click()
    mmcSound.Command = "Play"     'plays the sound
    mmcSound.Command = "Prev"     'sets track to the beginning
End Sub

Private Sub cmdDone_Click()
    Unload Me
End Sub

Private Sub Form_Unload(Cancel As Integer)
    'Closes the mmcSound WaveAudio device
    mmcSound.Command = "Close"
End Sub
```

Review 10 ⟳ ———————————————————————————————

Follow the instructions below to add sound to the Move Line application created in Review 7.

1) OPEN THE MOVE LINE PROJECT

Display the Move Line form if it is not already displayed.

2) ADD THE MMCONTROL TO THE TOOL BOX

a. From the Project menu, select the Components command. The Components dialog box is displayed.

b. Scroll down the list until the Microsoft Multimedia Control check box is displayed, then select it.

c. Click OK. The control is added to the bottom of the Tool box.

3) MODIFY THE APPLICATION INTERFACE

a. In the Tool box, double-click on the MMControl control (🖳). A multimedia object is placed on the form.
b. Move the multimedia object near the top of the form.
c. Change the Name property of the multimedia object to mmcSound.
d. Change the Visible property of the multimedia object to False.

4) MODIFY THE PROGRAM CODE

a. Display the Code Editor window.
b. Modify the Form_Load procedure as shown below:

```
        Private Sub Form_Load()
            Randomize

Add         mmcSound.DeviceType = "WaveAudio"
Add         mmcSound.FileName = "Laser.wav"
Add         mmcSound.Command = "Open"
        End Sub
```

c. Modify the tmrMoveLine_Timer() procedure as shown below:

```
        Private Sub tmrMoveLine_Timer()
Add         mmcSound.Command = "play"                    'plays the sound
Add         mmcSound.Command = "prev"                    'sets sound back to the beginning
            linMoveLine.X1 = Int(Me.Width * Rnd + 1)  'high number is width of form
            linMoveLine.Y1 = Int(Me.Height * Rnd + 1) 'high number is height of form
            linMoveLine.X2 = Int(Me.Width * Rnd + 1)
            linMoveLine.Y2 = Int(Me.Height * Rnd + 1)
        End Sub
```

d. Add the following Form_Unload procedure:

```
        Private Sub Form_Unload(Cancel As Integer)
            mmcSound.Command = "Close"
        End Sub
```

5) RUN THE APPLICATION

Save the modified Move Line project and run the application. Test the application by clicking on the Start command button.

6) PRINT AND THEN REMOVE THE PROJECT

Case Study

In this Case Study a Race Track application will be created.

specification The specification for this Case Study is:

A Race Track application that races two cars and determines which car wins. When the user starts the race a simulated signal light should display a red, then yellow, and then green light. Once the green light is displayed the signal light should disappear and two cars should appear racing along the form. As the cars race, the sound of an engine is played. When one of the cars gets to the end of the form a message box should display which car won.

design   When designing the form for this Case Study, we need to consider how the signal light and two cars should be displayed. The signal light is composed of three different lights, so it can be created by drawing three different color circles in a picture box. The picture box can be cleared once the green light is displayed. Each car should also be placed in a picture box so the cars can be moved across the form to simulate the race.

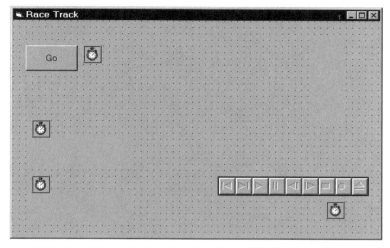

The interface design for the Race Track Case Study

The program code design for this Case Study is best done by listing the pseudocode for event procedures:

```
Private Sub Form_Load()
   Randomize
   Open Zoom.wav
End Sub

Private Sub cmdGo_Click()
   Enable tmrGo
End Sub

Private Sub tmrGo_Timer()
   Draw red circle if not already displayed
   Draw yellow circle if not already displayed
   Draw green circle if not already displayed
   If red, yellow, and green circles displayed Then
      Remove signal light
      Remove Go button
      Display cars
      Start sound
      Enable tmrSound
      Enable tmrCar1
      Enable tmrCar2
   End If
End Sub

Private Sub tmrSound_Timer()
   Play sound
   Rewind sound
End Sub
```

```
Private Sub tmrCar1_Timer()
   Move picCar1
   If picCar1 reaches end of form Then
      Display message that car 1 wins
      Reset form for new race
   End If
End Sub

Private Sub tmrCar2_Timer()
   Move picCar2
   If picCar2 reaches end of form Then
      Display message that car 2 wins
      Reset form for new race
   End If
End Sub

Private Sub Form_Unload
   Close mmc object
End Sub
```

coding   The interface and code for this Case Study are:

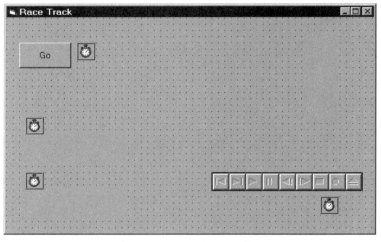

The Race Track interface

Object	Name	Caption	Visible
Form1	frmRaceTrack	Race Track	
Command1	cmdGo	Go	
MMControl1	mmcRaceSound		False

Object	Name	Enabled	Interval
Timer1	tmrGo	False	250
Timer2	tmrCar1	False	5
Timer3	tmrCar2	False	5
Timer4	tmrSound	False	1000

Object	Name	AutoRedraw	AutoSize	BorderStyle	Picture
Picture1	picSignalLight	True	False	None	None
Picture2	picCar1	False	True	None	None
Picture3	picCar2	False	True	None	None

An Introduction to Programming Using Microsoft Visual Basic

```
Option Explicit

Private Sub Form_Load()
  Randomize

  mmcRaceSound.DeviceType = "WaveAudio"
  mmcRaceSound.FileName = "Zoom.wav"
  mmcRaceSound.Command = "Open"
End Sub

Private Sub cmdGo_Click()
  tmrGo.Enabled = True
End Sub

Private Sub tmrGo_Timer()
  Static blnRed As Boolean, blnYellow As Boolean, blnGreen As Boolean

  If Not blnRed Then
    Call DrawRed(blnRed)
  ElseIf Not blnYellow Then
    Call DrawYellow(blnYellow)
  ElseIf Not blnGreen Then
    Call DrawGreen(blnGreen)
  Else                                        'start race
    tmrGo.Enabled = False
    picSignalLight.Cls                        'remove signal light
    blnRed = False
    blnYellow = False
    blnGreen = False
    cmdGo.Visible = False                     'remove Go button
    picCar1.Left = 350                        'race cars
    picCar2.Left = 350
    picCar1.Picture = LoadPicture("Car.wmf")
    picCar2.Picture = LoadPicture("Carsquare.wmf")
    mmcRaceSound.Command = "Play"
    mmcRaceSound.Command = "Prev"
    tmrSound.Enabled = True
    tmrCar1.Enabled = True
    tmrCar2.Enabled = True
  End If
End Sub

Sub DrawRed(ByRef blnRed As Boolean)          'draws solid red light
  picSignalLight.FillColor = vbRed
  picSignalLight.FillStyle = vbFSSolid
  picSignalLight.Circle (200, 200), 200, vbRed
  blnRed = True
End Sub

Sub DrawYellow(ByRef blnYellow As Boolean)    'draws solid yellow light
  picSignalLight.FillColor = vbYellow
  picSignalLight.Circle (200, 700), 200, vbYellow
  blnYellow = True
End Sub

Sub DrawGreen(ByRef blnGreen As Boolean)      'draws solid green light
  picSignalLight.FillColor = vbGreen
  picSignalLight.Circle (200, 1200), 200, vbGreen
  blnGreen = True
End Sub

Private Sub tmrSound_Timer()
  mmcRaceSound.Command = "Play"               'starts playing sound track
  mmcRaceSound.Command = "Prev"               'sets sound track to beginning
End Sub
```

```
Private Sub tmrCar1_Timer()
    picCar1.Move picCar1.Left + Int(41 * Rnd + 20)              'moves car

    'if car reaches the right side of the form restart
    If picCar1.Left >= (frmRaceTrack.Width - picCar1.Width) Then
        Call EndRace
        MsgBox "Car 1 wins!"
    End If
End Sub

Private Sub tmrCar2_Timer()
    picCar2.Move picCar2.Left + Int(41 * Rnd + 20)              'moves car

    'if car reaches the right side of the form restart
    If picCar2.Left >= (frmRaceTrack.Width - picCar2.Width) Then
        Call EndRace
        MsgBox "Car 2 wins!"
    End If
End Sub

'***************************************************************
'   Resets the form for a new race
'
'   Post: timers, mmc, and picture objects reset
'***************************************************************
Sub EndRace()
    tmrCar2.Enabled = False              'stop car timer
    tmrCar1.Enabled = False              'stop car timer
    tmrSound.Enabled = False             'stop sound timer
    mmcRaceSound.Command = "Stop"        'stop sound
    cmdGo.Visible = True                 'display Go command button
    picCar2.Picture = LoadPicture        'remove car graphic
    picCar1.Picture = LoadPicture        'remove car graphic
End Sub

Private Sub Form_Unload(Cancel As Integer)
    mmcRaceSound.Command = "Close"
End Sub
```

testing and debugging   Running the application and clicking on Go displays a red, then yellow, then green lights. The form below shows the red and yellow lights:

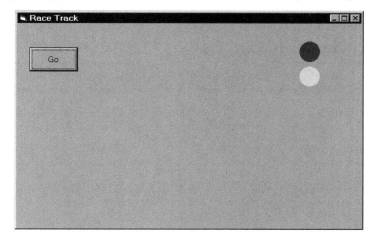

After the green light is displayed the signal light is removed and the cars begin to race:

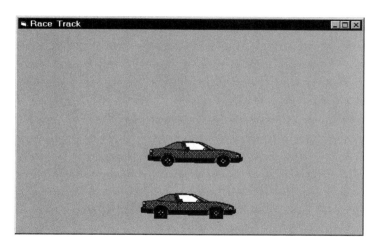

This Case Study should be tested by running it several times to make sure the animation appears as desired.

Chapter Summary

Applications are made easier to understand and more interesting with color and graphics. BackColor and ForeColor are two common color properties. The Visual Basic color constants can be used in assignment statements at run time to change color properties.

line

shape

Lines and shapes can be added to a form. A line is created using the Line control in the Tool box and has properties that can change the color, style, and thickness of the line. A shape is created using the Shape control in the Tool box and has properties that can change the color, style, and thickness of the outline of the shape as well as the color and style of the inside of the shape. When drawing shapes, the background color of the form should be set first.

picture box

Picture boxes are used to add graphics to an application. A picture box is created using the PictureBox control in the Tool box. Picture boxes can also be used as a container for drawing lines and shapes.

coordinate system

twips

The position of an object on its container is determined using a coordinate system with a horizontal x-axis and a vertical y-axis. The upper-left corner of the container is (0, 0). The unit of measurement is twips where a twip is 1/20 of a printer's point (1/577 of a centimeter).

Move method

The Left, Top, Width, and Height properties of a shape or picture box are used in combination with the Move method to move a shape or picture box. The X1, Y1, X2, and Y2 properties are used to move a line.

Line method
Circle method
PSet method
PaintPicture method
Cls method

Form and picture box objects support several methods to draw and manipulate graphics at run time. The Line method is used to draw a line, rectangle, or square. The Circle method is used to draw a circle, ellipse, or arc. The PSet method is used to change the color of an individual point. The PaintPicture method is used to paint a graphic at a specified location. The Cls method is used to clear all graphics. When using graphic methods the properties of the container object will affect the appearance of the graphics drawn on it.

timer
timer event

A timer object is used to execute code at specified intervals and is created using the Timer control in the Tool box. The timer event procedure is automatically called by the application and contains the code to be executed at regular intervals.

Animation can be simulated by cycling through a series of images with images being displayed quickly one after the other. A timer object is used to control the speed of the animation and a picture box control arrow is used to store the images. Animation can also be simulated by moving an object on the form.

multimedia

A multimedia object is used to play sound in an application and is created using the MMControl. The MMControl is added to the Toolbox using the Components command from the Project menu. The multimedia object appears similar to the controls used on a CD player.

Vocabulary

Coordinate system A two-dimensional grid that is used to determine the position of an object on its container.

Line A graphic object.

Multimedia An object used to play sound in an application.

Picture box An object used to place images and graphics on a form.

Shape A graphic object that can be a rectangle, oval, square, or circle.

Timer An object used to execute code at specified intervals.

Twip A unit of measurement used in the container coordinate system, where 567 twips = 1 cm.

Visual Basic

AutoRedraw Container object property that can be assigned True or False.

AutoSize Picture box property that can be assigned True or False.

BackColor Property used to change the background color of an object.

BackStyle Shape property used to display or not display the BackColor. Can be assigned 0 for transparent or 1 for opaque.

BorderColor Property used to change the color of a line or outline of a shape or line.

BorderStyle Property that can be set to transparent, solid, dash, dot, dash-dot, dash-dot-dot, or inside-solid for a shape or line.

BorderWidth Property used to change the thickness of a line or outline of a shape or line.

Circle Method used to draw a circle, ellipse, or arc.

Cls Method used to clear all graphics.

Command Multimedia object property used to open, close, play, stop, or reset the multimedia object.

Components command Displays a dialog box to select controls to add to the Tool box. Found in the Project menu.

DeviceType A multimedia object property used to change the type of device that is playing the sound.

DrawStyle Container object property that can be set to solid, dash, dot, dash-dot, dash-dot-dot, invisible, or inside-solid.

DrawWidth Container object property used to change the thickness of the line or outline of a drawn graphic.

FileName Multimedia object property used to select the sound file.

FillColor Property used to change the inside color of a graphic.

FillStyle Property that can be set to solid, transparent, horizontal line, vertical line, upward diagonal, downward diagonal, cross, or diagonal cross.

ForeColor Property used to change the color of text in an object or the color of graphics drawn on a container.

Height Property used to change the height of the object.

Interval Timer object property that can be assigned a numeric value from 0 to 64,767 milliseconds.

Left Property used to change the distance between the left edge of an object and the left edge of a container.

Line Method used to draw a line, rectangle, or square.

Line control Used to draw a line object. Found in the Tool box.

LoadPicture Function used to specify the graphic to display in a picture box.

MMControl Used to create a multimedia object. Must be added to the Tool box using the Components command.

Move Method used to move a shape or picture box to a new location.

PaintPicture Method used to paint a graphic at a specified location.

Picture Picture box property used to select a graphic.

PictureBox control Used to create a picture box object. Found in the Tool box.

PSet Method used to set the color of an individual point.

Shape Shape property that can be set to square, oval, circle, rounded rectangle, or rounded square.

Shape control Used to create a shape object. Found in the Tool box.

Timer control Used to create a timer object. Found in the Tool box.

Timer event Contains the code that is to be executed at regular intervals.

Top Property used to change the distance between the top edge of the object and the top edge of the container.

Width Property used to change the width of an object.

X1 Line property used to change the x coordinate of the starting point of the line.

X2 Line property used to change the x coordinate of the ending point of the line.

Y1 Line property used to change the y coordinate of the starting point of the line.

Y2 Line property used to change the y coordinate of the ending point of the line.

Exercises

Exercise 1

Create a House Color application that allows the user to select the color of the house, sun, sky, and door by clicking on an option button. The background color of the frames and option buttons should be the same color as the sky. When the sky is blue, all the text should be white, and when the sky is cyan the text should be black. The application interface should look similar to:

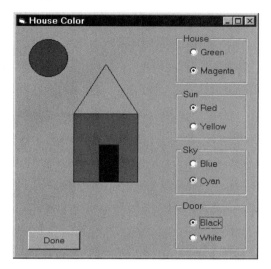

Exercise 2

Modify the Dice Game application created in Chapter Seven, Exercise 11 so that an image of the appropriate die is displayed. Use the Dice1, Dice2, Dice3, Dice4, Dice5, and Dice6 graphics. The application interface should look similar to the following after clicking on the Roll Dice button a few times:

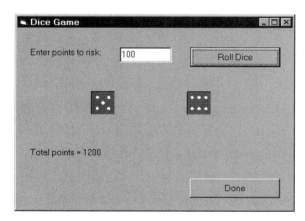

Exercise 3

Create a Celsius Thermometer application that moves the level of mercury (the red rectangle) in the thermometer up or down when the Hotter or Colder command button is clicked. The application interface should look similar to the following after clicking on the Hotter button several times:

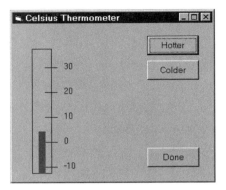

Exercise 4

Create a Draw Lines and Boxes application that allows the user to enter the information needed to draw a line or box (Hint: if the color of the line is stored in a variable, the variable must be assigned a Visual Basic color constant to work with the Line method and the user should not be able to select Yes in the Fill frame if No is selected in the Box frame). The application interface should look similar to:

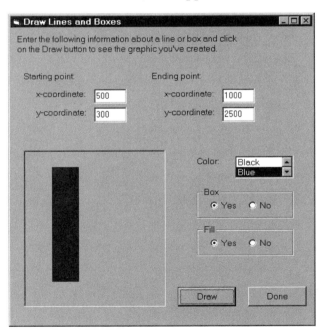

Exercise 5

Create a Draw Circles application that allows the user to enter the information needed to draw a circle (Hint: if the color of the circle is stored in a variable, the variable must be assigned a Visual Basic color constant to work with the Circle method). The application interface should look similar to:

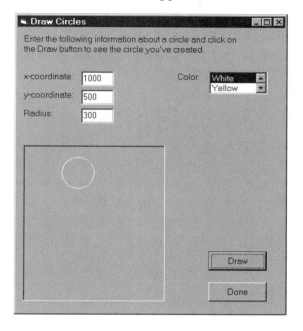

Exercise 6

Create a Draw Dots application that allows the user to enter the information needed to draw a dot (Hint: if the color of the dot is stored in a variable, the variable must be assigned a Visual Basic color constant to work with the PSet method). The application interface should look similar to:

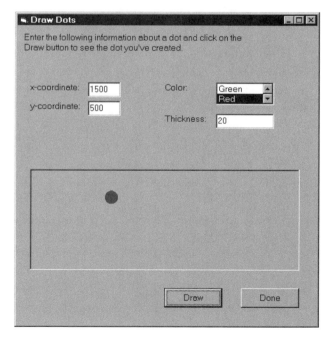

Exercise 7

Create a Breakfast Order application that allows the user to select the breakfast items by clicking on them and then displays the selected items on the plate in the middle of the form (Hint: use image objects to display the items at the top of the application and use four picture boxes to display the selected items on the plate). Use the Egg, Bacon, Toast, and Waffle graphics. The application interface should look similar to the following after clicking on the Bacon, Toast, and Waffle graphics:

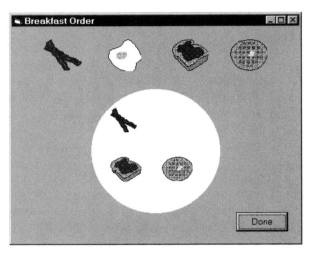

Exercise 8

Modify the Face application created in Review 6 to include a Wink button that, when clicked, winks an eye. The eye should change back to open after a moment. The application interface should look similar to the following after clicking on the Wink button:

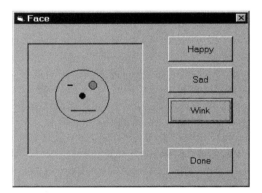

Exercise 9

Modify the Move Line application created in Review 7 so that the color of the line changes randomly at each timer event.

Exercise 10

Create a Sunset application that simulates the sun setting. When the sun hits to the water it should turn into a moon, stop moving, and then the sky should turn black (Hint: use arcs to create the water). The application interface should look similar to:

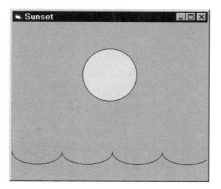

Exercise 11

Create a Tree Swing application that simulates a swing swaying (Hint: use three lines to create the swing, the middle line is stationary and the outer lines are displayed one at a time so that the swing appears to be moving). The application interface should look similar to:

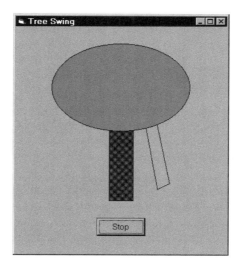

Exercise 12

Create a Turtle Run application that allows the user to control the speed of the animation by clicking on a command button. Use the Turtle1, Turtle2, and Turtle3 graphics. The three different animations should look similar to:

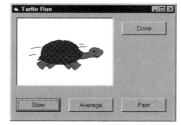 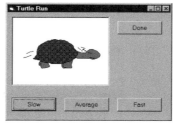 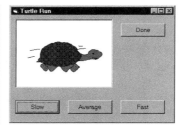

Exercise 13 ⚙

Modify the Dolphin application created in Review 9 so that the Splash.wav file is played during the animation.

Exercise 14

Create a Happy Birthday application that displays a birthday cake with candles on it. When the application starts, the flames on the candles should be displayed until the user clicks on the Blow Out Candles button (Hint: draw the flames in a picture box so that they can be cleared). When the Blow Out Candles button is clicked, the Applause.wav file should be played. The application interface should look similar to the following before clicking on the Blow Out Candles button:

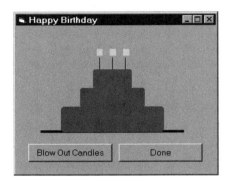

Exercise 15

Create a Bird Flying application that simulates a bird flying and plays the Bird.wav file. Use the Bird1, Bird2, and Bird3 graphics. The three different animations should look similar to:

Exercise 16 ⚙

Modify the Math Tutor application created in Chapter Five, Exercise 10 so that the Applause.wav file is played when the user enters a correct answer and the Buzzer.wav file is played when the user enters an incorrect answer.

Exercise 17

Create a Day and Night application that changes the background color of the form when the Day or Night button is clicked. When the Day button is clicked, the background should be a light color and the Bird.wav file played. When the Night button is clicked, the background should be a dark color, the Owl.wav file played, and the sun replaced by a moon. The application interface should look similar to the following after clicking on the Day button:

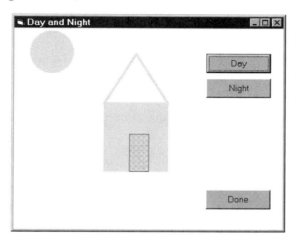

Exercise 18

Create an Animal Sounds application that plays the sounds of different animals when the associated animal button is clicked. Use the Dog, Cat, Horse, Pig, Cow, and Rooster.wav files. The application interface should look similar to:

Advanced
Exercise 19 ⚙

Modify the Draw Circles application created in Exercise 5 so that the user can enter the start and end values for an arc and the aspect ratio for an ellipse. Use combo boxes to enter the new information. The list for the start and end combo boxes should contain 3.14, 3.14/2, 0, and –3.14/2. The combo box for the aspect ratio should contain 0.5, 1, and 1.5, and the user should not be able to enter their own value. When the application is first run the start and end options should be 0 and the aspect ratio should be 1 (this creates a circle). Hint: you will need to convert the text "3.14/2" into a number before using it in the Circle method.

Advanced
Exercise 20 ⚙

Modify the Happy Birthday application created in Exercise 14 so that the user can enter the number of birthday candles displayed on the cake. The cake should be wide enough to display up to 10 candles, and the user should not be allowed to enter a number higher than 10 or less than 1.

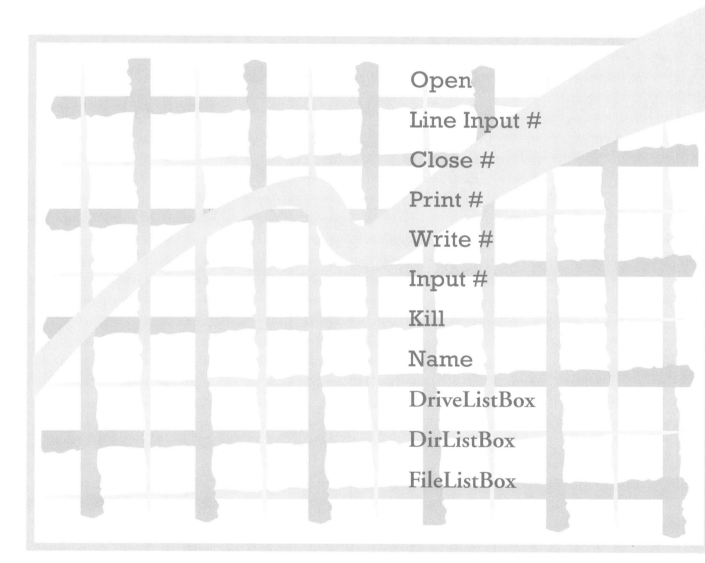

Open

Line Input #

Close #

Print #

Write #

Input #

Kill

Name

DriveListBox

DirListBox

FileListBox

Chapter Eleven Objectives

After completing this chapter you will be able to:

1. Understand files, plain text, and newline characters.
2. Understand a sequential access file.
3. Open a file and understand the FreeFile function.
4. Read text from a file to memory.
5. Use multiline text boxes.
6. Write text to a file.
7. Understand records and how they are written to a sequential access file.
8. Append data to a file.
9. Read, update, and delete records.
10. Delete and rename files.
11. Use the drive list box, the directory list box, and the file list box controls.

V isual Basic includes built-in file functions and statements for storing and retrieving data from files. In this chapter you will create applications that use sequential access files and include drive, directory, and file list boxes in the interface.

11.1 What is a File?

Up to this point, the applications created in this text have stored data in the computer's memory in the form of variables and arrays. However, memory is only temporary storage while the computer is turned on and an application is running. A *file* is a collection of related data stored on a persistent medium such as a hard disk, a CD, or a diskette. *Persistent* simply means lasting.

A file is separate from an application and can be read from and written to by more than one application. Files are often used to provide data to an application. Applications of any complexity usually require access to one or more files on disk.

A file that contains only plain text can be accessed sequentially. *Plain text* contains only ANSI text characters and the *newline character*, which is a carriage return-linefeed. Therefore, a *sequential access file* is plain text that is read one character at a time, and is sometimes thought of as a textstream:

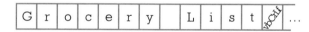

A sequential access file can be thought of
as a stream of characters

sequential access file

11.2 Opening a File

Open

Any operations performed on a file cannot take place until the file has been properly opened using the **Open** statement, which takes the form:

Open *pathname* **For** *mode* **As** #*filenumber*

pathname is the name of the file to be opened including its full path. *mode* is either **Input** for reading the contents of the file or **Output** or **Append** for writing text to a file. *filenumber* is a number used to refer to the file and should be determined using the Visual Basic built-in FreeFile function, which returns the next available integer for a file.

FreeFile

The following statements open a file named Grocery List.txt for input:

```
Dim intFileNum As Integer
intFileNum = FreeFile        'Get available file number
Open "Grocery List.txt" For Input As #intFileNum
```

When a file is open, Visual Basic maintains a file pointer to the current file position. When the **Open** statement is executed, the pointer is placed at the first character of the file, and can be visualized as:

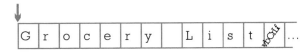

11.3 Reading Text from a File

Line Input #

The **Line Input #** statement is used to transfer one line of text from a sequential file to memory and takes the form:

Line Input #*filenumber, StringVariable*

filenumber is the number assigned to a file in a previous **Open** statement. *StringVariable* is a **String** variable that will store the line of text read from the file. **Line Input #** places in *StringVariable* the characters from the file pointer up to the newline character and then moves the file pointer to the first character after the newline.

The following statements read a line of text from the Grocery List.txt file:

```
. . .
Dim strTextLine As String
Open "Grocery List.txt" For Input As #intFileNum
Line Input #intFileNum, strTextLine        'Get a line of text
. . .
```

The statements above could be visualized as:

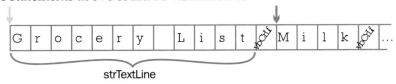

strTextLine

*The characters up to the newline are
assigned to strTextLine*

EOF

A run-time error is generated if an attempt is made to open a file that does not exist or an attempt is made to read past the end of a file. The Visual Basic built-in EOF function returns False until the end of a file is reached and takes the form:

EOF(*filenumber*)

programming style

filenumber is the number assigned to a file in a previous **Open** statement. It is good programming style to check for the EOF before trying to read from a file. The statements on the next page display the contents of the file in a label:

```
...
Dim strTextLine As String
intFileNum = FreeFile
Open "Grocery List.txt" For Input As #intFileNum
Do While Not EOF(intFileNum)      'Check for end of file
   Line Input #intFileNum, strTextLine
   lblFile.Caption = lblFile.Caption & strTextLine & vbCrLf
Loop
...
```

vbCrLf

Note that since the newline character is not read from the file, it must be appended to a line of text, it necessary, using & vbCrLf. A label is not the best method for displaying a file's contents because the file size is usually unknown. A text box is better for displaying file contents, as discussed in Section 11.5.

11.4 Closing a File

Close #

An open file should be closed when access is no longer needed by using the **Close #** statement, which takes the form:

Close #*filenumber*

filenumber is the number assigned to a file in a previous **Open** statement.

11.5 Multiline Text Boxes

A text box is usually best for displaying the contents of a file. For example, Windows Notepad is a text editor that uses a very large text box to display file contents.

A text box object has the MultiLine property that when set to True allows more than one line of text in a text box. The ScrollBars property allows scroll bars to be displayed in a text box. A text box with a vertical scroll bar wraps text to the next line when there is a newline character or if a line of text is too long to be displayed on one line of the text box. Note that if a horizontal scroll bar is displayed in a text box, text will not wrap. Other attributes of the MultiLine and ScrollBars properties are:

- **MultiLine** can be set to either True or False, but must be set to True for scroll bars, if any, are to appear. MultiLine can be changed at run time through assignment.

- **ScrollBars** can be set to none, horizontal, vertical, or both. Scroll bars are displayed only if the MultiLine property is True. Scroll bars can be changed at run time through assignment using the Visual Basic constants vbSBNone, vbHorizontal, VBVertical, and vbBoth.

The Sequential Access File application on the next page uses a text box to display the contents of a file named Recipe.txt:

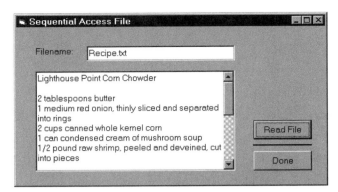

The Sequential Access File application includes the cmdReadFile_Click event procedure, which displays the Recipe.txt file in a text box:

```
Private Sub cmdReadFile_Click()
    Dim intFileNum As Integer, strTextLine As String

    intFileNum = FreeFile
    Open txtFilename.Text For Input As #intFileNum

    Do While Not EOF(intFileNum)      'Display file in text box
        Line Input #intFileNum, strTextLine
        'Add next line in file to text box
        txtViewFile.Text = txtViewFile.Text & strTextLine & vbCrLf
    Loop
    Close #intFileNum
End Sub
```

Review 1

Follow the instructions below to create the Sequential Access File application.

1) **CREATE A NEW PROJECT**

2) **ADD OBJECTS TO THE FORM**

Refer to the form below when placing and sizing the form and its objects. Use the table below to name and change the properties of the objects. Be sure to draw a line between the buttons as shown.

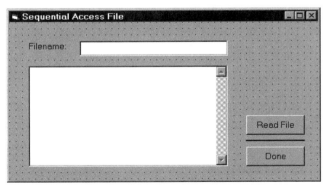

Object	Name	Caption	Text	MultiLine	ScrollBars	BorderWidth
Form1	frmSequentialAccessFile	Sequential Access File				
Label1	lblFilename	Filename:				
Text1	txtFilename		*empty*			
Text2	txtViewFile		*empty*	True	2-Vertical	
Command1	cmdReadFile	Read File				
Line1	linSeparator					2
Command2	cmdDone	Done				

An Introduction to Programming Using Microsoft Visual Basic

3) SAVE THE PROJECT

From the File menu, select Save Project. Save the form naming it frmSequentialAccessFile and save the project naming it Sequential Access File.

4) WRITE THE PROGRAM CODE

Display the Code Editor window and add the following event procedures:

```
Private Sub cmdReadFile_Click()
    Dim intFileNum As Integer, strTextLine As String

    intFileNum = FreeFile
    Open txtFilename.Text For Input As #intFileNum

    Do While Not EOF(intFileNum)      'Display file in text box
        Line Input #intFileNum, strTextLine
        'Add next line in file to text box
        txtViewFile.Text = txtViewFile.Text & strTextLine & vbCrLf
    Loop
    Close #intFileNum
End Sub

Private Sub txtFilename_Change()
    txtViewFile.Text = ""                  'Clear text box
End Sub

Private Sub cmdDone_Click()
    Unload Me
End Sub
```

5) RUN THE APPLICATION

a. Save the modified Sequential Access File project and then run the application.
b. Type Recipe.txt as the filename and then click Read File. The Recipe.txt file is displayed.
c. Click the Done button to close the application.

6) PRINT AND THEN REMOVE THE PROJECT

11.6 Writing Text to a File

Print #

The **Print #** statement is used to write text to a file and takes the form:

Print #*filenumber, output*

filenumber is the number of the file to be written to. *output* is data to be written and can be a series of numeric or **String** expressions or variables separated by spaces. A newline character is written to a file after *output*. If *output* is omitted, only a newline is written to the file. **Print #** writes *output* starting at the file pointer and then moves the pointer to the first character after the newline.

The following statements write text to a file. Note that the **Open** statement, which opens a file for output, creates one if it does not already exist:

Appending Data to a File

When a file is opened for **Output**, writing starts at the beginning of the file. To add data to the end of file, it must be opened for **Append**, discussed in Section 11.8.

```
...
Dim intFileNum As Integer
intFileNum = FreeFile
Open "My Text.txt" For Output As #intFileNum
Print #intFileNum, "text"
Print #intFileNum, "more"
Print #intFileNum, "more"
...
```

The statements on the previous page could be visualized as:

*Newlines are added with each Print # and the file pointer
is moved to the character after the last Print #*

A **Print** # statement may include a semicolon (;) which indicates that a newline character should not be written after the *output*. The following statements write text to a file without newline characters:

```
...
Dim intFileNum As Integer
intFileNum = FreeFile
Open "My Text.txt" For Output As #intFileNum
Print #intFileNum, "text";
Print #intFileNum, "more";
Print #intFileNum, "more"
...
```

The statements above could be visualized as:

*Newlines are not added when a semicolon
follows a Print # statement*

The Sequential Access File application can be modified to write text typed in a text box to a file:

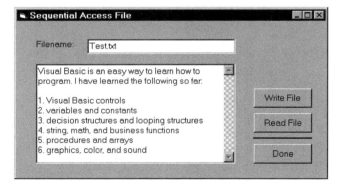

The modified Sequential Access File application includes the cmdWriteFile_Click event procedure which writes the text in a text box to a file:

```
Private Sub cmdWriteFile_Click()
    Dim intNewFile As Integer

    intNewFile = FreeFile
    Open txtFilename.Text For Output As #intNewFile
    Print #intNewFile, txtViewFile.Text
End Sub
```

Review 2

Follow the instructions below to modify the Sequential Access File application to write to a file.

1) OPEN THE SEQUENTIAL ACCESS FILE PROJECT

Display the Sequential Access File form, if it is not already displayed.

2) MODIFY THE FORM

Add a command button as shown below. Use the table below to name and change the properties of the object.

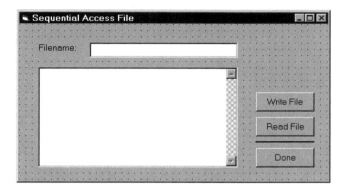

Object	Name	Caption
Command1	cmdWriteFile	Write File

3) ADD A CLICK EVENT PROCEDURE

Display the Code Editor window and add the cmdWriteFile_Click event procedure:

```
Private Sub cmdWriteFile_Click()
    Dim intNewFile As Integer

    intNewFile = FreeFile
    Open txtFilename.Text For Output As #intNewFile
    Print #intNewFile, txtViewFile.Text
    Close #intNewFile
    txtFilename.Text = ""     'Clear filename
    txtViewFile.Text = ""     'Clear file display
End Sub
```

4) RUN THE APPLICATION

a. Save the modified Sequential Access File project and then run the application.
b. Type Test.txt as the filename.
c. Type several lines of text and then click on the Write File button. A new text file named Test.txt is created containing the typed text.
d. Type Test.txt in the Filename text box and then click on the Read File button. The Test.txt file is displayed.
e. Click on the Done button to close the application.

5) PRINT AND THEN REMOVE THE PROJECT

11.7 Writing Records

record

Sequential access files are sometimes organized to contain records. A *record* is a set of fields where each field is one piece of data. For example, three book records with Title, Author, and In Stock fields would be:

Title	Author	In Stock
Peace in the Valley	Sage Ann	1
Swedish Customs	A Nilsson	14
How to be a Superhero	Tristan Brown	7

In a sequential access file, each record has the same fields in the same order, and one record sequentially follows another.

Records are generally associated with random access files, which are discussed in the next chapter. However, a sequential access file can be appropriate for storing records if the file size is kept small and the record structure is simple. Records can be written to a file sequentially with the *Write #* statement, which takes the form:

Write #

> Write #*filenumber, field1, field2, ...*

filenumber is the number of the file to be written to. *field1, field2, ...* are fields to be written and can be a series of numeric or string expressions or variables separated by commas. A newline character is written to a file after the field data. If *field1, field2, ...* are omitted, only a newline is written to the file. **Write #** writes field data starting at the file pointer and then moves the pointer to the first character after the newline. The **Write #** statement writes fields to a file in the following format:

- fields are separated by commas

- Strings are enclosed by quotation marks

- Boolean data is written as either #TRUE# or #FALSE#

- Dates are written in the universal date format as yyyy-mm-dd#

The Add Book Record application is used to add a new book to the current inventory:

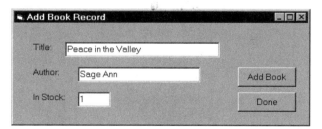

The Add Book Record application includes the cmdAddBook_Click event procedure which writes a book record to the file with filenumber intBookFile. Part of the cmdAddBook_Click procedure is:

```
...
Dim strTitle As String, strAuthor As String, intInStock As Integer

'Add record
strTitle = txtTitle.Text
strAuthor = txtAuthor.Text
intInStock = txtInStock.Text
Write #intBookFile, strTitle, strAuthor, intInStock

'Clear text boxes
txtTitle.Text = ""
txtAuthor.Text = ""
txtInStock.Text = ""
...
```

Note that the data from the text boxes is assigned to variables of the appropriate type before writing the record to a file. This is especially important with numeric data because it should not be treated as a string. The complete cmdAddBook_Click procedure is shown in the next section.

11.8 Appending Data to a File

Appending data to a file means to add data to the end of an existing file. When a file is opened for **Output**, data is written starting at the beginning of the file. However, when a file is opened for **Append**, data is written starting at the end of the file. For example, the Add Book Record application should open a file for **Append** rather than **Output** because existing book records need to be maintained. The cmdAddBook_Click procedure from the Add Book Record application is:

```
Private Sub cmdAddBook_Click()
    Dim intBookFile As Integer
    Dim strTitle As String, strAuthor As String, intInStock As Integer

    'Open file
    intBookFile = FreeFile
    Open "Books.txt" For Append As #intBookFile

    'Add record
    strTitle = txtTitle.Text
    strAuthor = txtAuthor.Text
    intInStock = txtInStock.Text
    Write #intBookFile, strTitle, strAuthor, intInStock

    'Clear text boxes
    txtTitle.Text = ""
    txtAuthor.Text = ""
    txtInStock.Text = ""

    'Close file
    Close #intBookFile
End Sub
```

Review 3

Follow the instructions below to create the Add Book Record application.

1) *CREATE A NEW PROJECT*

2) *ADD OBJECTS TO THE FORM*

Refer to the form on the next page when placing and sizing the form and its objects. Use the table on the next page to name and change the properties of the objects.

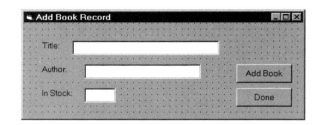

Object	Name	Caption	Text
Form1	frmAddBookRecord	Add Book Record	
Label1	lblTitle	Title:	
Text1	txtTitle		*empty*
Label2	lblAuthor	Author:	
Text2	txtAuthor		*empty*
Label3	lblInStock	In Stock:	
Text3	txtInStock		*empty*
Command1	cmdAddBook	Add Book	
Command2	cmdDone	Done	

3) SAVE THE PROJECT

From the File menu, select Save Project. Save the form naming it frmAddBookRecord and save the project naming it Add Book Record.

4) WRITE THE PROGRAM CODE

Display the Code Editor window and add the following event procedures:

```
Private Sub cmdAddBook_Click()
    Dim intBookFile As Integer
    Dim strTitle As String, strAuthor As String, intInStock As Integer

    'Open file
    intBookFile = FreeFile
    Open "Books.txt" For Append As #intBookFile

    'Add record
    strTitle = txtTitle.Text
    strAuthor = txtAuthor.Text
    intInStock = txtInStock.Text
    Write #intBookFile, strTitle, strAuthor, intInStock

    'Clear text boxes
    txtTitle.Text = ""
    txtAuthor.Text = ""
    txtInStock.Text = ""

    'Close file
    Close #intBookFile
End Sub

Private Sub cmdDone_Click()
    Unload Me
End Sub
```

5) RUN THE APPLICATION

a. Save the modified Add Book Record project and then run the application.

b. Add the following records:

Peace in the Valley	Sage Ann	1
Swedish Customs	A Nilsson	14
How to be a Superhero	Tristan Brown	7

c. Click on the Done button to close the application.

11.9 Reading Records

delimiter

Data written to a file using the **Write** # statement is stored as fields with delimiters. A *delimiter* is a character that is used as a separator. Visual Basic uses a comma delimiter to separate fields in a sequential access file. Another common delimiter is the tab character.

Input #

Records can be read from a file sequentially with the **Input** # statement, which takes the form:

> **Input** #*filenumber*, *field1*, *field2*, …

filenumber is the number of the file to be read. *field1*, *field2*, … will store the fields read from the file and should be a series of variables separated by commas. Each of the *field1*, *field2*, … variables need to be of the same type as the data being read or a run-time error may occur.

The following statement reads three fields from a file and can be visualized as follows:

> **Input** #intBookFile, strTitle, strAuthor, intInStock

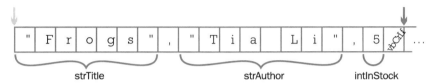

EOF

A run-time error is generated if an attempt is made to read past the end of a file. Therefore, the Visual Basic built-in EOF function should be used to verify that there are records to be read before trying to read the file.

The View Book Record application is used to view book inventory:

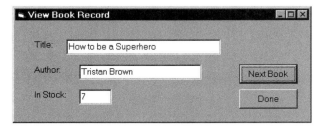

The View Book Record application includes the cmdNextBook_Click event procedure which reads a book record from the file with filenumber intBookFile and then displays the data in text boxes:

```
Private Sub cmdNextBook_Click()
    Dim strTitle As String, strAuthor As String, intInStock As Integer

    If Not EOF(intBookFile) Then
        'Read record
        Input #intBookFile, strTitle, strAuthor, intInStock

        'Display record
        txtTitle.Text = strTitle
        txtAuthor.Text = strAuthor
        txtInStock.Text = intInStock
    Else
        cmdNextBook.Enabled = False
    End If
End Sub
```

Note that the Books.txt file is not opened in the above event procedure. When a file is opened, the file pointer is placed at the beginning of the file. Therefore, if Books.txt were opened and closed each time cmdNextBook_Click were executed, the Input # statement would always read the first record. To allow cmdNextBook_Click to read records sequentially through the file, the file is opened in Form_Load and closed in cmdDone_Click. Also, when there are no more records to be read, the Next Book button is disabled so that the click event procedure can no longer be called.

Review 4

Follow the instructions below to create the View Book Record application.

1) CREATE A NEW PROJECT

2) ADD OBJECTS TO THE FORM

Refer to the form below when placing and sizing the form and its objects. Use the table below to name and change the properties of the objects.

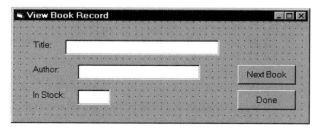

Object	Name	Caption	Text
Form1	frmViewBookRecord	View Book Record	
Label1	lblTitle	Title:	
Text1	txtTitle		*empty*
Label2	lblAuthor	Author:	
Text2	txtAuthor		*empty*
Label3	lblInStock	In Stock:	
Text3	txtInStock		*empty*
Command1	cmdNextBook	Next Book	
Command2	cmdDone	Done	

3) SAVE THE PROJECT

From the File menu, select Save Project. Save the form naming it frmViewBookRecord and save the project naming it View Book Record.

4) WRITE THE PROGRAM CODE

Display the Code Editor window and add the following code:

```
Option Explicit
Private intBookFile As Integer

Private Sub Form_Load()
    intBookFile = FreeFile
    Open "Books.txt" For Input As #intBookFile
End Sub

Private Sub cmdNextBook_Click()
    Dim strTitle As String, strAuthor As String, intInStock As Integer

    If Not EOF(intBookFile) Then
        'Read record
        Input #intBookFile, strTitle, strAuthor, intInStock

        'Display record
        txtTitle.Text = strTitle
        txtAuthor.Text = strAuthor
        txtInStock.Text = intInStock
    Else
        cmdNextBook.Enabled = False
    End If
End Sub

Private Sub cmdDone_Click()
    Close #intBookFile
    Unload Me
End Sub
```

5) RUN THE APPLICATION

a. Save the modified View Book Record project and then run the application.
b. Click on Next Book to display a record in the file. Continue to click on Next Book until all the records have been viewed.
c. Click on the Done button to close the application.

6) PRINT AND THEN REMOVE THE PROJECT

11.10 Updating and Deleting Records

updating

Updating a record means to change the data in one or more fields. To update a record in a sequential access file, the records in the original file are written to a new file until the record to be updated is accessed. This record is then updated and written to the new file. The remaining records in the original file are then written to the new file. The example below illustrates updating:

Original File

		New File
"Peace in the Valley", "Sage Ann", 1	copied →	"Peace in the Valley", "Sage Ann", 1
"Swedish Customs", "A Nilsson", 14	copied →	"Swedish Customs", "A Nilsson", 14
"How to be a Superhero", "Tristan Brown", 7	edited →	"How to be a Superhero", "Tristan Brown", 5
"Lobster Poetry", "Moses Biscotti", 4	copied →	"Lobster Poetry", "Moses Biscotti", 4
"Cooking with Wendy", "Wendy Li", 10	copied →	"Cooking with Wendy", "Wendy Li", 10

The new file now contains all the records, including the updated record, in the same order as the original file. The original file can now be deleted and the new file renamed to that of the original file.

deleting   Deleting a record requires a process similar to updating, except that when the record to be deleted is read, it is simply not written to the new file. The example below illustrates deleting:

Original File

		New File
"Peace in the Valley", "Sage Ann", 1	copied →	"Peace in the Valley", "Sage Ann", 1
"Swedish Customs", "A Nilsson", 14	copied →	"Swedish Customs", "A Nilsson", 14
"How to be a Superhero", "Tristan Brown", 7	not copied	"Lobster Poetry", "Moses Biscotti", 4
"Lobster Poetry", "Moses Biscotti", 4	copied ↗	"Cooking with Wendy", "Wendy Li", 10
"Cooking with Wendy", "Wendy Li", 10	copied ↗	

The Change Book Record application allows the user to update the In Stock field of a record or delete an existing record:

The Change Book Record code is shown in the next section.

11.11 Deleting and Renaming Files

The process of updating and deleting records generates two files: the original file and a new file with the current records. The original file should be deleted and the new file renamed to that of the original. The Kill statement is used to delete a file and takes the form:

Kill *filename*

filename is the name of the file to be deleted. The **Name** statement is used to change a file's name and takes the form:

Name *OldFilename* **As** *NewFileName*

OldFilename is the original name of the file and *NewFilename* is the name to give the file. For example, the statements below overwrite an existing file by deleting the file to be overwritten and then giving a new file the name of the deleted file:

```
Kill "Books.txt"
Name "Tempbooks.txt" As "Books.txt"
```

The Change Book Record application writes changes to the Books.txt file to a new file called Tempbooks.txt and then renames Tempbooks.txt. The Change Book application interface and code follow:

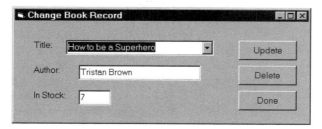

An Introduction to Programming Using Microsoft Visual Basic

```
Private Sub Form_Load()
  Call RefreshInterface
End Sub

Private Sub cboTitle_Click()
  Dim intBookFile As Integer
  Dim strTitle As String, strAuthor As String, intInStock As Integer

  'Open file
  intBookFile = FreeFile
  Open "Books.txt" For Input As #intBookFile

  'Display record
  Do While Not EOF(intBookFile)
    'Read record
    Input #intBookFile, strTitle, strAuthor, intInStock

    If strTitle = cboTitle.Text Then
      txtAuthor.Text = strAuthor
      txtInStock.Text = intInStock
    End If
  Loop

  'Close file
  Close #intBookFile
End Sub

Private Sub cmdChangeBook_Click(Index As Integer)
  Dim intBookFile As Integer, intNewBookFile As Integer
  Dim strTitle As String, strAuthor As String, intInStock As Integer

  If cboTitle.Text <> "" Then
    'Open original file
    intBookFile = FreeFile
    Open "Books.txt" For Input As #intBookFile

    'open new file
    intNewBookFile = FreeFile
    Open "Tempbooks.txt" For Output As #intNewBookFile

    'Process records
    Do While Not EOF(intBookFile)
      'Read record from original file
      Input #intBookFile, strTitle, strAuthor, intInStock

      If Index = 0 Then            'update stock
        If strTitle = cboTitle.Text Then
          intInStock = txtInStock.Text
        End If
        Write #intNewBookFile, strTitle, strAuthor, intInStock
      ElseIf Index = 1 Then        'delete book
        'Write record to new file if not displayed record
        If Not strTitle = cboTitle.Text Then
          Write #intNewBookFile, strTitle, strAuthor, intInStock
        End If
      End If
    Loop

    'Close files
    Close #intBookFile
    Close #intNewBookFile

    'Delete original file and rename new file
    Kill "Books.txt"
    Name "Tempbooks.txt" As "Books.txt"

    Call RefreshInterface
  End If
End Sub
```

```
'***************************************************************
' Clears the text boxes and current combo box list and
' adds an updated list of titles
'
' pre: Books.txt has records with Title, Author, and In Stock fields
' post: List of titles displayed in combo box
'***************************************************************
Sub RefreshInterface()
    Dim intBookFile As Integer
    Dim strTitle As String, strAuthor As String, intInStock As Integer

    txtAuthor.Text = ""  'Clear Author text box
    txtInStock.Text = ""   'Clear InStock text box

    'Open file
    intBookFile = FreeFile
    Open "Books.txt" For Input As #intBookFile

    'Add titles to combo box
    cboTitle.Clear
    Do While Not EOF(intBookFile)
        'Read record
        Input #intBookFile, strTitle, strAuthor, intInStock

        'Add title to combo box
        cboTitle.AddItem strTitle
    Loop

    'Close file
    Close #intBookFile
End Sub

Private Sub cmdDone_Click()
    Unload Me
End Sub
```

The RefreshInterface procedure clears the text boxes and combo box and adds the current titles to the combo box. The cboTitle_Click event procedure displays the author and in stock fields for the selected title.

The Update and Delete command buttons are a control array named cmdChangeBook. When either of these buttons is clicked, the Index of the button is passed to the cmdChangeBook_Click event procedure. Here, the Books.txt file (the original file) and Tempbooks.txt (the new file) are opened. After processing, the original file is deleted, the new file renamed, and the interface updated and cleared.

If the Update button had been clicked, the records in the original files are sequentially written to the new file until the title matching the modified record is read. At this point, the new In Stock value is read from the text box and this value written to the new file. Processing continues until the remaining records in the original file have been written to the new file.

If the Delete button had been clicked, the records in the original file are sequentially written to the new file until the title matching the record to be deleted is read. At this point, the record is not written to the new file. Processing is continued to write remaining records in the original file to the new file.

Review 5

Modify the Change Book Record application to include a Purge command button that when clicked deletes all the records that have 0 (zero) stock.

11.12 Using the File System Controls

The Sequential Access File application, created at the beginning of this chapter, includes a text box for typing a filename. This method of obtaining a filename forces the user to remember which drive, directory, and filename to use. A friendlier interface, such as the one shown below for the Display File application, includes a drive, directory, and file list box for obtaining a filename:

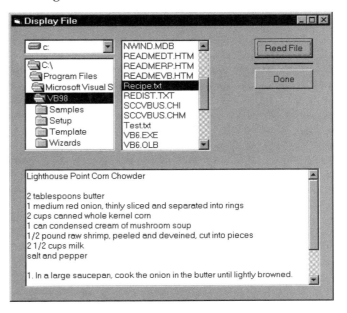

drive list box

A *drive list box* object is created using the DriveListBox control () in the Tool box and has the properties:

- **Name** identifies the object and is used by the programmer. It is good programming style to begin drive list box objects with drv.

- **Drive** changes automatically at run time to whatever the user selected in the list box. Drive is not available at design time.

directory list box

A *directory list box* object is created using the DirListBox control () in the Tool box and has the properties:

- **Name** identifies the object and is used by the programmer. It is good programming style to begin directory list box objects with dir.

- **Path** changes the path displayed in the list box. Path is not available at design time.

file list box

A *file list box* object is created using the FileListBox control () in the Tool box and has the properties:

- **Name** identifies the object and is used by the programmer. It is good programming style to begin file list box objects with fil.

- **Path** changes the path displayed in the list box. Path is not available at design time.

- **FileName** changes automatically at run time to whatever the user selected in the list box. FileName is not available at design time.

change event

When using drive, directory, and file list boxes in an application, a change event procedure should be coded for the drive and the directory list boxes. This is because the file list box should reflect what was selected in the directory list box, which should reflect what was selected in the drive list box. The following code demonstrates this:

```
Private Sub drvDrive_Change()
    dirDirectory.Path = drvDrive.Drive
End Sub

Private Sub dirDirectory_Change()
    filFilename.Path = dirDirectory.Path
End Sub
```

double-click event

A double-click event is often coded for the file list box object because it is a Windows standard that a file opens when it is double-clicked. The following code demonstrates how to use the Path and FileName properties of a file list box object to open the selected file for reading:

```
...
Dim strFilename As String

If Right(dirDirectory.Path, 1) = "\" Then        'path must end with a \
    strFilename = filFilename.Path & filFilename.FileName
Else
    strFilename = filFilename.Path & "\" & filFilename.FileName
End If

intFileNum = FreeFile
Open strFilename For Input As intFileNum
...
```

Review 6

Follow the instructions below to create the Display File application.

1) CREATE A NEW PROJECT

2) ADD OBJECTS TO THE FORM

Refer to the form below when placing and sizing the form and its objects. Use the table on the next page to name and change the properties of the objects.

Object	Name	Caption	Text	MultiLine	ScrollBars	BorderWidth
Form1	frmDisplayFile	Display File				
Drive1	drvDrive					
Dir1	dirDirectory					
File1	filFilename					
Text1	txtViewFile		*empty*	True	2 - Vertical	2
Command1	cmdReadFile	Read File				
Line1	linDividerLine					
Command2	cmdDone	Done				

3) SAVE THE PROJECT

From the File menu, select Save Project. Save the form naming it frmDisplayFile and save the project naming it Display File.

4) WRITE THE PROGRAM CODE

Display the Code Editor window and add the following event procedures:

```
Private Sub drvDrive_Change()
   dirDirectory.Path = drvDrive.Drive
End Sub

Private Sub dirDirectory_Change()
   filFilename.Path = dirDirectory.Path
End Sub

Private Sub filFilename_Click()
   txtViewFile.Text = ""
End Sub

Private Sub filFilename_DblClick()
   Call cmdReadFile_Click
End Sub

Private Sub cmdReadFile_Click()
   Dim intFileNum As Integer
   Dim strTextLine As String
   Dim strFilename As String

   'Assign strFilename the appropriate filename
   If Right(dirDirectory.Path, 1) = "\" Then
      strFilename = filFilename.Path & filFilename.FileName
   Else
      strFilename = filFilename.Path & "\" & filFilename.FileName
   End If

   'Open file for reading
   intFileNum = FreeFile
   Open strFilename For Input As intFileNum

   'Display file in text box
   txtViewFile.Text = ""                          'Clear any existing text
   Do While Not EOF(intFileNum)
      Line Input #intFileNum, strTextLine
      txtViewFile.Text = txtViewFile.Text & strTextLine & vbCrLf
   Loop

   'Close file
   Close #intFileNum
End Sub

Private Sub cmdDone_Click()
   Unload Me
End Sub
```

5) RUN THE APPLICATION

    a.   Save the modified Display File project and then run the application.

    b.   Select a drive, directory, and filename and then click Read File. The file is displayed.

    c.   Select a drive, directory, and then double-click on a filename. The file is displayed.

    d.   Click on the Done button to close the application.

6) PRINT AND THEN REMOVE THE PROJECT

Case Study

In this Case Study, the Display File application created in Review 6 will be modified to allow the user to choose display options and load previously set display options.

specification   The specification for this Case Study is:

The Display File application modified to allow the user to create a profile including the text box text color, background color, and text font size to display the file. This profile can then be loaded when the user runs Display File.

design   The form design for this Case Study is:

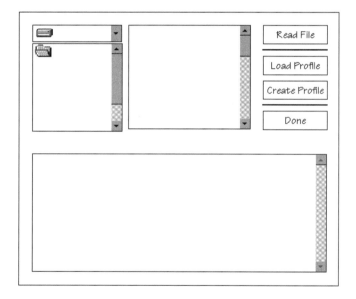

The Read File click event procedure should be coded as discussed in Section 11.12. The Load Profile and Create Profile click event procedures are described in the following pseudocode:

```
Private Sub cmdCreateProfile_Click()
    Open Dfprofile.txt, which has records with fields UserID,
        Backcolor, TextColor, and TextSize, for appending
    Get user ID and profile data and then write to file
End Sub
```

```
Private Sub cmdLoadProfile_Click()
   Open Dfprofile.txt, which has records with fields UserID,
      Backcolor, TextColor, and TextSize, for reading
   Search for user ID and then apply profile
End Sub
```

coding   The interface and code for this Case Study is:

Object	Name	Caption	Text
Form1	frmDisplayFile	Display File	
Drive1	drvDrive		
Dir1	dirDirectory		
File1	filFilename		
Text1	txtViewFile		*empty*
Command1	cmdReadFile	Read File	
Line1	linDividerLine1		
Command2	cmdLoadProfile	Load Profile	
Command3	cmdCreateProfile	Create Profile	
Line2	linDividerLine2		
Command4	cmdDone	Done	

```
Option Explicit

Private Sub drvDrive_Change()
   dirDirectory.Path = drvDrive.Drive
End Sub

Private Sub dirDirectory_Change()
   filFilename.Path = dirDirectory.Path
End Sub

Private Sub filFilename_Click()
   txtViewFile.Text = ""
End Sub

Private Sub filFilename_DblClick()
   Call cmdReadFile_Click
End Sub
```

```
Private Sub cmdReadFile_Click()
   Dim intFileNum As Integer
   Dim strTextLine As String, strFilename As String

   'Assign strFilename the appropriate filename
   If Right(dirDirectory.Path, 1) = "\" Then
      strFilename = filFilename.Path & filFilename.FileName
   Else
      strFilename = filFilename.Path & "\" & filFilename.FileName
   End If

   'Open file for reading
   intFileNum = FreeFile
   Open strFilename For Input As #intFileNum

   'Display file in text box
   txtViewFile.Text = ""   'Clear any existing text
   Do While Not EOF(intFileNum)
      Line Input #intFileNum, strTextLine
      txtViewFile.Text = txtViewFile.Text & strTextLine & vbCrLf
   Loop

   'Close file
   Close #intFileNum
End Sub

'*****************************************************************************
' Applies a user's text box styles to txtViewFile
'
' pre: intProfileNum file has records with fields UserID,Backcolor, TextColor, and TextSize
' post: txtViewFile.BackColor = BackColor, txtViewFile.ForeColor = TextColor, and
' txtViewFile.Font.Size = TextSize
'*****************************************************************************
Private Sub cmdLoadProfile_Click()
   Dim intProfileNum As Integer
   Dim strID As String, strUserID As String
   Dim strBackColor As String, strTextColor As String, intTextSize As Integer

   'Open file for reading
   intProfileNum = FreeFile
   Open "Dfprofile.txt" For Input As #intProfileNum

   'Apply profile if one exists
   strID = InputBox("Enter your User ID:", "Profile")
   If Not EOF(intProfileNum) Then              'get first record
      Input #intProfileNum, strUserID, strBackColor, strTextColor, intTextSize
   End If
   Do While (Not EOF(intProfileNum)) And strID <> strUserID
      Input #intProfileNum, strUserID, strBackColor, strTextColor, intTextSize
   Loop
   If strID = strUserID Then
      txtViewFile.BackColor = strBackColor
      txtViewFile.ForeColor = strTextColor
      txtViewFile.Font.Size = intTextSize
   Else
      MsgBox "No profile found."
   End If

   'Close file
   Close #intProfileNum
End Sub
```

```
'***********************************************************
'  Stores a user's desired text box styles in Dfprofile.txt
'
'  post: Dfprofile.txt contains a new record with fields UserID,
'  BackColor, TextColor, and TextSize
'***********************************************************
Private Sub cmdCreateProfile_Click()
   Dim intProfileNum As Integer
   Dim strID As String
   Dim strBackColor As String, strTextColor As String, intTextSize As Integer

   'Get user's ID
   strID = InputBox("Enter your User ID:", "Profile")

   'Open file for appending
   intProfileNum = FreeFile
   Open "Dfprofile.txt" For Append As #intProfileNum
   strBackColor = GetBackColor
   strTextColor = GetTextColor
   intTextSize = GetTextSize
   Write #intProfileNum, strID, strBackColor, strTextColor, intTextSize
   MsgBox "Profile created."

   'Close file
   Close #intProfileNum
End Sub

'***********************************************************
'  Returns a Visual Basic built-in color constant for the BackColor
'
'  post: a Visual Basic built-in color constant returned for BackColor
'***********************************************************
Function GetBackColor() As String
   Dim intColor As Integer

   intColor = InputBox("Enter a background color: 1 - White, 2 - Blue, 3 - Green, 4 - Black", "BackColor")
   If intColor = 1 Then
      GetBackColor = vbWhite
   ElseIf intColor = 2 Then
      GetBackColor = vbBlue
   ElseIf intColor = 3 Then
      GetBackColor = vbGreen
   ElseIf intColor = 4 Then
      GetBackColor = vbBlack
   Else                        'default color
      GetBackColor = vbWhite
   End If
End Function

'***********************************************************
'  Returns an integer for font size
'
'  post: an integer returned for font size
'***********************************************************
Function GetTextSize() As Integer
   Dim intSize As Integer

   intSize = InputBox("Enter a text size: 9, 10, 11, 12, 13, 14, 15, 16, 17, 18", "TextSize")
   If intSize >= 9 And intSize <= 18 Then
      GetTextSize = intSize
   Else                        'default size
      GetTextSize = 12
   End If
End Function
```

```
'**********************************************************
' Returns a Visual Basic built-in color constant for TextColor
'
' post: a Visual Basic built-in color constant returned for TextColor
'**********************************************************
Function GetTextColor() As String
   Dim intColor As Integer

   intColor = InputBox("Enter a text color: 1 - Black, 2 - Yellow, 3 - Red, 4 - White", "TextColor")
   If intColor = 1 Then
      GetTextColor = vbBlack
   ElseIf intColor = 2 Then
      GetTextColor = vbYellow
   ElseIf intColor = 3 Then
      GetTextColor = vbRed
   ElseIf intColor = 4 Then
      GetTextColor = vbWhite
   Else                          'default color
      GetTextColor = vbBlack
   End If
End Function

Private Sub cmdDone_Click()
   Unload Me
End Sub
```

Note that the GetBackColor and GetTextColor functions return a Visual Basic constant. These constants can be passed as strings without enclosing them in quotation marks.

testing and debugging

Running Display File, creating a profile, and then loading the profile displays the following:

This Case Study should be tested by creating several profiles and then loading each. There are several undesirable features of this application. For example, if there is no Dfprofile.txt file, as is the case before any profiles have been created, a run-time error occurs when the Load Profile button is clicked. Also, there are no options for changing or deleting an existing profile.

Review 7

Modify the Display File Case Study to display an input box asking for the user's ID when the application is started. If the user has no profile then the Load Profile and Create Profile buttons should be displayed on the interface. If the user has a profile, neither the Load Profile or Create Profile buttons should be displayed.

Chapter Summary

file
persistent
sequential access file

A file is a collection of related data stored on a persistent medium such as a hard disk, a CD, or a diskette. Applications of any complexity usually require access to one or more files on disk. A sequential access file contains only plain text and is accessed one character at a time.

Open

A file must be properly opened before it can be accessed. The **Open** statement is used to open a file for **Input, Output,** or **Append. Input** is for reading a file, **Output** is for writing to a file, and **Append** is for adding data to the end of an existing file.

Line Input #
Print #

EOF
Close #

The **Line Input #** statement is used to read one line of a sequential access file, and **Print #** is used to write one line of text to a file. When reading from a file it is important to first check for the end of file using the EOF function. When finished accessing a file, it should closed using the **Close #** statement.

A text box is usually best for displaying the contents of a file. The MultiLine and ScrollBars text box properties are used to wrap text and scroll the text in the text box.

record

Write #
delimiter

Sequential access files are sometimes organized to contain records. A record is a set of fields where each field is one piece of data. Records are written to a sequential access file with the **Write #** statement. Data written with the **Write #** statement is delimited with a comma. A delimiter is a character used to separate fields in a file.

Input #

Records are read from a sequential access file with the **Input #** statement. The EOF function should be used to check for the end of file before reading data.

updating

deleting

Updating a record means to change the data in one or more fields. To update a record in a sequential access file, the records in the original file are written to a new file until the record to be updated is accessed. This record is then updated and then the new record written to the new file. The remaining records in the original file are then written to the new file. Deleting a record requires a similar process. When the record to be deleted is read, it is simply not written to the new file.

A file is deleted from disk with the **Kill** statement. An existing file is renamed with the **Name** statement.

The drive, directory, and file list boxes can make an application easier to use by providing a simpler way for the user to select a filename.

Vocabulary

Append To add data to the end of existing data.

Delimiter A character that is used as a field separator in a sequential access file. The comma and tab characters are common delimiters.

Directory list box A list box that allows the user to select a directory on the computer.

Drive list box A list box that allows the user to select a computer drive.

File A collection of related data stored on a persistent medium.

File list box A list box that allows the user to select a file on the computer.

Newline character A carriage return-linefeed.

Persistent Lasting.

Plain text Text containing only ANSI characters and the newline character.

Record A set of fields where each field contains one piece of data. A set of records has the same fields in the same order.

Sequential access file A plain text file that is read one character at a time.

Update To change the data in an existing record.

Visual Basic

Append Keyword used in an **Open** statement to open a file for writing data after any existing data.

Close Statement used to close a file.

DirListBox control Used to create a directory list box object. Found in the Tool box.

Drive Drive list box property that changes automatically at run time to whatever the user selected in the list box.

DriveListBox control Used to create a drive list box object. Found in the Tool box.

EOF Function that returns True if the end of file has been reached for its filenumber argument.

FileListBox control Used to create a file list box object. Found in the Tool box.

FileName File list box property that changes automatically at run time to whatever the user selected in the list box.

FreeFile Function that returns the next available integer for a file.

Input Keyword used in an **Open** statement to open a file for reading.

Input # Statement used to read delimited data from a sequential access file.

Kill Statement used to delete a file.

Line Input # Statement used to read a line of text from a sequential access file.

MultiLine Text box property that allows more than one line of text in a text box.

Name Statement used to rename a file.

Open Statement used to open a file.

Output Keyword used in an **Open** statement to open a file for writing at the beginning of the file.

Path Directory and File list box property that changes the path in the list box.

Print # Statement used to write a line of text to a sequential access file.

ScrollBars Text box property that allows a text box to display one or more scroll bars.

Write # Statement used to write delimited data (records) to a sequential access file.

Exercises

Exercise 1

Create a Create Text File application that allows the user to enter text in a text box and save it to a file. The user should enter the filename in an input box after clicking on the **Create File** button. The application interface should look similar to:

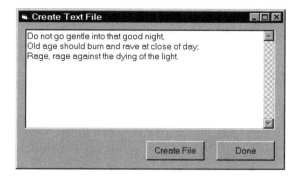

Exercise 2

Create a Read Text File application that displays the contents of a text file in a text box. The user should enter the filename in an input box after clicking on the **Read File** button. The application interface should look similar to:

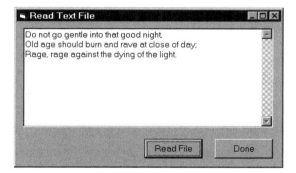

Exercise 3

Create a Text File Statistics application that allows the user to enter a filename and then displays the number of lines in the text file and the total number of characters. The application interface should look similar to:

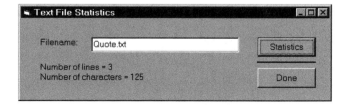

Exercise 4

Modify the Chapter Six Hangman Case Study so that the secret word is a word selected randomly from a text file containing 20 words. One algorithm for doing this is to generate a random number and the use the word that correlates to the number. For example, if 7 is the random number generated, then the word on the 7th line of the text file is used as the secret word.

Exercise 5

Create a Number Statistics application that computes the mean and mode of a set of numbers stored in a file. Have the application display the numbers in a list at form load time. The application interface should look similar to the following after the Mean and Mode buttons are clicked:

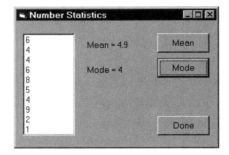

Exercise 6

A Mad-Lib story is a story where nouns and verbs in a sentence are randomly replaced with other nouns and verbs, usually with humorous results. Create a Mad-Lib application that displays a Mad-Lib sentence using the following text files:

- Sentences.txt which contains one sentence per line, each with # signs as noun placeholders and % signs as verb placeholders. For example:
    Gloria Martin's job is to % all of the #s.

- Verbs.txt which contains verbs, one per line. For example:
    run
    display
    eat

- Nouns.txt which contains nouns, one per line. For example:
    banana
    soprano
    elephants
    vegetable

The application interface should look similar to:

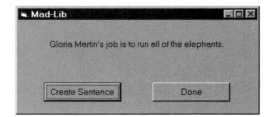

Exercise 7

a) Create an Add CD Record application that adds a new CD record to the current inventory. The application interface should look similar to:

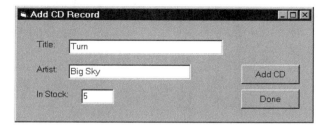

b) Create a View CD Records application that views the CD inventory records. The application interface should look similar to:

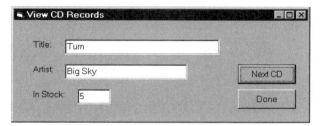

c) Create a Change CD Record application that allows the user to update the stock of a specific CD or delete a CD from the inventory. The application interface should look similar to:

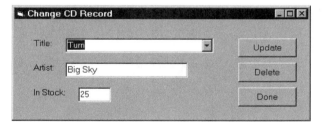

Exercise 8

a) Create an Add Birthday application that adds records containing the names and birthdays of your friends to a file. The application interface should look similar to:

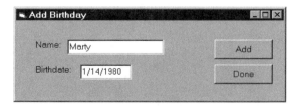

b) Create a View Birthdays application that displays the birthday records. The application interface should look similar to:

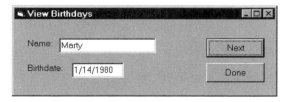

c) Create a Find Birthdays application that displays in a list box only the birthdays that match the month entered by the user in an input box when the Birthday button is clicked. The application interface should look similar to:

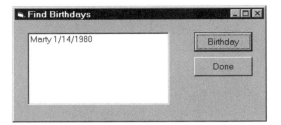

Exercise 9

a) Create an Add Car application that adds records to a car dealership inventory. The application interface should look similar to:

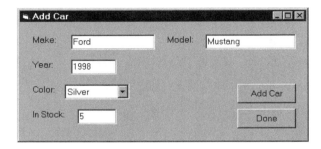

b) Create a View Cars application that displays the records of cars. The application interface should look similar to:

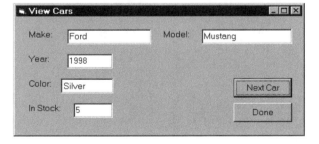

c) Create a Update Cars application that allows the user to update the car inventory. Keep in mind that the model of the cars depends on the make and that a unique record is made up of the make, model, year, and color. The application interface should look similar to:

An Introduction to Programming Using Microsoft Visual Basic

Exercise 10

Create an Append Files application that combines two files to create a new file. The application should use file controls to allow the user to select the first file and the second file. When the user selects the Append button an input box should be displayed asking the user for the name of the file to create and then display the file in the text box. The application interface should look similar to the following after selecting the Verbs.txt file and then the Nouns.txt file and clicking on the Append button:

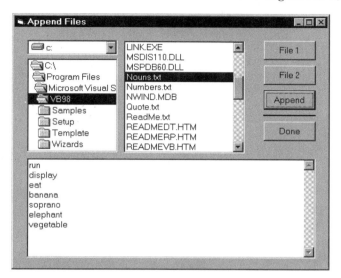

Advanced Exercise 11

Create three applications that are used to add student records, view student records, and update or delete a student record to a file. The student record should store the first and last names and the GPA for the student. The view student records application should also have options for quickly displaying the records for the students with the highest and lowest GPA.

Advanced Exercise 12

a) Create an application that is an on-line test. The application interface should display an input box at form load time that allows the user to enter his or her name. The form should display a question and four radio buttons with possible answers. When the user has selected an answer, a Next command button should be displayed to allow the user to display the next question. After an answer has been selected for the last question, a Done button should be displayed. The user's name should be written to a file followed by the selected answers, one answer per line. Each answer should be stored as A, B, C, or D to correspond to the first, second, third, or fourth radio button. The test questions should be read from a file that stores the questions each followed by four possible answers, on separate lines.

b) Create an application that scores the test answers entered by test takers. The application should read into an array the correct answers from a file that stores each answer on a separate line. The array should then be compared to the answers stored in the file created by the application in part (a). The application interface should display a list box with each test taker's name followed by the number of correct answers. The first line of the list should display the number of questions.

Advanced
Exercise 13

Create an application that merges two files of sorted numbers into a third file of sorted numbers. For example, if the two files of sorted numbers are similar to the following:

File 1	File 2
12	4
23	5
34	10
45	20

then the new file created should contain the following:

File 3
4
5
10
12
20
23
34
45

The application should not use an array to temporarily store numbers, but should merge the two files by taking one element at a time from each and writing it to the new file.

Chapter Twelve
Random Access Files

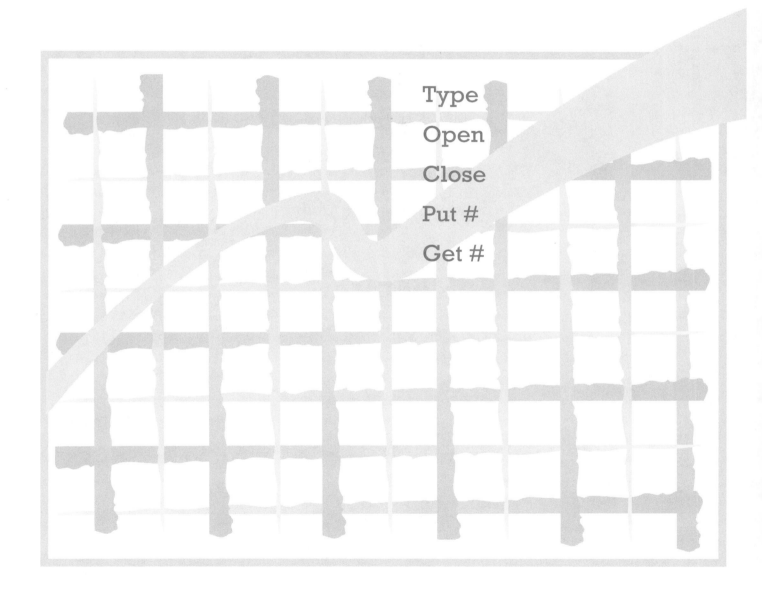

Type

Open

Close

Put #

Get #

Chapter Twelve Objectives

After completing this chapter you will be able to:

1. Understand user-defined types.
2. Understand user-defined type arrays.
3. Understand a random access file.
4. Open a random access file and understand the LenB function.
5. Close a random access file.
6. Write records to a random access file.
7. Calculate the number of records in a file and understand the LOF function.
8. Read, update, and delete records.

Visual Basic includes built-in file functions and statements for directly accessing data in a file. In this chapter you will create applications that store data in random access files and define user-defined types for variable declarations.

12.1 User-Defined Types

aggregate

member

A *user-defined type*, sometimes called an *aggregate*, defines a variable type that can store several related data items in one structure. Each of the data items is called a *member*, and can be data of any Visual Basic built-in type or other user-defined type.

Type

The **Type** statement is used to define a user-defined type and takes the form:

```
Private Type TypeName
    MemberName As DataType
    MemberName As DataType
    ...
End Type
```

Private indicates that the **Type** definition is local to the form module. *TypeName* is a valid identifier representing the user-defined type. *MemberName* is a valid identifier representing a member. *DataType* is a Visual Basic built-in data type or other previously defined user-defined type. A user-defined type can include many members. The **End Type** statement ends the **Type** statement. A **Type** statement must appear in the General section of a form module.

For example, a BookRecord type with strTitle, strAuthor, and intInStock members would be declared with the following **Type** statement:

```
Private Type BookRecord
    strTitle As String
    strAuthor As String
    intInStock As Integer
End Type
```

variable declaration

The following statement declares a variable of type BookRecord:

```
Dim udtNewBook As BookRecord
```

programming style

As a matter of good programming style, user-defined type variable identifiers should begin with udt.

12.2 Using User-Defined Types

accessing a member

A member of a user-defined type is accessed using dot notation, similar to accessing the property of an object. For example, the following statements declare a variable of type BookRecord and assign a value to the strTitle member of the variable:

```
Dim udtBookToChange As BookRecord
udtBookToChange.strTitle = "Peace in the Valley"
```

assignment

If all the members of one user-defined type variable are to be assigned to another variable of the same type, only the variable names need to be used in an assignment statement. For example, the following statements assign all the members of udtFoundBook to udtBookToDisplay:

```
Dim udtFoundBook As BookRecord, udtBookToDisplay As BookRecord
udtBookToDisplay = udtFoundBook
```

user-defined type array

An array of a user-defined type may also be declared. Each element of the array stores a set of the user-defined type members. For example, the following statements use an array of BookRecord:

```
Dim udtFictionBooks(5) As BookRecord
udtFictionBooks(0).strTitle = "The Secret Key"
```

user-defined type argument and parameter

User-defined types can be passed as arguments and declared as procedure parameters just as Visual Basic built-in data types. However, because user-defined types are large, they should be declared as **ByRef**.

Review 1 ───────────────────────

Write user-defined type declarations that hold information for each of the following:

a. Student information including student ID, full name, full address, and expected year of graduation.
b. Music CD stock information including CD ID, title, artist, and number in stock.

12.3 What is a Random Access File?

record

A *record*, as discussed in Chapter Eleven, is a set of related fields where each field is one piece of data. A *random access file* is a set of records of identical structure and size. Unlike sequential access files in which records are read one field at a time, random access files are read one record at a time. The file pointer that Visual Basic maintains in a random access file can be instantly moved to any record. For this reason, random access

direct access file

files are sometimes called *direct access files* and can be visualized as:

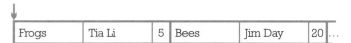

*The file pointer in a random access file can be
instantly moved to any record in the file*

An Introduction to Programming Using Microsoft Visual Basic

Throughout this chapter, applications will be developed for maintaining the inventory of a book store, similar to the applications in Chapter Eleven that were used to view, add, and change book records. However, with user-defined types and random access files, the applications developed in this chapter will use direct access for retrieving and writing records.

12.4 Opening a Random Access File

Open

Any operations performed on a random access file cannot take place until the file has been properly opened using the **Open** statement, which takes the form:

Open *pathname* **For Random As** #*filenumber* **Len** = *recordlength*

pathname is the name of the file to be opened including its full path. *filenumber* is the number used to refer to the file and should be determined using the Visual Basic built-in FreeFile function. *recordlength* is the size of a single record in the file, with each record being the same size. The **Open** statement opens a random access file for reading and writing and creates a file if one does not already exist.

12.5 Determining Record Length

LenB

The structure of a user-defined type naturally represents a record and is therefore used to represent the records of a random access file. The LenB function is used to determine the length in bytes of a variable representing a record. This length is used when opening the file. For example, the statements below define a BookRecord type and then declare a variable udtNewBook of this type. The length of udtNewBook is then used to open the random access file:

```
Option Explicit

Private Type BookRecord
    strTitle As String * 30        '30 character string
    strAuthor As String * 30       '30 character string
    intInStock As Integer
End Type

Private Sub cmdAddBook_Click()
    Dim udtNewBook As BookRecord
    Dim intBookFile As Integer, lngRecLength As Long

    'Open file
    intBookFile = FreeFile
    lngRecLength = LenB(udtNewBook)
    Open "Randbooks.dat" For Random As #intBookFile _
        Len = lngRecLength
...
```

> ### Data Storage
>
> Numeric and **Boolean** data types require a fixed number of bytes for storage. However, the storage requirements of a **String** data type vary depending on the number of characters in the string. A fixed-length string "fixes" the number of characters in a **String** variable, making it possible for the compiler to know how many bytes will be necessary for the variable.

fixed-length strings

Note that the BookRecord type declares members with fixed-length **Strings**. A *fixed-length string* contains an exact number of characters and is declared with an * and the number of characters after the **String** keyword. For example, in the BookRecord type, strTitle contains 30 characters. If strTitle is assigned a string less than 30 characters, the remaining portion of the string is automatically padded with space characters. If a string of more than 30 characters is assigned to strTitle, only the first 30 characters are stored and the remaining characters are truncated. Fixed-length strings are used with random-access files because each record in the file must be the same length in order to have direct access.

12.6 Closing a File

An open file should be closed when finished accessing it by using the **Close** statement, which takes the form:

> **Close** #*filenumber*

filenumber is the number assigned to a file in a previous **Open** statement.

Review 2

Write statements to open a random access file for the user-defined types declared in Review 1.

12.7 Writing Records

record number
Put #

The records in a random access file are automatically numbered, according to their position, starting with 1. The number of a record, called the *record number*, is used to move the file pointer to a record. The **Put #** statement is used to write a record to a random access file and requires the record number:

> **Put** #*filenumber, recordnumber, udtRecord*

filenumber is the number of the file to be written to. *recordnumber* is the position of the record. *udtRecord* is a user-defined type variable containing the record to be written. An error is generated if *udtRecord* exceeds the record length defined in the **Open** statement.

overwriting records
Seek

An existing record is overwritten by using its record number in the **Put #** statement. The Seek function returns the record number of the current record and takes the form:

> Seek(*filenumber*)

filenumber is the number assigned to a file in a previous **Open** statement.

appending records

To append a record to existing records, the record number in the **Put #** statement must be one more than the last record in the file. The number of records in a file can be determined by dividing the file size by the length of a single record, as in the following If...**Then** statement:

```
If LOF(intFileNum) Mod lngRecLength = 0 Then
    NumRecords = (LOF(intFileNum) \ lngRecLength)
Else
    NumRecords = (LOF(intFileNum) \ lngRecLength) + 1
End If
```

LOF

The LOF function returns the length in bytes of a file. Integer division is used because there can be only a whole number of records. An If...**Then** statement is used because there are three cases to consider when determining NumRecords. There may be no records in the file or the last record in the file may be exactly lngRecLength long, in which case the division will not have a remainder. However, Visual Basic pads all but the last record in a file. If the last record in the file is not exactly lngRecLength long, it must be accounted for by adding 1 to the result of the integer division.

Appending records to a random access file is demonstrated in the Add Book application, which is used to maintain a book inventory:

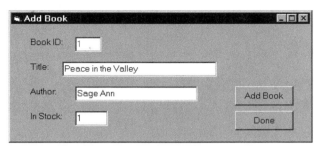

The Add Book application code follows:

```
Option Explicit

Private Type BookRecord
    strTitle As String * 30
    strAuthor As String * 30
    intInStock As Integer
End Type

Private Sub Form_Load()
    Dim udtBook As BookRecord
    Dim intBookFile As Integer, lngRecLength As Long, lngNextBookID As Long

    'Open file
    intBookFile = FreeFile
    lngRecLength = LenB(udtBook)
    Open "Randbooks.dat" For Random As #intBookFile Len = lngRecLength

    'Determine next record number
    lngNextBookID = NumRecords(intBookFile, lngRecLength) + 1
    txtBookID.Text = lngNextBookID    'Display next book ID
    txtBookID.Enabled = False         'User not allowed to change ID

    'Close file
    Close #intBookFile
End Sub

'******************************************************************
'   Adds a BookRecord record to a file
'
'   pre: The book ID for the next record is displayed
'   post: A new book record has been added to a file and the
'   next book ID displayed on the form
'******************************************************************
Private Sub cmdAddBook_Click()
    Dim udtNewBook As BookRecord
    Dim intBookFile As Integer, lngRecLength As Long, lngBookID As Long

    'Open file
    intBookFile = FreeFile
    lngRecLength = LenB(udtNewBook)
    Open "Randbooks.dat" For Random As #intBookFile Len = lngRecLength
```

```
'Add record
lngBookID = txtBookID.Text
udtNewBook.strTitle = txtTitle.Text
udtNewBook.strAuthor = txtAuthor.Text
udtNewBook.intInStock = txtInStock.Text
Put #intBookFile, lngBookID, udtNewBook

'Reset text boxes
txtBookID.Text = lngBookID + 1
txtTitle.Text = ""
txtAuthor.Text = ""
txtInStock.Text = ""

'Close file
Close #intBookFile
End Sub

'*******************************************************************
'  Returns the number of records in the file with intFileNum file number
'  containing records of length lngRecLength
'
'  pre: intFileNum is open
'  post: Number of records in intFileNum returned
'*******************************************************************
Function NumRecords(ByVal intFileNum As Integer, _
ByVal lngRecLength As Long) As Integer
   If LOF(intFileNum) Mod lngRecLength = 0 Then
      NumRecords = (LOF(intFileNum) \ lngRecLength)
   Else
      NumRecords = (LOF(intFileNum) \ lngRecLength) + 1
   End If
End Function

Private Sub cmdDone_Click()
   Unload Me
End Sub
```

Note that in the Add Book application the book ID for the next book is determined in the Form_Load event procedure by adding 1 to the value returned by the NumRecords function. The new book ID is then displayed in a text box, and this text box disabled so that the user cannot change its contents. The cmdAddBook_Click event procedure uses the book ID from the text box as the record number for the new book. This number is then incremented and a new book ID displayed in the text box.

Review 3

Create an Add Student application that maintains students records. Use the Add Book application as a guide. Include a NumRecords function, as used in the Add Book application, to determine the current number of student records. The application interface should look similar to that shown on the right after entering one record and typing data for a second record.

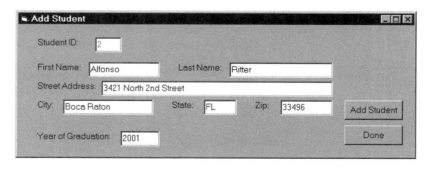

Review 4

Create an Add CD application that maintains a CD inventory. Use the Add Book application as a guide. Include a NumRecords function, as used in the Add Book application, to determine the current number of CDs. The application interface should look similar to that shown on the right after entering one record and typing data for a second record.

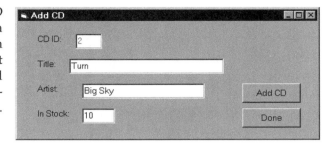

12.8 Reading Records

Get #

Records can be read from a random access file with the **Get #** statement, which takes the form:

Get #*filenumber, recordnumber, udtRecord*

filenumber is the number of the file to be read. *recordnumber* is the file position of the record. *udtRecord* is a user-defined type variable that will store the data read.

Reading records from a random access file is demonstrated in the View Book application, which is used to view book inventory:

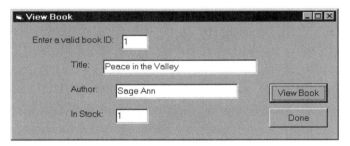

The View Book application code follows:

```
Option Explicit

Private Type BookRecord
    strTitle As String * 30
    strAuthor As String * 30
    intInStock As Integer
End Type

Private Sub Form_Load()
    Call InitializeForm
End Sub

'*********************************************************
'  Clears form
'
'  post: Book record text boxes on form are empty
'*********************************************************
Sub InitializeForm()
    txtBookID.Text = ""
    txtTitle.Text = ""
    txtAuthor.Text = ""
    txtInStock.Text = ""
End Sub
```

The RTrim Function

The Visual Basic built-in RTrim function removes trailing spaces from its string argument. RTrim can be used to remove the trailing spaces from a fixed-length string, as demonstrated in the following statements:

```
Dim strBig As String * 10
Dim strNewString As String

strBig = "Hello"
strNewString = strBig & _
" there!"         'Hello      there!
strNewString = RTrim(strBig) & _
" there!"         'Hello there!
```

```
Private Sub txtBookID_Change()
   txtTitle.Text = ""
   txtAuthor.Text = ""
   txtInStock.Text = ""
End Sub

Private Sub cmdViewBook_Click()
   Dim udtBookToView As BookRecord
   Dim intBookFile As Integer, lngRecLength As Long
   Dim lngTotalRecords As Long, lngBookID As Long

   'Open file
   intBookFile = FreeFile
   lngRecLength = LenB(udtBookToView)
   Open "Randbooks.dat" For Random As #intBookFile _
      Len = lngRecLength

   'Determine number of records
   lngTotalRecords = NumRecords(intBookFile, lngRecLength)

   'View record if valid
   If lngTotalRecords = 0 Then        'No records in file
      MsgBox "No records to view"
      cmdViewBook.Enabled = False 'Dim View Book button
   Else
      lngBookID = txtBookID.Text       'Get Book ID
      If lngBookID > 0 And lngBookID <= lngTotalRecords Then
         Get #intBookFile, lngBookID, udtBookToView
         txtTitle.Text = udtBookToView.strTitle
         txtAuthor.Text = udtBookToView.strAuthor
         txtInStock.Text = udtBookToView.intInStock
      Else
         Call InitializeForm
         MsgBox "Enter a valid book ID"
      End If
   End If

   'Close file
   Close #intBookFile
End Sub

'***********************************************************
'  Returns the number of records in the file with intFileNum
'  file number containing records of length lngRecLength
'
'  pre: intFileNum is open
'  post: Number of records in intFileNum returned
'***********************************************************
Function NumRecords(ByVal intFileNum As Integer, _
ByVal lngRecLength As Long) As Integer
   If LOF(intFileNum) Mod lngRecLength = 0 Then
      NumRecords = (LOF(intFileNum) \ lngRecLength)
   Else
      NumRecords = (LOF(intFileNum) \ lngRecLength) + 1
   End If
End Function

Private Sub cmdDone_Click()
   Unload Me
End Sub
```

The cmdViewBook_Click event procedure displays a book record corresponding to a valid record number entered by the user by reading just
that record from a random access file. Because of direct access, there is

no need to read every record in the file until the desired record is found. Note that if there are no records in the book file, the View Book button is dimmed so that the user can choose only the Done buton.

Review 5 ——————————————————————————————

Create a View Student application that displays the record of the student with the ID entered by the user. Use the View Book application as a guide. The application interface should look similar to that shown on the right after entering a valid student ID and clicking the View Student button.

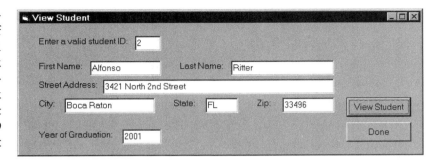

Review 6 ——————————————————————————————

Create a View CD application that displays the record of the CD with the ID entered by the user. Use the View Book application as a guide. The application interface should look similar to that shown on the right after entering a valid CD ID and clicking the View CD button.

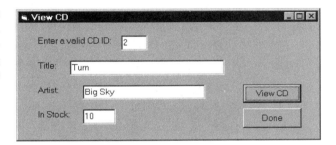

12.9 Updating and Deleting Records

A random access file record is updated by reading the record into a variable, making changes to the desired fields, and then writing the record back to the file in the appropriate record position.

There are two ways to delete random access file records. One method is similar to that used for deleting sequential access file records. All the records are read from the random access file and then all but the one to delete are written to another random access file. The original file is then deleted and the new file renamed to that of the original.

A second method for deleting a record is to simply mark the record as deleted. One way to do this is to set all the fields in the record to 0 or an empty string. Another method is to simply store the word DELETED in a **String** field. One reason for using this type of deletion process is to maintain the record numbering of the existing records. For example, the book inventory applications use the record number as the book ID for each book. The book IDs will not change if DELETED is stored in the strTitle field of deleted records.

Records marked as deleted may later be overwritten by a new record. This method of adding records requires additional code to first check for deleted records, rather than automatically appending new records to a file.

Updating and deleting records in a random access file is demonstrated in the Change Book application which is used to modify book inventory:

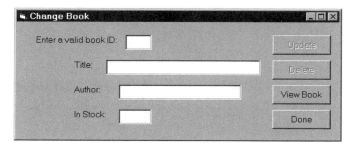

The View Book button is used to display the book that needs to be updated or deleted. The Update and Delete buttons are a control array and are dimmed until a book record is displayed. The Change Book application code follows:

```
Option Explicit

Private Type BookRecord
    strTitle As String * 30
    strAuthor As String * 30
    intInStock As Integer
End Type

Private Sub Form_Load()
    Call InitializeForm
End Sub

'*************************************************************
'   Clears text boxes on form and dims Update and Delete buttons
'
'   post: Text boxes on form are empty and Update and Delete
'   buttons are dimmed
'*************************************************************
Sub InitializeForm()
    txtBookID.Text = ""
    txtTitle.Text = ""
    txtAuthor.Text = ""
    txtInStock.Text = ""
    cmdChangeBook(0).Enabled = False  'Dim Update button
    cmdChangeBook(1).Enabled = False  'Dim Delete button
End Sub

Private Sub txtBookID_Change()
    txtTitle.Text = ""
    txtAuthor.Text = ""
    txtInStock.Text = ""
    cmdChangeBook(0).Enabled = False  'Dim Update button
    cmdChangeBook(1).Enabled = False  'Dim Delete button
End Sub

Private Sub cmdViewBook_Click()
    Dim udtBookToView As BookRecord
    Dim intBookFile As Integer, lngRecLength As Long
    Dim lngTotalRecords As Long, lngBookID As Long

    'Open file
    intBookFile = FreeFile
    lngRecLength = LenB(udtBookToView)
    Open "Randbooks.dat" For Random As #intBookFile _
        Len = lngRecLength
```

```
'Determine number of records
lngTotalRecords = NumRecords(intBookFile, lngRecLength)

'View record if valid
If lngTotalRecords = 0 Then          'No records in file
   MsgBox "No records to view"
   cmdViewBook.Enabled = False 'Dim View Book button
Else
   lngBookID = txtBookID.Text       'Get Book ID
   If lngBookID > 0 And lngBookID <= lngTotalRecords Then
      Get #intBookFile, lngBookID, udtBookToView
      txtTitle.Text = udtBookToView.strTitle
      txtAuthor.Text = udtBookToView.strAuthor
      txtInStock.Text = udtBookToView.intInStock
      cmdChangeBook(0).Enabled = True   'Enable Update button
      cmdChangeBook(1).Enabled = True   'Enable Delete button
   Else
      Call InitializeForm
      MsgBox "Enter a valid book ID"
   End If
End If

'Close file
Close #intBookFile
End Sub

'***********************************************************
'  Updates or deletes an existing BookRecord record in a file
'
'  pre: A valid book ID is displayed in the txtBookID text box
'  post: The displayed record is updated or deleted
'***********************************************************
Private Sub cmdChangeBook_Click(Index As Integer)
   Dim udtBookToChange As BookRecord
   Dim intBookFile As Integer, lngRecLength As Long
   Dim lngBookID As Long

   'Open file
   intBookFile = FreeFile
   lngRecLength = LenB(udtBookToChange)
   Open "Randbooks.dat" For Random As #intBookFile _
      Len = lngRecLength

   lngBookID = txtBookID.Text
   'Update record
   If Index = 0 Then
      udtBookToChange.strTitle = txtTitle.Text
      udtBookToChange.strAuthor = txtAuthor.Text
      udtBookToChange.intInStock = txtInStock.Text
      Put #intBookFile, lngBookID, udtBookToChange
   'Delete record
   ElseIf Index = 1 Then
      udtBookToChange.strTitle = "DELETED"
      udtBookToChange.strAuthor = ""
      udtBookToChange.intInStock = 0
      Put #intBookFile, lngBookID, udtBookToChange
   End If

   'Reset form
   Call InitializeForm

   'Close file
   Close #intBookFile
End Sub
```

```
'*********************************************************
'  Returns the number of records in the file with intFileNum file
'  number containing records of length lngRecLength
'
'  pre: intFileNum is open
'  post: Number of records in intFileNum returned
'*********************************************************
Function NumRecords(ByVal intFileNum As Integer, _
ByVal lngRecLength As Long) As Integer
    If LOF(intFileNum) Mod lngRecLength = 0 Then
        NumRecords = (LOF(intFileNum) \ lngRecLength)
    Else
        NumRecords = (LOF(intFileNum) \ lngRecLength) + 1
    End If
End Function

Private Sub cmdDone_Click()
    Unload Me
End Sub
```

If the Update button is clicked, the data in the text boxes is used to overwrite an existing record. If Delete is clicked, the strTitle field of the displayed record is assigned DELETED, the strAuthor field is assigned an empty string, and the intInStock field is assigned 0.

Review 7

Create a Change Student application that allows the user to update or delete a student record. Use the Change Book application as a guide. The application interface should look similar to that shown on the right after deleting and then viewing the first record.

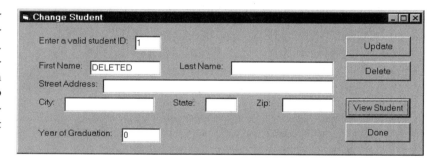

Review 8

Create an Change CD application that allows the user to update or change a CD record. Use the Change Book application as a guide. The application interface should look similar to that shown on the right after updating and then viewing the second record.

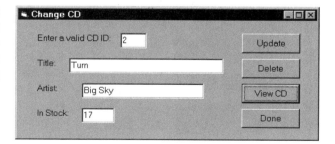

Case Study

The box office at a small theater needs an application for reserving seats. In this Case Study a Theater Box Office application is created.

specification   The specification for this Case Study is:

> The Theater Box Office application displays the arrangement of 50 theater seats for a small theater. The application should be able to display the seats sold for any show and allow the user to display information about a reserved seat and make a reservation for an empty seat.

design   The form design for this Case Study is:

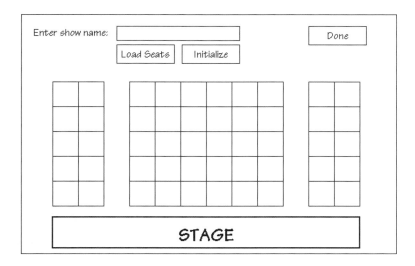

The application interface design for this Case Study includes a control array of 50 command buttons arranged to represent the seats in the theater. A rectangle shape and a label are used on the form to represent the stage. The user can enter the show name, which will be used as the name of the random access file, in a text box. The Initialize button writes empty seat records to the show file and changes the Caption of the seat buttons to display "---". The Load Seats button opens an existing file and changes the Caption of the seat buttons to display the status of the show's seats.

The program code design for this Case Study is best done by listing the pseudocode for the event procedures. Additionally, since the application should display seat information about any show, random access files will be used to store the seat information for each show. The user-defined type for the seat records is also defined below:

```
Private Type SeatRecord
    blnReserved As Boolean
    strName As String 15
    curPrice As Currency
End Type

Private cmdLoadSeats_Click()
    Read records from a file and update seat
        captions appropriately
End Sub

Private cmdInitialize_Click()
    Write to a file a SeatRecord record with blnReserved
        as False for each theater seat
    Update seat captions to display - - -
End Sub
```

```
Private cmdSeats_Click(Index As Integer)
    If seat caption is - - - then
        Display an input box to get name for reservation
        Make reservation
        Update seat caption to display R
    Else
        Display message box with name of reservation and
            seat price
    End If
End Sub
```

Since the cmdLoadSeats_Click, cmdInitialize_Click, and the
cmdSeats_Click event procedures update the seat caption, a general procedure UpdateSeatCaption should be coded. Both the cmdInitialize_Click
and the cmdSeats_Click event procedures write records to a file and therefore need a ReserveSeat procedure. Also to support other procedures,
SeatPrice and SeatName functions should be written.

coding   The interface and code for this Case Study is:

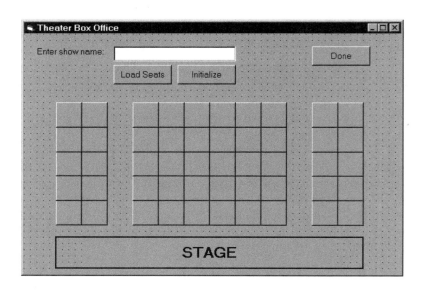

Object	Name	Caption
Form1	frmTheaterBoxOffice	Theater Box Office
Command1	cmdLoadSeats	Load Seats
Command2	cmdInitialize	Initialize
Command3	cmdDone	Done
Label1	lblStage	Stage

The rectangle in the Case Study is a shape named Shape1. The seats are
50 command buttons in a control array named cmdSeats with indexes 1
through 50.

```vb
Option Explicit

Private Const strEmptySeat As String = "---"
Private Const strReservedSeat As String = "R"
Private Const intNumSeats As Integer = 50

Private Type SeatRecord
   blnReserved As Boolean
   strName As String * 15
   curPrice As Currency
End Type

Private Sub cmdLoadSeats_Click()
   Dim udtTheaterSeat As SeatRecord
   Dim intShowFile As Integer, lngRecLength As Long
   Dim intSeatNum As Integer

   'Open file
   intShowFile = FreeFile
   lngRecLength = LenB(udtTheaterSeat)
   Open txtShowName.Text For Random As #intShowFile Len = lngRecLength

   'Read record and update seat button caption
   For intSeatNum = 1 To intNumSeats
      Get #intShowFile, intSeatNum, udtTheaterSeat
      Call UpdateSeatCaption(cmdSeats(intSeatNum), udtTheaterSeat.blnReserved)
   Next intSeatNum

   'Close file
   Close #intShowFile
End Sub

Private Sub cmdInitialize_Click()
   Dim intSeatNum As Integer

   'Initialize seats
   For intSeatNum = 1 To intNumSeats
      Call ReserveSeat(strEmptySeat, intSeatNum)
      Call UpdateSeatCaption(cmdSeats(intSeatNum), False)
   Next intSeatNum
End Sub

Private Sub cmdSeats_Click(Index As Integer)
   Dim strName As String

   If cmdSeats(Index).Caption = strEmptySeat Then
      strName = InputBox("Seat price is " & Format(SeatPrice(Index), "Currency") & _
         vbCrLf & "Enter last name of reservation:", _
         "Reserve a seat")
      If strName <> "" Then
         Call ReserveSeat(strName, Index)
         Call UpdateSeatCaption(cmdSeats(Index), True)
      End If
   Else
      MsgBox SeatName(Index) & vbCrLf & Format(SeatPrice(Index), "Currency")
   End If
End Sub
```

```
'***********************************************************
'  Writes a SeatRecord record to the file with the name
'  entered by the user.
'
'  pre: strName is the name of the reservation,
'  intSeatNum is a valid theater seat number
'  post: A seat reservation has been written to a file
'***********************************************************
Sub ReserveSeat(ByVal strName As String, ByVal intSeatNum As Integer)
   Dim udtTheaterSeat As SeatRecord
   Dim intShowFile As Integer, lngRecLength As Long

   'Open file
   intShowFile = FreeFile
   lngRecLength = LenB(udtTheaterSeat)
   Open txtShowName.Text For Random As #intShowFile Len = lngRecLength

   'Write record
   If strName = strEmptySeat Then
      udtTheaterSeat.blnReserved = False
   Else
      udtTheaterSeat.blnReserved = True
      udtTheaterSeat.strName = strName
      udtTheaterSeat.curPrice = SeatPrice(intSeatNum)
   End If
   Put #intShowFile, intSeatNum, udtTheaterSeat

   'Close file
   Close #intShowFile
End Sub

'***********************************************************
'  Changes the caption of cmdSeat button to reflect the seat status
'
'  pre: cmdSeat is a seat command button, blnReserved is True
'  if seat reserved, False otherwise
'  post: cmdSeat Caption indicates either empty or reserved
'***********************************************************
Sub UpdateSeatCaption(ByRef cmdSeat As Object, ByVal blnReserved As Boolean)
   If blnReserved Then
      cmdSeat.Caption = strReservedSeat
   Else
      cmdSeat.Caption = strEmptySeat
   End If
End Sub

'***********************************************************
'  Returns the price of seat intSeatNum
'
'  pre: intSeatNum is a valid seat
'  post: The Price of intSeatNum seat returned
'***********************************************************
Function SeatPrice(ByVal intSeatNum As Integer) As Currency
   Const intCenterSeatsStart As Integer = 1
   Const intCenterSeatsEnd As Integer = 30
   Const curCenterSeatPrice As Currency = 20
   Const curSideSeatPrice As Currency = 15

   If intSeatNum >= intCenterSeatsStart And intSeatNum <= intCenterSeatsEnd Then
      SeatPrice = curCenterSeatPrice
   Else
      SeatPrice = curSideSeatPrice
   End If
End Function
```

```
'********************************************************
'  Returns the name of the seat reservation
'
'  pre: intSeatNum is a valid reserved seat
'  post: The reservation name of intSeatNum seat returned
'********************************************************
Function SeatName(ByVal intSeatNum As Integer) As String
   Dim udtTheaterSeat As SeatRecord
   Dim intShowFile As Integer, lngRecLength As Long

   'Open file
   intShowFile = FreeFile
   lngRecLength = LenB(udtTheaterSeat)
   Open txtShowName.Text For Random As #intShowFile Len = lngRecLength

   'Read record and return strName
   Get #intShowFile, intSeatNum, udtTheaterSeat
   SeatName = udtTheaterSeat.strName

   'Close file
   Close #intShowFile
End Function

Private Sub cmdDone_Click()
   Unload Me
End Sub
```

testing and debugging   Running Theater Box Office and loading seats displays the following:

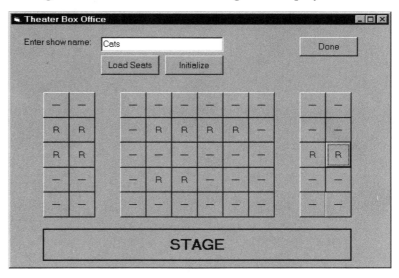

This Case Study should be tested by intializing and loading show files, reserving empty seats, and clicking on a reserved seat.

Review 9

The Theater Box Office Case Study application should not allow a user to click on a seat until the show file has been loaded or initialized. Modify the Case Study to dim all the seats (Enabled = False) when text is typed in the show name text box (a change event procedure).

Chapter Summary

Type

member

A user-defined type is declared using a **Type** statement and defines a variable type that can store several related data items in one structure. Variables of a user-defined type should have identifiers that begin with udt. Each data item of a user-defined type is called a member and is accessed using dot notation. All the members of one user-defined type can be assigned to another variable of the same type by using only the variable names in an assignment statement. An array of a user-defined type may also be declared. User-defined types can be passed as arguments and declared as parameters.

A random access file is a set of records of identical size and structure. Random access files are read one record at a time, and are sometimes called direct access files.

Open

LenB

Close #

A random access file is opened with the **Open** statement. The length of a record in the file must be included as part of the **Open** statement. The LenB function returns the length in bytes of a variable and is used to determine the size of a record. The **Close** # statement is used to close a file when access is no longer needed.

fixed-length strings

The structure of a user-defined type naturally represents a record and is therefore used to represent the records of a random access file. User-defined types representing records in a random access file must used fixed-length strings for **String** member. A fixed length string is declared with an * and the number of characters after the **String** keyword.

record number

The records in a random access file are automatically numbered, according to their position, starting with 1. The number of a record is called the record number and is used to move the file pointer to a record. The **Put** # statement writes a record to a file using a record number.

Seek

LOF

The Seek function returns the number of the current record. Records are appended to a file by first determining the total number of records in the file and then writing the new record using a record number 1 more than the last record in the file. The LOF function returns the length in bytes of a file and is divided by the length of a record to determine the number of records in a file.

Get #

Records are read from a random access file with the **Get** # statement. Records can be read from any position in the file by including the record number in the **Get** # statement.

A random access file record is updated by reading the record into a variable, making changes to the desired fields, and then writing the record back to the file in the appropriate position. A record can be deleted by writing all but the record to delete to a new file and then renaming the new file to that of the old file. Deleted records may also be marked as deleted to maintain the record numbering of existing records. Records marked as deleted may later be overwritten by a new record.

Vocabulary

Aggregate   A user-defined type.

Direct access file   A random access file.

Fixed-length string   A string that contains an exact number of characters.

Member   A data item in a user-defined type.

Random access file   A set of records of identical structure and size.

Record   A set of related fields where each field is one piece of data.

Record number   The number of a record in a random access file.

User-defined type   A variable type that can store several related data items in one structure.

Visual Basic

*   Used to declare a **String** variable of a fixed length.

Get #   Statement used to read a record from a random access file.

LenB   Function that returns the length in bytes of a variable.

LOF   Function that returns the length in bytes of a file.

Open   Statement used to open a random access file.

Put #   Statement used to write a record to a random access file.

Seek   Function that returns the number of the current record in a random access file.

Type   Statement used to define a user-defined type.

Exercises

Exercise 1

a) Create an Add Employee application that adds employee records to a random access file. The application interface should look similar to:

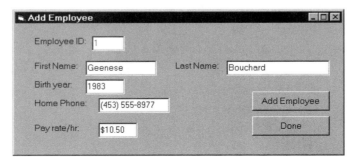

b) Create a View Employee application that displays the record for the employee with the ID entered by the user. The application interface should look similar to:

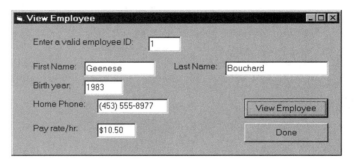

c) Create a Change Employee application that allows the user to update or delete an employee's record. The application interface should look similar to:

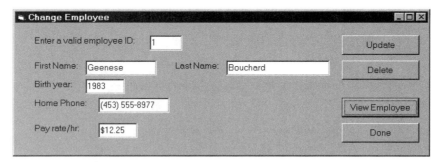

Exercise 2

Create an Update Birthday File application that append the records from the Newborn.dat file to Birthday.dat. The Birthday.dat and Newborn.dat files have records with a **String** * 30 first name field, **String** * 30 last name field, and **String** * 18 birthdate field. The application should first display the records of the Birthday.dat file in a list box, and then after clicking on the Append button display the records of the updated Birthday.dat file. The application interface should look similar to the following after clicking on Append:

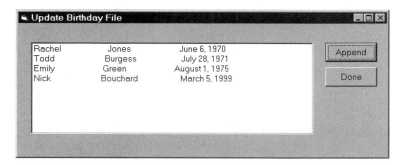

Exercise 3

Create an Academy Awards application that allows the user to display the winners from a specified year. The Academy.dat file has records with the following structure:

```
intYear As Integer
strPicture As String * 50
strStudio As String * 20
strDirector As String * 50
strActress As String * 50
strActor As String * 50
strSupActress As String * 50
strSupActor As String * 50
```

In the early years of the academy awards, there was no supporting actress and supporting actor awards, so these fields have an empty string in Academy.dat. The Academy.dat file uses the year for determining record number. Since the Academy Awards began in 1928, each record number is computed by subtracting 1927 from the year. The application interface should look similar to the following after entering 1929 and clicking View Winners:

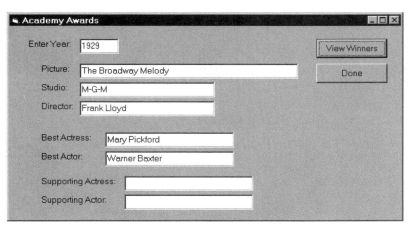

Exercise 4

Create a Special Occasion Meals application that displays an appetizer, a bread, a main course, two side dishes, a dessert, and a beverage for special occasions. The user should be able to enter a new special occasion meal and display a previously entered one. The application interface should look similar to:

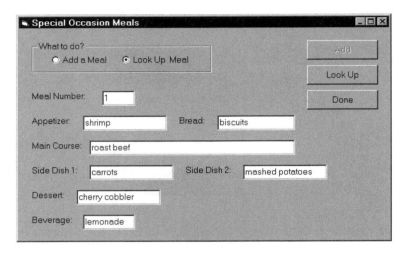

Exercise 5

a) Create a Find Book application that allows the user to enter the title of a book and then search for it by clicking on the Search by Title button. The application interface should look similar to:

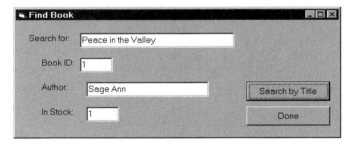

Your program code should use:

- FindBook function that has intFileNum, intTotalRecords, and strTitle value parameters and returns the record number of the record containing the title or –1 if the title was not found.
- ViewBook function that has a lngBookID and intFileNum parameter and displays the found record in text boxes on the form.

b) Modify the Find Book application to have a Search by Author button that allows the user to find a book by a specific author.

Exercise 6

Modify the Theater Box Office application created in the Case Study of this chapter so that the first row of the center section can only be reserved by season ticket holders. When one of these seats is selected, an input box should be displayed with the title "Season Ticket Holder" and the message This seat to be reserved by season ticket holders only--enter last name:. The named entered in the input box must be that of a season ticket holder in order to reserve the seat.

Your program should use a SeasonTicketHolder function that has a strName parameter and returns True if strName is in the Season.dat file (which contains just the last names of the season ticket holders).

Exercise 7

Create a January Rentals application that displays a command button control array for the nine cars and three vans owned by a car rental company. The buttons should be arranged to correspond to the parking places of the vehicles, as shown below. The application should allow the user to enter a day and change the status of all vehicles to not rented, or look up or rent vehicles for that day. Use the Case Study from this chapter as a guide when creating this application. The application interface should look similar to the following after a day has been typed and Look Up Day has been clicked:

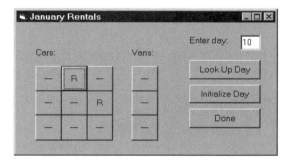

Exercise 8

Create a Survey application that uses a random access file to store surveys and allows the user to enter a survey and display a summary of the results (Hint: Use counters and accumulators if necessary). The application interface should look similar to:

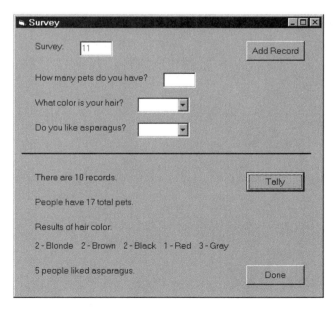

Exercise 9

Create an International Numbers application that displays the numbers one through ten in Spanish, French, and German. The number entered by the user should be used to display the appropriate record from the International Numbers.dat file. The International Numbers.dat file has records with a **String** * 20 French field, **String** * 20 German field, and **String** * 20 Spanish field. The application interface should look similar to:

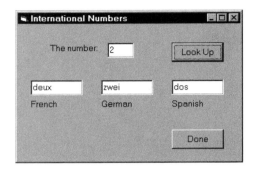

Advanced

Exercise 10

Modify the Theater Box Office Case Study from this chapter to automatically initialize a show file if necessary when the **Load Seats** button is clicked. For example, if the user enters Oliver as the show name and then clicks the **Load Seats** button, the application should intialize this file if there are no seats in it or load the seats if it contains seats.

Chapter Thirteen Objectives

After completing this chapter you will be able to:

1. Understand sorting and the bubble sort algorithm.
2. Use the Visual Basic built-in Timer function to determine the speed of sorts.
3. Understand the selection sort algorithm.
4. Understand the insertion sort algorithm.
5. Understand the binary search algorithm.

Sorting and searching algorithms are used in many applications for manipulating and analyzing data. In this chapter you will learn several of these algorithms.

13.1 Bubble Sort

sorting

Sorting is the process of putting items in a designated order, either from low to high or high to low. *Bubble sort* is a basic sorting algorithm that starts at the first element of a list of items and proceeds sequentially to the last, comparing each element with the next. If the first item is greater than the second, they are swapped. Then the second item is swapped with the third, if necessary, and so on until the end of the list is reached. This process is performed on each item in the list to "bubble" up items to their proper position.

For an array of integers, the BubbleSort procedure pseudocode is:

```
Sub BubbleSort(ByRef intArray() As Integer)
   For intItem = LBound(intArray) To UBound(intArray)
      For intIndex = LBound(intArray) To UBound(intArray) - 1
         If intArray(intIndex) > intArray(intIndex+1) Then
            swap intArray(intIndex) with intArray(intIndex+1)
      Next intIndex
   Next intItem
End Sub
```

The Bubble Sort application below uses the BubbleSort procedure to sort a list of randomly generated numbers:

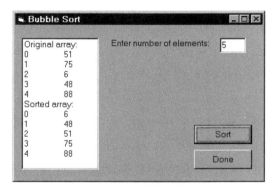

```
Option Explicit

Private Const intMaxNumber As Integer = 100

Private Sub Form_Load()
    Randomize
End Sub

Private Sub cmdSort_Click()
    Dim intDataArray() As Integer
    Dim intNumDataItems As Integer 'Number of items in intDataArray

    'Create array of random numbers
    intNumDataItems = txtNumElements.Text
    Call GenerateArray(intDataArray(), intNumDataItems)

    'Display original array in list box
    lstArrayElements.Clear
    lstArrayElements.AddItem "Original array:"  'Title
    Call DisplayData(intDataArray(), lstArrayElements)

    'Sort array
    Call BubbleSort(intDataArray())

    'Display sorted array in list box
    lstArrayElements.AddItem "Sorted array:"  'Title
    Call DisplayData(intDataArray(), lstArrayElements)
End Sub

'****************************************************************
'  Modifies intArray() to contain intNumElements random integers
'  ranging from 1 to intMaxNumber
'
'  pre: Randomize called
'  post: intArray() contains intNumElements random integers
'  ranging from 1 to intMaxNumber
'****************************************************************
Sub GenerateArray(ByRef intArray() As Integer, _
ByVal intNumElements As Integer)
    Dim intIndex As Integer

    ReDim intArray(intNumElements - 1)

    For intIndex = LBound(intArray) To UBound(intArray)
        intArray(intIndex) = Int(intMaxNumber * Rnd + 1)
    Next intIndex
End Sub

'****************************************************************
'  Displays the contents of intArray() in a list box
'
'  pre: intArray() contains at least one element
'  post: intArray() items displayed in a list box
'****************************************************************
Sub DisplayData(ByRef intArray() As Integer, ByRef lstList As ListBox)
    Dim intIndex As Integer

    For intIndex = LBound(intArray) To UBound(intArray)
        lstList.AddItem intIndex & vbTab & intArray(intIndex)
    Next intIndex
End Sub
```

```
'******************************************************************
'  Sorts intArray from low to high
'
'  pre: intArray has at least one element
'  post: intArray() elements are sorted low to high
'******************************************************************
Sub BubbleSort(ByRef intArray() As Integer)
    Dim intItem As Integer, intIndex As Integer
    Dim intTemp As Integer

    For intItem = LBound(intArray) To UBound(intArray)
        For intIndex = LBound(intArray) To UBound(intArray) - 1
            If intArray(intIndex) > intArray(intIndex + 1) Then
                intTemp = intArray(intIndex)
                intArray(intIndex) = intArray(intIndex + 1)
                intArray(intIndex + 1) = intTemp
            End If
        Next intIndex
    Next intItem
End Sub

Private Sub cmdDone_Click()
    Unload Me
End Sub
```

13.2 Timing Code

Timer

When choosing a sorting algorithm, one consideration is its efficiency. One measure of the efficiency of a sorting algorithm is the speed at which it can complete a sort. The Visual Basic built-in Timer function returns a **Single** representing the number of seconds that have elapsed since midnight. The following statements determine the time required for a sort:

```
...
Dim sglStart As Single, sglFinish As Single, sglTime As Single

sglStart = Timer
Call BubbleSort(intDataArray())
sglFinish = Timer
sglTime = sglFinish - sglStart
...
```

Review 1

Modify the Bubble Sort application to display a label with the time required for a sort. Test the application with 100, 500, 1000, and 2000 elements.

13.3 A More Efficient Bubble Sort

The BubbleSort procedure could be made more efficient by using a **Do…Loop** instead of a **For…Next** to process items. The **For…Next** processes every element in the array, even when no more swaps are needed to sort the list. By using a flag and a **Do…Loop**, processing need only be done until the list is sorted:

```
'***********************************************************
' Sorts intArray from low to high
'
' pre: intArray() contains at least one element
' post: intArray() elements are sorted low to high
'***********************************************************
Sub BubbleSort(ByRef intArray() As Integer)
    Dim intItem As Integer, intIndex As Integer
    Dim blnSwapRequired As Boolean          'Flag
    Dim intTemp As Integer

    blnSwapRequired = True
    Do While blnSwapRequired
        blnSwapRequired = False
        For intIndex = LBound(intArray) To UBound(intArray) - 1
            If intArray(intIndex) > intArray(intIndex + 1) Then
                intTemp = intArray(intIndex)
                intArray(intIndex) = intArray(intIndex + 1)
                intArray(intIndex + 1) = intTemp
                blnSwapRequired = True
            End If
        Next intIndex
    Loop
End Sub
```

Note the blnSwapRequired flag is True upon entering the loop and then immediately made False. If values are swapped, blnSwapRequired is made True to indicate that the list was still not sorted. When one pass can be made through the list without any swaps, the loop is exited.

Review 2

Modify the Bubble Sort application to include the more efficient BubbleSort procedure in Section 13.3. Test the application with 100, 500, 1000, and 2000 elements.

13.4 Selection Sort

Another sorting algorithm is *selection sort*, which starts by finding the lowest item in a list and swapping it with the first. Next, the lowest item among items 2 through the last is found and swapped with item 2, and then the lowest item among items 3 through the last is swapped with item 3. This process is continued until the last item is reached, at which point all the items will be sorted.

For an array of integers, the SelectionSort procedure pseudocode is:

```
Sub SelectionSort(ByRef intArray() As Integer)
    For intIndex = LBound(intArray) To UBound(intArray)
        Search intArray elements intIndex to UBound(intArray) for
            lowest element
        Swap lowest element with element at position intIndex
    Next intIndex
End Sub
```

The Selection Sort application on the next page includes the SelectionSort procedure:

An Introduction to Programming Using Microsoft Visual Basic

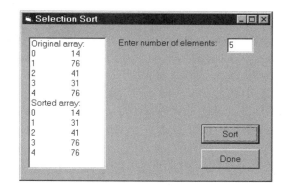

Option Explicit

Private Const intMaxNumber **As Integer** = 100

Private Sub Form_Load()
  Randomize
End Sub

Private Sub cmdSort_Click()
  Dim intDataArray() **As Integer**
  Dim intNumDataItems **As Integer** 'Number of items in intDataArray

  'Create array of random numbers
  intNumDataItems = txtNumElements.Text
  Call GenerateArray(intDataArray(), intNumDataItems)

  'Display original array in list box
  lstArrayElements.Clear
  lstArrayElements.AddItem "Original array:"   'Title
  Call DisplayData(intDataArray(), lstArrayElements)

  'Sort array
  Call SelectionSort(intDataArray())

  'Display sorted array in list box
  lstArrayElements.AddItem "Sorted array:"   'Title
  Call DisplayData(intDataArray(), lstArrayElements)
End Sub

'***
' Fills intArray() with intNumElements random integers ranging
' from 1 to intMaxNumber
'
' pre: Randomize called
' post: intArray() contains intNumElements random integers
' ranging from 1 to intMaxNumber
'***
Sub GenerateArray(**ByRef** intArray() **As Integer**, _
ByVal intNumElements **As Integer**)
  Dim intIndex **As Integer**

  ReDim intArray(intNumElements - 1)

  For intIndex = LBound(intArray) **To** UBound(intArray)
    intArray(intIndex) = Int(intMaxNumber * Rnd + 1)
  Next intIndex
End Sub

```
'*************************************************************************
' Displays the contents of intArray() in a list box
'
' pre: intArray() contains at least one element
' post: intArray() items displayed in a list box
'*************************************************************************
Sub DisplayData(ByRef intArray() As Integer, ByRef lstList As ListBox)
    Dim intIndex As Integer

    For intIndex = LBound(intArray) To UBound(intArray)
        lstList.AddItem intIndex & vbTab & intArray(intIndex)
    Next intIndex
End Sub

'*************************************************************************
' Sorts intArray() from low to high
'
' pre: intArray() contains at least one item
' post: intArray() sorted from low to high
'*************************************************************************
Sub SelectionSort(ByRef intArray() As Integer)
    Dim intIndex As Integer
    Dim intLowItemIndex As Integer, intTemp As Integer

    For intIndex = LBound(intArray) To UBound(intArray)
        intLowItemIndex = FindLowest(intArray, intIndex, UBound(intArray))
        intTemp = intArray(intIndex)
        intArray(intIndex) = intArray(intLowItemIndex)
        intArray(intLowItemIndex) = intTemp
    Next intIndex
End Sub

'*************************************************************************
' Returns the index of the lowest item in elements intLow
' to intHigh of intArray()
'
' pre: intArray() has at least one element
' post: Index of the lowest item in range intLow to intHigh
' returned
'*************************************************************************
Function FindLowest(ByRef intArray() As Integer, ByVal intLow As Integer, _
ByVal intHigh As Integer) As Integer
    Dim intIndex As Integer, intLowSoFar As Integer

    'Make first element the lowest
    intLowSoFar = intLow

    For intIndex = intLow To intHigh
        If intArray(intIndex) < intArray(intLowSoFar) Then
            intLowSoFar = intIndex
        End If
    Next intIndex
    FindLowest = intLowSoFar
End Function

Private Sub cmdDone_Click()
    Unload Me
End Sub
```

Note that several of the procedures are similar to those used in the Dynamic Array Demo from Chapter Nine.

An Introduction to Programming Using Microsoft Visual Basic

Review 3

Modify the Selection Sort application to display a label with the time required for a sort. Test the application with 100, 500, 1000, and 2000 elements.

13.5 Insertion Sort

More efficient than the bubble or selection sort algorithms is the insertion sort algorithm. An *insertion sort* starts by removing the second item of a list and shifting the first item up, if necessary, to position the removed element as the lowest in the list so far. The third item is then removed and previous items shifted up until the item can be placed in the appropriate position relative to the first two items. This process is repeated for the remaining items.

For example, in a low to high order sort for the list of items below, the 10 is removed, compared to the value in the previous position (40), 40 is shifted into position 2, and then 10 is placed at position 1. Next, the 30 is removed, compared to the value in the previous position (40), 40 is shifted into position 3, 30 compared to the value in the previous position (10), and then 30 is placed at position 2. This process repeats for the remaining items. The sort can be illustrated as:

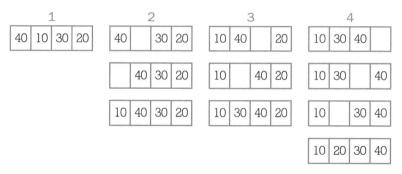

For an array of integers, the InsertionSort procedure pseudocode is:

```
Sub InsertionSort(ByRef intArray() As Integer)
  For Index = 2 To UBound(intArray)
    Temp = intArray(Index)
    PreviousPosition = Index – 1
    While Temp > intArray(PreviousPosition) _
      And PreviousPosition >= 1
      intArray(PreviousPosition + 1) = intArray(PreviousPosition)
      PreviousPosition = PreviousPosition – 1
    Loop
    intArray(PreviusPosition + 1) = Temp
  Next element
End Sub
```

The Insertion Sort application on the next page includes the InsertionSort procedure:

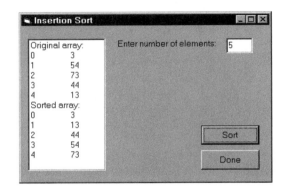

```
Option Explicit

Private Const intMaxNumber As Integer = 100

Private Sub Form_Load()
   Randomize
End Sub

Private Sub cmdSort_Click()
   Dim intDataArray() As Integer
   Dim intNumDataItems As Integer    'Number of items in intDataArray

   'Create array of random numbers
   intNumDataItems = txtNumElements.Text
   Call GenerateArray(intDataArray(), intNumDataItems)

   'Display original array in list box
   lstArrayElements.Clear
   lstArrayElements.AddItem "Original array:"       'Title
   Call DisplayData(intDataArray(), lstArrayElements)

   'Sort array
   Call InsertionSort(intDataArray())

   'Display sorted array in list box
   lstArrayElements.AddItem "Sorted array:"         'Title
   Call DisplayData(intDataArray(), lstArrayElements)
End Sub

'*******************************************************************
'  Fills intArray() with intNumElements random integers ranging
'  from 1 to intMaxNumber
'
'  pre: Randomize called
'  post: intArray() contains intNumElements random integers
'  ranging from 1 to intMaxNumber
'*******************************************************************
Sub GenerateArray(ByRef intArray() As Integer, _
ByVal intNumElements As Integer)
   Dim intIndex As Integer

   ReDim intArray(intNumElements - 1)

   For intIndex = LBound(intArray) To UBound(intArray)
      intArray(intIndex) = Int(intMaxNumber * Rnd + 1)
   Next intIndex
End Sub
```

```
'*************************************************************
' Displays the contents of intArray() in a list box
'
' pre: intArray() contains at least one element
' post: intArray() items displayed in a list box
'*************************************************************
Sub DisplayData(ByRef intArray() As Integer, ByRef lstList As ListBox)
    Dim intIndex As Integer

    For intIndex = LBound(intArray) To UBound(intArray)
        lstList.AddItem intIndex & vbTab & intArray(intIndex)
    Next intIndex
End Sub

'*************************************************************
' Sorts intArray from low to high
'
' pre: intArray() contains at least one element
' post: intArray() elements are sorted low to high
'*************************************************************
Sub InsertionSort(ByRef intArray() As Integer)
    Dim intItem As Integer, intPreviousItem As Integer
    Dim intTemp As Integer

    For intItem = LBound(intArray) + 1 To UBound(intArray)
        intTemp = intArray(intItem)
        intPreviousItem = intItem - 1
        Do While intPreviousItem > LBound(intArray) _
            And intArray(intPreviousItem) > intTemp
            intArray(intPreviousItem + 1) = intArray(intPreviousItem)
            intPreviousItem = intPreviousItem - 1
        Loop
        If intArray(intPreviousItem) > intTemp Then
            intArray(intPreviousItem + 1) = intArray(intPreviousItem)
            intArray(intPreviousItem) = intTemp
        Else
            intArray(intPreviousItem + 1) = intTemp
        End If
    Next intItem
End Sub

Private Sub cmdDone_Click()
    Unload Me
End Sub
```

Note that in the InsertionSort procedure, the Do...Loop moves up, if necessary, all but the element at the lower bound position. An If...Then statement is then used to move the lower bound position element up if necessary.

Review 4

Modify the Insertion Sort application to display a label with the time required for a sort. Test the application with 100, 500, 1000, and 2000 elements.

13.6 Binary Search

Lists are sorted in order to perform a more efficient search. A *binary search* is used with a sorted list of items to quickly find the location of a value. The binary search algorithm can be thought of as a "divide and conquer" approach to searching. It works by examining the middle item of an array sorted from low to high, and determining if this is the item sought, or if the item sought is above or below this middle item. If the item sought is below the middle item, then a binary search is applied to the lower half of the array; if above the middle item, a binary search is applied to the upper half of the array, and so on.

For example, a binary search for the value 5 in a list of items 1, 2, 3, 4, 5, 6, and 7 could be visualized as:

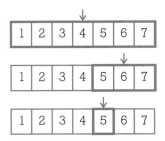

The binary search algorithm is very efficient. For example, in an array of 100 elements no more than 8 elements would be checked in a search, and in an array of one million items no more than 20 checks would be made. If a list of the entire world's population were to be searched using this algorithm, less than 40 checks would need to be made to find any one person.

The BinarySearch function below returns the index of the first occurrence found of value or a −1 if the value was not found:

```
'************************************************************
'  Returns the index of intNumToFind if found or a -1 if not found
'
'  pre: intArray() contains at least one element
'  post: index of intNumToFind is returned. -1 returned if not found
'************************************************************
Function BinarySearch(ByRef intArray() As Integer, _
ByVal intNumToFind As Integer) As Integer
   Dim intHighIndex As Integer, intMidIndex As Integer, _
   intLowIndex As Integer, blnFound As Boolean

   intHighIndex = UBound(intArray)
   intLowIndex = LBound(intArray)
   blnFound = False
   Do While Not blnFound And intLowIndex <= intHighIndex
      intMidIndex = Int((intHighIndex + intLowIndex) / 2)
      If intArray(intMidIndex) = intNumToFind Then
         blnFound = True
      ElseIf intArray(intMidIndex) > intNumToFind Then
         intHighIndex = intMidIndex - 1
      Else
         intLowIndex = intMidIndex + 1
      End If
   Loop
   If blnFound Then
      BinarySearch = intMidIndex
   Else
      BinarySearch = -1
   End If
End Function
```

An Introduction to Programming Using Microsoft Visual Basic

The Binary Search application generates an array of random numbers and then sorts the numbers using an insertion sort. The user can then enter a number to search for in the text box and click Search to display the index of the number, if found:

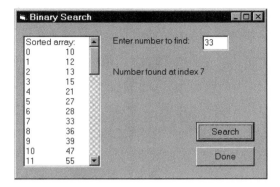

```
Option Explicit

Private Const intMaxNumber As Integer = 200
Private Const intNumElements As Integer = 50

Dim intDataArray() As Integer

Private Sub Form_Load()
    Randomize
    'Generate array of random numbers
    Call GenerateSortedArray(intDataArray(), intNumElements)

    'Display sorted array in list box
    lstArrayElements.AddItem "Sorted array:"          'Title
    Call DisplayData(intDataArray(), lstArrayElements)
End Sub

'***********************************************************
'  Fills intArray() with intNumElements random integers ranging
'  from 1 to intMaxNumber
'
'  pre: Randomize called
'  post: intArray() contains sorted intNumElements random integers
'  ranging from 1 to intMaxNumber
'***********************************************************
Sub GenerateSortedArray(ByRef intArray() As Integer, _
ByVal intNumElements As Integer)
    Dim intIndex As Integer

    ReDim intArray(intNumElements - 1)

    For intIndex = LBound(intArray) To UBound(intArray)
        intArray(intIndex) = Int(intMaxNumber * Rnd + 1)
    Next intIndex

    Call InsertionSort(intArray())          'Sort array
End Sub
```

```
'*************************************************************
' Displays the contents of intArray() in a list box
'
' pre: intArray() contains at least one element
' post: intArray() items displayed in a list box
'*************************************************************
Sub DisplayData(ByRef intArray() As Integer, ByRef lstList As ListBox)
  Dim intIndex As Integer

  For intIndex = LBound(intArray) To UBound(intArray)
    lstList.AddItem intIndex & vbTab & intArray(intIndex)
  Next intIndex
End Sub

'*************************************************************
' Sorts intArray() from low to high
'
' pre: intArray() has at least one element
' post: intArray() elements are sorted low to high
'*************************************************************
Sub InsertionSort(ByRef intArray() As Integer)
  Dim intItem As Integer, intPreviousItem As Integer
  Dim intTemp As Integer

  For intItem = LBound(intArray) + 1 To UBound(intArray)
    intTemp = intArray(intItem)
    intPreviousItem = intItem - 1
    Do While intPreviousItem > LBound(intArray) _
      And intArray(intPreviousItem) > intTemp
      intArray(intPreviousItem + 1) = intArray(intPreviousItem)
      intPreviousItem = intPreviousItem - 1
    Loop
    If intArray(intPreviousItem) > intTemp Then
      intArray(intPreviousItem + 1) = intArray(intPreviousItem)
      intArray(intPreviousItem) = intTemp
    Else
      intArray(intPreviousItem + 1) = intTemp
    End If
  Next intItem
End Sub

Private Sub cmdSearch_Click()
  Dim intNumToFind As Integer, intNumFoundIndex As Integer

  'Get item to find
  intNumToFind = txtNumToFind.Text
  intNumFoundIndex = BinarySearch(intDataArray(), intNumToFind)
  If intNumFoundIndex = -1 Then
    lblFoundMessage.Caption = "Number not found."
  Else
    lblFoundMessage.Caption = "Number found at index " & _
    intNumFoundIndex
  End If
End Sub

Private Sub txtNumToFind_Change()
  lblFoundMessage.Caption = ""
End Sub
```

```
'************************************************************
'  Returns the index of NumToFind if found or a -1 if not found
'
'  pre: intArray() contains at least one element
'  post: index of NumToFind is returned; -1 returned if not found
'************************************************************
Function BinarySearch(ByRef intArray() As Integer, _
ByVal intNumToFind As Integer) As Integer
   Dim intHighIndex As Integer, intMidIndex As Integer, _
   intLowIndex As Integer, blnFound As Boolean

   intHighIndex = UBound(intArray)
   intLowIndex = LBound(intArray)
   blnFound = False
   Do While Not blnFound And intLowIndex <= intHighIndex
      intMidIndex = Int((intHighIndex + intLowIndex) / 2)
      If intArray(intMidIndex) = intNumToFind Then
         blnFound = True
      ElseIf intArray(intMidIndex) > intNumToFind Then
         intHighIndex = intMidIndex - 1
      Else
         intLowIndex = intMidIndex + 1
      End If
   Loop
   If blnFound Then
      BinarySearch = intMidIndex
   Else
      BinarySearch = -1
   End If
End Function

Private Sub cmdDone_Click()
   Unload Me
End Sub
```

Review 5

Modify the Binary Search application to display the indexes of items checked in a search.

Chapter Summary

Sorting is the process of putting items in a designated order, either from low to high or high to low. The bubble sort starts at the first item of a list and proceeds sequentially to the last, comparing each item with the next and swapping items as necessary. The selection sort repeatedly finds the lowest item from a portion of a list and swaps it with the item at index, which is incremented until index is equal to that of the last element. The insertion sort sequentially removes items from a list and adds them back to the list in the appropriate position relative to the previous items in the list.

Timer

One measure of efficiency with sorting algorithms is the time it takes the implemented algorithm to sort a list of items. The Visual Basic built-in Timer function returns a **Single** representing the number of seconds that have elapsed since midnight and can be used to time a sort.

A binary search is a very efficient way to search a sorted list of elements. The binary search takes a "divide and conquer" approach to searching a list of items.

Vocabulary

Binary search A searching algorithm that searches for an item in a sorted list by repeatedly checking for the item as the middle item in a portion of a list.

Bubble sort A sorting algorithm that starts at the first item of a list and proceeds sequentially to the last, comparing each item with the next and swapping items as necessary.

Insertion sort A sorting algorithm that sequentially removes items from a list and adds them back to the list in the appropriate position relative to the previous items in the list.

Selection sort A sorting algorithm that repeatedly finds the lowest item from a portion of a list and swaps it with the item at index, which is incremented until index is equal to that of the last element.

Sorting The process of putting items in a designated order, either low to high or high to low.

Visual Basic

Timer Function that returns the time in seconds that have elapsed since midnight.

Exercises

Exercise 1

Create an Alphabetize Names application that allows the user to type in any number of names and then displays them in a list box sorted alphabetically. The application interface should look similar to:

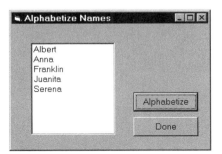

Exercise 2

Create a Sort by Field application that allows the user to enter first name, last name, and age information for any number of people and then displays the data in a list box sorted by the field selected by the user. Hint: use a user-defined type for storing data entered. The application interface should look similar to:

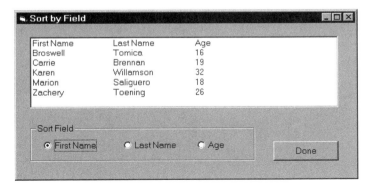

Exercise 3

One variation of binary search is called the *interpolation search*. The idea is to look in a likely spot, not necessarily the middle of the array. For example, if the value sought is 967 in an array that holds items ranging from 3 to 1022, it would be intelligent to look near the end of the array. Mathematically, the position to start searching at is a position 95% of the way down the array, because 967 is about 95% of the way from 3 to 1022. For example, if the array holds 500 elements, the first position to examine is 475 (95% of the way from 1 to 500). The search then proceeds to a portion of the array (either 1 to 474 or 476 to 500) depending upon whether 967 is greater or less than the 475th element.

Modify the Binary Search application to use the interpolation search.

Exercise 4

Create a Ternary Search application, similar to the Binary Search application, that divides the array into three pieces rather than two. Ternary Search finds the points that divide the array into three roughly equal pieces, and then uses these points to determine where the element should be searched for. Add code to time the ternary search to compare it to the binary search.

Advanced
Exercise 5

a) Create a Slang Dictionary application that allows the user to add words and their definitions to a random access file. The application should have a Search button that sorts the records in the file and then searches for a word entered by the user. If the word is found, the word and its definition are displayed, otherwise a message box is displayed indicating the word was not found. The application interface should look similar to:

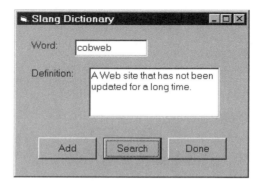

b) Currently, the Slang Dictionary application sorts the random access file every time the Search button is clicked. Modify the application to be more efficient by storing the sorted status in the first record. for example, when Add is clicked the first record should store Unsorted and the new word record appended. When Search is clicked, the first record should be checked for the sort status. If unsorted, then the records should be sorted, the first record changed, and then the file searched. If sorted, then only searching need be done.

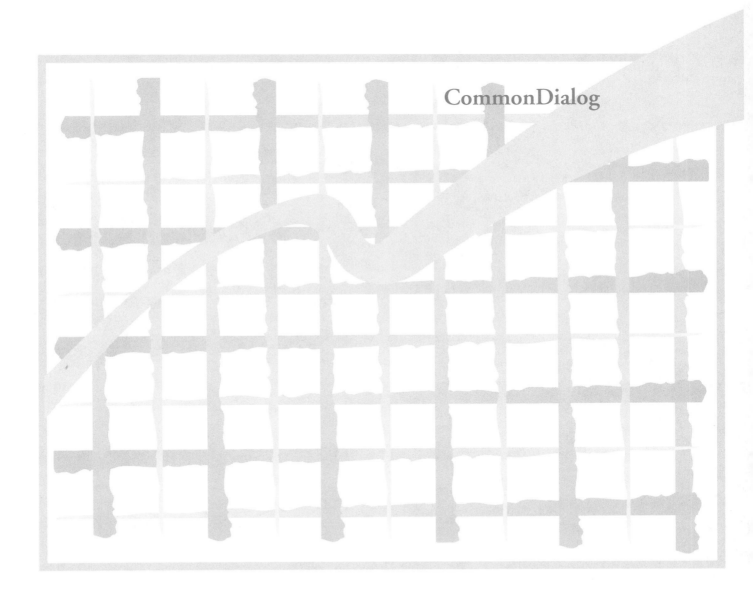

CommonDialog

Chapter Fourteen Objectives

After completing this chapter you will be able to:

1. Add menus to applications.
2. Understand common dialogs.
3. Add common dialog objects to applications.
4. Add a new form to a project.
5. Use multiple forms.
6. Add an about dialog to a project and understand template forms.
7. Add a splash screen to a project.
8. Understand the Sub Main procedure.
9. Add an existing form to a project.

$\mathbf{I}$n this chapter you will learn how to add menus to an application interface and create applications that use dialog boxes and multiple forms.

14.1 Menus in Windows Applications

menu A *menu* provides a set of commands to the user. When menus are added to an application a menu bar is displayed just below the title bar. For example, the Hello World application can be modified to contain menus:

The File menu is displayed

click event When the user selects a command from a menu, a click event occurs. Therefore, a click event procedure should be coded for each command.

Menus in your applications will be easier for users to understand if they are similar to menus in other Windows applications, which have the features:

- commands grouped and placed in an appropriately named menu

- access keys defined for each menu name and each command

- shortcuts created for commonly used commands

- an ellipses (…) displayed after a command name that displays a dialog box

- a separator line between groups of related commands in a menu

- if appropriate, a check mark next to a selected command

For example, most Windows applications place a Print command in the File menu with the P key as its access key and Ctrl+P as its shortcut.

14.2 Adding Menus to a Visual Basic Application

Menus and their commands are added to an application using the Menu Editor dialog box, which is displayed by selecting the Menu Editor command (Ctrl+E) from the Tools menu:

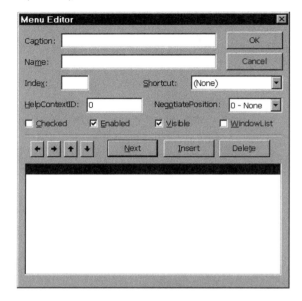

- Caption Text box for typing the menu or command name using the & to define the access key. A dash (-) is typed to create a separator line.

- Name Text box for typing the menu or command identifier used by the programmer. It is good programming style to begin menu names with mnu and to begin command names with mnu*Menu* where *Menu* is the name of the menu containing the command.

- Shortcut Combo box where a command shortcut, if appropriate, is selected.

- Checked Checkbox that is selected if a command should display a check mark next to it when the application starts. Menu objects also have a Checked property that can be changed at run time through assignment to either True to display a check mark or False to remove a check mark.

- Enabled Checkbox that is deselected if a menu or command should be dim when the application starts. Menu objects also have an Enabled property that can be changed at run time through assignment.

- ► Button that is clicked to move the current menu or command down one level in the text box shown below.

- ◄ Button that is clicked to move the current menu or command up one level in the text box shown below.

- Next Button that is clicked to show the menu or command in the text box below.

- Insert Button that is clicked to insert a new menu or command before the current menu or command shown in the text box below.

- Delete Button that is clicked to remove the current menu or command from the text box below.

- OK Button that is clicked to add or modify menus and remove the dialog box.

- Cancel Button that is clicked to cancel menus or changes to existing menus.

For example, a File menu with an Exit command is added by following the steps below:

1. Type &File in the Caption text box and mnuFile in the Name text box. The menu name is shown in the text box below.
2. Select the Next button.
3. Type E&xit in the Caption text box and mnuFileExit in the Name text box.
4. Select Ctrl+X in the Shortcut combo box.
5. Select OK to remove the dialog box.

Review 1

Follow the instructions below to modify the Hello World application created in Chapter Three to include menus and commands.

1) OPEN THE HELLO WORLD PROJECT

Display the Hello World form if it is not already displayed.

2) ADD THE FILE MENU AND ITS COMMANDS

a. From the Tools menu, select the Menu Editor command. The Menu Editor dialog box is displayed.
b. In the Caption text box, type &File. The text is added to the text box below.
c. In the Name text box, type mnuFile.
d. Select the Next button. The options are cleared and the next line, a blank line, is selected in the text box below.
e. In the Caption text box, type &Print. The text is added to the text box below.
f. In the Name text box, type mnuFilePrint.
g. In the Shortcut combo box, select Ctrl+P.
h. Click once on the right arrow button (▸). Print is moved down one level to be a command in the File menu.
i. Select Next. The options are cleared and the next line is selected in the text box below.
j. In the Caption text box, type -. The text is added to the text box below.
k. In the Name text box, type mnuSeparator.
l. Select Next. The options are cleared and the next line is selected in the text box below.
m. In the Caption text box, type E&xit. The text is added to the text box below.
n. In the Name text box, type mnuFileExit.
o. In the Shortcut combo box, select Ctrl+X.
p. Select Next. The options are cleared and the next line is selected in the text box below.
q. Select OK to remove the dialog box. Note the menu bar on the application interface.

3) RUN THE APPLICATION

Save the modified Hello World project and then run the application. Note the menu bar. Click on the File menu and note the commands and separator line. Click on Done to end the application and go back to Design view.

4) ADD OTHER MENUS AND COMMANDS

a. Display the form.
b. Display the Menu Editor dialog box. In the text box at the bottom of the dialog box, click in the blank line just below E&xit.
c. In the Caption text box, type &Style. The text is added to the text box below.
d. In the Name text box, type mnuStyle.
e. Deselect the Enabled check box so that the command is dim at run time.
f. Select the Next button. The options are cleared and the next line, a blank line, is selected in the text box below.
g. Add the Style commands below. Be sure they are indented to the appropriate level.

Caption	Name	Shortcut	Checked
&Bold	mnuStyleBold	Ctrl+B	yes
&Italic	mnuStyleItalic	Ctrl+I	

h. Add the Size menu and its commands shown below:

Caption	Name	Enabled
Si&ze	mnuSize	no
8	mnuSize8	
14	mnuSize14	
18	mnuSize18	
Other...	mnuSizeOther	

i. Add the Help menu and its commands shown below:

Caption	Name
&Help	mnuHelp
&About...	mnuHelpAbout

5) MODIFY THE PROGRAM CODE

a. Display the Code Editor window and add the following event procedures:

```
Private Sub mnuFilePrint_Click()
   Me.PrintForm
End Sub

Private Sub mnuFileExit_Click()
   Call cmdDone_Click
End Sub

Private Sub mnuStyleBold_Click()
   If mnuStyleBold.Checked = True Then    'determine if command is selected
      lblMessage.FontBold = False
      mnuStyleBold.Checked = False         'remove check mark
   Else
      lblMessage.FontBold = True
      mnuStyleBold.Checked = True          'display check mark
   End If
End Sub
```

```
Private Sub mnuStyleItalic_Click()
    If mnuStyleItalic.Checked = True Then        'determine if command is selected
        lblMessage.FontItalic = False
        mnuStyleItalic.Checked = False           'remove check mark
    Else
        lblMessage.FontItalic = True
        mnuStyleItalic.Checked = True            'display check mark
    End If
End Sub

Private Sub mnuSize8_Click()
    lblMessage.FontSize = 8
End Sub

Private Sub mnuSize14_Click()
    lblMessage.FontSize = 14
End Sub

Private Sub mnuSize18_Click()
    lblMessage.FontSize = 18
End Sub

Private Sub mnuSizeOther_Click()
    lblMessage.FontSize = InputBox("Enter font size:", "Font Size")
End Sub
```

    b.   Modify the imgGlobe_Click procedure as shown below:

```
Private Sub imgGlobe_Click()
    lblMessage.Caption = "Hello, world!"
    mnuSize.Enabled = True
    mnuStyle.Enabled = True
End Sub
```

6) RUN THE APPLICATION

Save the modified Hello World project and then run the application. Test the application by selecting each of the commands, using the access keys, and using the shortcut. The About command in the Help menu will be coded later in the chapter.

7) PRINT THE PROJECT

Review 2

Modify the Hello World application from Review 1 to include an Underline command in the Style menu and 10, 12, and 16 commands in the Size menu. You will need to use the Insert button in the Menu Editor dialog box.

14.3 Common Dialogs

Visual Basic provides a set of predefined dialog boxes called *common dialogs* that are used to perform an operation, such as opening a file. You can use these predefined dialog boxes in your applications instead of having to create them from scratch. The Open dialog box allows the user to select a file to open:

Open dialog box

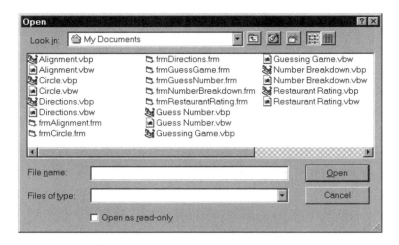

Save As dialog box   Similarly, the Save As dialog box allows the user to specify the filename to save a document as:

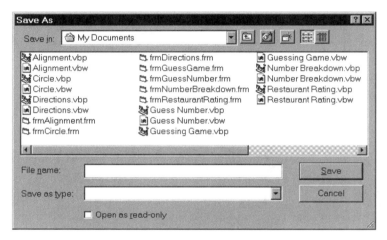

common dialog   Predefined dialog boxes can be used in an application by adding a common dialog object to a form. A *common dialog* object is created using the CommonDialog control (⊞) and has the properties:

- **Name** identifies the object and is used by the programmer. It is good programming style to begin common dialog object names with cdl.

- **FileName** automatically changes at run-time to the complete path and filename that the user selected in the dialog box.

- **FileTitle** automatically changes at run-time to the filename that the user selected in the dialog box.

- **DefaultExt** sets the default file extension of the file being saved. The user can enter an extension that is different than the default extension, but the default extension is used if no extension is entered.

- **InitDir** sets the directory (folder) that will be displayed when the dialog box is displayed.

CommonDialog Control

The CommonDialog control is added to the Toolbox by first selecting the Components command from the Project menu to display the Components dialog box. Then the Microsoft Common Dialog Control 6.0 is selected from the list. Selecting OK removes the dialog box and adds the control to the Tool box.

- **Filter** sets the allowed file types and extensions, which are displayed in the File of type or Save as type collapsible lists. For example

  cdlDialogBox.Filter = "Text files (*.txt)|*.txt|Data files (*.dat)|.dat"

  specifies that only .txt and .dat files can be saved or opened.

- **Flags** changes how the dialog box behaves based on the following Visual Basic constants:

  cdlOFNCreatePrompt – the user is prompted to create a new file
  cdlOFNFileMustExist – the user can enter only names of existing files
  cdlOFNLongNames – enables the use of long file names
  cdlOFNOverwritePrompt – Save As dialog box prompts user to overwrite an existing file
  cdlOFNPathMustExist – displays a warning if the user enters an invalid file path

A common dialog object is similar to a timer object in that it does not appear on the form at run-time. The common dialog control needs to be added to the Tool box using the Components command (refer to the CommonDialog Control sidebar).

A common dialog object uses methods to display a particular dialog box. For example, the ShowOpen method is used to display the Open dialog box and takes the form:

ShowOpen method

cdlDialogBox.ShowOpen   'Displays the Open dialog box

cdlDialogBox is the name of the common dialog object.

ShowSave method

The ShowSave method is used to display the Save As dialog box and takes the form.

cdlDialogBox.ShowSave   'Displays the Save As dialog box

cdlDialogBox is the name of the common dialog object.

Even though the dialog box is displayed and the user selects a file, code must be written to do something with what the user selected. For example, the statements below use the Open dialog box to determine which file to open:

```
Private Sub mnuOpen_Click()
    Dim intNewFile As Integer
    Dim strTextLine As String
    intNewFile = FreeFile

    cdlDialogBox.InitDir = "C:\My Documents"
    cdlDialogBox.Filter = "Text files (*.txt)|*.txt"
    cdlDialogBox.Flags = cdlOFNFileMustExist
    cdlDialogBox.ShowOpen

    If cdlDialogBox.FileName <> "" Then   'Cancel button not clicked
        Open cdlDialogBox.FileName For Input As #intNewFile

        Do While Not EOF(intNewFile)        'Display file in text box
            Line Input #intNewFile, strTextLine
            txtFile.Text = txtFile.Text & strTextLine & vbCrLf
        Loop
        Close #intNewFile
    End If
End Sub
```

The following statements use the Save As dialog box to determine the name to use when saving a text file:

```
Private Sub mnuSave_Click()
    Dim intNewFile As Integer
    intNewFile = FreeFile

    cdlDialogBox.InitDir = "C:\My Documents"
    cdlDialogBox.Filter = "Text files (*.txt)|*.txt"
    cdlDialogBox.Flags = cdlOFNOverwritePrompt
    cdlDialogBox.ShowSave

    If cdlDialogBox.FileName <> "" Then    'Cancel button not clicked
        Open cdlDialogBox.FileName For Output As #intNewFile
        Print #intNewFile, txtFile.Text
        Close #intNewFile
    End If
End Sub
```

An application that uses both Open and Save As dialog boxes require only one common dialog object to be added to the form.

Print dialog box

The Print dialog box is another Visual Basic predefined common dialog that is often used in Windows applications:

Common Dialog Object

The CommonDialog object has many more properties and Visual Basic constants that can be used in the Flags property. For example, you can set the **From** and **To** options in the Print dialog box. Refer to Visual Basic's help for more information.

The Print dialog box can be used in an application by adding a separate common dialog object to the form. The common dialog object property used with the Print dialog box is:

- **Copies** automatically changes at run-time to whatever the user selects for the **Number of copies**. Copies can be set at design-time to display a default number of copies.

ShowPrinter method

The ShowPrinter method is used to display the Print dialog box and takes the form:

```
cdlDialogBox.ShowPrinter          'Displays the Print dialog box
```

cdlDialogBox is the name of the common dialog object.

The Print dialog box does not print anything, it only stores the values entered by the user, so code must be written to do something with what the user selected. The Printer.**Print** and Printer.EndDoc statements send output to the printer and take the form:

Printer.Print	'sends the text in the text box as output to the printer object Printer.**Print** txtFile.Text
Printer.EndDoc	'sends the output to the default printer Printer.EndDoc

The following statements use the Print dialog box to print the text in a text box:

```
Private Sub mnuPrint_Click()
    Dim intLoop As Integer

    cdlPrinter.ShowPrinter

    For intLoop = 1 To cdlPrinter.Copies
        Printer.Print txtFile.Text      'output is all the text in the text box
        Printer.EndDoc                  'sends the output to the printer
    Next intLoop
End Sub
```

Review 3

Create a Notes application that contains a text box and a File menu with New, Open, Save, Print, and Exit commands. The New command should clear the contents of the text box. The Open command should use the Open dialog box to open an existing text file and then display it in the text box. The Save command should use the Save As dialog box to save the contents of the text box to a text file and warn the user if an existing file is being overwritten. The Print command should use the Print dialog box to allow the user to specify how many copies to print. The Exit command should end the application. Use the code from section 14.3 in your program. The application interface should look similar to that shown on the right.

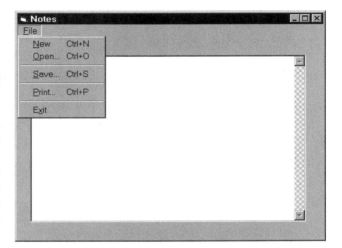

14.4 Adding a New Form to a Project

The applications you have created so far have used only one form, while most Windows applications use multiple forms. Each form in an application can be displayed or hidden depending on a user's action. For example, the Hello World application can be modified to display another form when the user clicks on an image:

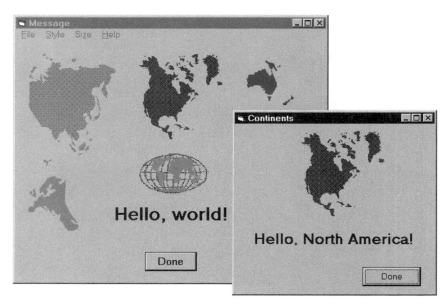

Clicking on a continent image displays a new form

A new form is added to a project by selecting the Add Form command from the Project menu which displays the Add Form dialog box:

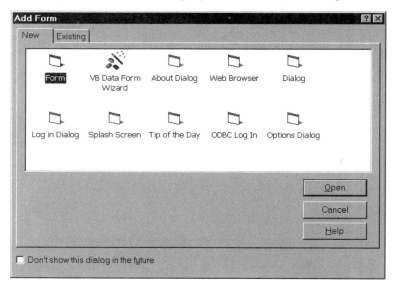

Forms are added to an application using this dialog box

A new, empty form is created by selecting the Form icon and then clicking on the Open button.

When a new form is added to a project, it is displayed in the Project Explorer window:

All the files in a project are displayed in this window

Removing Forms

A form can be removed from a project by first selecting the form in the Project Explorer window and then selecting the Remove frmFormName.frm command from the Project menu.

An Introduction to Programming Using Microsoft Visual Basic

Form Events

When a form is displayed using the Show method, the Form_Load event and then the Form_Activate event execute automatically. The Form_Load event loads the form module into memory. The Form_Activate event occurs each time the form gets the focus. Only the Activate event occurs each time a loaded form is displayed using the Show method.

Double-clicking on the form's name displays the form. The form module for that form can then be displayed by clicking on the View Code button. Keep in mind that for every form interface in the application there is an associated form module that contains program code.

It is helpful to think of a Visual Basic project as a collection of files that make up an application. The project file (.vdb) stores links to all the files used in the project. Each form in a project is saved in its own file (.frm), which contains the interface and code for that form.

14.5 Using Multiple Forms

Methods are used to display and hide the different forms in an application. The Show method is used to display a form and takes the form:

Show method

> *frmObject*.Show

frmObject is the name of the form to be displayed.

Hide method

The Hide method is used to hide a form and takes the form:

> *frmObject*.Hide

frmObject is the name of the form to hide. The Hide method only hides the form from the user, it does not remove the form from memory. The Unload statement should be used to remove a form from memory when it is no longer needed.

accessing objects on another form

When using multiple forms, it is possible to access the objects on another form using dot notation:

> *frmFormName*.*ObjectName*

frmFormName is the name of the form you want to access and *ObjectName* is the name of an object on that form. For example, in the modified Hello World application, clicking on the North America image executes the following event procedure. Note how the properties of image and label objects on the frmHelloContinents form are accessed using dot notation:

Variable Scope

A variable that is declared with the **Public** keyword in the General section of a form module is visible to every form in the project.

```
Private Sub imgNorthAmerica_Click()
    frmHelloContinents.imgContinent.Picture = imgNorthAmerica.Picture
    frmHelloContinents.lblMessage.Caption = "Hello, North America!"
    frmHelloContinents.Show
End Sub
```

Review 4

Follow the instructions below to modify the Hello World application from Reviews 1 and 2 to include a new form.

1) OPEN THE HELLO WORLD PROJECT

> Display the Hello World form if it is not already displayed.

2) MODIFY THE FORM

Add six image objects and resize the form as shown below. Use the table below to name and change the properties of the image objects.

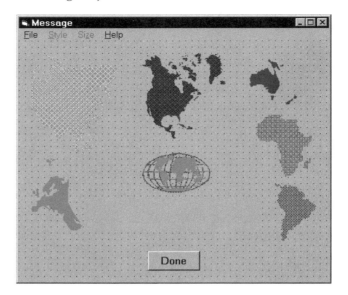

Object	Name	Picture
Image1	imgEurope	Europe
Image2	imgAsia	Asia
Image3	imgNorthAmerica	North America
Image4	imgAustralia	Australia
Image5	imgAfrica	Africa
Image6	imgSouthAmerica	South America

3) ADD A NEW FORM TO THE PROJECT

A form will be displayed each time a continent is clicked.

a. From the Project menu, select the Add Form command. A dialog box is displayed.
b. Select the Form icon and then click on the Open button. A new form is added to the project.
c. Refer to the form below when placing and sizing the form's objects. Use the table below to name and change the properties of the objects.

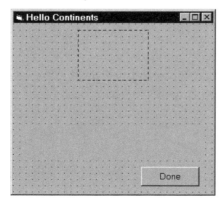

Object	Name	Caption	Alignment	Font	Visible
Form1	frmHelloContinents	Hello Continents			
Image1	imgContinent				
Label1	lblMessage	*empty*	2 - Center	14 point, Bold	False
Command1	cmdDone	Done			

d. From the File menu, select the Save frmHelloContinents command. Save the form naming it frmHelloContinents. The new form is saved with the Hello World project.

4) WRITE THE PROGRAM CODE FOR THE FRMHELLOCONTINENTS FORM

a. Double-click on frmHelloContinents in the Project Explorer window if the form is not already displayed.

b. Click on the View Code button and add the event procedures below:

```
Private Sub imgContinent_Click()
    lblMessage.Visible = True
End Sub

Private Sub cmdDone_Click()
    Me.Hide
    frmHelloWorld.Show
    lblMessage.Visible = False
End Sub
```

5) MODIFY THE PROGRAM CODE FOR THE FRMHELLOWORLD FORM

a. Display the frmHelloWorld form.

b. Display the Code Editor window and add the following event procedures:

```
Private Sub imgEurope_Click()
    frmHelloContinents.imgContinent.Picture = imgEurope.Picture
    frmHelloContinents.lblMessage.Caption = "Hello, Europe!"
    frmHelloContinents.Show
End Sub

Private Sub imgAsia_Click()
    frmHelloContinents.imgContinent.Picture = imgAsia.Picture
    frmHelloContinents.lblMessage.Caption = "Hello, Asia!"
    frmHelloContinents.Show
End Sub

Private Sub imgNorthAmerica_Click()
    frmHelloContinents.imgContinent.Picture = imgNorthAmerica.Picture
    frmHelloContinents.lblMessage.Caption = "Hello, North America!"
    frmHelloContinents.Show
End Sub

Private Sub imgAustralia_Click()
    frmHelloContinents.imgContinent.Picture = imgAustralia.Picture
    frmHelloContinents.lblMessage.Caption = "Hello, Australia!"
    frmHelloContinents.Show
End Sub

Private Sub imgAfrica_Click()
    frmHelloContinents.imgContinent.Picture = imgAfrica.Picture
    frmHelloContinents.lblMessage.Caption = "Hello, Africa!"
    frmHelloContinents.Show
End Sub

Private Sub imgSouthAmerica_Click()
    frmHelloContinents.imgContinent.Picture = imgSouthAmerica.Picture
    frmHelloContinents.lblMessage.Caption = "Hello, South America!"
    frmHelloContinents.Show
End Sub
```

c. Modify the cmdDone_Click event procedure as shown below:

```
Private Sub cmdDone_Click()
    Unload frmHelloWorld
    Unload frmHelloContinents
End Sub
```

6) RUN THE APPLICATION

    a. Save the modified Hello World project and then run the application.

    b. Test the application by clicking on one of the images to display the new form. Click on the image in the new form to display the message. Select Done to remove the form.

    c. Repeat part (b) for each image on the form.

    d. Select Done in the main form to end the application.

7) PRINT THE PROJECT

14.6 Adding a Template Form to a Project

about dialog

    An *about dialog* is a form that describes an application. For example, the Hello World application can be modified to display an about dialog form when the user selects the About command from the Help menu:

Hello World's about dialog form

adding an about dialog template form

    The about dialog is created from a Visual Basic *template form* that has a standard Windows interface and program code. A template form is added to a project by selecting Add Form from the Project menu to display the Add Form dialog box. Selecting the About Dialog icon and then the Open button adds a template form to the current project:

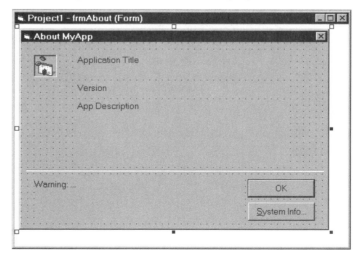

The application's description needs to be entered in the lblDescription label (App Description) and a disclaimer needs to be entered in the lblDisclaimer label (Warning...) . The title bar, application title label, and the version label have already been coded to display the name of the project and version 1.0.0.

Review 5

Follow the instructions below to modify the Hello World application from Review 4 to include an about dialog form.

1) OPEN THE HELLO WORLD PROJECT

Display the Hello World form if it is not already displayed.

2) ADD THE ABOUT DIALOG TO THE APPLICATION

a. From the Project menu, select Add Form. A dialog box is displayed.
b. Click on the About Dialog icon and then select Open. An about dialog template form is displayed.
c. Change the name of the form to frmAboutHelloWorld.
d. From the File menu, select the Save frmAboutHelloWorld command. Save the form naming it frmAboutHelloWorld. The form is saved with the Hello World project.
e. Refer to the form and table below to change the properties of the objects.

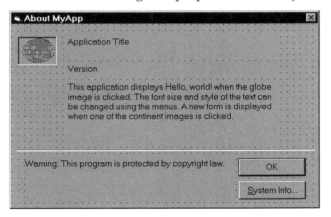

Name	Caption	Picture	AutoSize
lblDescription	*see above*		
lblDisclaimer	*see above*		
picIcon		Globe	False

f. Resize the globe image as shown above.
g. Double-click on the form. The form module for the frmAboutHelloWorld is displayed. Note that the form module contains code because the form was created from a template form.

3) MODIFY THE PROGRAM CODE

a. Double-click on frmHelloWorld in the Project Explorer window. The form is displayed.
b. Display the Code Editor window and add the mnuHelpAbout_Click procedure:

```
Private Sub mnuHelpAbout_Click()
    frmAboutHelloWorld.Show
End Sub
```

4) RUN THE APPLICATION

Save the modified Hello World project and then run the application. Test it by selecting the About command from the Help menu.

5) PRINT THE PROJECT

14.7 Splash Screen

A *splash screen* is a form that is briefly displayed on the screen while an application is being loaded. A splash screen template form is added to a project by selecting Add Form from the Project menu to display the Add Form dialog box. Selecting the Splash Screen icon and then the Open button adds a template form to the current project:

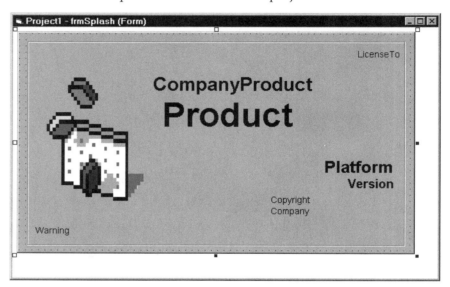

The license, company product name, platform, copyright, company, and warning information needs to be added or deleted. The product label and the version label have already been coded to display the name of the project and version 1.0.0. The form module already contains code that unloads the form when the user clicks on it.

14.8 Startup

Sub Main

standard code module

An application can be coded using a top-down design approach by using a Sub Main procedure. The *Sub Main* procedure contains statements that explicitly load and unload a splash screen and other forms used in an application. A Sub Main procedure is created in a *standard code module* which contains only code and is not associated with any form.

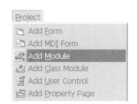

A standard code module is added to an application using the Add Module command from the Project menu. A standard code module should be named with a mod prefix and saved in its own file using the Save modModuleName command from the File menu. For example, the statements on the next page are in a standard code module and display the frmSplashHelloWorld form when the application is started and loads the frmHelloWorld form into memory without displaying it:

An Introduction to Programming Using Microsoft Visual Basic

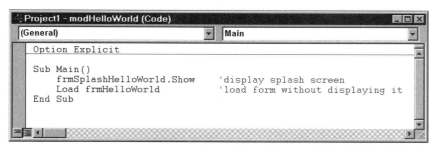

A standard code module

An application that contains a Sub Main must have the Sub Main procedure designated as its startup object. The startup object can be changed by selecting the Project Properties command from the Project menu which displays the Project Properties dialog box:

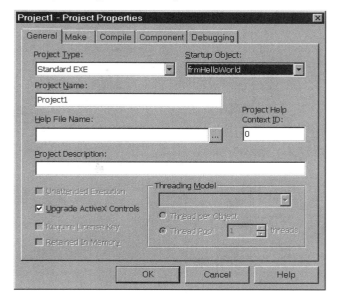

Sub Main must then be selected from the Startup Object combo box and then OK selected.

Review 6

Follow the instructions below to modify the Hello World application from Review 5 to include a splash screen.

1) *OPEN THE HELLO WORLD PROJECT*

Display the Hello World form if it is not already displayed.

2) *ADD A SPLASH SCREEN TO THE PROJECT*

a. From the Project menu, select Add Form. A dialog box is displayed.
b. Select the Splash Screen icon and then select Open. A splash screen template form is displayed.
c. Change the name of the form to frmSplashHelloWorld.
d. From the File menu, select the Save frmSplashHelloWorld command. Save the form naming it frmSplashHelloWorld. The form is saved with the Hello World project.

e. Use the table below to change the properties of the objects:

Object	Caption	Picture	Stretch
lblLicenseTo	License To *your name*		
lblCompanyProduct	*empty*		
lblPlatform	Windows 98		
lblCopyright	Copyright *year*		
lblCompany	*your school name*		
lblWarning	*empty*		
imgLogo		Globe	False

f. Resize the globe image if necessary.

g. Display the Code Editor window and add the following statement after the Unload Me statement in the Frame1_Click event procedure:

```
frmHelloWorld.Show      'displays frmHelloWorld after splash screen is unloaded
```

3) ADD A SUB MAIN IN A STANDARD CODE MODULE

a. From the Project menu, select the Add Module command. A dialog box is displayed.

b. Select the Module icon and then Open. A standard module is displayed.

c. Change the Name of the module to modHelloWorld.

d. From the File menu, select the Save modHelloWorld command. Save the module naming it modHelloWorld. The new standard code module is saved with the Hello World project.

e. Add the following code:

```
Sub Main()
    frmSplashHelloWorld.Show      'display splash screen
    Load frmHelloWorld            'loads frmHelloWorld without displaying it
End Sub
```

4) CHANGE THE STARTUP OBJECT

a. From the Project menu, select the Project1 Properties command. A dialog box is displayed.

b. In the Startup Object combo box, select Sub Main.

c. Select OK to remove the dialog box.

5) RUN THE APPLICATION

Save the modified Hello World project and then run the application. Test it by clicking on the splash screen to unload the splash screen and display the Hello World form.

6) PRINT AND THEN REMOVE THE PROJECT

14.9 Adding an Existing Form to a Project

Because forms are saved in their own file, they can easily be used in more than one application. An existing form is added to an application by selecting Add Form from the Project menu and then selecting the Existing tab in the Add Form dialog box:

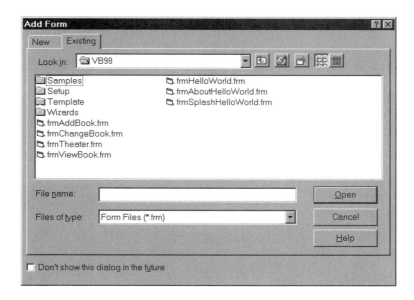

Selecting the form file and then Open adds the form to the current project. If changes are being made to the form that should only affect the current project, the form needs to be saved under a new name so the changes will not affect the application that originally used the form. The Save As frmFormName command form the File menu is used to save a form under a new name.

Save As

DBMS

A *database* is a file that contains a set of records. A *DBMS* (Database Management System) contains the tools needed to manipulate a database. In Chapter Twelve the Add Book, Change Book, and View book applications were used to add, delete, update, and view the book records stored in the Randbooks.dat file. With the use of multiple forms, a DBMS application can be created:

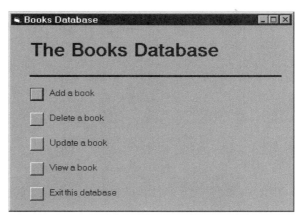

In the application above, when the user clicks on the Add a book button the Add Book form is displayed using the statements:

```
Private Sub cmdAddBook_Click()
    Me.Hide
    frmAddBook.Show
End Sub
```

Similarly, when the user clicks on the Delete a book button the Change Book form is displayed using the statements:

```
Private Sub cmdDeleteBook_Click()
    Me.Hide
    'hide Update button
    frmChangeBook.cmdChangeBook(0).Visible = False
    frmChangeBook.Caption = "Delete Book"
    frmChangeBook.Show
End Sub
```

Note that the Update button is hidden from the user because the user should only be given the option of deleting a book record.

Review 7

The Books Database application interface has already been created. Follow the instructions below to complete the application.

1) OPEN THE BOOKS DATABASE PROJECT

Display the Books Database form if it is not already displayed.

2) ADD EXISTING FORMS TO THE PROJECT

a.   From the Project menu, select Add Form. A dialog box is displayed.
b.   Select the Existing tab.
c.   Select the frmAddBook.frm file from the appropriate folder and then Open. The form is added to the application.
d.   Double-click on the form name in the Project Explorer window. The form is displayed.
e.   From the File menu, select the Save frmAddBook As command and save the form in the appropriate folder naming it frmAddBookDatabase. The form is saved under a new name so any edits will not affect the Add Book project used in Chapter Twelve.
f.   Repeat steps (a) through (d) to add the frmChangeBook.frm and frmViewBook.frm form files.

3) MODIFY THE PROGRAM CODE

Display the Code Editor window and modify the cmdDone_Click event procedures in the three forms just added to the project as shown below:

```
Private Sub cmdDone_Click()
    Unload Me
    frmBooksDatabase.Show
End Sub
```

4) WRITE THE PROGRAM CODE FOR THE FRMBOOKSDATABASE FORM

a.   Display the frmBooksDatabase form.
b.   Display the Code Editor window and add the following procedures. Note that the Add Book, Change Book, and View Book forms created in Chapter Twelve are used in this code.

```
Private Sub cmdAddBook_Click()
    Me.Hide
    frmAddBook.Show
End Sub
```

```
Private Sub cmdDeleteBook_Click()
    Me.Hide
    frmChangeBook.cmdChangeBook(0).Visible = False  'hide Update button
    frmChangeBook.Caption = "Delete Book"
    frmChangeBook.Show
End Sub
```

```
Private Sub cmdUpdateBook_Click()
    Me.Hide
    frmChangeBook.cmdChangeBook(1).Visible = False 'hide Delete button
    frmChangeBook.Caption = "Update Book"
    frmChangeBook.Show
End Sub

Private Sub cmdViewBook_Click()
    Me.Hide
    frmViewBook.Show
End Sub

Private Sub cmdExitDatabase_Click()
    Unload Me
End Sub
```

5) RUN THE APPLICATION

Save the modified Books Database project and then run the application. Test the application by selecting each command button and adding, viewing, updating, and deleting records using the different forms that are displayed.

6) PRINT AND THEN REMOVE THE PROJECT

Case Study

The gift department at a local bookstore needs an application that customers can use to print out an order form for books they wish to send as gifts. In this Case Study a Gift Order Form application will be created.

specification   The specification for this Case Study is:

> The Gift Order Form application should display application information at startup and then allow the user to enter his or her name and phone number, select the books to be sent as gifts, and enter the recipients information in a form that can be printed.

design   The application information should be displayed in a splash screen at startup and then display a gift order form. Because of the multiple forms, *Sub Main design*   this Case Study will use a standard code module and a Sub Main. The design of this Case Study will start with pseudocode for the Sub Main, which allows a top-down design approach:

```
Sub Main()
    Show splash screen
    Load gift order form
End Sub
```

frmSplashGiftOrderForm design

The form design for the splash screen is:

LicenseTo A. Student

Product

Windows 98
Version
Copyright 1999
Home Town University

The form design for the frmSplashGiftOrderForm form

The code design for the splash screen is:

```
Private Sub Frame1_Click()
    Unload frmSplashGiftOrderForm
    Display frmGiftOrderForm
End Sub
```

frmGiftOrderForm design

The form design for the main form, the gift order form, is:

File   Help

Sender: First Name [   ]   Last Name [   ]
             Phone [   ]

Books ordered:

[Select a Book]   [   ]

☐ Gift Wrap
☐ Gift Message [   ]

Ship To: First Name [   ]   Last Name [   ]
             Street Address [   ]
             City [   ]   State [▼]   Zip [   ]
             Phone [   ]

Shipping Method:

┌─Big Brown Truck────────────┐   ┌─Regular Mail────────────────┐
│ ○ Ground   ○ 2-Day   │   │ ○ First Class   ○ Book Rate │
└────────────────────────────┘   └──────────────────────────────┘

The form design for the frmGiftOrderForm

The form design for the gift order form includes menus with commands for clearing the form, printing the form, exiting the application, and displaying an about dialog box. Since the user should be able to select a book, a command button has been included that when clicked will display a form for viewing and selecting a book.

The code design for the gift order form is:

```
Private Sub cmdSelectABook_Click()
  Display frmDisplayBooks
End Sub

Private Sub mnuFileNewOrder_Click()
  Clear form
End Sub

Private Sub mnuFilePrint_Click()
  Print the form
End Sub

Private Sub mnuFileExit_Click()
  Unload form
End Sub

Private Sub mnuHelpAbout_Click()
  Display frmAboutGiftOrderForm
End Sub
```

frmDisplayBooks design   When the user clicks on the Select a Book button, a new form is displayed for viewing and selecting books. This form's design is:

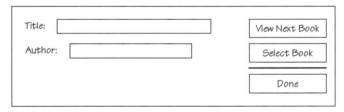

The form design for the frmDisplayBooks form

```
Create BookRecord user-defined data type

Private Sub cmdViewNextBook_Click()
  Open random access file
  Read current record
  Display record in the text boxes on the form
  Close the file
End Sub

Private Sub cmdSelectBook_Click()
  Add currently displayed book record to the list box on
  frmGiftOrderForm
End Sub

Private Sub cmdDone_Click()
  Unload form
End Sub
```

frmAboutGiftOrderForm design

The last form used in the application is an about dialog form that is displayed when the user selects the About command from the Help menu. The frmAboutGistOrderForm design is:

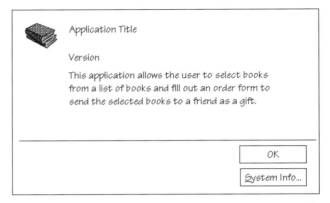

The form design for the frmAboutGiftOrderForm form

coding

The interface and code for this Case Study follow.

Sub Main coding

The Sub Main is coded in a standard form module and then specified as the startup object:

```
Sub Main()
    frmSplashGiftOrderForm.Show
    Load frmGiftOrderForm
End Sub
```

frmSplashGiftOrderForm coding

The splash screen interface and click event procedure are:

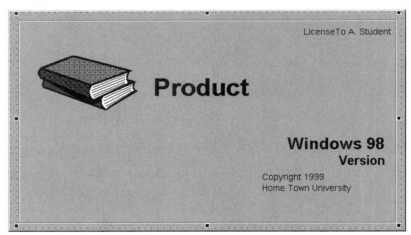

Object	Name	Caption	Picture	Stretch
frmSplash	frmSplashGiftOrderForm			
	lblLicensedTo	Licensed To *your name*		
	lblCompanyProduct	*empty*		
	lblPlatform	Windows 98		
	lblCopyright	Copyright *year*		
	lblCompany	*your school name*		
	lblWarning	*empty*		
	imgLogo		Books	False

```
Private Sub Frame1_Click()
    Unload Me
    frmGiftOrderForm.Show
End Sub
```

frmGiftOrderForm coding   The Gift Order Form interface and code are:

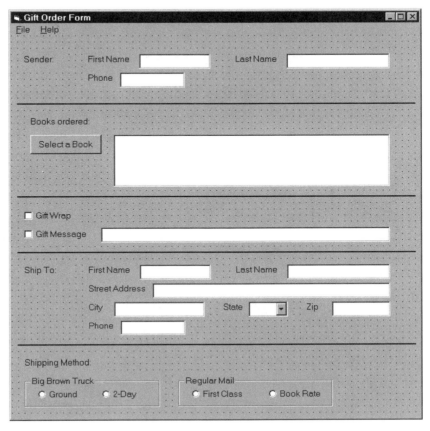

Object	Name	Caption	Text
Form1	frmGiftOrderForm	Gift Order Form	
Label1	lblSender	Sender:	
Label2	lblFirstNameSender	First Name	
Text1	txtFirstNameSender		*empty*
Label3	lblLastNameSender	Last Name	
Text2	txtLastNameSender		*empty*
Label4	lblPhoneSender	Phone	
Text3	txtPhoneSender		*empty*
Label5	lblBooksOrdered	Books ordered:	
Command1	cmdSelectABook	Select a Book	
List1	lstBooksOrdered		
Check1	chkGiftWrap	Gift Wrap	
Check2	chkGiftMessage	Gift Message	
Text4	txtGiftMessage		*empty*
Label6	lblShipTo	Ship To:	
Lable7	lblFirstName	First Name	
Text5	txtFirstName		*empty*
Label8	lblLastName	Last Name	
Text6	txtLastName		*empty*
Label9	lblAddress	Street Address	
Text7	txtAddress		*empty*

Object	Name	Caption	Text
Label10	lblCity	City	
Text8	txtCity		*empty*
Label11	lblState	State	
Combo1	cboState		
Label12	lblPhone	Phone	
Text9	txtPhone		*empty*
Label13	lblShippingMethod	Shipping Method:	
Frame1	fraBigBrownTruck	Big Brown Truck	
Option1	optGround	Ground	
Option2	opt2Day	2-Day	
Frame2	fraRegularMail	Regular Mail	
Option3	optFirstClass	First Class	
Option4	optBookRate	Book Rate	

Menu Name	Caption	Shortcut
mnuFile	&File	
mnuFileNewOrder	&New Order	Ctrl+N
mnuFilePrint	&Print	Ctrl+P
mnuFileExit	E&xit	Ctrl+X
mnuHelp	&Help	
mnuHelpAbout	&About…	

```
Option Explicit

Private Sub cmdSelectABook_Click()
   frmDisplayBooks.Show
End Sub

Private Sub mnuFileNewOrder_Click()
   txtFirstNameSender.Text = ""
   txtLastNameSender.Text = ""
   txtPhoneSender.Text = ""
   lstBooksOrdered.Clear
   chkGiftWrap.Value = vbUnchecked
   chkGiftMessage.Value = vbUnchecked
   txtGiftMessage.Text = ""
   txtFirstName.Text = ""
   txtLastName.Text = ""
   txtAddress.Text = ""
   txtCity.Text = ""
   txtState.Text = ""
   txtZip.Text = ""
   txtPhone.Text = ""
   optGround.Value = False
   opt2Day.Value = False
   optFirstClass.Value = False
   optBookRate.Value = False
End Sub

Private Sub mnuFilePrint_Click()
   Me.PrintForm
End Sub

Private Sub mnuFileExit_Click()
   Unload Me
End Sub

Private Sub mnuHelpAbout_Click()
   frmAboutGiftOrderForm.Show
End Sub
```

An Introduction to Programming Using Microsoft Visual Basic

frmDisplayBooks coding The cmdSelectABook_Click event procedure displays the Display Books form. The Display Books interface and code are:

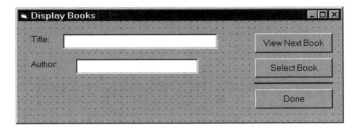

Object	Name	Caption	Text
Form1	frmDisplayBooks	Display Books	
Label1	lblTitle	Title:	
Text1	txtTitle		*empty*
Label2	lblAuthor	Author:	
Text2	txtAuthor		*empty*
Command1	cmdViewNextBook	View Next Book	
Command2	cmdSelectBook	Select Book	
Command3	cmdDone	Done	

```
Option Explicit

Private Type BookRecord
    strTitle As String * 30
    strAuthor As String * 30
End Type

Private Sub Form_Load()
    Call InitializeForm
End Sub

'**************************************************
'  Clears form
'
'  post: Text boxes on form are empty
'**************************************************
Sub InitializeForm()
    txtTitle.Text = ""
    txtAuthor.Text = ""
End Sub

Private Sub cmdSelectBook_Click()
    frmGiftOrderForm.lstBooksOrdered.AddItem txtTitle.Text
End Sub

Private Sub cmdViewNextBook_Click()
    Dim udtNewBook As BookRecord
    Dim intBookFile As Integer, lngRecLength As Long
    Dim lngTotalRecords As Long, lngRecLength As Long
    Static lngRecNum As Long

    'Open file
    intBookFile = FreeFile
    lngRecLength = LenB(udtNewBook)
    Open "Giftbooks.dat" For Random As #intBookFile _
        Len = lngRecLength

    'Determine number of records
    lngTotalRecords = NumRecords(intBookFile, lngRecLength)
```

```
'View record if valid
If lngRecNum < lngTotalRecords Then
   lngRecNum = lngRecNum + 1
Else
   lngRecNum = 1
End If
Get #intBookFile, lngRecNum, udtNewBook
txtTitle.Text = udtNewBook.strTitle
txtAuthor.Text = udtNewBook.strAuthor

'Close file
Close #intBookFile
End Sub

'*************************************************************
' Returns the number of records in the file with intFileNum
' file number containing records of length lngRecLength
'
' pre: intFileNum is open
' post: Number of records in intFileNum returned
'*************************************************************
Function NumRecords(ByVal intFileNum As Integer, _
ByVal lngRecLength As Long) As Integer
   If LOF(intFileNum) Mod lngRecLength = 0 Then
      NumRecords = (LOF(intFileNum) \ lngRecLength)
   Else
      NumRecords = (LOF(intFileNum) \ lngRecLength) + 1
   End If
End Function

Private Sub cmdDone_Click()
   Unload Me
End Sub
```

frmAboutGiftOrderForm coding

The last form used in the Gift Order Form application is the about dialog. The frm GiftOrderFormAbout interface is shown below. Since it is a template form there is no additional coding that needs to added.

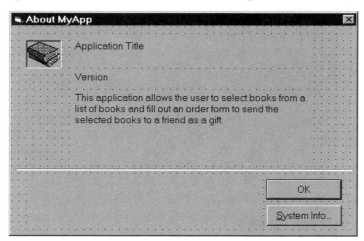

Object	Name	Caption	Picture	AutoSize
frmAbout	frmAboutGiftOrderForm			
	lblDescription	*see above*		
	lblDisclaimer	*empty*		
	picIcon		Books	False

An Introduction to Programming Using Microsoft Visual Basic

This Case Study should be tested by running the application and verifying that the splash screen is displayed first and the main form is displayed after clicking on the splash screen. Each menu item should be selected to make sure it works correctly. Also, books should be selected by clicking on the Select a Book command button and then selecting the books in the Display Books form.

Review 8

Modify the Gift Order Form Case Study to be password protected. Add the Welcome form created in Chapter Five Review 14 to the Case Study project and then modify the Sub Main appropriately.

Chapter Summary

menu

Menus can be added to a Visual Basic application using the Menu Editor command from the Tools menu. It is important that the menus you add to your applications are similar to other Windows applications. A click event procedure is coded for each command in a menu.

common dialogs

A common dialog is a Visual Basic predefined dialog box. This chapter introduced the Open, Save As, and Print dialog box. These dialog boxes are used in an application by adding a common dialog object to the form. A common dialog object is created using the CommonDialog control ( ). The common dialog object uses the ShowOpen, ShowSave, and ShowPrint methods to display a specific dialog box. Code must be written to do something with what the user selected in the dialog box.

ShowOpen, ShowSave,
ShowPrint methods

Add Form
template form

The Add Form command from the Project menu is used to add a new form, template form, or existing form to a project. A template form has a standard Windows interface and program code. The Project Explorer window is used to switch between the different forms in a project. The Show method is used to display a form and the Hide method is used to hide a form. An object on a form can be accessed by another form using dot notation.

Show method
Hide method
accessing objects on
another form

Sub Main
standard code module

A Sub Main procedure can be coded in a standard code module and be used as the startup object. A standard code module is added to a project using the Add Module command from the Project menu. The Project Properties command from the Project menu is used to change the startup object.

Vocabulary

About dialog A form that describes an application.

Common dialog A set of Visual Basic predefined dialog boxes.

Database A file that contains a set of records.

DBMS Contains the tools needed to manipulate a database.

Menu A set of commands.

Splash screen A form that is briefly displayed on the screen while an application is being loaded.

Standard code module Contains only code and is not associated with any form.

Template form A form that has a standard Windows interface and program code.

Visual Basic

Add Form command Used to add a new, template, or existing form to a project. Found in the Project menu.

Common dialog control Used to create a common dialog object. Must be added to the Tool box.

Copies Common dialog property that automatically changes at run-time to what the user entered in the Number of copies option of the Print dialog box.

DefaultExt Common dialog property that sets the default file extension of the file being saved. If the user enters an extension that is different than the default extension, it is used, but the default extension is used if no extension is entered.

FileName Common dialog property that automatically changes at run-time to the complete path and filename that the user selected in the dialog box.

FileTitle Common dialog property that automatically changes at run-time to the filename that the user selected in the dialog box.

Filter Common dialog property that sets the allowed file types and extensions.

Flags Common dialog property that changes how the dialog box behaves based on a Visual Basic constant.

Hide Method used to hide a form.

InitDir Common dialog property that sets the directory (folder) that will be displayed when the dialog box is displayed.

Menu Editor command Used to add menus to an application. Found in the Tools menu.

Printer.**Print** Statement used to send output to the printer.

Printer.EndDoc Statement used to send output to the printer.

ProjectPropeties command Used to change the startup object. Found in the Project menu.

Save As command Used to save a form under a different name. Found in the File menu.

Show Method used to display a form.

ShowOpen Method used to display the Open dialog box.

ShowPrinter Method used to display the Print dialog box.

ShowSave Method used to display the Save As dialog box.

Sub Main A special procedure added to a standard code module that can be used as the startup object.

Exercises

Exercise 1 ⚙

Modify the Chapter Four Case Study to include a File menu and a Help menu. The File menu should contain an Exit command. The Help menu should contain a Directions and an About command. The Directions command should display a new form with directions on how to use the calculator and the About command should display an about dialog form. The application interface should no longer display a Done button.

Exercise 2 ⚙

Modify the Chapter Five Case Study to include a File menu. The File menu should contain a Print and an Exit command. The application should display a splash screen at startup and the interface should no longer display the Print and Done buttons.

Exercise 3 ⚙

Modify the Chapter Six Case Study to include a File menu and a Help menu. The File menu should contain a Play Game and an Exit command. The Help menu should contain a Directions and an About command. The Directions command should display a new form with directions on how to play hangman and the About command should display an about dialog form. The application interface should no longer display the Play Game and Done buttons.

Exercise 4 ⚙

Modify the Chapter Seven Case Study to include a File menu and a Help menu. The File menu should contain a Play Game and an Exit command. The Help menu should contain a Rules and an About command. The Rules command should display a new form with the rules for the game of 21 and the About command should display an about dialog form. The application should display a splash screen at startup and the interface should no longer display the Play Game and Done buttons.

Exercise 5 ⚙

Create a Business Functions application that contains the Installment Loan Payments, How Much Can I Borrow, and Watch Your Money Grow forms from Chapter Eight. When the application starts, the form should display options for using the Pmt, PV, and FV functions. Based on the option selected by the user, one of the forms from Chapter Eight should be displayed.

Exercise 6 ⟳

Modify the Chapter Nine Case Study to include a File menu and a Language menu. The File menu should contain a New Order and an Exit command. The Language menu should contain an English and a Spanish command. The English command should display the menu items in English when clicked and the Spanish command should display the menu items in Spanish when clicked. A check mark should appear next to the selected command. The application interface should no longer display the New Order, English, and Quit buttons.

Exercise 7 ⟳

Modify the Chapter Eleven Case Study to include a File menu and Tools menu. The File menu should contain a Print and an Exit command. The Print command should use the Print dialog box to print the contents of the text box. The Tools menu should contain a Read File, a Load Profile, and a Create Profile command. The Read File command should use the Open dialog box to display the file in the text box. The application interface should only display a large text box.

Exercise 8 ⟳

Create a Sequential Books DBMS application that uses the Add Book Record, View Book Record, and Change Book Record forms from Chapter Eleven. Use the Books Database application from this chapter as a guide.

Exercise 9 ⟳

Modify the Chapter Twelve Case Study to include a Tools menu and a Help menu. The File menu should contain a Print and an Exit command. The Print command should use the Print dialog box to print the form. The Tools menu should contain an Initialize command. The application interface should no longer display Initialize and Done buttons.

Advanced
Exercise 10 ⟳

Modify an exercise from a previous chapter so that it:

- contains a menu bar with at least two menus and four commands
- uses a new form
- displays a splash screen at startup
- uses one of the common dialogs (Open, Save As, Print)

Using Microsoft Office with Visual Basic
Applications

OLE

Data

Chapter Fifteen Objectives

After completing this chapter you will be able to:

1. Understand OLE.
2. Embed a new or existing Excel spreadsheet into a Visual Basic application.
3. Link an existing Excel file to a Visual Basic application.
4. Link and embed Word documents to a Visual Basic application.
5. Use relational databases in Visual Basic applications.

In this chapter you will incorporate Microsoft Office applications in Visual Basic applications. Spreadsheets and word processor documents will be embedded in and linked to a Visual Basic application using the OLE control. The Data control will be used to view database data. You will need Microsoft Excel, Word, and Access to complete this chapter.

15.1 OLE

OLE is a technology that allows an application to contain an object created by another Windows application. For example, you can create a Visual Basic application that contains an Excel spreadsheet and chart:

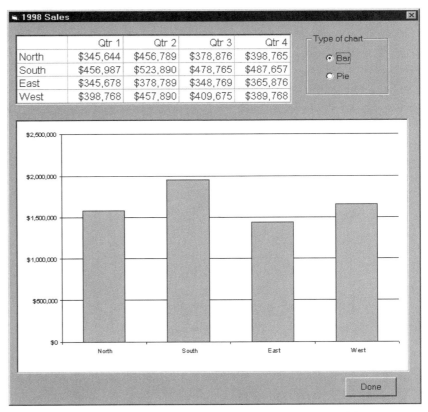

This Visual Basic application contains a spreadsheet and chart that were created by Excel

OLE allows the user to access the Excel spreadsheet program from within the Visual Basic application.

Object Linking and Embedding

OLE originally stood for Object linking and Embedding. However, it is now referred to as just OLE.

Copy and Paste

The Copy and Paste commands from the Edit menu can be used to embed an object. The Paste Link command can be used to link an object.

---

container application
server application

A *container application* contains an object from another application, called the *server application*. In the previous example, the Visual Basic application is the container and Excel the server.

15.2 Embedding a New Excel Spreadsheet

embedded object

OLE container

A new, empty Excel spreadsheet can be embedded into a Visual Basic application by adding an OLE container object to a form, which acts as a placeholder for the spreadsheet object. An *embedded* object is created by the server application but is only stored in the container application. An *OLE container* object is created using the OLE control ( ) in the Tool box. Creating an OLE container object on the form displays the Insert Object dialog box:

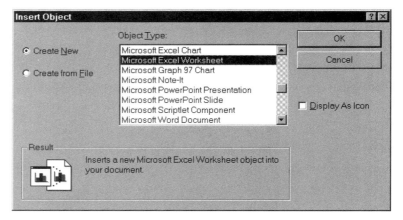

Selecting the Create New option button, and Microsoft Excel Worksheet from the Object Type list, and then OK inserts a new, empty spreadsheet object into the OLE container on the form.

An OLE container has the properties:

- **Name** identifies the object and is used by the programmer. It is good programming style to begin OLE container object names with ole.

- **SizeMode** changes how the OLE container and its object is sized. SizeMode can be set to clip, stretch, autosize, or zoom. SizeMode can be changed at run time through assignment using the Visual Basic constants:

  vbOLESizeClip – object is displayed in actual size. When the object is larger than the OLE container, the image is clipped by the OLE container's borders

  vbOLESizeStretch – object is resized to fill the OLE container, but the image may not be proportionally resized

  vbOLESizeAutoSize – the OLE container is resized to display the entire object

  vbOLESizeZoom – object is resized to fill the OLE container as much as possible while still remaining proportional

entering new spreadsheet data at design-time

When a new spreadsheet object is first placed in the OLE container at design time, Visual Basic's menu bar is replaced with Excel's menu bar, and column letters and row numbers are displayed in the spreadsheet object to indicate that the programmer can enter data:

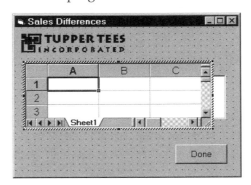

The data initially entered into the spreadsheet at design time will be displayed each time the application is run. The data can be changed at design time by right-clicking on the OLE container and selecting the Edit command from the pop-up menu.

activating an embedded object

in-place activation

When the Visual Basic application is run, double-clicking on the OLE container activates it. When an embedded OLE object is *activated*, the server application is started within the Visual Basic application which is called *in-place activation*. The interface of the Visual Basic application changes to that of the server application. For example, running the Sales Differences application and double-clicking on the spreadsheet displays the Excel menu bar:

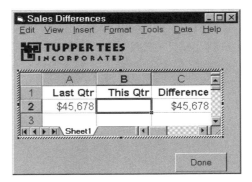

In-place activation

deactivating

An OLE object can be deactivated by pressing the Escape key.

Any changes made to an embedded spreadsheet at run time are not saved.

Review 1

Tupper Tees manufactures and sells college t-shirts and needs a Visual Basic application that allows its salespeople to compare their current sales to their last quarter sales. Follow the instructions below to create the Sales Differences application shown in the previous section.

1) CREATE A NEW PROJECT

2) ADD OBJECTS TO THE FORM

Refer to the form below when placing and sizing the form and its objects as instructed in the steps following:

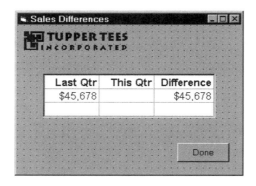

a. Use the table below to name and change the properties of the objects.

Object	Name	Caption	Picture
Form1	frmSalesDifferences	Sales Differences	
Image1	imgTupperTees		Tuppertees
Command1	cmdDone	Done	

b. In the Tool box, click the OLE control (▥) and then drag the cross-hairs pointer on the form to create an OLE container as shown above. It may take a few seconds for the Insert Object dialog box to be displayed.
c. In the Insert Object dialog box, select Microsoft Excel Worksheet from the Object Type list.
d. Select OK to remove the Insert Object dialog box and embed a new spreadsheet in the application.
e. Note that the menu bar of the IDE has changed and the cell cursor is in the spreadsheet. Enter the data shown above into the spreadsheet starting at cell A1 and using the formula =A2-B2 in cell C2.
f. Using the Cells command from the Format menu, format the data as shown above.
g. Click on an empty portion of the form. The OLE container object is no longer active.
h. Click once on the OLE container object and use the table below to name and change its properties.

Object	Name	SizeMode
OLE1	oleSpreadsheet	2 - AutoSize

3) SAVE THE PROJECT

From the File menu, select Save Project. Save the form naming it frmSalesDifferences and save the project naming it Sales Differences.

4) WRITE THE PROGRAM CODE

Display the Code Editor window and add the following event procedure:

```
Private Sub cmdDone_Click()
    Unload Me
End Sub
```

5) RUN THE APPLICATION

a. Save the modified Sales Differences project and then run the application.
b. Double-click on the spreadsheet data. Notice how the interface changes to include the Excel menu bar. Enter $23,456 in cell B2. Notice how the contents of cell C2 change.
c. Press the Escape key to deactivate the object.

d. Select Done to end the application.

e. Run the application again. Note that the changes just made were not saved.

15.3 Embedding an Existing Excel File

An existing Excel spreadsheet or chart can be embedded into a Visual Basic application using an OLE container object. Selecting the Create from File option button in the Insert Object dialog box displays the following options:

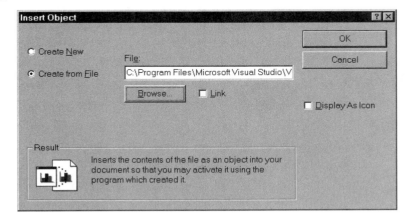

The Browse button is used to locate the existing Excel file, and selecting OK displays the selected file in the OLE container.

SourceDoc

The OLE container's embedded object can be changed at design time from what was originally selected by using the OLE container's SourceDoc property. The SourceDoc property displays a dialog box for selecting the file to be embedded (the source document).

CreateEmbed method

At run time, the embedded object can be changed using the CreateEmbed method that takes the form:

oleObject.CreateEmbed (*filepath*)

oleObject is the name of the OLE container and *filepath* is a **String** variable or a string enclosed in quotation marks that specifies the location of the file.

It is important to note that any changes to an object in the server application are not reflected in the container application. For example, if you embed a spreadsheet into a Visual Basic application and then modify the spreadsheet in Excel, the changes will not appear in the spreadsheet in the Visual Basic application. Also, remember that any changes made to the spreadsheet at run time are not saved.

Review 2

Tupper Tees uses salespeople in four different regions (North, South, East, West) to sell their products and needs a Visual Basic application that displays last years total sales so that their employees can refer to it. Follow the instructions below to create the 1998 Sales application.

1) **CREATE A NEW PROJECT**

2) **ADD OBJECTS TO THE FORM**

Refer to the form below when placing and sizing the form and its objects as instructed in the steps following:

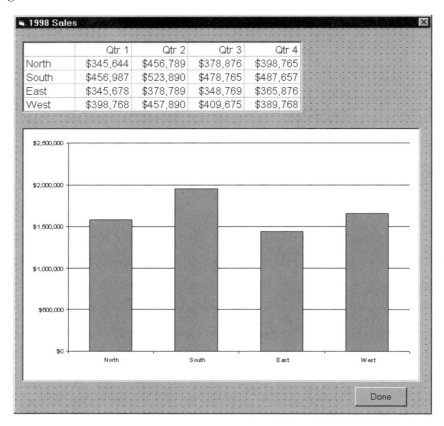

a. Use the table below to name and change the properties of the objects.

Object	Name	Caption
Form1	frm1998Sales	1998 Sales
Command1	cmdDone	Done

b. In the Tool box, click the OLE control ( ) and then drag the cross-hairs pointer to create an OLE container near the top of the form. It may take a few seconds for the Insert Object dialog box to be displayed.

c. In the Insert Object dialog box, select the Create from File option button.

d. Select the Browse button and then select the 1998 Sales.xls file from the appropriate folder.

e. Select the Insert button to select the file.

f. Select OK to remove the Insert Object dialog box and embed the file in the application.

g. Use the table below to name and change the properties of the OLE container object.

Object	Name	Enabled	SizeMode
OLE1	oleNumbers	False	2 - AutoSize

h. Repeat steps b through f to embed the 1998 Sales Bar Chart.xls file in the application.
i. Use the table below to name and change the properties of the OLE container object.

Object	Name	Enabled	SizeMode
OLE1	oleChart	False	3 - Zoom

3) SAVE THE PROJECT

From the File menu, select Save Project. Save the form naming it frm1998Sales and save the project naming it 1998 Sales.

4) WRITE THE PROGRAM CODE

Display the Code Editor window and add the following evet procedure:

```
Private Sub cmdDone_Click()
    Unload Me
End Sub
```

5) RUN THE APPLICATION

a. Save the modified 1998 Sales project and then run the application.
b. Double-click on the spreadsheet data. It cannot be activated because it has been disabled.
c. Double-click on the chart. It is also deactivated because the data should not be changed.

6) MODIFY THE FORM

Add a frame and two option buttons as shown below. Use the table below to name and change the properties of the objects.

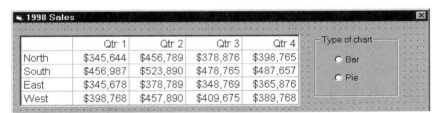

Object	Name	Caption
Frame1	fraChartType	Type of chart
Option1	optBar	Bar
Option2	optPie	Pie

7) ADD EVENT PROCEDURES

Display the Code Editor window and add the following event procedures:

```
Private Sub Form_Load()
    optBar.Value = True
End Sub

Private Sub optBar_Click()
    oleChart.CreateEmbed ("1998 Sales Bar Chart.xls")
End Sub

Private Sub optPie_Click()
    oleChart.CreateEmbed ("1998 Sales Pie Chart.xls")
End Sub
```

8) RUN THE APPLICATION

Save the modified 1998 Sales project and then run the application. Test the application by clicking on each option button.

9) PRINT AND THEN REMOVE THE PROJECT

15.4 Linking an Existing Excel File

An existing Excel spreadsheet or chart can be linked to a Visual Basic application using the OLE container object. A *linked* object is an object that is created and stored in the server application and a link to that object is stored in the container application. Selecting the **Create from File** option button in the Insert Object dialog box displays the following options:

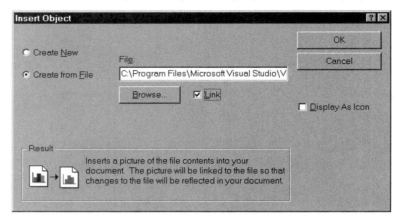

Selecting the Link check box creates a linked object

Selecting the Link check box and then OK displays a copy of the linked file in the OLE container object.

Any changes made to a linked object in the server application are reflected in the container application. For example, if you link a spreadsheet to a Visual Basic application and then modify the spreadsheet in Excel, the changes will also appear in the object in the Visual Basic application. Similarly, any change made to the linked object by first activating it from the Visual Basic application are saved.

The OLE container's linked object can be changed at design time from what was origingally selected by using the OLE container's SourceDoc property.

Update method

The Update method is used to update a linked object and takes the form:

> *oleObject*.Update

oleObject is the name of the OLE container to update. The Update method should be placed in the form load procedure so that each time the application is run the linked object is current.

CreateLink method

At run time, the linked object can be changed using the CreateLink method that takes the form:

> *oleObject*.CreateLink (*filepath*)   'linked object

oleObject is the name of the OLE container and *filepath* is a **String** variable or a string enclosed in quotation marks that specifies the location of the file.

When a linked OLE object is activated, the server application is started and displays the source document. The source document must be saved within the server application for any edits to be retained to the file on disk.

Review 3

Tupper Tees needs an application that allows its employees to enter their current sales amount. Follow the instructions below to create the Current Sales application.

1) **CREATE A NEW PROJECT**

2) **ADD OBJECTS TO THE FORM**

Refer to the form below when placing and sizing the form and its objects as instructed in the steps following:

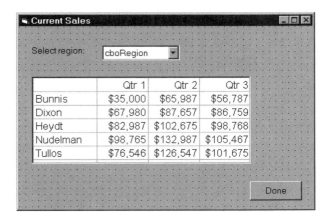

a. Use the table below to name and change the properties of the objects.

Object	Name	Caption	Style
Form1	frmCurrentSales	Current Sales	
Label1	lblRegion	Select a region:	
Combo1	cboRegion		2 - Dropdown List
Command1	cmdDone	Done	

b. In the Tool box, click the OLE control ( ) and then drag the cross-hairs pointer to create an OLE container.
c. In the Insert Object dialog box, select the Create from File option button.
d. Select the Browse button and then select the North Region Current Sales.xls file from the appropriate folder.
e. Select the Insert button to select the file.
f. Select the Link check box in the Insert Object dialog box.
g. Select OK to remove the Insert Object dialog box and link the file to the application.
h. Use the table below to name and change the properties of the OLE container object.

Object	Name	SizeMode
OLE1	oleSpreadsheet	0 - Clip

3) **SAVE THE PROJECT**

From the File menu, select Save Project. Save the form naming it frmCurrentSales and save the project naming it Current Sales.

4) **WRITE THE PROGRAM CODE**

Display the Code Editor window and add the following event procedures:

```
Private Sub Form_Load()
    cboRegion.AddItem "North"
    cboRegion.AddItem "South"
    cboRegion.AddItem "East"
    cboRegion.AddItem "West"
```

```
    cboRegion.Text = "North"
    oleSpreadsheet.Update
End Sub

Private Sub cboRegion_Click()
    If cboRegion.Text = "North" Then
        oleSpreadsheet.CreateLink ("North Region Current Sales.xls")
    ElseIf cboRegion.Text = "South" Then
        oleSpreadsheet.CreateLink ("South Region Current Sales.xls")
    ElseIf cboRegion.Text = "East" Then
        oleSpreadsheet.CreateLink ("East Region Current Sales.xls")
    Else
        oleSpreadsheet.CreateLink ("West Region Current Sales.xls")
    End If
End Sub

Private Sub cmdDone_Click()
    Unload Me
End Sub
```

5) RUN THE APPLICATION

    a. Save the modified Current Sales project and then run the application.

    b. Test the application by selecting each region in the combo box and then activating the spreadsheet for that region by double-clicking on it.

6) PRINT AND THEN REMOVE THE PROJECT

Review 4

Modify the Current Sales application created in Review 3 so that there is a Total column displayed in the spreadsheet. Edit the spreadsheet from within the Visual Basic application. The application interface should look similar to that shown on the right after activating the OLE object, adding the new Total column, and saving the changes to the spreadsheet file. Make sure to edit each region's spreadsheet file.

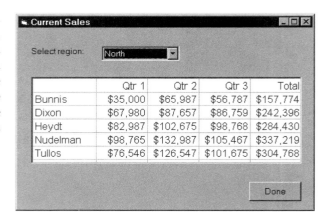

15.5 Linking and Embedding Word Documents

The OLE container object can also be used to link and embed new or existing Word documents the same way Excel spreadsheets were embedded and linked in a Visual Basic application.

In addition to displaying the actual contents of a file, an icon representing the file can be inserted into an OLE container:

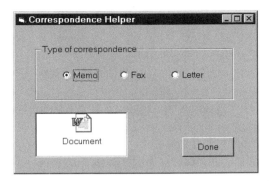

An OLE container can display an icon of a file

Selecting the file to link or embed and then the Display As Icon check box in the Insert Object dialog box displays the following options:

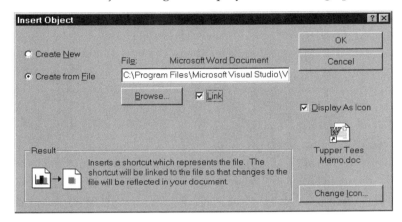

The icon image or the label describing the icon (filename) can be edited using the Change Icon button. The Display As Icon check box can be selected for new files and embedded files.

Double-clicking on the icon at run time displays the linked or embedded file in the server application.

Review 5

Follow the instructions below to create the Correspondence Helper application.

1) **CREATE A NEW PROJECT**

2) **ADD OBJECTS TO THE FORM**

   Refer to the form on the next page when placing and sizing the form and its objects as instructed in the steps following:

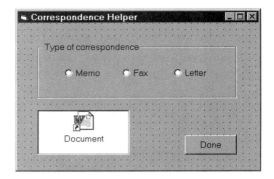

a. Use the table below to name and change the properties of the objects.

Object	Name	Caption
Form1	frmCorrespondenceHelper	Correspondence Helper
Frame1	fraCorrespondence	Type of correspondence
Option1	optMemo	Memo
Option2	optFax	Fax
Option3	optLetter	Letter
Command1	cmdDone	Done

b. In the Tool box, double-click the OLE control ( ).
c. In the Insert Object dialog box, select the **Create from File** option button.
d. Select the **Browse** button and then select the Tupper Tees Memo.doc file from the appropriate folder.
e. Select the **Insert** button to select the file.
f. Select the **Link** check box and the **Display As Icon** check box.
g. Select the **Change Icon** button to display the Change Icon dialog box.
h. Enter Document in the **Label** text box and then select **OK**.
i. Select **OK** to remove the Insert Object dialog box and link the file to the application.
j. Use the table below to name and change the properties of the OLE container object.

Object	Name	SizeMode
OLE1	oleDocument	2 - AutoSize

3) SAVE THE PROJECT

From the File menu, select Save Project. Save the form naming it frmCorrespondenceHelper and save the project naming it Correspondence Helper.

4) WRITE THE PROGRAM CODE

Display the Code Editor window and add the following event procedures:

```
Private Sub Form_Load()
    optMemo.Value = True
End Sub

Private Sub optFax_Click()
    oleDocument.CreateLink ("Tupper Tees Fax.doc")
End Sub

Private Sub optLetter_Click()
    oleDocument.CreateLink ("Tupper Tees Letter.doc")
End Sub

Private Sub optMemo_Click()
    oleDocument.CreateLink ("Tupper Tees Memo.doc")
End Sub
```

```
Private Sub cmdDone_Click()
    Unload Me
End Sub
```

5) RUN THE APPLICATION

a. Save the modified Correspondence Helper project and then run the application.
b. Test the application by selecting each option button and double-clicking the icon to start the Word program and display the appropriate document.

6) PRINT AND THEN REMOVE THE PROJECT

15.6 Databases and the Data Control

The computer's fast retrieval and large storage capabilities make it an ideal tool for managing information in the form of a database. A *relational database* provides a way of organizing and storing data. A relational database contains many *tables* where each table is a unique set of records. Business and organizations use relational databases in many ways: a bank keeps track of accounts and transactions, and a college organizes student records, faculty information, and class schedules.

relational database

Data from a database can be viewed and manipulated in a Visual Basic application by adding a data object to a form. For example, a data object is used in the Employees application below:

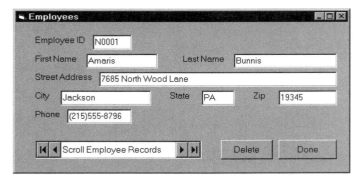

The data object is used to scroll through records

The Visual Data Manager

Visual Basic includes an application called Visual Data Manager (VisData) that can be used to create or modify a relational database. VisData can be started by selecting the Visual Data Manager command from the Add-Ins menu.

A record, as discussed in Chapters Eleven and Twelve, is a set of fields. The field entries for a record are displayed using text blocks in the example above. These text boxes are called *bound objects* because they are bound (linked) to a specific field in the Employees table. Clicking on one of the buttons on the data object scrolls through the records of the Employees table:

bound objects

Move First — Move Last
Move Previous   Move Next

data object

A *data object* is created using the Data control ( ) in the tool box and has the properties:

- **Name** identifies the object and is used by the programmer. It is good programming style to begin data object names with dat.

- **Caption** changes the text displayed in the data object.

- **DatabaseName** is used to display a dialog box for selecting the database file to bind to the data object.

- **RecordSource** changes the name of the table in the database that the data control will be bound to.

- **EOFAction** can be set to Move Last, EOF, or Add New to specify how the data control acts when the Move Next button is clicked and the last record is displayed. EOFAction can be changed at run time through assignment using the Visual Basic constants:

    vbEOFActionMoveLast – the last record remains as the current record
    vbEOFActionEOF – the MoveNext button is disabled
    vbEOFActionAddNew – a new empty record is displayed

After adding a data object to the form and setting its properties, the DataSource and DataField properties need to be set for each text box so that the field entries will be displayed. The DataSource property is set to the name of the data object and the DataField property is set to the name of the field in the database table that contains the entries to be displayed.

adding a record

A new record is added to the database by displaying the last record and clicking on the Move Next button (▶) on the data object to display a new, empty record. The record is automatically saved when it is typed in the text boxes. Note that the EOFAction property of the data object has to be set to Add New.

updating a record

A record is updated by simply editing the displayed record. Any edits are automatically saved in the database file.

deleting a record

A currently displayed record is deleted using the Delete method, which takes the form:

Delete method

datObject.Recordset.Delete

datObject is the name of the data object displaying the record to be deleted.

Refresh method

The Refresh method updates the records and displays the first record of the database and takes the form:

datObject.Refresh

datObject is the name of the data object displaying the records to be refreshed.

The following statements use the Delete method and the Refresh method to delete the currently displayed record and then refresh the database:

```
Private Sub cmdDelete_Click()
    datEmployees.Recordset.Delete
    datEmployees.Refresh
End Sub
```

Review 6

Tupper Tees uses the Employees application to view employee records stored in a database. Follow the instructions below to complete the Employees application.

1) OPEN THE EMPLOYEES PROJECT

Display the Employees form if it is not already displayed.

2) ADD A DATA OBJECT TO THE FORM

Refer to the form below when placing and sizing the data object as instructed in the steps following:

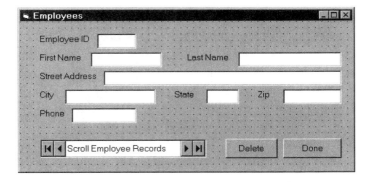

a. In the Tool box, double-click on the Data control (🖳). A data object is added to the form. Resize the object as shown above.

b. Use the table below to name and change the properties of the data object:

Object	Name	Caption	DatabaseName	RecordSource	EOFAction
Data1	datEmployees	*see above*	Tupper Tees	Employees	2 - Add New

3) SET PROPERTIES TO BOUND THE TEXT BOXES TO THE APPROPRIATE FIELDS

Use the table below to change the properties of each text box to bind it to the data object:

Name	DataSource	DataField
txtEmployeeID	datEmployees	Employee ID
txtFirstName	datEmployees	First Name
txtLastName	datEmployees	Last Name
txtAddress	datEmployees	Address
txtCity	datEmployees	City
txtState	datEmployees	State
txtZip	datEmployees	Zip
txtPhone	datEmployees	Phone

4) WRITE THE PROGRAM CODE

Display the Code Editor window and add the following event procedures:

```
Private Sub cmdDelete_Click()
    datEmployees.Recordset.Delete
    datEmployees.Refresh
End Sub

Private Sub cmdDone_Click()
    Unload Me
End Sub
```

5) RUN THE APPLICATION

a. Save the modified Employees project and then run the application. Test the application by scrolling through the records. Update and delete some of the records.
b. Select Done to end the application.
c. Run the application again. Note that the changes were saved.

6) PRINT AND THEN REMOVE THE PROJECT

Chapter Summary

container application
server application
embedded object
linked object

OLE is a technology that allows an application to contain an object created by another Windows application. A container application contains the object and the server application is the application that created the object. An embedded object is an object that is created by the server application but is only stored in the container application. A linked object is an object that is created and stored in the server application and a link to the object is stored in the container application.

OLE container

activating, deactivating
CreateEmbed method
CreateLink method

The OLE container object is used to embed or link a spreadsheet or word processor document into a Visual Basic application. An OLE container object is created using the OLE control () in the Tool box. An OLE object is activated by double-clicking on it. It is deactivated by pressing the Escape key. The CreateEmbed method and the CreateLink method are used to change the source document at run time.

data object

adding a record
updating a record
deleting a record
Delete method

The data object is used to view, add, update, and delete database records in a Visual Basic application. A data object is created using the Data control () in the Tool box. Field entries for a record are displayed in bound text boxes. A record is added by displaying the last record and clicking on the Move Next button to display a new, empty record. Editing a displayed record automatically updates it. The Delete method is used to delete the currently displayed record.

Vocabulary

Activating Double-clicking an OLE object so that it can be edited using the server application.

Bound object An object that is linked to a specific field in a database table.

Container application An application that contains an object from another application.

Data An object that is used to add, view, update, and delete database records.

Deactivating Pressing the Escape key to deactivate an OLE object.

Embedded object An object that is created by a server application but is only stored in the container application.

In-place activation An embedded OLE object that can be edited with the server application interface in the Visual Basic application.

Linked object An object that is created and stored in a server application and a link to that object is stored in the container application.

OLE A technology that allows an application to contain an object created by another Windows application.

OLE container An object that acts as a placeholder for another object.

Record A set of fields.

Relational database Contains many tables.

Server application An application that creates an object that is embedded or linked to another application.

Table A unique set of records.

Visual Basic

CreateEmbed Method used to change an embedded object at run time.

CreateLink Method used to change a linked object at run time.

Data control Used to create a data object. Found in the Tool box.

DatabaseName Data object property that is used to display a dialog box for selecting the database file to bind to the data object.

Delete Method used to delete the current record.

EOFAction Data object property used to specify how the data object acts when the Move Next button is clicked and the last record is displayed.

OLE control Used to create an OLE container object. Found in the Tool box.

RecordSource Data object property that is used to change the name of the table in the database that the data control will be bound to.

Refresh Method used to update records and then display the first record.

SizeMode OLE container object property that changes how the OLE container and its object is sized.

SourceDoc OLE container object property that is used to display a dialog box for selecting the source document.

Update Method used to update a linked OLE object.

Exercises

Exercise 1

Create an Elaine's Bakery application that displays the Elaine's Bakery.xls, Elaine's Bakery Revenue Chart.xls, and Elaine's Bakery Income Chart.xls files as embedded OLE objects. The revenue chart and income chart files should be displayed on separate forms when the user clicks the appropriate command button. The application interface for the startup form should look similar to:

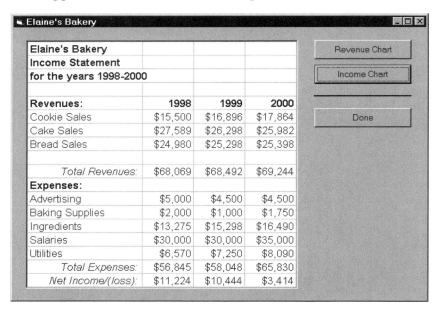

Exercise 2

Create a Payroll Calculator application that calculates payroll taxes. The application should display the Taxes.xls spreadsheet file as an embedded OLE object. The application interface should look similar to:

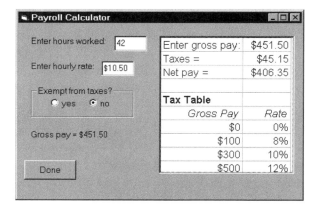

Exercise 3

Create a Brochure Printing Costs application that displays the Brochure Costs.xls spreadsheet file as a linked OLE object. The application interface should look similar to:

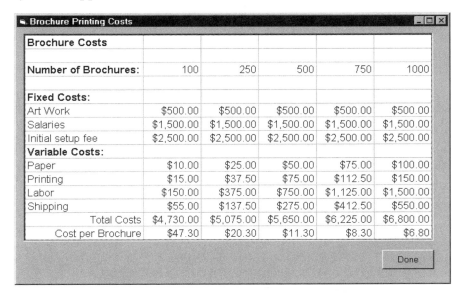

Exercise 4

Create a Personal Finances application that displays the Personal Finances.xls spreadsheet file as a linked OLE object. Update the data in the spreadsheet file with your own personal transactions. The application interface should look similar to:

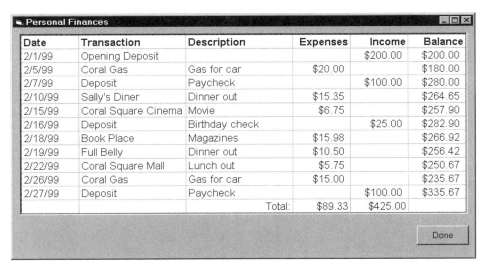

Exercise 5

Create a Create Embedded File application that displays a new Excel Spreadsheet or Word document based on which icon the user double-clicks. The application interface should look similar to:

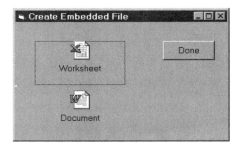

Exercise 6

Create a My Paper Helper application that displays in a combo box the names of five papers you have written and then displays the paper in an embedded OLE object when the user selects the paper. The application interface should look similar to:

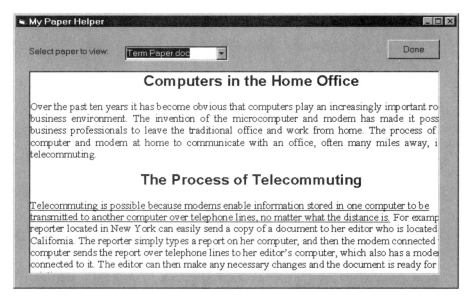

Exercise 7

Create a Presidents application that displays the Presidents.doc file in a linked OLE object. Update the list in the document to include the current president. The application interface should look similar to:

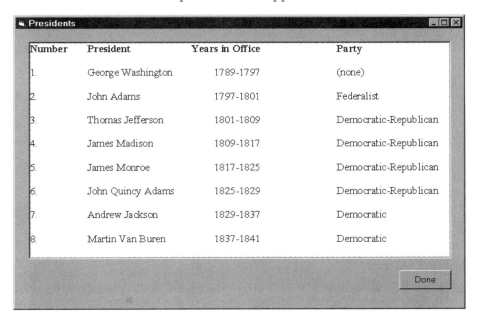

Exercise 8

a) Create a Solar System application that displays the records in the Solar System table of the Space Exploration.mdb relational database file. The application interface should look similar to:

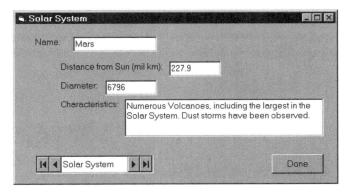

b) The Space Exploration.mdb database also contains an Explorations table. Create a multiform application called Space Exploration that allows the user to view the Solar System form created in (a) or an Explorations form that is used to view the Explorations table of the database. The Explorations table contains Date, Vehicle, Country, Destination, and Mission fields.

Exercise 9

a) Create an Animals application that displays the records in the Animals table of the Seaquarium.mdb relational database file. The application interface should look similar to:

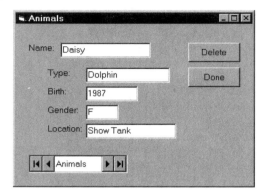

b) The Seaquarium.mdb database also contains a Tanks table and a Shows table. Create a multiform application called Sea Attraction that allows the user to view the Animal form created in (a), a Tank form used to view the Tanks table, or a Shows form that is used to view the Shows table of the database. The Shows table contains Show, Early Show, Late Show, and Tank fields. The Tanks table contains Tank, Size, Cleaning, and Inspected fields.

Advanced
Exercise 10

Create an application that displays the records of a table you created using Microsoft Access and at least one linked or embedded spreadsheet file that you have also created that is related to the data in the database.

Visual Basic Naming Conventions and Keywords

T his appendix discusses good programming style naming conventions for variables, constants, and objects. Also listed are the keywords used in this text.

Naming Conventions for Constants and Variables

The identifiers of constants and variables should be descriptive and in mixed case, using capital letters for the beginning of each word, with no spaces between words. Identifiers should have an all lowercase prefix that indicate the type of data stored:

Type	Prefix	Type	Prefix
Boolean	bln	Long	lng
Currency	cur	Single	sgl
Double	dbl	String	str
Integer	int	User-defined	udt

Naming Conventions for Objects

The Name property for an object should be descriptive and in mixed case, using capital letters for the beginning of each word, with no spaces between words. Object names should have an all lowercase prefix that indicates the object type:

Object	Prefix	Object	Prefix
check box	chk	label	lbl
combo box	cbo	line	lin
command button	cmd	list box	lst
common dialog	cdl	multimedia	mmc
data object	dat	OLE	ole
directory list	dir	option button	opt
drive list	drv	picture box	pic
file list	fil	shape	shp
frame	fra	text box	txt
form	frm	timer	tmr
image	img		

Keywords

Append Keyword used in an **Open** statement to open a file for writing data after any existing data. Introduced in Chapter Eleven.

Boolean A data type used to represent True or False. Introduced in Chapter Four.

ByRef Keyword used to declare a reference parameter in a general procedure. Introduced in Chapter Seven.

ByVal Keyword used to declare a value parameter in a general or function procedure. Introduced in Chapter Seven.

Call Statement used to execute a general procedure. Introduced in Chapter Seven.

Close Statement used to close a file. Introduced in Chapter Eleven.

Const Statement used to delare a variable. Introduced in Chapter Four.

Currency A data type representing positive or negative numbers that are money values with up to four digits to the right of the decimal place and 15 digits to the left. Introduced in Chapter Four.

Debug.Print Statement used to display output to the Immediate window. Introduced in Chapter Four.

Dim Statement used to declare a variable. Introduced in Chapter Four.

Do...Loop Statement that repeatedly executes code as long as a condition is True. Introduced in Chapter Six.

Double A data type representing positive or negative integer numbers up to $1.8e^{308}$. Introduced in Chapter Four.

End Function Statement used to end the **Function** statement. Introduced in Chapter Seven.

End Sub Indicates the end of a procedure. Introduced in Chapter Three.

For...Next Statement that executes a loop body a fixed number of times. Introduced in Chapter Six.

Function Statement used to declare a function procedure. Introduced in Chapter Seven.

Get # Statement used to read a record from a random access file. Introduced in Chapter Twelve.

If...Then Statement that executes code when a condition is true. Introduced in Chapter Five.

If...Then...Else Statement that executes code in the **Else** clause when a condition is false. Introduced in Chapter Five.

If...Then...ElseIf Statement that is used to decide among three or more actions. Introduced in Chapter Five.

Input Keyword used in an **Open** statement to open a file for reading. Introduced in Chapter Eleven.

Input # Statement used to read delimited data from a sequential access file. Introduced in Chapter Eleven.

Integer A data type representing positive or negative integer numbers up to 32,767. Introduced in Chapter Four.

Kill Statement used to delete a file. Introduced in Chapter Eleven.

Like Operator used to perform textual comparison on strings and pattern matching using characters such as ?, *, #, []. Introduced in Chapter Six.

Line Input # Statement used to read a line of text from a sequential access file. Introduced in Chapter Eleven.

Long A data type representing positive or negative integer numbers over 32,767. Introduced in Chapter Four.

Mod Arithmetic operator used to perform modulus division. Introduced in Chapter Four.

Name Statement used to rename a file. Introduced in Chapter Eleven.

Open Statement used to open a file. Introduced in Chapter Eleven.

Option Explicit Statement used to require a variable declaration before a variable is used. Introduced in Chapter Four.

Output Keyword used in an **Open** statement to open a file for writing at the beginning of the file. Introduced in Chapter Eleven.

Preserve Keyword used in a **ReDim** statement to keep the existing values of an array when it is resized. Introduced in Chapter Nine.

Printer.EndDoc Statement used to send output to the printer. Introduced in Chapter Fourteen.

Printer.**Print** Statement used to send output to the printer. Introduced in Chapter Fourteen.

Print # Statement used to write a line of text to a sequential access file. Introduced in Chapter Eleven.

Private Indicates the procedure cannot be accessed outside of the form module. Introduced in Chapter Three.

Put # Statement used to write a record to a random access file. Introduced in Chapter Twelve.

ReDim Statement used to allocate space for the elements of a dynamic array. Introduced in Chapter Nine.

Single A data type representing positive or negative real numbers up to $3.4e^{38}$. Introduced in Chapter Four.

Static Keyword used in place of **Dim** to declare a static variable. Introduced in Chapter Seven.

Step Used in a **For...Next** statement to increment or decrement the counter by a set amount. Introduced in Chapter Six.

String A data type representing a string. Introduced in Chapter Four.

Sub Indicates the beginning of a procedure. Introduced in Chapter Three.

Type Statement used to define a user-defined type. Introduced in Chapter Twelve.

Write # Statement used to write delimited data (records) to a sequential access file. Introduced in Chapter Eleven.

Program Index

In Order of Appearance

Calculator (Case Study) 4-20
Guessing Game (version 1) 5-2
Guessing Game (version 2) 5-11
Guessing Game (version 3) 5-17
Pizza Order (Case Study) 5-25
Hangman (Case Study) 6-21
Game of 21 (Case Study) 7-21
Mortgage Analyzer (Case Study) 8-18
Dice Rolls 9-5
Letter Occurrences 9-7
Dynamic Array Demo 9-10
Tic-Tac-Toe 9-17
Lucy's Cuban Cafe (Case Study) 9-21
Race Track (Case Study) 10-23
Change Book Record 11-15
Display File (Case Study) 11-21
Add Book 12-5
View Book 12-7
Change Book 12-10
Theater Box Office (Case Study) 12-15
Bubble Sort 13-2
Selection Sort 13-5
Insertion Sort 13-8
Binary Search 13-11
Gift Order Form (Case Study) 14-24

Alphabetical

Add Book 12-5
Binary Search 13-11
Bubble Sort 13-2
Calculator (Case Study) 4-20
Change Book 12-10
Change Book Record 11-15
Dice Rolls 9-5
Display File (Case Study) 11-21
Dynamic Array Demo 9-10
Game of 21 (Case Study) 7-21
Gift Order Form (Case Study) 14-24
Guessing Game (version 1) 5-2
Guessing Game (version 2) 5-11
Guessing Game (version 3) 5-17
Hangman (Case Study) 6-21
Insertion Sort 13-8
Letter Occurrences 9-7
Lucy's Cuban Cafe (Case Study) 9-21
Mortgage Analyzer (Case Study) 8-18
Pizza Order (Case Study) 5-25
Race Track (Case Study) 10-23
Selection Sort 13-5
Theater Box Office (Case Study) 12-15
Tic-Tac-Toe 9-17
View Book 12-7

Index

' 3-13
& operator 6-15
&, access key 8-12
() 3-17, 9-1
\ operator 4-13
_ 7-2

A

ABC (Atanasoff-Berry Computer) 1-4
about dialog 14-14
About Dialog icon 14-14
Abs function 8-1
access key 8-12
access key, creating 8-12
accessing a member of a user-defined type 12-2
accessing an element of an array 9-2
accessing objects on other forms 14-11
accumulators 6-5
activated 15-3
activating an embedded object 15-3
Ada 1-6
Add Form command 14-10, 14-14, 14-18
Add Module command 14-16
adding a control to the Tool box 10-18
adding a new form to a project 14-9
adding a record with the data object 15-14
adding a template form to a project 14-14
adding an existing form to a project 14-18
adding menus to a Visual Basic application 14-2
AddItem method 8-7, 8-10
address 1-11
aggregate 12-1
Aiken, Howard 1-3
algorithm 5-13
Allen, Paul 2-1, 3-1
Alt key 2-7
Altair 1-8, 3-1
ALU (Arithmetic Logic Unit) 1-10
amortization 8-4

Analytical Engine 1-2
And 5-12
animation 10-15
ANSI 1-11, 6-16, 6-17, 11-1
appending 11-9
appending data to a sequential access file 11-5, 11-9
appending records to a random access file 12-4
Apple computer 1-8
Apple Computer, Inc. 1-9
application event 3-12
application online help 2-21
application, running 3-6
applications 1-9, 1-13
applications software 1-9, 1-13, 2-1
arc 10-9
arc, drawing 10-9
arccosine 8-23
arcsine 8-23
arctangent 8-23
argument 7-4
arguments, omitted in a function 10-8
Arithmetic Logic Unit (ALU) 1-10
array 9-1
array declaration 9-1
array initialization 9-1
array parameter 9-4
array, control 9-12
array, dynamic 9-9
array, searching 9-8
array, two-dimensional 9-15
arrow keys 2-7
Asc function 6-16
ASCII 1-11, 6-16
ASCII codes 6-17
assignment statement 3-12
Atanasoff-Berry Computer (ABC) 1-4
Atansoff, John 1-4
Atn function 8-23
AutoList 3-12
automatic type conversion 4-11

An Introduction to Programming Using Microsoft Visual Basic

B

Babbage, Charles 1-2
Backspace key 2-8
backup 2-16
Backus, John 1-6
Bardeen, John 1-6
base 10 1-10
base 16 1-11
base 2 1-10
base unit 1-8
BASIC 1-6, 3-1
Bell Laboratories 1-6
Berry, Clifford 1-4
binary 1-10
binary number system 1-4, 1-10
binary representation 6-18
binary search 13-9
bit 1-10
BMP 3-5, 10-5
body 3-9
Boolean 4-6
Boolean expression 5-1
bound objects 15-13
Brittain, Walter 1-6
bubble sort 13-1
built-in data types 4-5
business functions 8-3
button 2-6
ByRef 7-8
ByVal 7-4
Byron, Ada 1-2
byte 1-10

C

Call statement 7-1
Case Studies 4-18
CD 1-12
CD-ROM drive 1-8, 1-12
central processing unit 1-5, 1-8, 1-9, 1-10
change event 4-11, 8-10, 11-18
changing property values through assignment 3-11
character data storage 6-16
check box 2-6, 5-19
check box object properties 5-19
CheckBox control 5-19
chip 1-7
Chr function 6-16
Circle method 10-8, 10-9
circle, drawing 10-9
classes 3-1, 7-17
Clear method 8-7, 8-10
click event 14-1
click event 3-15, 4-15, 8-7, 8-10
clicking 2-2

Close # statement 11-3
Close button 2-4, 2-5
Close button in a dialog box 2-6, 2-7
Close command 2-10
Close statement 12-4
closing a document 2-10
closing a sequential access file 11-3
closing a random access file 12-4
closing a project 3-10
Cls method 10-8, 10-10
COBOL 1-6
Code Editor window 3-8
coding 4-19
collapsible list 2-6, 2-7
color properties 10-1
combo box 8-9
combo box object properties 8-9
ComboBox control 8-9
command 2-3, 2-5
command button 3-4
command button properties 3-5, 3-12
CommandButton control 3-4
comments 3-13
Common Business Oriented Language 1-6
common dialog object properties 14-6, 14-8
common dialogs 14-5
CommonDialog control 14-6
CommonDialog control, adding to the Tool box 14-6
compiler 3-18
Components command 10-18, 14-7
computer 1-5
concatenation 6-15
Const statement 4-4
constant 4-4
container application 15-2
container object 10-11
container object properties 10-11
control array 9-12
control array as parameter 9-13
control array, creating 9-12
control array, removing an object 9-13
Control key 2-6
control, adding to the Tool box 10-18
control, CheckBox 5-19
control, ComboBox 8-9
control, CommandButton 3-4
control, CommonDialog 14-6
control, Data 15-13
control, DirListBox 11-17
control, DriveListBox 11-17
control, FileListBox 11-17
control, Frame 4-15
control, Image 3-15
control, Label 3-4
control, Line 10-2
control, ListBox 8-6

control, OLE 15-2
control, OptionButton 4-15
control, PictureBox 10-5
control, Shape 10-3
control, TextBox 4-10
control, Timer 10-13
conversion, automatic type 4-11
converting degrees to radians 8-21
converting radians to degrees 8-21
coordinate system 10-8
Copy command 9-13, 15-1
Copy Disk command 2-15
copying 2-18
copying a diskette 2-15
copying a file 2-18
copying a folder 2-18
copying an object 9-13
Cos function 8-20
Count method 9-13
counter 5-17
Countess of Lovelace, Ada 1-2
CPU 1-5, 1-8, 1-9, 1-10
cracker 1-15
Create Shortcut(s) Here command 2-19
CreateEmbed method 15-5
CreateLink method 15-8
creating a control array 9-12
creating a general procedure 7-3
creating a new project 3-2
creating access keys 8-12
creating an executable file 3-17
Currency 4-6
cursor 2-7
cursor control keys 2-7
customizing the Desktop 2-3

D

Data control 15-13
data entry 8-12
data entry with business applications 8-4
data object properties 15-13
data storage 12-3
data type 4-1
data type memory requirements 4-5
data types, built-in 4-5
database 14-19
DBMS 14-19
deactivating 15-3
Debug.Print statement 4-8
debugged 1-6
debugging 4-8
debugging, history of 4-8
decision structures 5-1
default button 2-6, 2-7
degrees to radians, converting 8-21

Desktop shortcut 2-8
Delete key 2-8
Delete method 15-14
deleted file, recovering 2-20
deleting a file 2-18
deleting a folder 2-18
deleting a record 11-14
deleting a record with the data object 15-14
deleting files 11-14
deleting records in a sequential access file 11-13
deleting records in random access files 12-9
delimiter 11-11
Department of Defense (DOD) 1-6
design 4-19
design time 3-4
Desktop 2-3
Desktop, customizing 2-3
Details command 2-17
dialog box 2-1
dialog box, using 2-6
dialogs, common 14-5
Difference Engine 1-2
Dim statement 4-1, 9-9
Dimension 4-1, 9-9
dimmed 8-12
direct access file 12-2
directory list box 11-17
directory list box object properties 11-17
DirListBox control 11-17
disabled 8-12
disabling an object 8-13
disk operating system 2-1
diskette 1-12
diskette drive 1-8, 1-12
diskette, formatting 2-14
diskette, proper handling of 2-13
diskette, using 2-13
division operators, special 4-13
division, integer 4-13
division, modulus 4-14
Do...Loop 6-1
docking the Immediate window 4-9
document 7-6
documenting procedures 7-6
dots, drawing 10-10
Double 4-1, 4-6
double-click event 11-18
double-clicking 2-2
drag and drop 2-18
dragging 2-2
drive list box 11-17
drive list box object properties 11-17
DriveListBox control 11-17
dynamic array 9-9
dynamic matrix 9-17

E

Eckert, J. Presper 1-4, 1-5
EDSAC 1-5
EDVAC 1-5
Electronic Communications Privacy Act, 1986 . 1-14
element 9-1
element, accessing 9-2
ellipse, drawing 10-9
embedded object 15-2
embedded object, activating and deactivating 15-3
embedding a new Excel spreadsheet 15-2
embedding a Word document 15-10
embedding an existing Excel file 15-5
Enabled property 8-13
End button 3-6
End command 3-6
End Sub 3-9
ENIAC 1-4
Enter key 2-8
entering new spreadsheet data at design time 15-3
EOF function 11-11
EOF function 11-2
Escape key 2-8
ethics 1-15
event 3-1
event procedure 3-8, 7-1
event-driven program 3-1
e^x 8-24
Excel file, embedding an existing 15-5
Excel file, linking an existing 15-8
Excel spreadsheet 15-1
executable file 3-18
executable file, creating 3-17
Exit command 2-12
Exit command (Visual Basic) 3-18
exiting an application 2-12
exiting Visual Basic 3-18
Exp function 8-24
Exploring window 2-17
exponent 1-12
exponential function 8-24
expression 3-17

F

Fair Credit Reporting Act of 1970 1-14
Fairchild Semiconductor 1-7
False 5-1
file 2-1, 2-9, 11-1
file list 2-5
file list box 11-17
file list box object properties 11-17
file system controls 11-17
file system objects 11-2

file types 3-15, 10-5
file, copying 2-18
file, deleting 2-18
file, finding 2-21
file, moving 2-18
file, read-only 2-18
file, recovering deleted 2-20
file, renaming 2-19
FileListBox control 11-17
filenames 2-9
Files or Folders command 2-21
files, deleting 11-14
files, renaming 11-14
Financial Privacy Act of 1978 1-14
Find command 2-21
finding files 2-21
first generation computers 1-4
Fix function 5-7
fixed-length string 12-3
flag 6-5
floating point numbers 1-12
focus 8-12
Folder command 2-18
folder, copying 2-18
folder, deleting 2-18
folder, moving 2-18
folder, renaming 2-19
folders 2-17
For…Next statement 6-12
For…Next with array 9-2
form 3-4
form events 14-11
Form icon 14-10
Form Layout window 3-3
form module 3-8
form properties 3-5, 3-12
form, adding a template to a project 14-14
form, adding an existing to a project 14-18
form, adding to a project 14-9
form, removing from a project 14-10
Form_Load event procedure 3-12
Form_Unload event 10-19
Format command 2-14
Format function 8-3
formatting diskettes 2-14
formatting numeric output 8-3
forms, multiple 14-11
Formula Translator 1-6
FORTRAN 1-6
fourth generation computers 1-8
frame 4-15
Frame control 4-15
frame object properties 4-15
FreeFile function 11-1
FSO 11-2
function 5-5, 5-6, 7-13

function argument 5-6
function procedure 7-13
FV function 8-4

G

Gates, Bill 2-1, 3-1
GB 1-11
general procedure 7-1
Get # statement 12-7
GIF 3-15, 10-5
gigabyte 1-11
global declarations 5-9
graphical user interface 2-1
GUI 2-1

H

hard disk 1-12
hard disk array 1-12
hard disk drive 1-12
hardware 1-8
Help command 2-20
help, online Windows 98 2-20
hexadecimal 1-11
Hide method 14-11
hiding an object 8-13
high-level programming languages 1-6
history of debugging 4-8
Hoff, Marcian 1-8
Hollerith, Herman 1-3
Hollerith's tabulating machine 1-3
Hopper, Grace Murray 1-6, 4-8

I

IBM (International Business Machine) . 1-3, 1-6, 1-7
IC (integrated circuit) 1-7
ICO 10-5
icons 2-1
IDE 3-2
identifier 4-1, 4-5
If…Then 5-1
If…Then…Else 5-3
If…Then…ElseIf 5-4
Image control 3-15
image object 3-14, 3-15
Image object properties 3-15
Immediate Window command 4-8
Immediate window, docking 4-9
indenting code 5-3
index 9-1
Index property 9-12, 9-13
indexes, meaningful 9-5
infinite loop 6-2

information age 1-13
initializing a static variable 7-12
in-place activation 15-3
input 1-9
Input # statement 11-11
input box 6-4
input devices 1-8
InputBox function 6-4
insertion sort 13-7
InStr function 6-11
Int function 5-7
Integer 4-6
integer division 4-13
integers 1-12
integrated circuits 1-7
integrated development environment 3-2
Intel Corporation 1-7, 1-8
interface 2-1, 3-1
International Business Machine (IBM) . 1-3, 1-6, 1-7
interpreter 3-17
inverse trigonometric functions 8-23
investment 8-4
IsNumeric function 8-2
iteration 6-1

J

Jacquard, Joseph 1-2
Jobs, Steven 1-8
JPEG 3-15
JPG 10-5

K

K 1-11
Kemeny, John 1-6, 3-1
keyboard 1-8
keyword 4-5
Kilby, Jack 1-7
Kill statement 11-14
kilobyte 1-11
Kurtz, Thomas 1-6, 3-1

L

label 3-4
Label control 3-4
label properties 3-12
label properties 3-5
LBound 9-2, 9-13, 9-16
LCase function 6-8
Left function 6-9
Leibniz wheel 1-1
Len function 6-10
LenB function 12-3

lifetime 7-11
Like operator 6-19
line 10-1
line continuation 7-2
Line control 10-2
Line Input # statement 11-2
Line method 10-8
line object properties 10-2, 10-14
line objects, moving 10-14
linear search 9-8
lines, drawing 10-8
linked object 15-8
linking a Word document 15-10
linking an existing Excel file 15-8
list box 8-6
list box object properties 8-6
ListBox control 8-6
LoadPicture function 7-23, 10-5
loan 8-3
local declarations 5-9
LOF function 12-4
Log function 8-24
logarithmic function 8-24
logic error 5-14
logical operator 5-12
Long 4-6
looping structure 6-1
lower bound 9-1
lowercase string 6-8

M

machine language 1-5
Macintosh 1-9
magnetic tape 1-6
mainframe 1-7
mantissa 1-12
Mark I 1-3
mathematical functions 8-1
matrix 9-15
matrix, accessing its elements 9-16
Mauchly, John 1-4, 1-5
Maximize button 2-4, 2-5
MB 1-11
meaningful indexes 9-5
megabyte 1-11
member 9-1, 12-1
memory 1-8, 1-9
memory size 1-11
menu 2-5, 14-1
Menu bar 2-4, 2-5
Menu bar (Visual Basic) 3-3
Menu Editor command 14-2
Menu Editor dialog box 14-2
menu name 2-5

menus, adding to a Visual Basic application ... 14-2
message box 5-14
method 5-20
microcomputer 1-8
microprocessor 1-8
Microsoft Corporation 2-1
Microsoft Jet Engine Database 15-14
Mid function 6-10
Mid statement 6-10
Minimize button 2-4, 2-5
MMControl control 10-18
MMControl control, adding to the Tool box .. 10-18
Mod operator 4-13
Model 650 1-6
modulus division 4-14
monitor 1-8
mouse 1-8
mouse pointer 2-2
Move method 10-6
moving 2-18
moving the mouse pointer 2-2
moving a file 2-18
moving a folder 2-18
moving an object 3-6
moving line objects 10-14
moving picture boxes 10-6
moving shapes 10-6
MS-DOS 2-1
MsgBox statement 5-14
MultiLine Property 11-3
multimedia object 10-18
multimedia object button properties 10-19
multimedia object properties 10-18
multiple forms 14-11
multitasking 2-1
My Computer icon 2-14

N

Name statement 11-14
named constant 4-4
naming objects 3-9
nested For...Next, nested for matrix 9-16
nested If...Then...Else statements 5-4
New command 2-8, 2-18
New Project command 3-2
newline character 11-1
NII 1-14
Not 5-12
Noyce, Robert 1-7
number of characters in a string 6-10
numeric output, formatting 8-3

O

object 1-13
Object collapsible list 3-5
Object Linking and Embedding 15-1
object oriented programming 3-1
object parameter 7-17
object, disabling 8-13
object, resizing and moving 3-6
object, selecting 3-6
objects 3-1
objects, accessing on other forms 14-11
objects, naming 3-9
OLE 15-1
OLE container 15-2
OLE container object properties 15-2
OLE control 15-2
omitted arguments 10-8
online Windows 98 help 2-20
OOP 3-1
Open command 2-10
Open dialog box 14-5
Open Project button 3-13
Open Project command 3-13
Open statement (sequential access files) 11-1
Open statement (random access files) 12-3
opening a sequential access file 11-1
opening a file 2-10
opening a random access file 12-3
operating system 2-1
operating system software 1-9
operator precedence 3-17, 4-14
operators 3-17
operators, special division 4-13
Option Base 9-1
option button 2-6, 2-7
option button object properties 4-15
option buttons 4-14
Option Explicit 4-7
OptionButton control 4-15
Or 5-12
output 1-9
output devices 1-9
overflow error 1-12
overwrite 2-9
overwriting records 12-4

P

PaintPicture method 10-8, 10-10
parameter 7-4, 7-9
parameter, array 9-4
parameter, control array 9-13
parameter, object 7-17
parameter, reference 7-8
parameter, user-defined type 12-2
parameter, value 7-4
parentheses 3-17
Pascal, Blaise 1-1
Pascaline 1-1
passing data 7-4
PasswordChar property 5-15
Paste command 9-13, 15-1
Paste Link command 15-1
pasting an object 9-13
path 11-2
pattern matching 6-19
payment 8-3
PC 1-8
persistent 11-1
personal computer 1-8
picture box 10-5
picture box object properties 10-5, 10-6
picture boxes, moving 10-6
Picture property 3-15
PictureBox control 10-5
piracy 1-14
plain text 11-1
Pmt function 8-3
pointing 2-2
pointing with the mouse 2-2
postcondition 7-6
precondition 7-6
Preserve 9-9
Print # statement 11-5, 11-6
Print command 2-11
Print command (Visual Basic) 3-9
Print dialog box 14-8
printer 1-9
Printer.EndDoc 14-9
Printer.Print statement 14-9
PrintForm method 5-20
printing a document 2-11
Privacy Act of 1974 1-14
Private 5-9
procedure 7-1
procedure, creating a general 7-3
procedure, event 7-1
procedure, function 7-13
procedure, general 7-1
procedure, Sub 7-1
procedure, user-defined 7-1
procedures, documenting 7-6
program 1-5, 1-9
program code 3-1, 3-8
programming guidelines 3-19, 4-17, 5-22
project 3-2
Project Explorer window 3-3
Project Properties command 14-17
Project window 3-3
project, adding a new form to 14-9
project, adding a template form to 14-14

project, adding an existing form to 14-18
project, closing 3-10
project, creating 3-2
project, opening 3-13
project, printing 3-9
project, removing a form 14-10
project, saving 3-6
properties list 3-5
Properties window 3-3
properties, check box object 5-19
properties, combo box object 8-9
properties, command button object 3-5, 3-12
properties, common dialog object...................... 14-6
properties, container object 10-11
properties, data object 15-13
properties, directory list box 11-17
properties, drive list box 11-17
properties, file list box 11-17
properties, form 3-5, 3-12
properties, frame object 4-15
properties, Image object 3-15
properties, label object 3-5, 3-12
properties, line object 10-2, 10-14
properties, list box object 8-6
properties, multimedia object.......................... 10-18
properties, OLE container object 15-2
properties, option button object 4-15
properties, picture box object 10-5, 10-6
properties, shape object 10-3, 10-6
properties, text box object 4-11, 11-3
properties, timer object 10-13
property values, changing through assignment3-11
PSet method 10-8, 10-10
pseudocode 5-13
punched card... 1-2
Put # statement 12-4
PV function 8-4

Q

QuickBasic 3-1

R

radians to degrees, converting 8-21
radio buttons 4-14
RAM (Random Access Memory) 1-9
random access file 12-2
Random Access Memory (RAM) 1-9
random numbers 5-5, 5-7
Randomize 5-7
range errors 9-3
read 1-6
Read Only Memory (ROM) 1-9
reading records in sequential access files 11-11
reading records in a random access files 12-7

reading text from a file 11-2
read-only 2-18
read-only file 2-18
real numbers 1-12
record 11-8, 12-2
record number 12-4
record, adding with the data object 15-14
record, deleting with the data object 15-14
record, updating with the data object 15-14
records, appending 12-4
records, deleting in random access files 12-9
records, overwriting 12-4
records, reading 12-7
records, updating in sequential access files ...11-13
records, deleting in sequential access files 11-13
records, updating in random access files 12-9
Recycle bin 2-20
ReDim statement 9-9
reel-to-reel 1-6
reference parameters 7-8
Refresh method 15-14
relational database 15-13
relational operators 5-1
removable hard drive 1-12
Remove Project command 3-10
removing an object from a control array 9-13
renaming 2-19
renaming a file 2-19
renaming a folder 2-19
renaming files 11-14
repeat key 2-7
Resize tab 2-4, 2-5
resizing an object 3-6
RGB 10-1
Right function 6-10
right to privacy 1-13
right-clicking 2-2
Rnd function 5-5, 5-7
ROM (Read Only Memory) 1-9
Round function 8-2
rounding 4-11
roundoff error 1-12, 5-2
RTrim function 12-7
Ruby 3-1
run time 3-6
run-time error 4-7, 9-3

S

Save As command 14-19
Save As dialog box 14-6
Save command 2-9
Save project button 3-6
Save project command 3-6
saving a document 2-9
saving often 2-9

scope 5-9
screen scroll 2-11
screen tips 2-2, 3-3
scroll arrow 2-11
scroll bar 2-4, 2-5, 2-11
scroll box 2-11
search, binary 13-9
searching an array 9-8
second generation computers 1-6
Seek function 12-4
selecting 2-2
selecting an object 3-6
selection sort 13-4
sentinel 6-5
sequential access file 11-1
server application 15-2
setting tab order 8-12
Sgn function 8-1
Shape control 10-3
shape object properties 10-3, 10-6
shapes 10-3
shapes, moving 10-6
Shockley, William 1-6
shortcut 2-5, 2-19
Show method 14-11
ShowOpen method 14-7
ShowPrint method 14-8
ShowSave method 14-7
Shut Down command 2-3
Sin function 8-20
Single 4-6
software 1-9
sort, bubble 13-1
sort, insertion 13-7
sort, selection 13-4
sorting 13-1
sound 10-18
SourceDoc property 15-5
Space function 6-15
spec 4-18
specification 4-18
splash screen 14-16
Splash Screen icon 14-16
spreadsheet data, entering at design time 15-3
spreadsheet file, embedding an existing 15-5
spreadsheet file, linking an existing 15-8
spreadsheet, embedding a new 15-2
Sqr function 8-1
standard code module 14-16
Standard EXE icon 3-2
Start button 2-8, 3-6
starting Visual Basic 3-2
startup 14-16
statement 3-8
static variable 7-11
static variable, initializing 7-12

Status bar 2-4, 2-5
Step 6-13
Stepped Reckoner 1-1
stored program computer 1-5
StrComp 6-18
StrConv function 6-9
String 4-6
string conversion functions 6-8
String function 6-15
string, fixed-length 12-3
Sub 3-9
Sub Main 14-16
Sub procedures 7-1
subscript 9-3
substring 6-9
syntax error 4-7
System 360 1-7

T

tab order 8-12
tab order, setting 8-12
TabIndex property 8-12
tables 15-13
Tabulating Machine Company 1-3
Tan function 8-21
tape drive 1-12
Task bar 2-4
template form 14-14
terminal 1-7
testing and debugging 4-21
Texas Instruments 1-7
text box 2-6, 4-10
text box object properties 4-11, 11-3
TextBox control 4-10
textual comparison 6-18
third generation computers 1-7
timer 10-13
Timer control 10-13
timer event 10-13
Timer function 13-3
timer object for animation 10-15
timer object properties 10-13
Title bar 2-4, 2-5
Tool bar 3-3
Tool box 3-3
transistor 1-6
trigonometric functions 8-20
Tripod 3-1
True 5-1
Turing test 1-15
Turing, Alan 1-5, 1-15
twips 10-6
two-dimensional array 9-15
Type statement 12-1

U

U.S. Census 1-3
U.S. Census Bureau 1-3, 1-5
UBound 9-2, 9-13, 9-16
UCase function 6-9
Unicode 6-16
UNIVAC 1-5
Universal Automatic Computer 1-5
Unload 3-9, 10-19
Update method 15-8
updating 5-17
updating records in sequential access files 11-13
updating a record with the data object 15-14
updating records in random access files 12-9
upper bound 9-1
uppercase string 6-9
user events 3-8
user input, obtaining a value from 4-10
user-defined procedure 7-1
user-defined type... 12-1
user-defined type argument 12-2
user-defined type array 12-2
user-defined type parameter 12-2

V

value parameters 7-4
variable array 9-1
variable assignment 4-1
variable declaration of user-defined type 12-1
variable declarations 4-6
variable initialization 4-6
variable scope 14-11
variable, declaring multiple 4-6
variable, static 7-11
variables 4-1
vbCrLf 6-16, 11-3
vbTab 6-16
View Code button 3-8
View Object button 3-8
virus 1-15
Visible property 8-13
Visual Basic, exiting 3-18
Visual Basic, starting 3-2
von Leibniz, Gottfried Wilhelm 1-1
von Neumann, John 1-5

W

WAV 10-18
wave sound 10-18
What's This button 2-6, 2-7
window 2-1, 2-4
Windows 98 GUI 2-3
Windows application standards 8-12
Windows Explorer 2-17
Windows GUI 3-1
windows, using 2-4
WMF 3-15, 10-5
word 1-12
Word document, embedding 15-10
Word document, linking 15-10
word processor document, embedding 15-10
word processor document, linking 15-10
Work area 2-4, 2-5
WORM 1-12
Wozniak, Stephen 1-8
write 1-6
Write # statement 11-8
write-protect 2-16
write-protect tab 2-16
writing records to sequential access files 11-8
writing records to random access files 12-4
writing text to a file 11-5

Z

Zip drive 1-12

An Introduction to Programming Using Microsoft Visual Basic